Structural Slumps

STRUCTURAL SLUMPS

The Modern Equilibrium Theory of
Unemployment, Interest, and Assets

EDMUND S. PHELPS

In collaboration with

Hian Teck Hoon

George Kanaginis

Gylfi Zoega

HARVARD UNIVERSITY PRESS

Cambridge, Massachusetts, and London, England   1994

Library of Congress Cataloging in Publication Data

Phelps, Edmund S.
    Structural slumps : the modern equilibrium theory
of unemployment, interest, and assets / Edmund S.
Phelps, in collaboration with Hian Teck Hoon,
George Kanaginis, Gylfi Zoega.
        p.   cm.
    Includes bibliographical references (p.
    and index.
    ISBN 0-674-84373-8 (acid-free paper)
    1. Business cycles.   2. Depressions.
3. Equilibrium (Economics)   4. Unemployment.
5. Interest.   6. Money.   I. Title.
HB3711.P48   1994
338.5'42—dc20   93-15775
CIP

A000005353088

Contents

Part III   Small and Large Open Economies: Working Models

Part IV   Microtheoretic Formulations, Modern and Neoclassical

Part V   Empirical Evidence

Part VI   Concluding Notes

Preface

THE rise in recent decades of a modern economic theory, centered on the effects of a number of informational limitations within firms and markets, has had a liberating influence on macroeconomic thought. A diverse body of research has resulted, one belonging to neither the neoclassical nor the monetary schools, that adopts a radically different perspective on the determination of the level of economic activity. Movements in the unemployment rate, not in the size of the labor force, are the stuff of slumps and booms. The shifts and long swings in unemployment are an equilibrium phenomenon, not a matter of misperceptions or misforecasts and consequent wage-price misalignments. Behind the equilibrium path of unemployment are nonmonetary factors working through nonmonetary mechanisms: the propensity to quit or shirk, hysteresis effects of idleness, insider-outsider relationships, welfare-state subsidies, rent-seeking unions, balance-sheet factors in financial markets, and the institutional substructure. Despite their kindred spirit, however, the existing formulations do not offer a usable intertemporal general-equilibrium theory. The emerging school has lacked a unifying core model to which all the above mechanisms could ultimately be hooked up.

This book sets out what I hope will become the main paradigm of this school. The equilibrium path of the unemployment rate always approaches the natural rate, as before. But something has been added. The natural rate moves! I build a family of modern equilibrium models in which the natural rate, conceived along the lines I suggested in 1968, is seen to be a function of the real structure of the economy (and the corresponding structure overseas). The analytical task has been to determine exactly how the natural rate depends on this structure—on real sectoral demands, factor supplies and technology, rates of taxation, subsidies, and tariffs.

Believing does not make it so, of course. Hence the theory is followed by an econometric investigation of the empirical effects of these same determinants of the unemployment rate. The findings, as I see them, unmistakably support the paradigm here against its chief rivals, the Keynesian schools and the real business cycle school, though more evidence will be needed to convince their most loyal adherents. It will be enough, however, if this investigation reopens the subject of employment determination. Undoubtedly a great many secrets of prosperity and depression remain to be unlocked.

In turning from the monetary channels of Keynes back to real mechanisms, this theory resembles the real business cycle school. But in its modern view of employee incentives and resulting unemployment, and its view of industry in disaggregative and imperfect-market terms, it is obviously unlike that neoclassical school. Neither is this new theory always at odds with Keynesian doctrine. One of the surprises is the number of times a Keynesian proposition is obtained from a theoretical setting devoid of money, the essence of the Keynesian system.

That said, I feel a need to say a few words on the work's motivation and its relation to past work of mine and others'.

Why study slumps? This book and the other recent arrivals on unemployment come after a period when, in the New Classical theory then receiving attention, a long stretch of high unemployment did not fit, and there was nothing pathological about unemployment in any case. Yet, their theoretical inconvenience notwithstanding, long elevations of unemployment are a social problem, since much of what we measure as unemployment reflects job rationing, hence is involuntary and imposes private and social net burdens; the fact (if it is a fact) that there are some industries in which the wage moves to clear the market makes little difference. Furthermore, the vulnerability of Western economies to long stretches of high unemployment—to slumps—is again evident. The postwar streak of prosperity was broken with the stubborn decline suffered in the 1970s. The unusual slump over three continents in the 1980s was by far the deepest since the 1930s, and this Second World Depression was longer for some countries than the first one, still called the Great Depression. The 1990s have begun with another decline, also rather uneven, and increasingly this slump looks to be an extension of the preceding one, punctuated by a bubble in the late 1980s. On the now extensive postwar record, one would have to concede that the unemployment rate is capable of wide swings of decadal length or more, and that a series of structural shifts and developments have pushed the equilibrium path to new heights. The challenge of uncovering the structural changes behind these big swings and the worsening trend of the past twenty years has been the impetus for the present work.

Conceivably, this book might nevertheless have attempted to interpret the recent slumps by means of the antecedent theories. Twice in my career, in fact, I thought the missing "micro" element in the monetary approach to employment determination was finally in place so that we had at last a macroeconomics that could satisfactorily explain a preponderant part of unemployment fluctuations. In the latter half of the 1960s some of us introduced a microeconomics of expectations-based wage and employment decisions, and with it we sought to explain employment fluctuations in terms of disequilibrium (incorrect-expectations) deviations of the unemployment from the equilibrium (correct-expectations) steady-state level—the level that became known as the natural rate. In the latter half of the 1970s, the profession having revealed a preference for the rational-expectations version of the earlier models, some of us set out to build upon the idea that wage-setting is scheduled in a staggered fashion over the year, so that the employment effect of demand shocks and supply shocks is long-lasting—the return to the natural rate slow—and monetary stabilization policy can regulate the speed of recovery to the natural rate.

The Keynesian, monetarist, and New Keynesian schools all adopted the natural rate. But it was drafted into service when still underdeveloped. The earliest essays on the natural rate, such as my model based on labor turnover, touched on its causes but did not make it determinate. By default, the natural rate of unemployment was treated as a sort of constant: It might ebb and flow with time but it was conveniently independent of the usual macroeconomic shocks. The traditional "macro" shocks under analysis were taken to be neutral for the equilibrium unemployment-rate path.

Unfortunately, it now seems difficult to maintain that the monetary approach of these schools, with its premise of a fixed natural rate, is adequate for understanding the lengthy boom and the two major slumps of postwar history. Some years ago, after decades of research, much of it on the monetary approach to unemployment determination, I became aware that I was unable to explain persuasively why the unemployment rate was so remarkably low in most countries for more than two decades after the war, why unemployment remained high for so protracted a period in the 1970s, years after the first of the oil price shocks, and, most glaringly, why unemployment in many countries rose so stubbornly well into the mid-1980s despite vigorous recovery in other countries. The Keynesian schools predicted that the fiscal stimulants finally taken in the United States would boost European employment, not drag it further down; so, by the way, did the real business cycle school.

Any hope of accounting for the major swings in economic activity since the war, I decided, would require abandoning the simplification of a natural unemployment rate invariant to nonmonetary (not just monetary) macro shocks in favor of models making the equilibrium rate an endogenous variable determined by a variety of nonmonetary forces. The longer slumps and booms, at any rate, must be explained largely as *displacements of the equilibrium path of unemployment itself,* not as deviations of unemployment around an impervious equilibrium path. For me this goal became a personal imperative, as I could hardly leave macroeconomics knowing that my previous work on the natural rate had missed so promising an opportunity. It became necessary to return to the natural rate to try to realize its true potential.

But how, if at all, can structural shifts drive the natural rate? The conceptual challenge has been to hit upon and to model the nonmonetary mechanisms through which various nonmonetary shocks may plausibly have important effects on the path of equilibrium unemployment. It was gratifying finally to see that the conception of the natural rate I had proposed in the late 1960s, in which firms cause unemployment by driving up the economywide wage in their efforts to discourage quitting, and the sister conception of wage-setting intended to combat shirking could be used for this purpose. I am not the first to work out the determination of the natural rate, conceived that way, in a proto-general-equilibrium model—Steven Salop was, later Joseph Stiglitz. Their models were not broad enough, though, particularly with regard to the role of assets and interest, to generate much of importance in the way of comparative-statics on the effects of relevant shocks. I am fortunate to have come in on the general-equilibrium research program in time to construct models that overcome two crucial difficulties that were blocking acceptance of the new theory.

Most previous models suffer the absurd implication that if (as in the Shapiro-Stiglitz model) a technological advance reduces the natural rate of unemployment, ongoing secular technical progress goes on reducing it— contrary to historical evidence that unemployment is (or was) trendless; if (as in the Salop model) secular progress is neutral for the natural rate, so is a permanent supply shock. The solution here is the construction of a theoretical model in which, though the natural rate may be disturbed when a productivity advance pulls up wages and incomes, the response of the natural rate is entirely transient. Thus formulated, the theory averts any implication that secular productivity growth puts the equilibrium unemployment rate on a trend while preserving for technological or natural-resource shocks a short-term role.

The other problem to be met was to release the demand side of the labor market from the marginal productivity straightjacket of the neoclassical aggregative school. Here I have taken a good deal of inspiration from the rustic parables of Austrian capital theory. Nearly all employment is governed by considerations of the future, so what firms will pay for labor generally depends importantly on real asset prices and thus on real rates of interest—and this is true even in the models omitting physical capital. Some of the illustrative models here lead to unexpected findings: some kinds of product demands actually lower interest rates, so the structure of demand matters. The resulting theory thus points to a panoply of nonmonetary forces—the configuration of real demands as well as supply conditions—capable of driving the natural rate.

It is far too soon to be sure that this theory is true. Yet it is, I believe, the only existing theory to show how certain structural shifts and mechanisms in the global economy may lie behind the major swings and worsening trend in business activity of recent decades. The monetary approach and the real business cycle approach cannot claim the same explanatory power.

Although I have tried hard not to claim too little for this theory—a fundamentally new approach needs all the boost it can get—I should also be wary of claiming too much. These days economics seems subject to a monistic tendency to imagine that one theory will triumph over the others, or ought to. The truth is that every one of the extant theories has something to tell us about some of the effects of some shocks over some time frame. The structuralist theory propounded here will, if it succeeds, push back the domain of some of the other theories, not eliminate any of them. The structuralist theory will gain a place at a pluralist table in recognition, if I am right, of its value in illuminating the areas it was designed to explore.

It is a pleasure to acknowledge the financial support and personal help provided to me over the five years of research for this volume.

A continuing association with the University of Rome, Tor Vergata, and its economic research arm, CEIS, has provided me with support and facilities for this research every summer since 1987. I owe a large debt of gratitude to Luigi Paganetto, dean of faculty and chairman of CEIS, for his commitment to this position for me in the faculty and center he has created.

Another association developed around the same time at the Institut d'Etudes Politiques, in the University of Paris, and the related Observatoire Français des Conjonctures Economiques (OFCE) where I have received recurrent financial support and research assistance. The International Policy Evaluation Group at OFCE, to which I was appointed when it was formed in 1990, provided more assistance to this project in financing the econometric tests of my theory; Chapter 17 is one of the products of these tests. I am much indebted to Jean-Paul Fitoussi, professor at "Science Po" and president of the OFCE, for his steady support at these attractive institutions.

This book, in fact, grew out of the work Professor Fitoussi and I began in late 1985 on the external real interest shock to Europe in the 1980s. I had argued earlier that the apparent fiscal stimulus overseas would drain Europe of its capital, but I had not figured out how to refute the Keynesian and neoclassical views that total employment and exports would nevertheless be expanded by the stimulus—the rising tide that lifts all boats. The three two-country models he and I developed in our book, *The Slump in Europe,* showing that European employment could instead contract— the Fitoussi-Phelps thesis—suggested the three models in the present volume. The value added here is to demonstrate that the lessons of the mixed monetary/real Fitoussi-Phelps models survive in the nonmonetary-equilibrium environment of the present models, and that unexpected implications arise from the closed-economy versions of applicability to the world as a whole.

Among my debts I must also mention a grant from the National Science Foundation that made possible the exploration of some early modeling and statistical work in 1987 and 1988. The research department of the International Monetary Fund offered its hospitality to what must have seemed a very alien enterprise for some time in the spring of 1988.

Several other contacts proved important. A paper presented by Jeffrey Sachs at the Brookings Institution in 1979, which I resisted at the time, was the first challenge I heard to the invariance of the natural rate to real shocks, and he was in turn the first convert to the Fitoussi-Phelps elevation of the capital market over the goods markets. Notes that Pentti Kouri showed me in 1984 brought home the scope that real-wage rigidity would create for real demand shifts to alter employment. An exchange with Joseph Stiglitz in 1985 caused me to rethink whether, as I had imagined, the natural rate was as likely increasing in the real wage as decreasing. An objection by Lawrence Summers expressed to me in 1986 that secular progress would soon undo contractionary disturbances led me to revise the models to include in them the incentive effects of employees' wealth. Conversations with Dennis Snower emphasized to me the importance of adducing evidence in favor of the theory as against rival theories. Criticisms by Olivier Blanchard have helped me to see in the rise of stock markets in the 1980s a puzzle for the theory. I am not sure I have met these latter challenges, but I have responded.

Early on, a few econometric studies were important signs that I might be on the right course. A model by Andrew Newell and James Symonds had the first results I had seen on the contractionary effects of the world real interest rate. A study by Giuseppe Tullio rejected the Keynesian theory of the locomotive, which was antithetical to the theory here. Finally, a dissertation published by Dirk Morris confirmed the effect of various global fiscal variables on the world real rate of interest. These reports came as intergalactic emissions encouraging me to believe that there is in fact something out there.

A gratifying aspect of this project has been that it attracted the participation of three of the best students I have taught. This volume has benefited from their collaboration at some key points. Hian Teck Hoon, now at the National University of Singapore, developed with me the dynamic turnover model of the natural rate (Chapter 7) and helped to get the two-sector model under better control (Chapter 9). George Kanaginis, with Three Crown Capital Partners, worked with me on the neoclassical investigation of structural shifts (Chapter 16) that stands as the analogue in real business cycle theory of what is attempted here using some elements of modern theory. Gylfi Zoega, now with Birkbeck College following his work at OFCE and the World Bank, contributed importantly to the design and carried out the extensive statistical estimations in the econometric analyses (Chapter 17). My thanks also go to a succession of advanced graduate students at Columbia who took the time to study and comment upon this research as it unfolded in my annual seminar.

The publishers of several journal articles and conference volumes containing material of mine have granted permission to recycle those pieces in the present volume: the *American Economic Review* for Chapter 7; the *Quarterly Journal of Economics* for Chapter 8; the conference volume edited by Anthonie Knoester, *Taxation in the United States and Europe: Theory and Practice* (Macmillan Ltd.), for Chapter 9; the *Journal of Economic Literature* for a portion of Chapter 10; the conference volume edited by Helmut Frisch and Andreas Wergoetter, *Open-Economic Macroeconom-*

ics (Macmillan Ltd.), for elements of Chapter 11; the *Rivista di Politica Economica* for the second half of Chapter 12; the conference volume edited by Anthony Atkinson, *Economics for the New Europe* (Macmillan Ltd.), for some elements of Chapter 13; the conference volume edited by Dennis Snower and Joseph Stiglitz, *Unemployment and Wages* (Cambridge University Press), for Chapter 15; the *Journal of Public Economics* for Chapter 16; and the Second Report of the Policy Evaluation Group of OFCE for Chapter 17.

I want to thank Michael Aronson for shepherding this project along so attentively at Harvard University Press. Kate Schmit did a splendid job overseeing the production of a complex book.

Finally, this book at several points brings back memories of the contributions to my thinking of the late Arnold Collery. My second teacher in economics at Amherst, later a dean and then my colleague and chairman at Columbia, a deep economic theorist from whom I gained much, and throughout an extraordinarily generous friend, he was a long and benevolent influence on my life. I dedicate this volume to his memory.

Edmund S. Phelps
McVickar Professor of Political Economy
Columbia University

Structural Slumps

Introduction

THE aim of this book is to uncover the nonmonetary mechanisms through which various nonmonetary forces are capable of propagating slumps and booms in the contemporary world economy. The approach is to synthesize out of some modern as well as neoclassical elements a theory of what could be called *structural unemployment* and its path through time. The theory is then tested against global data from the postwar period.

The theoretical sections are built around the *equilibrium* case in the expectational sense of the term: the case of *correct expectations* about the course of the economy. The product is therefore a theory of the equilibrium path of unemployment.

The prototype models of twenty-five years ago also possessed an equilibrium unemployment path. The equilibrium unemployment rate was shown to converge (gradually if it did not jump) to what was called the *natural* unemployment rate. In these models, though, the natural rate was treated as a constant or as a parameter that moves exogenously with time.

In a useful shorthand one may characterize the theory here as *endogenizing* the natural unemployment rate—defined now as the *current* equilibrium steady-state rate, given the *current* capital stock and any other state variables. (It is the unemployment rate that, if it were the actual rate at the moment, would make the current rate of change of the associated equilibrium unemployment rate path equal to zero.) In the new theory, then, the equilibrium path of the unemployment rate is driven by a natural rate that is a *variable* of the system rather than a constant or a forcing function of time. The endogenous natural rate becomes the moving target that the equilibrium path constantly pursues.

The theory here rests on a family of intertemporal micro-macro models, each of which revolves around a distinct kind of asset acquired by the firm that is of importance for its hiring decisions: the trained employee, the customer, and fixed capital equipment. Collectively these models provide a "structuralist story" of how the equilibrium unemployment path is determined.

Seeing the natural rate and the associated equilibrium path of unemployment as endogenous, pushed by business forces as any other economic variable is, finally charms us into venturing a step further: to view actual unemployment as tending steadily and reliably to the equilibrium path described by the theory. With that step we arrive at a new paradigm in macroeconomics: *an equilibrium theory of unemployment movements*—hence a moving-natural-rate theory of movements in the *actual* rate of unemployment. Of course, the latter rate may not track the former rate at all closely; certainly a Keynesian would not suppose so. But it is plausible that the moving-natural-rate theory holds the solution to the mystery of what is behind the *shifts* and *long swings* of the unemployment rate.

The subsequent empirical section of this work finds that the theory of equilibrium unemployment developed here succeeds to an important degree in explaining the two nearly global slumps in the 1970s and 1980s. (The view of the 1990s it offers is not far off the mark either.) Other nonclassical representatives of the equilibrium approach to unemployment nonetheless exist: the insider-outsider models (especially their nonmonetary versions) and the still embryonic models based on modern finance notions of credit rationing to firms and households. Apportioning the truth among the rival claimants within the broad structuralist school would be difficult with only the present data.

In aiming to redirect attention to the long movements of the unemployment rate, away from the high-frequency vibrations of so much current-day analysis, this book is not striking out in a novel direction but is actually returning to the main tradition of earlier business cycle theorizing, of which there is no greater example than Keynes's *General Theory*.[1]

It could also be argued that the function of the relatively formal body of microeconomic general-equilibrium modeling here is to provide theoretical support for relationships that several leading practitioners in macroeconomics, for more than a dozen years now, have been explicitly positing or implicitly assuming on intuitive grounds in their analyses of current macro disturbances.

The nonclassical elements in the theory make it a *modern* rather than a neoclassical theory. The most central of these is the relationship between the firm and the employee springing from their incentives in the modern setting of asymmetric information. The resulting economics of incentive pay, or efficiency wages, plays a key role here, as it does in a growing number of models, in generating involuntary unemployment and shaping its equilibrium path. The theoretical structure is further strengthened if we use a modern treatment of the product market, though the general framework does not require it. The relevance of modern views of the capital market is also noted but they could not be imbedded into the framework on this occasion.

The *neoclassical* element is the role of interest rates determined in the capital market. In the general-equilibrium theory built up here, the path of the natural unemployment rate is intertwined with the path of the natural rate of interest. A correct analysis of the unemployment effects of any structural shift or other nonmonetary shock requires an understanding of the mechanism simultaneously determining them. Once their interaction is understood, and only then, one can see how a given structural shift or other nonmonetary shock pushes the economy toward slump or boom, in the equilibrium scenarios of the theory, and simultaneously sets in motion an adjustment process leading to complete or partial recovery.

The emerging general-equilibrium theory makes demand shocks as much as supply shocks the great movers and shakers of the economy's equilibrium path. In the version constructed here, the theory sees shifts in profitability and thrift, and possibly shifts in productivity and population growth rates, as prime sources of disturbances. Adjustments of domestic assets and of wealth operate to amplify or ultimately to dampen or erase the early effect on unemployment.

The results obtained echo pre-Keynesian doctrine in sounding the theme of slump through "undersaving": public debt and other fiscal stimuli to consumer spending are seen as contractionary. Yet the results have in common with Keynesian doctrine the theme of slump through "underinvestment": in particular, government armaments purchases (and in all but special cases manpower buildups too), as occur in wartime, and more generally any government spending on goods produced by the capital-goods sector of the economy are implied to be expansionary—without any reference to the liquidity of a money economy, which is crucial to the Keynesian analysis.

Introducing country-specific demand stimuli in a multinational world adds further twists to the story. It is found to be theoretically possible for such stimuli to have an expansionary effect at home—a result more Keynesian than that obtained by some Keynesian models—while having a contractionary effect abroad. This is the same "locomotive" in reverse, or "crowding out" at a distance, previously found in the partly monetary models of Fitoussi and Phelps.[2]

At some point, if only for working purposes, it becomes necessary to have a name for the theory. It might well be called the *structuralist* theory of unemployment movements: The object under its study is a kind of structural unemployment. It prepares us for long-persisting and even nonvanishing disturbances owing to permanent shocks, unlike theories of vibrations around a fixed trend path. It sees unemployment as (much of the time) an equilibrium phenomenon varying with real demand and supply rather than with the supply of money in relation to the temporary nominal wage or price level of the moment (which we don't think of as part of the deep structure of the economy). Finally, as just noted, the theory describes how unemployment responds to alterations in the structure of goods demands and of goods supplies; composition matters. Whatever we finally call the theory, however, it is not a reestablishment on different theoretical ground of the doctrine of Keynes or of any other monetary school. The occasional resemblance between a structuralist finding and a Keynesian one is purely coincidental.

Part I begins with a review and defense of the leading modern conceptions of the employer-employee relation—the turnover, or quitting, model and the supervision, or shirking, model. The discussion proceeds to the usual analysis of the equilibrium level of the incentive pay, or "efficiency wage," that firms are driven to establish in their efforts to discourage quitting and shirking. The implied equilibrium wage curve in the (un)employment rate–wage plane is derived. This relationship and "labor demand" determine the equilibrium rate of unemployment. The treatment of labor demand, though, must also depart from the neoclassical treatment—must also be modernized—if it is to be compatible in spirit with the modern treatment of wage setting and if the whole apparatus is to have wide empirical applicability: The demand price of labor is a function of employment, the unemployment rate, and the real prices of assets, some of which exist because of modern elements in the economy.

Part II studies three working models corresponding to three distinct assets in which the firm invests: customers, functional employees, and physical capital. The focus here is the case of the closed economy in which the path of the unemployment rate is determined simultaneously with the real interest rate path. The first chapter takes up the model of turnover in employees in whom the firm has invested firm-specific training. The next chapter treats in a parallel way an economy in which a firm's stock of assets is not its firm-oriented employees but rather its stock of customers. The last chapter here treats in the same way an economy in which a firm's stock of assets is its stock of capital, such as its accumulated plant measured in floor space. A summary chapter discussing the main results and informally tying the models together closes this part.

Part III takes up the nature of the economic interdependencies among national economies to which the structuralist theory points. Are the transmissions positive or negative? For each kind of economy studied in Part II there is a chapter here on the case of the small open economy, meaning an economy so small as to take as given the world real interest rate, and on the international transmission mechanisms in a two-country model of two such economies. The analysis of these working models is again followed by a discussion of the main results of the theory thus far developed.

Part IV addresses the weakness of the working models—that they take for granted the nature of the behavioral functions, in particular the quitting and shirking functions that play a key role in the modeling of incentive wage setting, without any explicit microtheoretic underpinnings. A key concern here is the unwelcome implication of some previous microtheoretic formulations that secular progress in productivity and real wage rates generates a secular decline of the unemployment rate. The flaw of the previous microtheoretic formulations of incentive (efficiency) wages in this regard is their neglect of the effect of employees' wealth—or income from wealth—on their propensity to quit and to shirk. The first chapter here constructs an intertemporal model of shirking, in which the agents accumulate or decumulate wealth as described by a dynamic programming problem. With this intertemporal model in hand we proceed to explore the existence of conditions under which productivity increases are ultimately neutral for the equilibrium unemployment rate, thus escaping the implication that was to be avoided. The results in fact show the microtheoretic possibility that the propensities to shirk and to quit do indeed possess the "homogeneity" properties that they were assumed to have in the working models.

The previous working models are also vulnerable in their disregard of any possible effect on the propensity to shirk of the real rate of interest—other than its effect through wealth or the income from wealth. (Two key themes regarding the employment effect of higher real interest through certain demand shocks would fall to the ground if the propensity to shirk and to quit were affected strongly enough in the "wrong" way.) A simulation analysis of the intertemporal model finally yields some reassurance on that real interest rate question.

Part V confronts the "structuralist" theory of unemployment developed over the course of the previous chapters with two kinds of empirical evidence. The first of the chapters here reports on some econometric findings, drawn from world time series as well as national series, bearing on the empirical validity of the structuralist theory, especially its emphasis on demand shocks. The second weighs the extent to which the structuralist theory serves to explain the historical record of unemployment over recent decades. This chapter speculates on a structuralist interpretation of the global history of unemployment, with emphasis on the period since the Second World War and the differing experience of the three main regions of the OECD countries.

Part VI contains the closing chapters, one on some precursors of the theory and the other a rumination on the sorts of policies toward structural disturbances to which the theory might lead.

I

CONCEPTS AND AGENDA

1

Modern Equilibrium Theory

SOME twenty-five years ago, a radically novel perspective on individual behavior began to invade economics. This quintessentially modern outlook brought into play assumptions about the costliness or existence of information quite foreign to (neo)classical theory.[1] The new slant on market transactions finally set in motion the development of a modern paradign of market equilibrium to challenge the competitive equilibrium of neoclassical theory. This book, if successful, will help to carry that development toward maturity in the area of macroeconomics.

With the advent of the new paradigm, as Kuhn observed of paradigm shifts in all fields, even some of the terms of discourse have undergone a change of meaning. The term "equilibrium" is a case in point. Earlier, several theorists had come to mean by the term a state or path along which all markets (or the market in question) clear—where no buyer or seller is rationed, is involuntarily limited, in the quantity that may be bought or sold. Those of an econometric bent, on the other hand, tended to mean by the term a stationary state or a stochastic stationary state—with static-expectations equilibrium, rational-expectations equilibrium, and so forth all being admissible members of the class. In contrast, those working with the new paradigm have found it convenient to use the term as it had been employed by Marshall, Myrdal, Hayek, and several other major theorists in this century: *equilibrium* is a state or path along which *expectations* are in an appropriate sense *correct,* so that, absent an unanticipated shock, they will be ratified or fulfilled by experience. This volume will always use "equilibrium" in that expectational sense.

The pioneering contributions to the new paradigm were all analyses of what Marshall called *partial* equilibrium. Arrow, arguing that in the equilibrium of the insurance industry buyers cannot obtain as much insurance as they would like, located certain information conditions leading to moral hazard as the source of the nonclassical phenomenon.[2] The implied equilibrium displays an undersupply of insurance, as less is provided than found in the neo-neoclassical equilibrium of a model without informational deficiencies. Vickrey, arguing that the government sector does not generally supply every project whose benefit exceeds the cost, saw the sand in the classical machine to be the incentive of each citizen to conceal the benefits that would accrue.[3]

The hallmark of these modern analyses is that they see in these situations the presence of asymmetric information, one or both parties being unable to detect whether the other is telling the truth or keeping his word about his preferences, intentions, or conduct. A consequence of these modern models is that, even in equilibrium, there is an "excess demand" for insurance and for public goods (other considerations aside), contrary to classical theory. Centuries ago Hume had written of moral hazard, and Marx had glimpsed the employee information problem of the capitalist firm, yet economics had resisted those early insights.

The new equilibrium paradigm reached the labor market later in the 1960s. In my 1968 paper on wage behavior and labor-market equilibrium—where, again, labor-market equilibrium is not defined by market clearing but simply means a state of correct expectations—there is a moral hazard in the association between the firm and the employee.[4] The hazard faced by the firm is that an employee whom the firm has given firm-specific training so that he or she can function within the firm may quit and thus impose on the firm the investment-like costs of finding and training a replacement. The firm hopes that the employee will not quit except for cause (the employer paying less or demanding more than the industry standard) but knows that it cannot typically enforce such an understanding, and so it will aim to motivate reduced turnover by taking whatever steps are cost-effective.[5] One such measure is to raise its wage above the market-clearing level, calculating that a small wage premium would be repaid by the *incentive* it created to quit less readily.

A consequence is that there will be involuntary unemployment—a pool of workers in excess supply, rationed out of a job.[6] The equilibrium steady-state unemployment rate at each moment is just large enough that if the actual unemployment rate should happen to be lower, employees can find similar jobs at other firms so quickly and hence are so ready to quit their existing employers that the firms are thrown into a wage competition:

[T]he increase of [the firm's] quit rate will impose costs: The firm must either allow its output to decrease, thus losing profits, or incur the recruit-

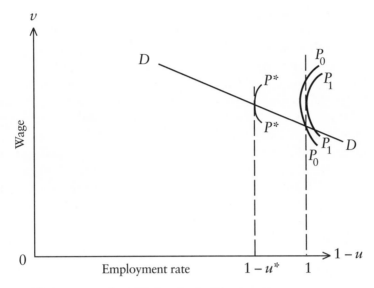

Figure 1.1 The property of equilibrium in the labor market

ment, processing, and training costs of replacing the departing workers (or choose some combination of these two losses). At [the] high quit rate corresponding to a [sufficiently] low unemployment rate, the firm will want to [establish] a differential between the wage it pays and the average wage paid elsewhere, on the ground that the savings from the lower turnover costs [thereby obtained] will more than pay for the extra wage bill. As all firms attempt to [establish] this differential, the general wage index rises.[7]

With all firms paying more in expectation of achieving the incentive effect of a wage differential and none gaining it, the firms will be in a state of disappointment—a state of disequilibrium. Only at a sufficiently large unemployment rate will each of the homogeneous firms find its quit rate small enough that it is willing to set its *wage* equal to the wage it assumes in its calculation the others will pay—to the *expected* economywide wage. Thus the equilibrium steady-state unemployment rate—or *natural rate* as it came to be called—is just large enough to make the turnover problem manageable in the sense that it does not drive firms to a futile attempt to outpay one another.

This basic property of labor-market equilibrium, some details aside, may be conveyed in a somewhat impressionistic way by the diagram of labor demand and labor force per firm shown in Figure 1.1. The labor market clears where the labor demanded equals the labor force. But at that market-clearing point, the individual firm's wage-employment isoprofit contour (P_0P_0) that goes through it and takes the other firms' wage to be given at the market-clearing wage is not vertical—the firm can move to a better profit contour (the best being P_1P_1) by raising its wage; hence the point of market clearing is not an equilibrium. An equilibrium occurs up the labor demand curve at a point where the intersecting isoprofit contour (P^*P^*) that takes as given that the other firms stick to the higher wage corresponding to this new point is locally vertical—so the firm can do no better than to offer the same wage.

Another model deducing the non-market-clearing property of labor-market equilibrium, one appearing about a decade later, is based on another incentive problem faced by firms. This is the problem of shirking, or slacking, by employees, which was introduced into theoretical analysis of wages and employment by Calvo and Bowles.[8] Continuous monitoring of every employee would be prohibitively expensive for the firm. The suggested solution is to motivate employees to shirk with reduced frequency by the same means that it motivates employees to quit with reduced frequency: by offering the employee incentive pay. By giving the employee more to lose in the event of dismissal, the firm will reason, the threat (certain or uncertain) of dismissal in the event the employee is caught shirking is made a stronger deterrent for the employee. Up to a point, then, raising the wage will generally gain more in output per man-hour than it will lose in wages per man-hour, with the result that the wage cost of producing a given output is decreased on balance.[9]

The logic of the shirking story parallels that of the turnover model: As each firm finds out that all the other firms in the economy have pushed up their wages as well in the same hope of reducing costs, each must now pay more just to stay even with its rival employers and still more if it would offer premium pay to discourage shirking. The result of the increased cost of labor is that firms' production managers cut output and employment. The equilibrium is reached when the general level of wages has risen just enough that the individual firm is content not to seek a wage higher than the wage it expects the other firms are going to offer.

According to either of these *incentive-wage* models, to use a term that will be used interchangeably with *efficiency wage,* labor-market equilibrium is marked by *job rationing,* thus involuntary unemployment. An unemployed person, both in labor-market equilibrium and generally in disequilibrium as well, has to wait passively until some firm, on reaching into the figurative fishbowl, finds that it has his number. The unemployed worker is helpless to underbid for a job because he cannot persuade any prudent firm, no matter how solemn his promises, that if hired at the same wage as the others he would exhibit a lesser propensity to quit or to shirk than other employees with similar attributes are estimated to possess. The firm cannot observe his preferences, intentions, or character. The information on the quit behavior to which he would be willing to commit himself does not exist and cannot be produced. Similarly, the firm cannot observe the probability with which the employee shirks, it can only (hope to) observe instances of shirking and draw inferences accordingly or possibly act without any inferences as an object lesson to the others. From the perspective of the present theory, the wage-employment offers of the firms in the contrasting neoclassical equilibrium fail to be incentive-compatible, as they assume a willingness not to quit or not to shirk that is contrary to the actual and unobservable motives of the workers as long as firms behave classically.

How well or badly, we may ask, has incentive-wage theory performed when compared with empirical observations? This is not the best place for an extensive evaluation of incentive-wage models. A brief commentary may forestall some objections, however.

It might be asked why, if these models are valid, it should be the case that unemployment rates are lowest among the best paid. Don't they quit and shirk too? The answer, it seems, is that there are such strong nonpecuniary penalties that owners can present to the upper echelons of a firm that there is not a proportional impulse to push up the rewards of such workers to hold down their shirking and quitting.[10]

Or it might be asked why incentive-wage theory should be applied to the simpler tasks that are typically performed by the least-skilled workers. Does McDonalds have to worry about quitting or shirking? This view stands opposite to that just considered in that it suggests the theory explains unemployment only among workers holding the most sophisticated or crucial jobs. The answer here, it seems, is that even McDonalds must concern itself with the deportment and reliability of its workforce. To be nearly certain the workers will not amuse themselves by inserting unpleasant ingredients into the burgers, the employer must give the workers something to lose in the event there is evidence warranting suspicion of such behavior. The tendency to see low-skilled jobs as essentially neoclassical, as perfectly and costlessly monitorable and measurable in every respect at all times, stems from a weakness of the imagination.

The more deleterious objections that have beset incentive-wage theory, curiously, have not been empirical so much as a priori, or methodological, in nature. Some of these are the subject of the next chapter.

2

Contrary Postulates of the Neoclassical Schools

THE neoclassical theory regards the information problems on which the modern theory is centered, though real enough perhaps, as somehow surmounted by the participants in the market. On this premise it proceeds to show that equilibrium (in the expectational sense) implies market clearing: As long as the labor market does not clear, the argument goes, there are disappointed sellers or else disappointed buyers, hence disequilibrium. (In the modern setup, the unemployed expect that only a certain proportion of them will be lucky enough to be hired and in equilibrium the actual statistical experience bears out that expectation.) A thorough theoretical grounding of the modern view that equilibrium leaves many or all labor markets uncleared, with excess supplies, must therefore reply to the neoclassical objections. The present chapter is at least a small gesture in that direction.[1]

Theorists defending the neoclassical paradigm, such as Stigler and Alchian, have often argued that the equilibrium it portrays is self-enforcing, successfully overcoming moral hazards in general and, by implication, excessive quitting and shirking in particular.[2] If the owner of a factory were to leave it in a condition in which the risks of fire, say, were excessive, in the sense that the willingness of those working there to pay for a lessening of those risks through a wage reduction would exceed the cost of lessening those risks, the actuarial experience accumulated in the marketplace would soon enough cause workers to exact a wage premium for working at the riskier factory; so the owner must comply with the interests of the workers to work in a safer factory or be forced out of business.[3] Analogously, there is the argument that if an employee were to choose to quit without sufficient reason or to risk dismissal on the grounds of inadequate attention to duties, he or she would anticipate having to carry the evidence of this experience in his or her employment résumé, and the prospect of this black mark (or a sufficient number of them at any rate) would be a tolerably effective deterrent against such behavior.

The reply to that defense from the perspective of the modern theory is that it exaggerates the reliability with which employers can monitor the past employment relations of potential or actual employees. An applicant for employment at a firm can claim that the record has been lost or that a previous employer was retaliating for some grudge or that the previous employer was under a misapprehension in bringing the accusation. What seems like a workable device for enforcing good behavior by employees, if it were relied upon to the degree imagined, would require a costly institution to administer—a court system or some other public agency of third-party adjudicators to resolve the various issues in each worker's past employment record.

A second kind of defense of the neoclassical position, one receiving greater weight perhaps, argues that there is always some arrangement or institution by which any persons who are in the excess supply predicted by the modern analysis of equilibrium can reach an agreement with one or more employers for a mutual gain—for an Edgeworth improvement.[4] A modified position is that such arrangements or institutions could exist at any rate and only legal prohibitions bar some of them from being put into practice.

The shirking model of efficiency wages, for example, invites the objection that the firm could deter substandard performance by making it a policy to dock a worker's salary in proportion to the estimated shortfall from the stated norms of performance; if no more salary is due, the firm could demand return of past salary, and to guard against the infeasibility of collecting the firm could require that a security deposit be held in escrow during the employee's stay at the firm. It is not immediately obvious that there will not exist a labor-market equilibrium in which all firms follow such policies, no firm finding it in its self-interest to deviate along the modern lines of incentive pay. If it were replied that many workers, especially the young, would lack the wealth to put up such a security deposit, it could be answered that prospective workers could obtain funds from a bondsman in the same way that prisoners without vast wealth are able to put up bail to obtain freedom pending trial.

The modernist's reply to this line of argument is that, if the initial conditions are taken to be the modern equilibrium, a firm attempting to strike such an agreement with a worker in excess supply would be met with suspicion by the worker: the employer is possibly a scoundrel who already plans to make false claims against the worker once employed in order to defraud him of wages to which he will be entitled or defraud him of the security deposit he has made; or perhaps the employer will be normally prey to temptations to exaggerate claims or not to recognize extenuating circumstances or give the benefit of the doubt, and so forth. The worker would therefore have to anticipate the possibility or likelihood (with unknown probability) of costly litigation. Workers in excess supply may generally shy away from firms seeking to hire with these neoclassical personnel policies, therefore. Furthermore, many workers will be unable to finance the envisioned security deposit because bondsmen will know that for a worker so insured there would be a high degree of moral hazard, as the penalty for shirking would not be the employee's loss, so firms will likewise find it risky to count on the feasibility of compensation for employee underperformance. The kind of employment contract envisioned by neoclassical theory appears to be unenforceable or to make enforcement so costly and full of imponderables as to be unattractive to one or the other party or both.

The same conclusion could be reached by supposing instead that the initial conditions were somehow those of market clearing and arguing that in that situation, with its attendant legal costs and distrust, the adoption by some firms of a policy of incentive pay—the carrot, not simply the stick—would attract employees away from the other firms. Both lines of analysis will reach the conclusion that incentive wages will be endemic and that excess supplies will be a side effect. It might be remarked, however, that workers with large levels of wealth, since they can better finance, would have an advantage in that respect over the less wealthy; but their greater ability to pay litigation costs and more generally the "price" of shirking makes them prime candidates for early involuntary retirement.

The firm's task of motivating the employee not to quit except when the aggregate benefit to the two parties to the employment contract exceeds the cost is also problematic, perhaps more so, than motivating employees not to shirk. Here again the neoclassical theorists often speak of a scheme to combat excessive quitting in which, as a condition of being hired by the firm, a worker must post a refundable deposit to indemnify the firm against the cost it would suffer in the event he quit. But again such a scheme would be subject to abuse by the employer: in unprofitable conditions the employer could harass the employee into quitting with the objective of obtaining the deposit, so the employee might have trouble enforcing the terms of the deposit. In addition, the employer might not be able to enforce the agreement because a worker might be able to claim that the firm harassed him into quitting as a means of taking the deposit.

How then to interpret the vision of equilibrium, with its market-clearing feature, presented by neoclassical theory? To say that the neoclassical system abstracts from the problems of information is one way, and well known. It is reasonable to understand the neoclassical system as describing a society in which all participants have a decent respect for a set of rights protecting people against deceptive dealing, fraud and theft of property. Institutions, including private firms, work only because there are people in them who would suffer a costly loss in their integrity if they did not adhere to the understandings in their implicit employment contract.[5]

But while the notion that there exist mechanisms and utility functions serving to motivate prosocial behavior undoubtedly has an important role to play in permitting us to grasp why social cooperation is as widespread as it is in organizations and society, antisocial phenomena of uncooperativeness are also sufficiently widespread as to create a pattern to be explained. That the neoclassical paradigm takes us as far as it does is remarkable; it is the paradigm on which much of the success of economics rests. But if we are to address the shortfall of reality from the neoclassical paradigm, some room must also be made for the modern paradigm.

Another issue divides neoclassical and modern proponents. The neoclassicals can point to the fact that there is no quitting problem and no shirking problem at all in an important submarket for labor services—the self-employment submarket—so in that submarket there is no tendency for equilibrium to entail a wage above the market-clearing level. There is held to be a sense in which the labor market as a whole can be said to clear under conditions of equilibrium because, in equilibrium, the "wage" for selling apples on street corners must be sufficiently low that there is no excess supply for such services; any excess supply is strictly a disequilibrium phenomenon (resulting from incorrect expectations). Some models conjure up an entire "secondary" sector in which the wage is posited to clear the market; wages are above-clearing only in the "primary" sector, and those in excess supply there work in the secondary sector while keeping their names in the pool or their places in the queue for a job in the primary sector. In such models no involuntary unemployment results from the nonclearing of wages for incentive reasons in the primary sector.

A richer model of a market generally possesses advantages, of course, but it is not clear that for purposes of macroeconomic analysis the benefits of the two-submarket model are substantial enough to outweigh the costs of the complications. Even if, when labor demand drops in the job-rationed submarket, all of those losing their jobs turn to selling services in the submarket that clears, the significance of this observation is not obvious: when those rationed jobs are eliminated, workers are involuntarily forced out of employments in which there is already excess supply to begin with because of efficiency wages, so they suffer a first-order loss of welfare; society as a whole suffers a similar loss as well since there must have been underemployment in the submarket with the excess supply as a result of the high wages used to combat excessive quitting and shirking. It is true in this case, with all the disemployed successfully reallocated to selling apples, that there will be no measured unemployment on this account, but there is still the involuntary reduction of employment in the preferred jobs.

For various reasons, however, not everyone losing a job will choose to move to the market-clearing sector: for some it would pay too little; some would be stigmatized for doing the kind of work available in the secondary market; others would not want to lose the possibility of immediately accepting a preferred job in the event it suddenly becomes available—there must be many considerations at work here. Hence, despite the choice of some to take up work in the market-clearing submarket, there will be an increase of measured unemployment, and this measured unemployment is the counterpart of an involuntary decrease of employment in the preferred submarket where the job rationing goes on. So the aggregate treatment of the labor market used throughout the present study, following most of the early models of the incentive-wage type, does seem to capture in a qualitative way the main features to be represented when there is an economywide contraction in the demand for labor: the involuntariness of the job losses and the increase of measured unemployment.

None of this discussion should be confused with a quite different question: whether the neoclassical theory, properly developed, can arrive at the same predictions with regard to employment and wages that the structuralist theory based on job rationing reaches. Later in this work there will be an opportunity to contrast the neoclassical predictions with the structuralist ones in this regard. But this much is clear: the neoclassical theory will not be able to explain fluctuations in involuntary unemployment in any ordinary sense of the term. The neoclassical models in which employees have contracts permitting them to be furloughed in the event of certain contingencies does suggest a kind of "unemployment." But the workers who are parties to such labor contracts with their employer remain employees during the spell of idleness, as they continue to draw some kind of salary and do not lose any rights of seniority that may have accumu-lated. Indeed, a frequently cited objection to this neo-neoclassical modeling of unemployment is that the "employed" are implied to envy the "unem-ployed."

It is hard to see how it is possible to escape the conclusion that the distinct perspective of the modern theory is needed alongside that of the neoclassical tradition if we are to understand the fluctuations of what we commonly regard as involuntary unemployment.

3

The Labor-Market Equilibrium Locus
in Modern Models

THE originators of the various notions of the natural unemployment rate did not investigate the influence on the natural rate of shifts in either the demand for labor or the supply of labor. It was recognized that an exogenous increase in the propensity to quit, for example, or in the rate of inflow of new workers, either of which would increase steady-state turnover, would tend directly to increase the natural rate. Yet for more than a decade the models containing a natural rate were a long way from addressing the usual array of nonmonetary shocks. By default, the natural unemployment rate, though not conceived a constant, came to be treated in applied work as one of the great "constants" of economics: it could drift with *time* somehow, but it was not allowed to move with the shock under analysis.

This situation began to change in the late 1970s. Open-economy and closed-economy models appeared based on the postulate of real-wage rigidity instead of a natural rate invariant to real shocks.[1] These models portray real shocks that reduce the real demand price of labor as contracting equilibrium employment, not just (or not at all) the equilibrium real wage. An empirical study by Jeffrey Sachs, taking for granted that real shocks lay behind employment disturbances, sought the explanation in varying degrees of real-wage resistance—an intermediate case between rigidity and accommodation leaving the equilibrium unemployment rate unchanged.[2]

A prototype general-equilibrium model of the natural rate was first developed by Steven Salop, a model based on the turnover story of Phelps and Stiglitz.[3] A richer second-generation model in a similar spirit by Shapiro and Stiglitz followed a few years later, this one based on the parallel shirking story proposed by Calvo and Bowles.[4] These models determine the equilibrium wage level at each given unemployment rate when every firm is optimally taking into account incentive considerations and the wage at the other firms. The aspect of interest is the relationship between the equilibrium wage and the given unemployment rate. The analyses reveal the theoretical possibility that the equilibrium wage is an increasing function of the employment rate.[5] But these models of labor-market equilibrium conditions do not really establish that the natural rate is driven down by shocks pulling up the derived demand for labor and thus lifting the real wage. The reason, which will become apparent in this chapter, is that the wage-setting curve is not generally invariant to shocks that shift the labor demand curve.

The notion of a relationship between the equilibrium incentive wage and the unemployment rate—to be called here the *labor-market equilibrium locus* or simply the *equilibrium wage curve*—was clearly a critical step. It provides a kind of surrogate labor supply curve, or employment supply curve, to be juxtaposed against some sort of demand curve. The supply block containing this relationship, when combined with any labor-demand block of one's choice, jointly determines the equilibrium unemployment rate and equilibrium wage. A new paradigm was taking shape, whether or not it would prove viable. On the other hand, some pitfalls remained to be identified and circumvented for further progress to occur.[6]

This chapter is devoted to deriving an example of the equilibrium wage locus drawn from the turnover model and another example of the wage locus based on the shirking model. Although a few features of these illustrative formulations foreshadow some results from the utility-theoretic analysis appearing later, this introductory exposition cannot of course deduce all the theoretical propositions derivable from a microtheoretic general-equilibrium model. The micromodeling of the behavior of employees on which any incentive-wage model must ultimately be based will be studied in Part IV.

3.1 Quitting and the Equilibrium Wage Curve

Consider the turnover model of incentive wages introduced in Chapter 1. In this model, an employee is with some frequency seized by the urge to leave his or her job for the unemployed pool in order to be available for employment in some newly preferred location. The exploration here is confined to firms with a large and apparently homogeneous work force from the standpoint of their productivity and propensity to quit.

The proportionate quit rate, or propensity to quit as we may call it,

experienced at such a firm, it will be argued in Chapter 15, can be written
as a function of the firm's own wage; the wage that the firm's employees
expect will be offered at the other firms—with allowance made for the
employment rate to reflect the possibility of actually obtaining the wage
rate elsewhere; and the average wealth level of the employees—to be more
precise, the income from their average asset holdings. Known by the names
income from wealth, unearned income, and *independent income,* it is the
income from stocks and bonds and other property or, as in a later chapter,
annuity income.

The first two considerations affecting the quit rate are obvious enough.
An increase of the ith firm's own real wage, v^i, clearly operates to reduce
the propensity to quit; the opportunity cost of quitting to join the unemployment pool in a newly preferred location is increased. Symmetrically,
an improvement in the wage-income prospect of persons in the unemployment pool, due either to an increase in the expected wage rate elsewhere,
v^e, or to a decrease of the unemployment rate, u, clearly operates in the
opposite direction; the expected value of the benefit from quitting to join
the unemployed in the newly desired location is increased. This prospect
will be proxied, as is nearly standard practice, by the product $(1 - u)v^e$,
which is taken to be identical across firms. Of course, this product is only
an approximation of the theoretically correct representation.[7]

The third consideration is the workers' average independent income,
to be denoted y^w. In intertemporal models of any realism, the employees'
average wealth, w, and their income from wealth, y^w, are there—they exist—and, in principle, they have a rightful place in the quit-rate function
as well as in the various demand and supply functions. The substantive
rationale for this third argument of the quit-rate function is that the higher
the independent income of workers, the better they are able to get along
without employment in order to travel and present themselves as available
for employment at firms in some other area. In the simplified formulation
here, only the income from assets is introduced in the quit-rate function;
the capitalized real value of assets is excluded, which is very natural if,
as in the more formal analyses of the later chapters, it is assumed that
all assets are exchanged for insurance policies paying annuities and life-
insurance dividends. A small point is worth being quite clear about: if we
conceive of the wage rates as real wages—measured in consumer goods,
that is—the corresponding average income y^w should be thought of as real
nonwage income after nonwage transfers and nonwage taxes; then the impact of an increase in the value-added tax rate would be to lower real wage
rates and real unearned income in the same proportion; if instead the wage

rates are conceived as *product* wages—measured in capital goods, intermediate goods, exports, or whatever—it is again natural to define independent income in the same units as the wage, here the good produced.

To sum up: At each firm the propensity to quit, or rate of attrition, is given by a quit-rate function $\zeta(v^i, (1 - u)v^e, y^w)$, the first derivatives of which are respectively negative, positive, and positive.[8]

Quitting matters to firms in the turnover model of incentive pay for a chain of reasons. Newly hired workers at a firm are not productive there until they have received a requisite amount of orientation and familiarization with the firm. In providing this training the firm is making an investment, diverting the efforts of a portion of its existing employees from the production of output to "breaking in" the newly hired. It will be supposed that training cost, measured in product, per unit of time is a constant-returns-to-scale function of hiring and the stock of (trained) employees. Let E^i denote the stock of employees and h denote the hire rate. Current hiring, and hence training, per unit of time is therefore hE^i. In these terms, it will be supposed that current training costs are a linear homogeneous function $T(hE^i, E^i; \Lambda)$ having positive first derivatives with respect to its two arguments. Since $T(\cdot)$ measures the opportunity cost in foregone output of diverting functional employees to the orientation of the stream of new recruits, it is measured in units of the firm's output; for the same reason, the function T must be indexed by the marginal product of functional employees, which will be denoted by Λ.[9] An equivalent expression for current hiring costs is $E^i T(h^i, 1; \Lambda)$. The derivative of $T(h^i, 1; \Lambda)$ with respect to h^i may be called *marginal training cost* and will be denoted $T'(h^i, 1; \Lambda)$. It is positive and nondecreasing.

This investment cost is borne by the firm, not by the worker, in the sense that the worker does not write a check to pay the cost of the training. That is because what that worker gains is not knowledge of general use in raising his or her wage prospects, which is the sort of investment the worker would undertake up to a point unilaterally, but information specific to the individual firm; the cost of this information is rather like a tax levied on the transaction, and the incidence of the "tax" similar. Hence the firm stands to lose the unamortized part of its investment in an employee should he or she decide eventually to quit the firm.[10]

One way of characterizing the firm's optimal policy is to find the product wage, v^i, and the hire rate, h^i, that at each point in time maximize current "cash flow" in terms of product *plus* an appropriate allowance for the rate of growth of trained employees, which will be of profit in the future; this growth rate may be written as $[h^i - \zeta(v^i, (1 - u)v^e, y^w)]$.[11] An equivalent procedure is to find the wage and hire rate that minimize current total costs in terms of product, including the opportunity costs incurred by training *minus* the same allowance for the rate at which trained employees are being accumulated. In this formulation the precise expression to be minimized is

(3.1) $\{v^i + T(h^i, 1; \Lambda) - q^i[h^i - \zeta(v^i, (1 - u)v^e, y^w)]\}E^i \equiv \mathcal{H}(v^i, h^i)$

This is a Hamiltonian function in which q is the shadow price of trained employees, reflecting their present discounted value per employee, which multiplies the current rate of accumulation in the square brackets.[12] The first-order condition for the optimum wage to combat quitting is

(3.2a) $-\zeta_1(v^i, (1 - u)v^e, y^w)q = 1$

and the optimum hiring rate is given by

(3.2b) $T'(h^i, 1; \Lambda) = q$

At the minimum with respect to v^i, in (3.2a), the cost per functional employee of a unit increase of the wage, given by the righthand side and equal to one, would be just counterbalanced by the marginal benefit, given by the lefthand side, which is the consequent reduction in turnover multiplied by the shadow price of employees, q, or, equivalently in view of (3.2b), by marginal training cost.[13]

If we suppose that all firms have the same training technology and are otherwise in an identical situation as well, so that they are equal in every respect, condition (3.2a) becomes an equation in the economywide wage, v, given its expectation, v^e. In an equilibrium scenario, the case with which we are concerned, we also have

(3.3) $v^e = v$

at each moment along the equilibrium path. Upon replacing v^e by v, equation (3.2a) determines the equilibrium v as a function of $1 - u$ and q.

Another relationship is that determining the equilibrium level of nonwage income per worker as a function of the equilibrium wage, the employment rate (taken to be equal to E/L), and the shadow price:[14]

(3.4) $y^w = (1 - u)[\Lambda - q\zeta(v, (1 - u)v, y^w) - v]$

The level of assets per worker (denoted generically by a), which is here E/L, is multiplied by the quasirent per asset (denoted generically by R).[15]

A question that will be investigated here is how the equilibrium wage varies with the employment rate. In one of the elementary general-equilibrium models to be presented below, that in Chapter 7, the question of how the equilibrium v varies with increasing $1 - u$ is analyzed while holding constant the value of q. In that exercise the value of $T'(\cdot)$ must be correspondingly constant to satisfy (3.2b). Another exercise is to determine how the equilibrium wage depends on the employment rate when instead it is assumed that marginal training cost is a functional constant, to be denoted T', contrary to the model here. In that exercise q must adjust to that constant to satisfy (3.2b). These two exercises must lead to the same answer.

Taking q to be constant and using (3.3), equation (3.2a) becomes

(3.5) $1 = -\zeta_1(v, (1 - u)v, y^w)q \qquad q = \text{constant} > 0$

Since (3.4) determines y^w as a function of v and u, given q, the system of (3.4) and (3.5) together determine the equilibrium supply wage, or optimal incentive wage, as a function of $1 - u$, given q. This relationship is the labor-market equilibrium locus.

Total differentiation of this system yields the following result for the slope of the equilibrium locus with respect to the employment rate:

(3.6) $$\frac{dv}{d(1 - u)} = \frac{-(\zeta_{12}v + \zeta_{13}y^w_{1-u})}{\zeta_{11} + \zeta_{12}(1 - u) + \zeta_{13}y^w_v}$$

where y^w_{1-u} denotes the total derivative of y^w with respect to $1 - u$ and y^w_v denotes the total derivative with respect to v (using $v^e = v$ already incorporated in (3.4)). What, in view of this result, are the implications of the model for the slope of the locus?

THE SLOPE OF THE LOCUS WITH y^w CONSTANT

Let us begin the analysis of the slope of the equilibrium wage locus in (3.5) as if y^w were independent of v and $1 - u$. We disregard the derivatives of y^w.

Then, in evaluating the numerator in (3.6) we look only at the first term, which, taken with the minus sign in front, measures how the decrease of the quit rate induced by a given absolute increase of the firm's own wage is altered by an improvement in income prospects elsewhere generated by an increase of the employment rate. Presumably this decrease goes up as prospects elsewhere are improved; that is, $-\zeta_{12}v > 0$. This is the germ of the intuition that firms are motivated to choose a higher wage the higher is the employment rate: the marginal effectiveness of a wage increase is potentiated by an increase in the likely quit rate brought about by reduced unemployment. But we are not done

The denominator in (3.6), still taking nonwage income to be invariant, is unambiguously positive at least at near-zero employment rates. The reason is that $\zeta_{12}(1 - u)$ is small at low employment rates and $\zeta_{11} > 0$ by virtue of the second-order condition for a cost minimum: if the wage is pushed up by successive equal amounts, the successive reductions of the quit rate are diminishing in the neighborhood of the minimum. This is the diminishing marginal effectiveness of the firm's own wage. But since ζ_{12} < 0 by the argument of the previous paragraph on the numerator, meaning that a given absolute wage increase would have greater marginal effectiveness the higher the going wage at other firms, the algebraic sign of the denominator looks problematic at high employment rates.

The difference model. The accustomed practice in analyzing such an incentive-wage model, a practice begun by Calvo and adopted in many subsequent formulations, is to specify that the employee behavior that firms are offering incentive pay to discourage, here the quitting behavior described by the function ζ, depends on the two wage rates simply through the *difference* between income prospects if employed and if unemployed, $v - (1 - u)v^e$. In that linear case, ζ_{11} and ζ_{12} are equal in absolute size and of opposite sign, so that $\zeta_{11} + \zeta_{12}(1 - u)$ reduces to $-\zeta_{12}u > 0$, so the denominator is then everywhere positive. Since the numerator, taken with the minus sign, was seen to be positive as well, the implication is that the slope of the locus is positive, income from wealth aside. This is the now-standard result.[16]

Such an equilibrium locus is illustrated in Figure 3.1. This locus is asymptotic to the vertical line representing full employment—an employment rate of one.[17]

The objection to the linear specification just discussed is that it is ad hoc not just in the sense of being arbitrary—a model, after all, abstracts arbitrarily from some mechanisms to highlight others, so an arbitrary specification, if well chosen, may be equally acceptable—but in the sense that it is not clear that v and $(1 - u)v^e$ could enter that way if the quit-rate function were derived from a microeconomic model making the traditional

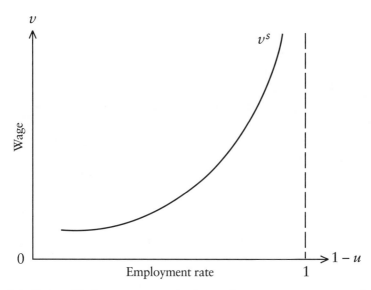

Figure 3.1 The equilibrium wage curve in the employment rate–wage rate plane: The employee turnover-training story

rationality postulates. It is hard to imagine how a utility-theoretic formulation could deliver such linearity, since one would expect in any tolerably complete modeling that a given difference between v and $(1 - u)v^e$ would have less significance for an employee the greater is their level. Maybe some specification of a utility-theoretic model would imply that it is the *ratio* between v and $(1 - u)v^e$ that matters for the quit rate, nonwage income aside, not the difference.

The ratio model. If we specify the quit rate to be a function of the ratio, and if furthermore we banish income from wealth, the denominator in the righthand side of (3.6) becomes zero in value. The numerator remains nonzero. In this ratio case, therefore, the slope of the equilibrium wage locus is infinite at every wage. Undoubtedly this was precisely the case in the minds of macroeconomists in the 1970s when it became implicit in their modeling that changes in the general level of wages had no significant effect on the equilibrium value of the unemployment rate.[18] However it will not do for our purposes, since a sloping equilibrium wage curve must lie at the heart of any model showing how shifts in the derived demand for labor have effects, at least transient ones, on both the equilibrium wage and, as a by-product, the equilibrium employment rate.

A plausible solution to this specification question, and one that is indirectly supported by the utility-theoretic model in Chapter 15, is to suppose that the things that matter for the quit rate are the wage *relative* to the income from wealth of the employees, v/y^w, and (our proxy for) wage prospects elsewhere *relative* to income from wealth, $(1 - u)v^e/y^w$. The hypothesis to be adopted here, one that is empirically plausible and will be shown to be theoretically admissible as well, is that an equiproportionate increase or decrease in all three arguments of the quit-rate function leaves the quit rate unchanged.

The homogeneity specification. The restriction we are introducing, then, is that the function ζ is homogeneous of degree zero in its three arguments, given certain other factors that will remain in the background in the present chapter. Hence the quit-rate function can be written, among other ways, as on the righthand side:

(3.7) $\zeta(v^i, (1 - u)v^e, y^w) = \zeta(1, (1 - u)v^e/v^i, y^w/v^i)$

On this homogeneity specification, the first-order condition becomes[19]

(3.2a') $1 = -(1/v^i)\zeta_1(1, (1 - u)v^e/v^i, y^w/v^i)q$

upon making use of the zero-degree homogeneity property that the first partial derivatives weighted by their corresponding arguments add up to zero: $\zeta_1 v^i + \zeta_2(1 - u)v^e + \zeta_3 y^w = 0$.[20]

As before, we impose $v^i = v$ and use $v^e = v$ in differentiating (3.2a') to obtain the slope of the equilibrium wage curve:

(3.6') $$\frac{dv}{d(1 - u)} = \frac{-(\zeta_{12}v + \zeta_{13}y^w_{1-u})}{-\zeta_1 - \zeta_{13}(y^w/v) + \zeta_{13}y^w_v}$$

Remembering still to disregard the terms involving the derivatives of the y^w function, we find that the strictly positive slope of the equilibrium locus is now unambiguous. Here the denominator can clearly be taken to be positive, since the spirit of the homogeneous quit function makes ζ_{13} as well as ζ_{12} of opposite sign to ζ_{11} and hence negative: both an increase in expected wages elsewhere and an increase in nonwage income potentiate the marginal effectiveness of an increase in the firm's wage at any given level of that wage. In effect, the ambiguity over whether $[\zeta_{11} + \zeta_{12}(1 - u)]$ in (3.6) is positive or zero or negative is resolved by calculating that it equals $-\zeta_1 - \zeta_{13}(y^w/v)$ and ensuring that the latter be positive by requiring ζ_{13} to be negative in the spirit of the stipulation that ζ_{12} is negative. Note finally that, with both ζ_{13} and ζ_{12} negative, the numerator is also positive. So the righthand side of (3.6′) is positive, as was to be shown.

The mechanism underlying this result should be clear: An increase of the employment rate, with q and the parameters of the model held constant, makes the wage prospects consequent upon quitting more favorable and it also raises the nonwage income available on stocks held by employees. One result of each of these effects is an increase in the rate of quitting for given wages at the employees' own firm and elsewhere. The crucial result, however, is that the effect of a given wage increase by the individual firm on employee quitting is strengthened, thus heightening the marginal cost-effectiveness for the firm of raising its pay scale; it is somewhat as if the firm had accidentally *reduced its own wage rate* relative to others' and to nonwage income. The response of firms is to raise their own wage rates, which tends to bring the marginal effectiveness of increased pay back down to its previous and optimal level. Through this mechanism the equilibrium level of the product wage is driven up.[21]

THE SLOPE WHEN NONWAGE INCOME IS ALSO CONSIDERED

To complete this rudimentary analysis of the slope of the equilibrium wage curve, it is necessary to bring in the effects of the wage and the employment rate on employees' average nonwage income. It will be assumed here that the average nonwage income of employees is satisfactorily measured by nonwage income per worker, though the average quantity of assets held by employees might change with a change of the employment rate.[22] So y^w, defined as the nonwage income per capita and per unit of the labor force, proxies for employees' average unearned income.

Consider first the denominator in (3.6′). It can be grasped immediately from consideration of equation (3.4) that $y_v^w < 0$, meaning that increased wages reduce nonwage income per share. It might be thought that, locally, a small increase of the wage would have no effect, as each firm in labor-market equilibrium is using its wage to achieve a maximum of its own nonwage income. However, the increase of the other firms' wages increases the quit rate at the individual firm, and thus exposes it to increased turnover costs. The fact that the wage reaction of the individual firm to the increase of wages has no effect itself, by the envelope theorem, and the same applies to the speed with which it feeds new workers to the training department, in no way avoids the first-order effect on its costs. With $y_v^w < 0$ and $\zeta_{13} < 0$, as required earlier, it follows that this added factor only fortifies the positive sign of the denominator in (3.6′).

Now the numerator in (3.6'). Here it can be seen from (3.4) that in the range of low enough employment rates, $y^w_{1-u} > 0$. It might be thought that necessarily, in the neighborhood of labor-market equilibrium, the opposite sign applies, since the competitive firms here overproduce from the perspective of profit; a thoroughly cartelized industry would curtail output. However, the partial derivative y^w_{1-u} holds constant the real wage, and hence the labor price of the product, so it takes no account that the market is being "spoiled" a little by the increase of output produced by the increase of employment. If the turnover rate were invariant to the employment rate, the derivative would be a constant, and a positive one, since firms must cover their training costs with gross profits if they are to be viable. The ambiguity arises once the turnover rate has risen with increased employment to a level such that a further small increase of employment, in increasing the turnover rate more, might increase costs by as much as or more than output. At this point and even more markedly at higher employment rates, we may suppose, the individual firm is willing to produce more (at an unchanged wage) because that action by itself only increases its profit, equiproportionately in fact; but the similar actions of the other firms will cause its profit to drop. So we may think of two intervals. In the low employment range, $y^w_{1-u} > 0$. Hence the positive sign of the numerator in (3.6') is reinforced. In the high employment range, the sign is opposite, being negative, and as we go into the interval the sign of the numerator becomes theoretically ambiguous.

Of course, as an empirical matter, we observe that there are large overhead costs at each firm, so that firms are actually making considerable losses at depression or even recession levels of output; the firms are in business because they know that, between depression and a normal level of activity, increased output and employment tends over a very large range to have a huge positive effect on profit, as wages are much below the marginal productivity of labor (even net of interest and amortization on training costs). In a more general model capturing that element, therefore, nonwage income would increase with employment over nearly all of its range and very likely at all observed employment levels.

The turnover model thus provides strong support for the notion of an upward-sloping labor-market equilibrium locus in the employment rate–product wage rate plane.

3.2 Shirking and the Equilibrium Wage Curve

The other incentive-wage model is based on shirking. In the formulation adopted in this volume, paid labor—represented by the number of persons employed, all of them technically identical and behaving alike—has to be multiplied by the "effort" of workers to obtain a measure of effective labor input in production. For costs to be at a minimum at any given employment level, the wage at the ith firm must be high enough to minimize the ratio of its wage, v^i, to effort at the firm, say, $\varepsilon(v^i, (1 - u)v^e, y^w)$.

The minimization problem at such a firm may be described as

$$(3.8) \qquad \varsigma^i(1 - u; v^e) = \min_{v^i} [v^i/\varepsilon(v^i, (1 - u)v^e, y^w)]$$

Here $1 - u$ is again the employment rate, N/L, where N denotes the number of workers employed and L is the total supply of workers to the labor market.

Upon applying the same homogeneity postulate to the present example that we used before, and viewing the firm as choosing the v^i/y^w ratio, to be denoted θ^i, and the other firms as choosing the corresponding v/y^w, θ, the expectation of which is the v^e/y^w ratio, θ^e, the minimization can be written

$$(3.8') \qquad \varsigma^i(1 - u; \theta^e) = \min_{\theta^i} [\theta^i y^w (1 - u, \theta)/\varepsilon(\theta^i, (1 - u)\theta^e, 1)]$$

The first-order condition is then[23]

$$(3.9) \qquad 0 = \theta^i \varepsilon_1(\theta^i, (1 - u)\theta^e, 1) - \varepsilon(\theta^i, (1 - u)\theta^e, 1)$$

With $\theta^i = \theta$ for all i, as before, and the equilibrium condition that $\theta = \theta^e$, as in (3.3), there results an equation determining the equilibrium θ as a function of $1 - u$, which will not be displayed.

The nature of the equilibrium relationship between θ and $1 - u$ can be investigated through an analysis of (3.9) with the use of the equilibrium condition $\theta = \theta^e$ and hence $d\theta = d\theta^e$. Total differentiation of (9) yields

$$(3.10) \qquad d\theta = \{[\theta\varepsilon_{12}(1 - u) - \varepsilon_2(1 - u)]/(-\theta\varepsilon_{11})\}d\theta^e$$
$$+ \{[\theta\varepsilon_{12}\theta^e - \varepsilon_2\theta^e]/(-\theta\varepsilon_{11})\}d(1 - u)$$

A small increase of the employment rate, $d(1 - u)$, has a positive impact effect on θ since, in the denominator of the pertinent coefficient, $\varepsilon_{11} < 0$ by the second-order condition for a cost minimum, while in the numerator we have $-\varepsilon_2 > 0$ and we specify $\varepsilon_{12} > 0$. Of course, since y^w is also in-

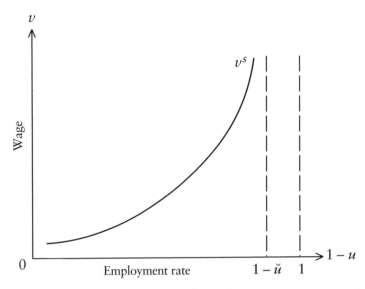

Figure 3.2 The equilibrium wage curve in the employment rate–wage rate plane: The shirking story

creased by the stimulus to the employment rate, the absolute wage, v, must also show a positive (and proportionately greater) increase.

An interesting wrinkle in the shirking model concerns the magnitude of the equilibrium effect on the wage—and the very existence of an equilibrium effect. Suffice it to say that over a range of unemployment rates sufficiently high, there exists a (finite) wage for labor-market equilibrium. The matter is perhaps best left for an endnote to those wishing to pursue it.[24]

An equilibrium wage locus like the one just discussed is shown in Figure 3.2. The critical employment rate is denoted by $1 - \breve{u}$.

This chapter has introduced the concept of the labor-market equilibrium locus, or equilibrium wage curve. It has investigated rather informally some properties of typical equilibrium wage curves. The models in Part II provide a less informal analysis. An explicit dynamic utility-theoretic derivation awaits the middle part of this volume.

The labor-market equilibrium locus is just one of the building blocks of the modern theory of unemployment determination under construction here. Another one is the labor demand–price function, an introductory examination of which is the purpose of the next chapter.

4

The Product-Market Equilibrium Locus and Partial-Equilibrium Unemployment Determination

THIS chapter reaches a partial-equilibrium view of the determination of the (equilibrium path of the) unemployment rate. The subsequent chapter will introduce a general-equilibrium perspective on unemployment. Several equations will parade by, yet the discussion is informal and the emphasis is on the underlying ideas rather than rigorous details.

This partial-equilibrium determination of the path of the employment rate is obtained by adding to the condition for labor-market equilibrium, introduced in Chapter 3, the condition for product-market equilibrium. The function of the present chapter is to discuss the notion of product-market equilibrium in each of the three models studied in this volume.

What is product-market equilibrium? It will be recalled that labor-market equilibrium, as that term is used here, requires, among other expectational conditions, that each of the firms have correct expectations about the product wage at the other firms, an expectation of which their own product-wage offer is a function.[1] Analogously, product-market equilibrium requires, among other expectational conditions, that each of the firms has correct expectations about the price to be received by the others relatively to its own, the price being expressed in terms of the asset, a convenient numeraire.[2]

In the case of customer markets, in which the firm does not know the current-period price being charged by the other firms, the application of the idea of product-market equilibrium is clear: the firm's own price-quantity decision depends on its expectation of the price-quantity decision of the others. In auction-type product markets, the possibility of a product-market disequilibrium of any consequence requires firms' employment and production decisions in the current period to be based to a degree on their expectation of the going price to emerge at the end of the current period

or subsequent periods: they might then offer a wage expressed in units of
the asset numeraire that was expected to yield the optimal product wage
from the standpoint of incentives, then hire and produce accordingly, only
to find that the price level in units of the numeraire and hence the actual
product wage turned out to be different from their expectation.[3]

Thus product-market equilibrium entails that firms are supplying in the
current period what they would do under correct expectations about actual
prices (over the industry or various industries). This means that firms are
currently "on" their output supply curve, more precisely, their *correctly
informed* supply curve or, better, their *equilibrium* supply curve.

Since labor demand is a derived demand, as Marshall put it, deriving
from the supply of output, the property of being on the output supply
curve can be translated to the condition of being on the labor demand
curve. Equilibrium with regard to labor demand requires equilibrium in
the supply of output produced by the labor—hence product-market equilibrium. More precisely, the equilibrium level of work force that is demanded (or, taking training costs into account, the equilibrium growth of
the work force that is demanded) at a given real wage can be interpreted
to mean the employment level (or employment growth) needed to gain the
capacity for supplying output that the firms would want at that wage under
correct price expectations. The firms must have correct expectations in
order to be able to estimate correctly the worth of having a marginal increase in the level (or the growth) of employment.

Accordingly, the equilibrium curve that would normally be labeled "labor demand curve" is, when translated to the employment rate–wage
plane, labeled the *product-market equilibrium locus* to emphasize the connection to the product market. A more informal name is the *equilibrium
employment-rate curve* or, in models where the employment rate is not a
jump variable, the *demand-wage relationship*.

It follows from all this that the partial equilibrium studied in this chapter requires that the firms' wage be "on" the equilibrium wage-setting locus, which is the labor-market equilibrium condition, *and*—the product-
market condition—that the firms be "on" the labor demand curve, hence
in equilibrium with respect to the level of their work forces or, in models
with rising marginal training costs, to the growth in their stocks of employees. In models without rising training or other hiring costs, therefore, the
current partial-equilibrium employment rate is indicated by the intersection of the wage curve and the labor demand curve. In models with rising
training costs, it is not quite so simple, of course.

We finally arrive at the question to which this chapter aims to give an introductory answer: What features of an economy determine the position and the slope of its equilibrium employment curve, or product equilibrium locus, in the employment rate–wage rate plane? What is wanted is a treatment of that curve, at least that curve in special cases, that is in the same modern spirit underlying the equilibrium wage curve of the previous chapter.

For modeling the labor-demand function, most economists have usually been content to use a neoclassical and aggregative approach based on perfect information in both product and labor markets, the aggregation of products, and an aggregate production function exhibiting constant returns to scale and diminishing returns. Inverting the labor-demand function, one obtains for the "demand wage" labor's marginal product, which is a decreasing function of employment.

The great movers and shakers of this neoclassical aggregative labor-demand function are supply shocks in the broad sense—technological shocks and capital stock shocks as well as oil shocks and land fertility shocks, shocks which are representable as shifts of the production function. Since the present-day proponents of what they call the "real business cycle" theory have been united in adopting exclusively the neoclassical aggregate marginal-product-of-labor function as the demand curve, it is these supply-side shocks which have been the focus of attention in their analysis of employment fluctuation. In that framework, demand shocks can transmit disturbances to the labor market through the labor-demand function only if they somehow affect the stocks of knowledge, capital, oil, or land—or else the relevant service flows from these assets.[4] As a consequence, the real business cycle theory has constrained itself to the position, which has become a part of its identity, that demand shocks can disturb the labor market only through income or interest-rate effects operating through the supply of labor. Hence, in this view, public expenditure expands employment if and only if it drives down the real wage, inducing enterprises to take on more labor, by dampening workers' estimates of their lifetime overall wealth after deduction of expected taxes.[5]

What follows is a discussion of the properties of labor demand emerging from three kinds of models of the modern type, all of which take into account informational problems of one sort or another. These models should be thought of as additive in the sense of being integrable into a comprehensive model preserving their common features and resolving (with a net resultant to be determined empirically) their opposing features.

4.1 Labor Demand and Firms' Investment in Employees

The turnover-training model of the incentive wage introduced in the previous chapter presents a mechanism of labor demand that has some distinctive features. This model can make use of the simplest possible conception of the product market, namely the perfectly competitive model of the product market, without losing the properties that the turnover model of the labor market tends to impart to the labor demand curve. Under correct expectations, as commented earlier, this perfectly competitive product market is always in equilibrium. Despite perfect competition, however, product-market equilibrium in the model is not characterized by "price (in terms of the asset) equals marginal cost," and marginal product equals real wage, as a result of turnover and the costs of training.

What exactly is the relationship generated by the turnover model between aggregate employment demanded, expressed as a ratio to labor supply, and the economywide wage? It is necessary to delve into the anatomy of the firm's maximization problem. As observed in the previous chapter, the ith firm, aiming to maximize the present discounted value of the stream of estimated profits over time, may be interpreted as calculating the appropriate shadow price, q^i, to impute to its trained employees, E^i in number, and forming a Hamiltonian function corresponding to this price,

$$(4.1) \quad \{\Lambda - v^i - T(h^i, 1; \Lambda)$$
$$+ q^i[h^i - \zeta(v^i, (1 - u)v^e, y^w)]\}E^i \equiv \mathcal{H}(v^i, h^i; q^i)$$

the current value of which it maximizes at each point in time with respect to the gross hiring rate, h^i, defined as hires per unit time per employee, and to the wage; the wage optimization was studied in the previous chapter. The bracketed expression, being the excess of the hiring rate over the quit rate, equals the current growth rate of the employee stock, g^i. As before, all the firms here are taken to be alike, save possibly for the happenstance scale of their initial stock of employees, which is of no consequence.

A relevant finding regarding the optimal hiring rate was obtained in the previous chapter. Each firm equates marginal training cost to the shadow price of a trained employee. The first-order condition for a maximum of (4.1) with respect to the hiring rate is identical. This condition determines the economywide hiring rate, h, as an increasing function of q. Upon substitution $\zeta(\cdot) + g_t$ for h_t, we have an equation for the economywide growth rate,

$$(4.2) \quad 0 = -T'(\zeta(\cdot) + g_t, 1; \Lambda) + q_t$$

where $T'(\cdot)$ denotes, as in Chapter 3, the derivative of per-employee train-ing cost with respect to the hiring rate, the first argument of the function. The firms at each moment push up the rate of growth of their stock of employees to the point where the marginal cost of training equals the shadow price (or value) placed on having one more worker in their stock of functional employees.

Equation (4.2) is itself a powerful tool for understanding "labor de-mand" in this model and particularly its relationship to the asset price and thus interest rates. It says that, given the wage and the current (predeter-mined) unemployment rate, and hence the corresponding nonwage income figuring in the quit-rate function, an increase of q signals firms to step up the growth rate by increasing their hiring rate. Thus a rise of interest rates, other things equal, in reducing the present discounted value (and shadow price) of the existing stock of employment, has the effect of reducing the growth of employment. This result foreshadows one of the main proposi-tions of the structuralist theory: shifts in consumer demand or government demand that drive up the interest rate and thus drive down asset prices operate to shift down the demand for labor. Yet a caveat is in order. Some shocks driving up interest rates, such as productivity shocks, may have a countervailing impact on the shadow price through another channel, such as the expected stream of returns obtainable from the asset, or they may also impact on the marginal-training-cost function or on the quit-rate func-tion. One must not jump to the conclusion that all shocks raising interest rates shrink employment.

The dynamics can be pursued by studying a diagram plotting the quit rate and the hiring rate against the employment rate. The former is an increasing reduced-form function of the employment rate, since the firms defend against increased turnover by raising their wage but not by so much as to prevent altogether a rise of turnover. The latter, the hiring rate, is a constant corresponding to the given q. Hence, at a low employment rate, hiring exceeds quitting, so the employment rate will be rising; and vice versa at a high employment rate. We need not take up the details in this purely conceptual chapter.

The determination of the asymptotic level to which the employment rate converges is needed for a general-equilibrium analysis. We want to study the wage-unemployment relation such that g_t equals the (exogenous) growth rate of the labor force, γ, so that the unemployment rate is un-changing. Replacing g_t with γ_t in (4.2) yields the equation

$$(4.3) \qquad 0 = -T'(\zeta(v, (1 - u)v, y^w) + \gamma_t, 1; \Lambda) + q_t$$

This relationship is one view, at any rate, of the labor demand curve expressed as a ratio to the (fixed) labor force—the desired employment rate, or employment rate demanded, in other terminology. What does it say? It implies, first of all, that, given the wage, an increase of the shadow price, q, in entailing a higher marginal training cost and hence a greater hiring rate, causes the employment demanded (expressed as a rate) to increase, since that is what will increase the quit rate and thus the hiring rate. Surprisingly, it also implies that, given the value of q to which this demand curve is indexed, an increase in the wage, v, must be accompanied by an increase of the employment rate, not a decrease as we are accustomed to see. The explanation is that, at any given employment rate, an increased wage has a net negative effect on the quit rate;[6] at any given rate, an increased employment rate has a positive effect on the quit rate; since (4.3) requires that the employment rate adjust to keep the quit rate at the level of the hiring rate corresponding to the specified level of q, the employment rate must increase to offset the effect on the quit rate of an increased wage. The reason for this unexpected result is that in holding q constant one is abstracting from the deterrent effect of the wage on firms' willingness to employ that lies behind the usual models' characteristically negative slope of the labor demand curve; for example, a tax on labor, in raising labor cost to the firm, would cause q to drop and thus to contract employment.[7]

Another view of employment from the demand side is obtained from another of the conditions for an optimal policy. This is the intertemporal Pontyragin requirement that the shadow price satisfy an arbitrage condition involving the capital gain, dq/dt, and the current rate of interest, r_t:[8]

$$(4.4) \qquad r_t q_t - dq_t/dt = \Lambda - v - T(\zeta(\cdot) + g_t, 1; \Lambda) + q_t g_t$$

Since firms are choosing g to maximize the righthand side, a small variation in it can be disregarded. The same is not true of the wage, however, since each firm in choosing its wage level considers only the effect of its wage on its own turnover; a general wage increase, given the employment rate, would undoubtedly decrease the quit rate by less than enough to compensate for the higher wage, so the righthand side would decrease.[9] Recall also that an increase of the employment rate, given the wage rate, would increase turnover, hence raising turnover costs appearing on the righthand side. It follows that, given the own rate of interest, $r_t - q^{-1} dq/dt$, and the shadow price, q, an increase of the employment rate (which decreases the righthand side) must be accompanied by a drop of the general wage (which increases the righthand side) in order that the righthand side remain at the level given by the lefthand side. Hence the negatively sloped labor demand curve is obtained. It can also be seen that an upward shift of the own rate of interest, in raising the required return earned per unit of time from a newly trained worker, $(r_t - q^{-1}dq/dt)q$, which gives the required return on the acquisition of a newly trained worker, requires a larger righthand side—hence a drop of the wage at a given employment rate to boost profitability through its external effect on turnover, or a lower employment rate at a given wage to boost profits through its effect on turnover. It is at first puzzling that an increase of q likewise shifts down this kind of labor demand curve. The resolution is that if the underlying shock is a decrease of demand lowering the own interest rate, the increase of q will only be an incomplete offset—the net effect is lower employment at any given wage—but readers will have to study Chapter 7 to see that.

A third view of labor demand is obtained if we eliminate q from (4.4) by substituting for it from (4.2). The result is an equation determining the employment growth rate as a function of the real wage and the own rate of interest.[10] This equation can be used to examine how the wage needed to generate a specified growth rate varies with the level of the employment rate. It is natural to fix attention on the wage-unemployment conditions under which g_t equals the (exogenous) growth rate of the labor force, γ, so that the unemployment rate is unchanging at the current moment:

$$(4.5) \qquad \Lambda - v - T(\zeta(\cdot) + \gamma_t, 1; \Lambda)$$
$$= T(\zeta(\cdot) + \gamma_t, 1; \Lambda)(r_t - q^{-1}dq_t/dt - \gamma_t)$$

The unambiguous implication of this version of the labor-demand relationship is that, again, an increase of the own rate of interest rate, in increasing the righthand side, requires, given the wage, a decrease of the employment rate: by reducing marginal training cost it operates to decrease the righthand side, and by reducing training costs it operates to increase cash flow and hence increase the lefthand side. The presence of the same feature in a rather wide range of models will warrant a good deal of attention later in this volume. This point about the effect on labor demand of the rate of interest is made, however primitively, in an early turnover model of employment by the present author.[11]

As could be anticipated, the relationship here between the employment rate and the wage is ambiguous. A higher employment rate, in increasing the quit rate, raises training costs and hence lowers cash flow, on the lefthand side; a reduction of the wage would serve to restore cash flow and

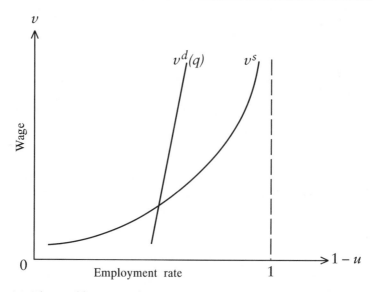

Figure 4.1 The equilibrium employment-rate curve, or "demand wage" relation, indexed by the shadow price of functional employees in the turnover-training model

thus go in the direction of restoring the equality of lefthand and righthand sides. On the other hand, the higher employment rate, in raising the quit rate, also raises the marginal training cost on the righthand side; an increase of the wage, in reducing the quit rate, would serve to bring the marginal training cost back down. For small rates of interest, the former effect is decisive, in which case the demand curve is downward-sloping.

Figure 4.1 provides a partial-equilibrium analysis of the natural rate of employment and the associated wage. This particular view uses equation (4.3) to obtain the labor demand curve, which is upward-sloping given q, Λ, and the various functions. Under rising marginal training cost, the case under discussion, the demand wage curve there corresponds to a given current growth rate—the growth rate of the labor force. Under the same increasing marginal training cost, the equilibrium wage curve should also be interpreted as the particular curve corresponding to a growth rate of zero. Given the right q, the one satisfying the general equilibrium path, the corresponding intersection of the steady-employment-rate demand wage curve and the steady-employment-rate wage curve determines the *current* value of the *natural* rate of employment—meaning now by that term the employment rate that, if initially occurring, will have no tendency to be rising or falling at the moment. (Another, perhaps safer term is the current stationary employment rate.) Under *stationary*-equilibrium or steady-equilibrium growth conditions, of course, the corresponding equilibrium value of q in the apparatus of Figure 4.1 partially characterizes the *stationary*-state or steady-growth employment rate.

4.2 Derived Labor Demand and Firms' Investment in Customers

When we want to focus on other kinds of capital than investment in a functional work force, it is simplest to use an incentive-wage model that does not come with its own capital in addition. The model founded on shirking rather than quitting is therefore very convenient.

The departure from the neoclassical aggregative habit in this section is a customer-market treatment of the product market.[12] In this view, buyers gradually stumble on to or hear by word of mouth of the existence and location of suppliers other than the one they know. A buyer would not be instantaneously attracted from his current supplier by an epsilon advantage currently on offer by one or more suppliers elsewhere since he would at first be unaware of the opportunity; further, a buyer would not instantaneously desert his supplier if that supplier raised his price epsilon about the level believed to prevail elsewhere since he would not at first know a better source. Hence each supplier recognizes that those buying from him are *customers*: having been buyers yesterday, hence accustomed to buy there, they will continue buying there today if the supplier remains competitive and will drift away only gradually if not. This friction in the flow of information about firms and hence in the migration of customers gives rise to an imperfectly competitive equilibrium in which the atomistic competitors do not find it profitable to compete the going price all the way down to marginal cost. The size of the price markup over marginal cost is determined by the degree of informational friction arising from the structure of the product market and by the real rates of interest found in the capital market.

In the convenient formulation of the Phelps-Winter model, each buyer is currently a customer at just one among the fixed number of firms. Each firm's stock of customers is a continuous variable that can grow or decline only gradually. Accumulating (or decumulating) this stock is the only investment (or disinvestment) the firm makes. The firm sets its own price with an eye to the consequences for the growth or erosion of its stock of customers. The customer market is conceived as having a single consumer good; the firms' products are differentiated in some other dimension, such as their locations or fax numbers. So any positive differential between a firm's price and that of the other identical firms would not be indefinitely sustainable—it would cause its stock of customers ultimately to vanish—and a maintained negative differential would gain market share until the firm had all the customers in the market.

Here attention is confined to the case of an equilibrium path (correct expectations) in a closed economy in which the customer market encompasses the whole output of the economy, and output is produced by labor alone under conditions of constant costs at the individual firm.

In this model, the problem of the individual firm is to find the price at each point that maximizes the value of the firm—the present discounted value of the stream of profits—and thus also the price of its shares. The optimal price markup over marginal cost balances the immediate benefit in increased cash flow that would result in the short term (given its existing stock of customers) from a small increase of price on the one hand against the suitably discounted sum of the costs that would gradually be incurred as a result of that small price increase in the form of lost customers (on each of whom it is making a profit). In this maximization, the balance struck depends upon the shadow price (or worth) assigned to customers: a higher real price of customers, q, would cause the optimal markup of a firm to be lower.

The precise maximization can be described in terms similar to those arising in the previous model. With regard to the ith firm, we let x^i, a continuous variable, denote (the size of) its customer stock, let y^i denote the amount of consumer output it supplies per customer, and let p^i denote its nominal price (in units of the *numeraire*, the economy's homogeneous shares, or common stock). Then, following the previous convention, p will denote the price at the other firms, and p^e the price that the firm and its customers expect is being charged elsewhere. Similarly, y is the supply per customer at the rest of the firms, which is equal to output per capita in the economy, and y^e is the expected level. In this notation, the firm's real price, p^i/p, is a decreasing function of its per-customer supply relative to that of the other firms, $f(y^i/y)$, $f'(\cdot) < 0$, $f(1) = 1$. (Two firms supplying the same per customer would have to be at the same point on the identical per-customer demand curve and thus be charging the same nominal price, and a firm supplying more would have to be lower on that demand curve.) Correspondingly, the growth rate of the firm's stock of customers, g_i, is likewise determinable by a function $g(y^i/y)$, $g'(\cdot) > 0$, $g(0) = 0$, under zero growth in the economywide population of customers. Finally, ς will denote unit cost, an increasing function of output per unit of labor force (and hence per unit of customers) in the economy. In these terms, the optimal price policy of the *i*th firm is the supply policy in which at each point in time *t* the current output supplied per customer y_i maximizes a Hamiltonian function that is the sum of current profit plus value-weighted customer inflow, where the weight assigned to the growth rate of the customer stock is the shadow price *q*:

(4.6) $x^i\{y_i[f(y^i/y) - \varsigma(y)] + q^i g(y^i/y)\} \equiv \mathcal{H}(y^i, x^i; q^i, y)$

The first-order condition for this maximum is

(4.7) $0 = f(y^i/y) - \varsigma(y) + y^i f'(y^i/y)y^{-1} + q^i g'(y^i/y)y^{-1} \equiv \mathcal{H}_{y^i}(\cdot)$

On the righthand side, the first and third terms add up to marginal revenue and the second term subtracts marginal cost. Hence this condition expresses a feature of customer-market equilibrium, that as long as the shadow price of customers is positive, so the fourth term is also positive, the firm operates at an output level beyond the textbook monopolist's output level for the sake of its long-run interest—in gaining more or losing fewer customers.

Now product-market equilibrium is easily characterized. The foregoing formulation of the maximization presupposes that the individual firm is in equilibrium—with correct expectations about its competitors' *p* and *y*. Supposing also that firms are identically situated, so they behave identically in equilibrium conditions, it follows that every firm's real price, p^i/p, and the per-customer supply ratio, y_i/y, are equal to one. Thus (4.7) yields the following characterization of product-market equilibrium:

(4.8) $0 = 1 - \varsigma(y) + f'(1) + qy^{-1}g'(1)$

Clearly an increase of *y*, in reducing the profit margin, $1 - \varsigma(y)$, implies that *q* increases—and by more proportionately than *y* increases. Hence the amount of output per customer that firms want to supply in equilibrium conditions is increasing, and less than unit-elastic, in the shadow price.

What does this equilibrium condition imply with regard to the derived demand for labor? To express this equilibrium condition in terms of the wage and the employment rate, we can use the structural relationship in our constant-costs shirking model giving unit cost, ς, as a function of the economywide wage and the employment rate. Further, we can regard output per customer, or family, as essentially employment per family times employee effort. This leads to the product-market equilibrium condition in labor-market terms:

(4.9) $0 = 1 - \varsigma(1 - u, v) + f'(1)$

$\qquad + g'(1)q/(1 - u)\varepsilon(v, (1 - u)v, y^w(1 - u, v; a))$

A principal point of interest about this equilibrium condition is the dependence of the equilibrium employment rate upon the shadow price of customers. An increase of q increases the righthand side. At given v, an increase of $1 - u$ decreases the righthand side by lifting unit cost and, assuming that some increase of $(1 - u)\varepsilon(\cdot)$—output per customer—is eked out despite the weakening of effort, by raising output. Hence the employment rate for product-market equilibrium is increased by an increase in the value of additional customers, given the wage.

One is naturally curious about the slope of this relationship in the employment rate–wage plane. The effect of the wage on the righthand side is ambiguous. At a given employment rate, an increase of the wage, given nonwage income, unambiguously increases effort, by the zero-degree homogeneity of the function ε, and the indirect effect via the implied contraction on nonwage income further stimulates effort; the resulting increase of output per customer acts to decrease the righthand side of (4.9). Somewhat surprisingly, the wage has an ambiguous effect on unit cost,

(4.10) $\varsigma^i(1 - u; v) = \min_{v^i} [v^i/\varepsilon(v^i, (1 - u)v, y^w(1 - u, v; a)]$

An increased economywide wage has three impacts. The impact on the firm's own wage is nil since, being optimized, it has no marginal significance—the envelope theorem. Each firm suffers decreased effort by its employees through the impact of a higher wage at the other firms. But each firm enjoys improved effort through the impact on the nonwage income of employees:

(4.11) $\partial \varsigma^i/\partial v = \varepsilon^{-2}[\varepsilon - v\varepsilon_1 + v(1 - u)\varepsilon_2 + y_v^w]$

$\qquad = \varepsilon^{-2}[v(1 - u)\varepsilon_2 + \varepsilon_3 y_v^w]$

It will be assumed that the net effect is positive at employment rates in the moderate or high range. Then the wage effect via unit costs fortifies the decrease of the righthand side already found. In this range, therefore, the product-market equilibrium curve in (4.9) is negatively sloped.

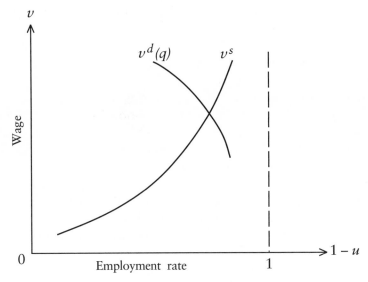

Figure 4.2 The equilibrium employment-rate curve, or "demand wage" relation, indexed by the shadow price of customers in the customer-market model

A plausible depiction of this equilibrium demand–wage relationship, indexed by the shadow price of customers, is presented in Figure 4.2.

The corresponding relationship indexed instead by the own interest rate can be derived from the intertemporal condition,

$$(4.12) \quad rq - (dq/dt) = [1 - \varsigma(y)]y + qg$$

which is analogous to that in equation (4.4).

4.3 Derived Labor Demand and Investment in Physical Capital

In this, the third and last model of the goods market, physical capital makes its long-awaited appearance. A capital good is produced alongside the consumer good. The product-market model is conjoined to the shirking model of the labor market in preference to the turnover model (as in section 4.2) in order not to bring in a second kind of capital, functional employees, on top of the capital presented by the goods market.

As capital theorists are fond of observing, a snapshot of any contemporary closed economy operating at any given moment would show little production of final consumer goods. The preponderance of output is in-

tended to permit or facilitate the production of consumer goods in the
future, a long stretch of the future in the case of fixed capital of the point-
input flow-output type. How to model this important feature? In important ways the most suitable model we could construct would build on one
or another representation of the idea of the period of production in Austrian capital theory—growing trees or maturing wine being the classic examples. Instead we may use the more conventional model, which can be
traced back to Marx, of a "two-sector" economy: one activity produces
the consumer good with capital and labor, the other activity produces the
capital good.[13] Capital and labor are instantaneously shiftable between
these two activities, so it is natural to think that, far from being in different
regions of the economy, the two activities are carried on within every firm.
Upon making the conventional specification that the capital-producing activity is the more labor-intensive, the model replicates all the main insights
of the Austrian approach.

Consider then a population of enterprises that are perfect competitors
in the product market. They all take the real price of the capital good as
given, with the consumer good serving as the numeraire. A firm with a
total amount of capital, K^i, may allocate it between producing the consumer good and producing the capital good. Letting q_t denote the real
price of the capital good prevailing in the perfect goods market, the maximand for the ith firm can be written as

$$(4.13) \quad \{F^C(K^i_C, \varepsilon^i N^i_C) - v^i(N^i_C + N^i_I)$$
$$+ q_t[F^I(K^i - K^i_C, \varepsilon^i N^i_I) - \delta K]\} \equiv \mathcal{H}(\cdot)$$

where each F denotes a production function and δ denotes the exponential
rate of decay of the capital stock.

It is clear that the function to be maximized is formally analogous to
the Hamiltonian functions maximized in the two previous models. In the
present model, capital is tradable, but it is not necessarily traded between
firms. If all the firms are similar in the sense of having the same technology,
a firm could constrain itself to start with the capital it has to begin with
and to produce itself its future stocks of the capital good, no more and
no less, without doing anything nonoptimal. Then it could maximize the
Hamiltonian above with q_t being interpreted as the shadow price to be
used in valuing whatever growth in the capital stock is produced.

The first-order conditions with regard to labor and employment input—the well-known marginal equivalences—generate the Samuelson-

Stolper result that, on the conventional differential factor intensity assumption stated above, an increase of the real price of the capital good, which is the relative price of the more labor-intensive good, increases the equalized marginal value productivity of effort-weighted labor in both uses. The latter is in turn equated to the effort-adjusted wage. Hence the latter is an increasing function, say V_*, of the capital good price:

$$(4.14) \quad v^i/\varepsilon(v^i, (1 - u)v, y^w(1 - u, v; a)) = V_*(q) \qquad V'_*(q) > 0$$

In the classic example in which capital is produced by means of labor alone, $V_*(q)$ is proportional to q, the factor of proportionality being the marginal physical product of labor in producing capital:

$$(4.14') \quad v^i/\varepsilon(v^i, (1 - u)v, y^w(1 - u, v; a)) = \Lambda q$$

This characterization of product-market equilibrium determines the shifts and the shape of the equilibrium employment rate curve, or demand-wage relationship.

Again we find that an increase of the real price of the asset—in the present case shares are backed by physical capital rather than by functional employees or customers—increases the employment rate necessary for product-market equilibrium at any given real wage. This follows from the fact that the lefthand side is unambiguously increasing in $1 - u$.

Once again there is some ambiguity about the slope of this demand-wage relationship in the employment rate–wage plane. Nevertheless, one is inclined to presume that there exists a region of sufficiently high employment rates such that a firm's unit cost is increasing in the economywide wage on balance (because the positive shirking effect of higher wages paid by competitors in the labor market outweighs the negative effect of the reduction in nonwage income resulting from higher wages); in that region the equilibrium employment curve is negatively sloped. However, there definitely exists another region of sufficiently low employment rates with the opposite slope.

For completeness, Figure 4.3 records this equilibrium employment curve.

Finally, by the factor-price-frontier relation, there also is a demand-wage relation indexed by the unit rental on capital, R:

$$(4.15) \quad v^i/\varepsilon(v^i, (1 - u)v, Ra) = Y(R) \qquad R \equiv rq - dq/dt, Y'(R) < 0$$

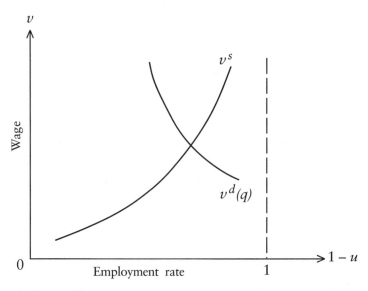

Figure 4.3 The equilibrium employment-rate curve, or "demand wage" relation, indexed by the shadow or market price of capital in the two-sector model

With regard to the righthand side, an increase of R, which equals the marginal product of capital in the consumer-good producing activity, unambiguously reduces the marginal product of labor in the same activity, thus reducing the righthand side. On the lefthand side, an increase of R encourages shirking, reducing effort, increasing costs, and thus increasing the lefthand side. As v^i has no effect at the margin, there must therefore be an unambiguous decrease in the quantity $(1 - u)v$ in order that effort be increased so that the wage adjusted by efficiency is reduced. This rental-indexed demand-wage relationship is a rectangular hyperbola.

Three models of the derived demand for labor have been introduced. When the demand-wage relationship that these models generate in the employment rate–wage plan is juxtaposed against the equilibrium wage curve of the previous chapter, we obtain a partial-equilibrium view of the determination of either the level or the growth of the employment rate. It is apparent that a general-equilibrium view requires modeling the capital market in order to endogenize the rate of interest and thus to make possible the determination of the path of the shadow price.

5

Capital-Market Equilibrium, Neoclassical and Modern, and General-Equilibrium Employment

THE illustrative models introduced in the previous chapter brought out the important feature that as soon as we leave the neoclassical aggregative conception of the derived demand for labor, in which the demand price for labor is the marginal product of labor in the aggregate production function, the labor demand price relationship (whether it exists as a stock relation or only as a flow relation) corresponding to product-market equilibrium must be indexed by the own rate of interest borne by the real asset of the economy or, more conveniently, by the shadow price imputed optimally to the asset by the firms in their intertemporal maximization. This is not the only variable to which this demand-type relation must be indexed. However, this particular dependence does mean that the general-equilibrium determination of the (path of the) unemployment rate requires simultaneously solving for the path of the shadow price of the asset and, except in extremely special cases that could arise in small open economies operating in a perfect world capital market, the path of the real rate of interest. In short, general equilibrium requires capital-market equilibrium.

The first objective here is to identify the conceptions of the capital market that will be employed in the analysis of the working models in Part II. It is hoped that some feel for the determination of general equilibrium can also be imparted here as a preview of the analyses to come. The details corresponding to each of the three models under analysis—the quitting model cum perfectly competitive aggregative product market, the shirking model cum customer frictions in the product market, and the shirking model cum two-sector production—are sufficiently diverse, however, that it would be difficult or impossible in this chapter to do much more than provide an impression of how general equilibrium is determined.

This chapter begins with a discussion of the determination of the path

of the shadow price—under perfect foresight this is essentially equivalent
to the path of the real share price in the economy. Here the path of the
real rate of interest is given. We then move on to discuss the mechanisms
brought into play in the present study for determining the path of the real
rate of interest. The emphasis is on neoclassical mechanisms in the capital
market, as they are the mechanisms used in the simple working models of
dynamic equilibrium in Part II. However, the chapter concludes with some
remarks on the consequences of going to modern conceptions of the capital
market based on equity rationing and other informational notions.

5.1 Neoclassical Mechanisms in Capital-Market Equilibrium

There are two dimensions to the capital market, asset price and interest
rate, and the equilibrium paths—the paths exhibited in equilibrium scenarios—of these two variables are simulataneously determined.

DETERMINATION OF THE EQUILIBRIUM REAL ASSET PRICE

A basic condition on the shadow price of the asset met in Chapter 4 is the
differential equation

$$(5.1) \quad dq/dt = rq_t - (R + g^A q_t)$$

where, as before, R is the return, or quasirent, per unit of the asset held
by firms, r denotes the current instantaneous real rate of interest, the time
subscript suppressed, and g^A denotes the own-rate of growth of the stock
of assets at the firm—the rate at which the assets are multiplying.[1] This
equation appeared earlier, in sections 4.1 and 4.2. What exactly is its economic meaning?

   An interpretation of this condition is that the forward-looking firm correctly forecasts with regard to any additional asset that it might choose to
accumulate the path of the unit quasirent on it plus whatever additional
growth (properly valued) in assets that having an additional unit of the
asset would yield at each future date s. So returns are correctly anticipated.
Then the firm correctly forecasts the path of the real rate of interest in
order to calculate its present discounted value, q_t. The current total rate
of return from holding the asset will be continuously equal to the current
instantaneous real rate of interest. This is the condition for firms to be in
equilibrium in the capital market.

   In a world with a perfect capital market, which the relatively formal models of Part II imagine, q can also be interpreted as the price of shares under the convention that the firm keeps issuing stock dividends or retiring stock as necessary to ensure that the number of shares continues to equal the number of homogeneous assets owned by the firm. In such a neoclassical share market, therefore, the price of shares representing ownership claims to identical amounts of assets of the homogeneous firms—such as one employee or one customer or one unit of capital backing every one share outstanding—is identical to the shadow price calculated by firms. The obvious interpretation is that households, as they also have correct expectations in any equilibrium scenario, use the same path of the real interest rate as firms use; and they are also supposed to have all the information needed to make the same projection of future returns on assets as firms make. Thus on both sides of the capital market, valuations of shares are identical.

The household needs to know the market value of its shares in order to plan correctly the path of its consumption or, if the shares are directly held by financial intermediaries, it needs to know its wealth level (always defined here in real-value terms) as determined by its positions with its intermediaries. To be in equilibrium households also have to have correct expectations about future rates of interest. In the neoclassical view there is a perfect consumption-loan market through which anyone without financial wealth but the prospect of positive wages in the future could borrow in order to finance consumption during unemployment or, more generally, to finance consumption beyond wage earnings. In principle, the Fisher-Ramsey formulation of optimal saving by the infinite-horizon household, with its well-known Euler equation in the growth rate of the marginal utility of consumption, would serve well enough for a great many of the questions we will want to pose. Instead, in order to study the effects of public debt but not only for that reason, we use the now-familiar Blanchard-Yaari generalization to finite-horizon households having access to an insurance market, with occasional reference to subsequent additions to that model.[2]

In Blanchard's model without either population growth or productivity growth, aggregate consumption, C, is given by a derived aggregate consumption function,

$$(5.2) \qquad C = (\rho + \mu)(H + W)$$

in which μ denotes the death rate, ρ denotes the rate of pure time preference, or utility discount rate, W denotes (financial) wealth, and H denotes "human" wealth. In the present volume financial wealth is generally defined by

(5.3) $W = qA + D$

where A is the stock of assets held, q their real price, and D the stock of public debt. Saving (per unit of time) is then

(5.4) $dW/dt = rW + V - T - C$

where V denotes the real wage bill and T the tax bill. The accumulation of human wealth (per unit of time) is

(5.5) $dH/dt = (r + \mu)H - V$

Unless indicated elsewhere, the term *wealth* in this study will refer only to W.[3] Differentiation of the consumption equation and some substitutions then gives the useful Euler-like differential equation

(5.6) $dC/dt = (r - \rho)C - \mu(\rho + \mu)W$

or, equivalently,

(5.7) $r - g^C = \rho + \mu(\rho + \mu)W/C$

This analysis has been extended to a setting of population or productivity growth, though this extension will not be previewed in this chapter.[4]

DETERMINATION OF THE EQUILIBRIUM INTEREST RATE

The simplest small open economy. In a one-consumer-good world having both a perfect world product market and a perfect world capital market, the so-called small open economy—one that is too small to affect the world real rate of interest (though not generally without influence over all of its own relative prices)—would have the same consumer good, obey the law of one price, and accordingly have the same real rate of interest as prevails in the rest of the world. Hence

(5.8) $r = r^*$ a positive constant at each t

Then the path of the share price remains to be determined from the other equations of the open-economy model that we construct from any of the three models introduced in the above chapters. The problem is to derive the reduced-form relationship giving the real asset price, q, as a function of the state of the open economy, as summarized by its state variables—the stock of functional employees, the stock of domestic customers, the nontradable domestic capital stock, *and* (in general) its national wealth—its ownership claims to the aforementioned physical assets and similar assets overseas (as well a; public debt). This problem for a fixed r^* over time appears in the first and third working models in Part III, sections 11.1 and 13.1.

Another small open economy. Not all small open economies are incapable of affecting the home real rate of interest, which is to say, the rate of interest in terms of the consumer good *produced* at home. Let e denote the real exchange rate, meaning the nominal price of the foreign-produced consumption good in terms of the home currency as a ratio to the price of the home-produced consumption good, hence the cost of the former in terms of the latter; in these terms an increase of the real exchange rate is a real depreciation, or a rise in the real cost of the good produced abroad. Then if e is rising along an equilibrium path, so that e is at each point being expected to rise, the real rate required on loans expressed in the home-produced good will be higher on that account, and the real prices of assets in terms of the home-produced good will be lower in order to afford the higher rate of algebraic real appreciation needed to offer the higher overall real yield in terms of the home good. The general relationship is

$$(5.9) \qquad r = r^* + e^{-1}(de/dt)$$

In such economies there are two real jump variables, or co-state variables, driven generally by two slow-moving state variables representing domestic assets and national wealth. The small open economy version of the second working model, that of a customer-market economy, is of this type.

The closed economy. What of the world as a whole? It is natural to begin by modeling a single—and implicitly homogeneous—closed economy.

Clearly if the actual and expected share price are equal but, say, above equilibrium, that will cause excess demand for the consumption-good market and excess supply for shares (assuming that either shares or consumer goods are the medium of exchange)—or conceivably the reverse—with the result that the share price will abruptly seek a new level disappointing those expectations about the goods price of shares. Hence a basic condition for capital-market equilibrium is that the price of shares, actual and ex- pected, be such as to equate the supply of consumption arising from the labor-and-product market analysis to the demand for consumption arising from the model of household-consumption planning just reviewed.[5] The previous models of the labor and product markets have the property that, in the closed economy, they make the supply of consumption a function, say Y^C, of q and A. As the first step, therefore, to determining the interest rate, we may write

$$(5.10) \quad r = \rho + \mu(\rho + \mu)[(qA + D)/Y^C(q, A)] + g^C$$

It then remains to determine the path of q.

TEMPORARY AND STATIONARY-STATE GENERAL EQUILIBRIUM

For an analysis of the general equilibrium determination of q we can pro- ceed to combine (5.1) and (5.7), equating r in the one to r in the other and obtaining

$$(5.11) \quad q^{-1}[R + dq/dt] + g^A = \rho + \mu(\rho + \mu)[(qA + D)/C)] + g^C$$

This equation shows how, given the two growth rates and also the (ex- pected) rate of change of q, households' valuation of shares is related to R and, in general, to the asset-consumption ratio, A/C, and the debt/con- sumption ratio, D/C.

A picture of temporary general equilibrium then swims into view. There is a supply-side relationship making consumer-good output a function of q and A, which is determinable from the equations appearing in the previous chapter. Increased q tends to bring an increased derived demand for labor and thus a higher employment rate though not necessarily a higher supply of consumer-good output; the latter may actually decrease. There is also, in the form of (5.11), a demand-side relationship describing the q deter- mined by the stock market as a (single-valued) function of consumer-good output as a ratio to the stock of assets. (This is not a monotone relation.) The intersection of the two relationships determines current q and current consumption. With q in hand, and with A, the current stock of the asset,

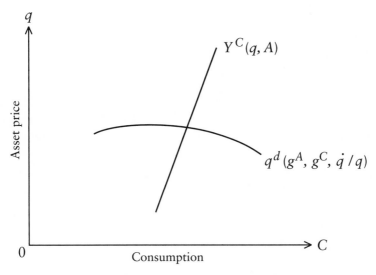

Figure 5.1 Determination of q in temporary general equilibrium

predetermined or parametrically given (depending on the model under analysis), the solutions for the other variables follow, including notably the employment rate.

Figure 5.1 conveys the way the above two relationships interact to determine the current equilibrium q and C, *given* the growth rates of C and A and the expected rate of change of q. Since each of the three models we will be analyzing differs in significant details, it would be hard to go beyond the statement that, in these models at least, there exists an intersection and, on some restrictions, the intersection is unique.

The picture provided by Figure 5.1 nicely represents the equilibrium stationary-state solution (in cases creating the existence of such an equilibrium), since in that case the two growth rates and the rate of change of q are equal to zero.

Another way of portraying general equilibrium, either the temporary equilibrium or the equilibrium stationary state, is to operate in the Hicksian employment–interest rate plane. This will sometimes be done.

The astute reader will have noticed another way to approach the general-equilibrium determination of the path of q. Equality of the supply of the consumer good and the demand yields

$$(5.12) \quad Y^C(q, A) = (\rho + \mu)(H + qA + D)$$

upon substituting for W as before. Evidently q is driven by H and, if a variable, by A. But since H is endogenous, using this result may present some dangers except in the hands of analysts who already understand the general-equilibrium solution.

5.2 Modern Mechanisms in Capital-Market Theory

It has long been argued by economic theorists keen on capturing important real-world features that the amount of equity a firm or a person has—the part of assets not offset by liabilities, hence net worth—is crucial for effective investment demand as it sets the quantity or the terms of available credit. Arnold Collery proposed a Keynesian model in which the greater the propensity of investors to save in order to build up equity, the higher will be aggregate demand and employment, as firms will bid the rate of interest to a higher level at any given level of output (or of investment) the larger the volume of investment they are qualified, so to speak, to make.[6] The notion that lenders impose some fixed ratio of credit to equity is perhaps too crude. Perhaps the modern models of credit rationing that have emerged in recent years also contain too many *if*s to be persuasive components of a macromodel. However, there is an antecedent idea that serves as well for most purposes. It is the notion that Kalecki called the principle of increasing risk.[7] Interpreted along the above lines, the principle is that, given the firm's stock of equity, the greater the investment to be made, and hence the larger the quantity of borrowing to be undertaken, the higher will be the rate of interest imposed by lenders on the firm. (The formulation was open to the criticism that it is the cumulative level of debt, not the growth, that presumably matters.)

Kalecki's principle, in one or another guise, has recently reappeared in two quite different theoretical models. Both are worth citing here for, although it would be a prodigious task to integrate these models with the three general equilibrium models used in this volume, which are already complex enough, they are suggestive of how the results of the three general equilibrium models would be modified or strengthened by that integration.

Aghion and Bolton have modeled a discrete-time economy in which, in the simplest case, a firm consists of one lumpy capital good, one manager, and a variable input of wage-earning workers.[8] Both capital and the manager live for one period. There is a continuum of persons within the present generation with respect to inherited wealth. Some invest and self-employ, the rest are wage earners. Those who are rich enough to buy the capital to establish a firm do so and lend any surplus wealth to others.

The borrowers are the middle-wealth people whose wealth is not enough to self-finance the capital in their firms. Finally, there are those too poor to be creditworthy and who therefore also lend their wealth to others—to the middle group. There is a schedule of interest rates facing the borrowers that rises with the amount that must be borrowed. The less the equity possessed, the higher the rate—until the equity is sufficiently small that lenders will refuse to lend at all in view of the moral hazard studied earlier in the Stiglitz-Weiss model.[9] The dynamic general equilibrium is worked out.

This model has the modern property that if a shock should occur to increase the equity of the middle, or borrowing, group, the result is a drop of interest rates and an increase in the number of middle-group persons who are then able to finance the needed investment to run a firm. An increase in the wealth of the rich is less efficacious, and unfortunately that is also true of the wealth of the poor. Thus the "structure" of wealth matters for the level of investment activity. This model could undoubtedly be integrated with, say, some modified version of the two-sector production model and the shirking model of the labor market in such a way as to preserve the property that an increase in the attractiveness of investment leads to an increase of the employment rate.

Another modern model of the capital market with clear implications for the structural theory of unemployment is that developed by Greenwald and Stiglitz.[10] The point stressed by them is a simple one though it has been resistant to any general equilibrium formulation that could be of use in macroeconomics. The point is that investing more, which means borrowing more when there is equity rationing (which is also posited in the Aghion-Bolten general equilibrium model), adds to the risk of bankruptcy borne by the managers. Owing to an adverse selection phenomenon, any manager with a bankruptcy on his or her record will be inferred more likely to be a bad manager than the others, and owing to moral hazard, managers cannot buy insurance against bankruptcy. Since to produce a firm must first invest in working capital and pay wage earners, and it must invest more the larger the volume of production to be carried on, the manager will chance a higher volume of output the farther the firm is from the brink of bankruptcy.

This model has a useful implication regarding any shock precipitating losses at the firm, and thus depleting the quantity of equity. This effect will force the firm to rein in the rate of production so as to keep the risk of bankruptcy within a tolerable level—increasingly so as the cumulative loss mounts. Another implication pertains to a shock driving up real interest rates. This effect will likewise have a dampening effect on the supply of output since, as the burden of the firm's loans and the other short-term debt is at once increased and the eventual burden of long-term debt is at once foreseen to be increased, the firm is placed nearer to the brink of bankrupty.

Though this chapter has not worked out the nature and existence of the intertemporal general equilibrium path of the three sorts of the models studied in this volume, even with the relatively transparent neoclassical treatment of the capital market described in this chapter, let alone the modern treatments acknowledged, it is immediately clear that there are important channels running from the capital market to the product market and thence to the labor market—channels acting on the supply of output and thus upon the supply of jobs through the derived demand for labor. There are also channels going directly to the labor market through employee incentives. Perhaps the centrality of the capital market is the distinctive feature of the structuralist unemployment theory. That does not mean, of course, that every shock owes its influence or its primary effect to its impact on real interest rates and capital-asset prices. It does mean, however, that the capital market must always be taken into account in the analysis.

6

Key Factors in the Structuralist Theory
of Unemployment Fluctuation

THE previous chapters have introduced the elements of the structuralist theory of unemployment whose development and evaluation is the purpose of this volume. It may be useful at this point to take stock. Readers
will likely want to pause for a moment to collect in their minds the causal
factors to which the theory points—the state variables and the parameters
arising in the set of models presented that seem to be especially important.

The set of causal influences—the shocks—compiled here are, in the
main, factors already brought to attention by one or more other theories
of economic activity. (So that no important factors will be overlooked, the
discussion has been arranged systematically, beginning with the shocks
with which the neoclassical aggregate theory has been occupied, moving
on to the concerns of supply-side doctrine, and concluding with the real
demand factors in Keynesian models.) However, there are at least two factors—real interest rates (external or induced internally by public debt or
time-preference shocks) and transfer payments—that have a central role
in the structuralist theory and yet play little or no part in any of the other
principal theories.

Productivity shocks and supply shocks. Though they have come to
seem the special preserve of the neoclassicals, these shocks constitute an
important category of factors in virtually every macroeconomic school of
thought. In one of the standard Keynesian models a permanent supply
shock may (under certain, not unrealistic parameter values) knock unemployment above the natural rate, thus requiring a downward adjustment
of nominal (as well as real) wages.[1] In the neoclassical settings of Barro
and of Prescott, temporary cost shocks are seen as sources of employment
fluctuation while there is no presumption that a permanent shock has such
effects.[2] (More on the latter below.) The static partial-equilibrium analyses

from a structuralist point of view by Bruno and Sachs conclude that permanent as well as temporary productivity shocks in the positive direction are expansionary for employment, contracting the unemployment rate, at least over the near term.[3]

In the structuralist models here, permanent productivity shocks are capable of having effects on the equilibrium path of employment and of all the other variables of the system. A positive shock to costs—a supply shock, in common parlance, implicitly in the adverse direction—arising from, say, a drying up of some natural resource, in shifting the production functions and contracting the derived demand for labor, tends *on this account* to contract the employment rate. A negative shock to costs—a positive productivity shock—arising from, say, a technological improvement, in boosting the derived demand for labor, operates on that account to pull up the employment rate.[4]

Yet the models here, though stripped down to essentials, are not so trivially analyzed. A shock seldom disturbs just one equation of the model: the above cost shocks also operate to shift the equilibrium labor-market locus—the wage curve—by impacting on the nonwage income of workers, which works in the opposite direction. Furthermore, in general a shock will disturb the path of the interest rate, the shadow price of the assets, and thus the derived labor demand.

The implied effect on the whole of the employment rate's time path is also of some importance. There would be something terribly wrong with a model that implied a permanent technical improvement to have a permanent effect on the employment rate—as if we would today be facing unemployment rates five or ten times what we have were it not for the progress brought by the industrial revolution and the postwar breakthroughs. A neoclassical analysis of the effects of a permanent productivity shock has been admirably worked out in King, Plosser, and Rebelo, who show the conditions under which the effects on the interest rate and the employment level vanish asymptotically.[5] If the three models here are correctly specified, it must similarly be that the initial employment effect, whichever its direction, contains in it the seeds of a return of the employment rate to the normal range. (There is also a distinction that sometimes needs to be made between the near term and the medium-range future.) Thus a dynamic general-equilibrium analysis of these cost shocks is required in order to determine correctly the theoretical consequences for the path of the employment rate.

In an open economy, of course, cost disturbances arise from a range of external shocks under such headings as real import costs, the terms of trade, and the real exchange rate. The exogeneity of the overseas interest rate facilitates the analysis, but the greater dimensionality of dynamic open-economy models hinders rigorous analysis.

Asset and wealth shocks. These two conceptually distinct shocks are closely connected in closed economies, clearly, differing only by the public debt, though they are independent of one another in open economies. The neoclassical analysis of the effects of a capital-wealth shock has been studied by King, Plosser, and Rebelo.[6] Obviously such a shock has effects in the structuralist theory, too. In the closed-economy case, a natural disaster or war that destroys assets and wealth operates to shift down the equilibrium wage curve by depriving people of income from wealth, but at the same time it tends to drag down the equilibrium demand wage curve by its effect on the marginal value productivity of labor (where real value is measured in consumer goods). An analysis is required to obtain the implications for employment, asset prices, and interest.

It should be mentioned that if the stock of wealth, and thus nonwage income, declines simply because of reduced saving, the reduced independence that workers will have as a result of the reduction in their unearned incomes will again operate to shift down the equilibrium wage curve, and the reduction in the stock of capital will again operate to shift down the derived labor demand curve. But with regard to a small open economy, a perfect world capital market will see to it that capital does not leave. Then only the downward shift of the national wealth is operative.

Exogenous interest rate shocks. In an open economy, a surge of investment opportunities external to the country presents it with an exogenous increase of interest rates. The consequent drop of the real exchange rate (real depreciation) and of the (real) shadow prices of the assets whose growth appears in the firms' Hamiltonian maximands operates to contract the labor demand price curve. While assets in the form of physical capital are depleted, migrating abroad, wealth is not, as nationals substitute overseas assets for disappearing domestic assets. The way seems wide open to the conclusion that the employment rate is contracted. That position was earlier developed in papers from the 1980s by Lal and van Wijnbergen, by Fitoussi and Phelps, and by Newell and Symonds.[7] These papers generally referred to a mix of monetary and nonmonetary channels, where they were explicit at all. It remains to be seen whether the dynamic, nonmonetary, general-equilibrium models have the same thrust as those earlier papers.

The question of the effect of an exogenous increase of the world real interest rate, a thought-experiment that large regions of the world went through in the 1980s, may be one of the few pivotal tests for judging the merits of the Keynesian, neoclassical, and structuralist approaches. In open-economy Keynesian theory, such an increase in interest rate foreordains a movement up the economy's "LM" curve, a movement that is achieved through a currency depreciation sufficient to boost the "IS" curve as required: this was the foundation for the view that a large country could be a "locomotive" to pull the global train.[8] In neoclassical theory, an increase of the real interest rate is hailed as an engine for pushing out the supply of labor and for stimulating an increase in the effective supply of capital-goods services by inducing firms to discount more heavily the future costs of earlier replacement.[9] The structuralist theory developed here focuses on other channels, so it will be important to see whether it may or must differ in its implications in this regard from the other two theories.

Steady population growth and productivity growth. These factors are well known to be buoyant in Keynesian doctrine.[10] The neoclassicals have been relatively silent on the question.[11]

The effects of a disturbance to productivity from a one-time permanent technological shock were already put on the agenda for analysis. The effects of sustained, in fact steady, technological progress are not going to be quite the same. If a one-time technological improvement produces a boom that slowly fades away, it might be thought that a steady rate of technological progress produces ultimately a steady elevation of the employment rate, as the forces tending to drive it back to normal are never able to catch up with more than a fraction of the cumulative technological improvement. (Similarly, if a one-time population increase produces a slump that vanishes asymptotically, it might be guessed that steady population growth would tend over time to leave some permanent lowering of the employment rate.) But such guesswork overlooks the observation that a permanent change in the rate of actual and henceforth expected technical progress involves also an immediate increase in expectations of future incomes, which translates to an immediate boost to consumer demand, which in turn has employment consequences.[12]

The "welfare state": Transfer payments. Many commentators have suggested that the transfer payments made to or indirectly available to the population, and the poorer population in particular, have the side effect of decreasing employment. Econometric evidence drawn from the recent experience of southern Italy by Micossi and Tullio is quite striking.[13] Yet no explanation in terms of modern theory is offered why such payments increase the equilibrium unemployment rate. The formulations here suggest, however, a channel through which some of these transfers have the hypothesized effect.

The models of incentive wages in Chapter 3 give a place for the average nonwage income of workers—of the employed, to be more accurate. In fact, if one looks at the formulation underlying the optimal wage condition in the shirking model, in section 3.2, it may be seen that if workers' average nonwage income, now treated as an exogenous shift variable, were to be increased, the optimal incentive wage at any given unemployment rate would increase in the same proportion, no matter how unimportant the elasticity of shirking with respect to nonwage income—as long as that elasticity is greater than zero.[14] In the minimalist version expounded there, this average unearned income is just quasirent per unit of savings times savings per worker. In principle, though, the unearned income of employed persons includes their receipt of transfer payments from the government, and this transfer component ought to be interpreted broadly so as to reflect the gain to the employed from pension and disability income received by retired parents, benefits to unemployed or ill spouses, and various children's allowances up through university. The independence from having to earn wages or at any rate to earn them soon must be a powerful determinant of the heights to which the personnel managers of firms find it necessary to drive up the wage in order to reach the point of cost minimization.

Distortionary tax rates. Supply-side doctrine indicts distortionary taxation as a cause of decreased employment. The pioneering work of Knoester on what he calls the "inverted Haavelmo effect" is well known.[15] But the theory of the effects, if any, on the equilibrium unemployment path has been left hazy at best. It is clear from the same incentive-wage equation that a flat tax rate on wage and nonwage income alike—a proportional income tax, say—will have no effect on the incentive wage required at any given unemployment rate. It would not shift up or down the equilibrium wage curve.[16] However, the equilibrium wage curve will definitely be shifted up by employee-paid social security taxes, or by tax hikes on wage earnings in excess of tax hikes on unearned income or, *a fortiori,* in combination with tax cuts on unearned income. Here there is forward shifting. Employer-paid payroll taxes on employment or excise taxes on production will have the effect of shifting down the derived demand for labor.

Protective Tariffs. When we come to open economies, small and large, we will want some understanding of the effects of tariffs on economic activity in the near and far term. Keynesian theory sees protection against imports as expansionary through its encouragement of expenditure switching to import substitutes. Of course, it is rather harder to see expansion in the steady state if that state exhibits no imbalance in the balance of trade.

Structuralist theory presents a different perspective. If protection against labor-intensive economies abroad serves to lower the returns to national wealth, being largely invested in the home country, and to raise the rents earned on human capital, one would guess that protectionism would operate to expand employment—an answer in harmony with Keynesian doctrine. Yet the representative country does not face hordes of cheap labor beyond its borders; it has the representative share of cheap labor. Modeling a world of representative countries, their factor proportions the same, all vying with one another for market share, is better suited to the more representative countries.

A key insight in analyzing the effect of protection on a representative country, it may be conjectured, is the point that protective hurdles put before potential foreign entrants into the domestic market operate in some degree to shelter a firm serving the domestic market from the consequences in terms of customer losses that would result from raising its price. A firm in expectational equilibrium will see that all such firms will be induced to set a higher price in the domestic market, so the collective effect will be much larger than if each firm imagined the others would not join it. Of course, to drive a harder bargain with buyers means offering a restricted supply at the old terms, which in turn implies trimming the derived demand for labor; the demand wage in terms of domestic product is reduced. Is the supply wage reduced too, and by the same proportionate amount? Some reflection suggests that if the workers' portfolios give disproportional weight to shares in firms predominantly in the domestic market, which would be rational for them to do if their consumer purchases are predominantly from those firms, the increased shelter from foreign entrants, in increasing the profits flowing to domestic operations, will operate to boost the nonwage income of domestic workers and thus to push up the required incentive wage—certainly not to pull down the supply wage in a full or partial accommodation of the reduced demand wage. According to this line of reasoning, then, protectionism is contractionary for the representative country.

Rate of pure time preference. In Keynesian theory, consumer spending is generally a stimulus to aggregate demand, which is an expansionary factor. Even in neoclassical theory or in the folklore, at any rate, a surge of time preference would drive up real interest rates, which—taken alone—would present an incentive to supply more labor in order to have extra income to save, thus to take advantage of the higher interest rates.

In the structuralist theory, however, there is at least one channel through which an increase of time preference operates in a contractionary direction: the increase of real interest rates causes the shadow prices of the assets of firms to drop, which shifts down the labor demand price curve.

Of course, the analysis of a small open economy will undoubtedly go somewhat differently. Except in the context of a one-good perfect market, the real rate of interest will be driven up at home, as in the closed-economy case. But in a customer-market setting, the increased demand of nationals among the domestic customers will have another impact.

Public debt shocks. Studies by Morris and by Beenstock find evidence of a powerful effect of world debt on world real interest rates, and a revised analysis by Barro finds a weaker effect.[17] Beenstock also finds a contractionary effect on output and employment.

The structuralist models here highlight a channel through which the public debt seems to be contractionary for the employment rate. A "helicopter drop" of public debt is an analytically attractive case to examine. There is an impact, excluding the case of Ricardian equivalence, on the required real rate of interest along any given path of consumption supply through the Euler-like equation of Blanchard. The induced disturbance of real interest rates ramifies through the system, and in particular has an effect on the derived demand for labor, as with an exogenous interest rate shock.[18]

Public expenditures. The central role accorded public expenditure by the Keynesian school is well known, and so pervasive is this habit of thinking that proponents of other theoretical perspectives have generally been keen to show that their doctrines are not un-Keynesian in this regard, at least on the whole. Keynes himself began by arguing that public works programs—including balanced-budget programs, so far as one can tell—would be expansionary for employment.[19] This property was universalized to all public expenditure in his *General Theory.*

Advocates of the neoclassical aggregative school agree that an increase of government purchases foreseen to be temporary is expansionary for employment through a positive effect on the supply of labor. A revised analysis concludes that this is even more strongly true of permanently increased public expenditure.[20]

Looking to see where the structuralist theory is "Keynesian" in its conclusions and where it is "counter-Keynesian" is an important item on the agenda; structuralism's relation to the neoclassical doctrine is also important. It is immediately rather clear that if the government makes purchases of output from firms that would have otherwise sold it to consumers, it will create an excess demand in the consumer-goods market, which will have to be corrected by an abrupt increase of interest rates and a drop of asset prices—in the same way as if increased consumer demand were the cause of the excess demand. The only difference is that the government will be collecting increased taxes to continue balancing the budget, which implies a drop of human wealth but one not as large as the increase of financial wealth.

It is clear, though, that an increase of public expenditure from the capital-goods-producing sector is radically different in its impact on the product markets—even if the output purchases are thrown away or "consumed" by the government as in the previous case. There is no necessary crowding out of consumer demand here—quite the reverse, as consumers now feel poorer in anticipation of higher tax bills in the future. How does a maintained increase in the rate of purchase of the capital good by the government (for uses having no effects on other parameters) affect interest rates, the derived demand for labor, and employment? It would seem that the government through such a measure is capable of driving up the real price of the capital good and thereby stimulating the derived demand for labor (under our two-sector comparative-factor intensiveness assumption). Perhaps Keynes had it right enough the first time—with no need to have brought in money. It would also seem that such an expenditure plan, in driving up the real price of the capital good along the way to stimulating the demand for labor, will in so doing decrease real interest rates, not push them up. That would fit in with what has been observed about the behavior of real interest rates in time of war—that they are usually depressed, not elevated as Keynesian theory and the neoclassical theory both imply.[21]

If we accept as a stylized fact that increased government purchase of capital goods for military purposes tends, even in a closed economy, to bring at least a transient elevation in the path of the equilibrium employment rate, and if we further accept as a stylized fact that the real rate of interest is reduced by high government expenditures during wartime, the analysis of the employment-rate and interest-rate effects of such public expenditures will be an interesting test for the structuralist theory.

II

THE CLOSED ECONOMY: WORKING MODELS

7

A Turnover-Training Model

THE turnover, or quitting, model of the labor market, it will be recalled, is based on the concept of the investment cost incurred in providing a new worker with the firm-specific training, or breaking-in, needed to transform the worker into a functional employee, able to be productive within the firm. This chapter builds a general-equilibrium system around this element in order to provide a model, however rudimentary, of the determination of the natural rate of unemployment. (The latter means the unemployment rate that, if it prevailed at first, would be steady at least temporarily, tending for the moment neither to rise nor to fall, along the subsequent equilibrium path. In the simple setting here, that is the steady-state rate.) The model also generates the equilibrium dynamics of the unemployment rate in its approach to the natural rate following shocks to the actual unemployment rate or to the natural rate or both.[1]

The model here can be seen as a theoretical revision and completion of the proto-model of equilibrium wages and unemployment by Salop, which in turn grew out of the theory of incentive wages in defense against quitting and consequent job rationing begun by Phelps and Stiglitz.[2] The model is recast in its naturally intertemporal terms. Since training is an investment decision, and the decision to stay or quit is repeated, an intertemporal analysis will portray more accurately the full implications of the model than will Salop's formulation, in which firms are imagined to make a timeless choice over alternative stationary profiles of wage rate and employment—a sort of Golden Rule of wage policy. The model is completed by recognizing that firms have a value residing in their assets—their employees—so workers and consumers must be represented as choosing their propensities to consume and to quit with a view to this wealth or to the income from this wealth, which will be the only wealth, other than public debt, in the model.

Analysis of the resulting model shows that the derived demand for labor shifts up not only with increased productivity, as in the static version, but with reduced real interest costs as well. The equilibrium incentive-wage locus is in turn lowered by the resulting reduction of nonwage income. The way is opened for a vastly richer understanding of the natural rate.

The general-equilibrium analysis here uncovers a number of shocks that drive the equilibrium unemployment rate by disturbing the real rate of interest: some raising unemployment by forcing up interest rates, others lowering unemployment despite raising interest rates. In what might be called the paradox of demand, we find that increased demand for the output of the consumer good (or other output produced by the same processes), whether induced by an increase of the public debt or the result of a spontaneous increase of pure time preference, cannot coax firms to employ more at the initial real price vector; in fact, the rise of the real interest rate and the associated drop in real asset values needed to eliminate the excess consumer demand has the perverse side effect of curtailing investment in new employees, thus swelling the equilibrium rate of unemployment and ultimately shrinking output and consumption. It is not just a principal Keynesian lesson that is turned upside down but a major tenet of the neoclassical real business cycle theory too, for both of those approaches find an expansionary effect in all demand shocks that lift interest rates.

The chapter is organized as follows. Section 7.1 develops the basic structure of the economy. Section 7.2 solves the general-equilibrium closed-economy model, with the term structure of real interest rates determined endogenously, and studies various macroeconomic shocks: technology shocks, as well as stimuli to aggregate demand arising from an exogenous rise in time preference or an increase in public debt. Section 7.3 makes some concluding remarks.

7.1 The Structure of the Model

The background is familiar enough to readers of modern theory. Production requires a team of workers who must be introduced to one another for the teamwork to take place. Any such ongoing enterprise constitutes a firm. Production and employment are carried out by many identical competitive firms. But employees are prone to quit in order to find employment in some newly preferred location—East Coast to West Coast, West Coast to East Coast.

In this setting each of the many identical, atomistic firms seeks wage and hiring policies to maximize the value of the firm's equity. Each firm faces a time path of interest rates $\{r_t\}_{t=[0,\infty]}$. The discount factor $e^{-\int_0^t r_v dv}$ gives the rate at which output at time t can be traded for output at time zero. The firm maximizes the expected present discounted value of its cash flows given by

$$\int_0^\infty \left[f(\Lambda E_t) - v_t E_t - E_t T\left(\frac{H_t}{E_t}; \Lambda\right) \right] e^{-\int_0^t r_s ds} dt \equiv Q_0$$

by choosing at each moment the current investment in new workers, H_t, and the real wage rate, v_t, paid to its stock of employees, E_t. We shall, in fact, suppose that labor is the only factor of production, and, with constant returns to scale, write $f(E_t)$ as ΛE_t. The variables E_t, H_t, and $f(E_t)$ are measured per unit of population per firm. With all firms identical and population (all of whom are in the labor force) constant in a Blanchard-Yaari setup, E_t gives us the rate of employment while $1 - E_t$ gives us the rate of unemployment; v_t is the real wage measured in terms of output while H_t is the number of trainees (new workers) per capita.

The total cost of training H_t new workers per capita is measured in terms of output and denoted $E_t T(H_t/E_t; \Lambda)$. Note that this is the opportunity cost of training and it is necessarily shifted up by an increase in the productivity parameter Λ since increased Λ raises the output forgone in allocating a given number of employees to the training of new hires. Thus modeled, training cost is implied to be a linear homogeneous function of E_t and H_t. Defining $h = H/E$ as the gross hiring rate, $T(h; \Lambda)$ has the following properties: $T(0) = 0$, $T'(h) > 0$, and $T''(h) > 0$, where it is understood that the derivatives are taken with respect to the gross hiring rate while the productivity parameter is held unchanged. This specification of the training-cost function together with the assumption of a constant-returns-to-scale production function allows us to equate the shadow price of trained workers, q, to the per-employee value of the firm, V/E.

The maximization problem is subject to the constraint

$$\dot{E}_t = H_t - \hat{\zeta}(\cdot) E_t$$

which gives the change of employment per unit of time as the difference between the number of employees hired and the number of employed workers that quit. The quit rate, $\hat{\zeta}$, experienced by any firm will be written as a function of its own real wage, v; an indicator, z, of the expected value of wage earnings for a worker who quits; and the average nonwage income of workers—to be more precise, the average income from wealth, y^w. (We abstract from the annuity-income component of nonwage income appropriate to the Blanchard-Yaari setup.) The indicator z gives the income prospects resulting from an employee's decision to join the unemployment pool in order to be available for employment in some newly preferred location. A plausible specification of the quit function is that it depends upon the firm's real wage relative to the income from wealth of the employees, v/y^w, and the prospective real wage earnings obtainable upon quitting relative to income from wealth, z/y^w. The hypothesis to be adopted here, one that is empirically plausible and that can be shown to be theoretically admissible as well, is that an equiproportionate increase or decrease in all three arguments of the quit-rate function leaves the quit rate unchanged. The quit-rate function can, therefore, be written as $\hat{\zeta}(z/v, y^w/v)$ with the properties: $\hat{\zeta}_1 > 0$ and $\hat{\zeta}_2 > 0$. (In terms of the notation used in Chapter 3, $\hat{\zeta}(z/v, y^w/v) = \zeta(1, z/v, y^w/v)$.) Employees are, therefore, more likely to quit when job prospects elsewhere improve relative to the real wage they currently receive; an increase in their nonwage income relative to their current real wage also raises the quit propensity.

To solve the firm's problem, we set up the current-value Hamiltonian given by

$$E\{\Lambda - v - T(h) + q[h - \hat{\zeta}(z/v, y^w/v)]\}$$

where q is the shadow value of a trained employee. Our first-order necessary conditions (which are also sufficient under our assumptions) are given by:

(7.1) $T'(h_t) = q_t$

(7.2) $E_t\left[-1 + q_t\left(\dfrac{\hat{\zeta}_1 z_t}{v_t^2} + \dfrac{\hat{\zeta}_2 y_t^w}{v_t^2}\right)\right] = 0$

(7.3) $\dot{q}_t - r_t q_t = -[\Lambda - v_t - T(h_t) + h_t T'(h_t) - q_t \hat{\zeta}(z_t/v_t, y_t^w/v_t)]$

(7.4) $\lim_{t \to \infty} e^{-\int_0^t r_v dv} q_t E_t = 0$

Consider (7.1). The lefthand-side term is the marginal opportunity cost of training a new worker. Thus, the condition states that investment in new workers takes place until the marginal training cost equals the shadow value of a trained worker. Noting that the lefthand side of (7.1) is increasing in h under our specification of the training-cost function, we can invert the equation to give h as an increasing function of q, in a manner similar to Tobin's q theory of investment. Thus,

$$(7.5) \qquad h_t = \Phi(q_t) \qquad \Phi'(\cdot) > 0$$

Equation (7.2) gives us the real wage–turnover cost tradeoff. It tells us that if the firm raises its real wage by one unit, the direct wage costs per employee rise by E, while the turnover cost declines by $q[(\hat{\zeta}_1 z/v^2) + (\hat{\zeta}_2 y^w/v^2)]E$ since turnover falls by $[(\hat{\zeta}_1 z/v^2) + (\hat{\zeta}_2 y^w/v^2)]E$ and each additional worker is worth q. These two values are equated at the optimum.

Equation (7.3) can be rewritten as:

$$(7.6) \qquad \Lambda - T(h_t) + h_t T'(h_t) + \dot{q}_t = v_t + q_t[r_t + \hat{\zeta}(z_t/v_t, y_t^w/v_t)]$$

In (7.6), $hT'(h)$ is the reduction in the opportunity cost of training a new worker made possible by an additional employed worker while $T(h)$ is the output lost from diverting an employee's time from its production activity to its training activity. Therefore, $\Lambda - T(h) + hT'(h)$ is the total marginal product of the employed worker. The marginal benefit of having one more employee is the total marginal product of the worker plus the capital gain, $\dot{q}$. The marginal cost, on the other hand, is given by the real wage paid per worker, plus the real interest and turnover cost evaluated at the shadow price of a worker. We can solve for q in (7.6), using the transversality condition to obtain

$$(7.7) \qquad q_t = \int_t^\infty [\Lambda - T(h_s) + h_s T'(h_s) - v_s] e^{-\int_t^s (r_v + \hat{\zeta}(z_v/v_v, y_v^w/v_v)) dv} ds$$

Equation (7.7) states that the shadow price of a trained worker is equal to the present discounted value of the stream of marginal cash flow attributable to an additional worker trained at time t. At each future date s, the marginal cash flow consists of three components: (i) $\Lambda - T(h)$ is the extra revenue measured in terms of output attributable to having an additional employee; (ii) $hT'(h)$ is the reduction in the opportunity cost of training made possible by having an additional employee; and (iii) v is the real wage that has to be paid to the additional worker. The (instantaneous) rate at which marginal cash flows at date s are discounted is equal to $r + \hat{\zeta}$ rather than simply r because each employed worker is subject to attrition at the rate $\hat{\zeta}$.

After paying wages to current trained employees, the firm has to decide how to distribute its profit and finance the training of new workers. We may assume that firms finance the training of new workers by issuing new shares but independently of the method of financing we take the nonwage income per capita y^w to be given by the per-capita rent on the firm's investment

$$(7.8) \qquad y^w_t = E_t(\Lambda - v_t)$$

Also, under our assumptions that the production function is constant returns to scale in E, and the training-cost function being homogeneous of degree one in E and H, there is a simple relation between the value of the firm, V, the shadow price of a trained worker, q, as well as the stock of employed workers, E. In particular, $V = qE$.

UTILITY MAXIMIZATION BY CONSUMER-WORKERS

To give force to the conventional measures of fiscal stimulus such as the size of the public debt, we adopt the Blanchard-Yaari setup of finite-lived households. In that model, the economy is in a demographic stationary state so that the population size of every age is stable. Each agent is assumed to be a supplier to the labor market, and to avoid the considerations of risk, we may assume that each agent is a unified household with a large number of members suffering the same unemployment rate as the population as a whole.

As in Blanchard, the critical equation describing the law of motion of per-capita aggregate consumption is given by

$$(7.9) \qquad \dot{C}_t = (r_t - \rho)C_t - \mu(\mu + \rho)W_t$$

where C is per-capita aggregate consumption, ρ is the rate of time preference, μ is the probability of death, and W is nonhuman wealth, that is, the wealth traded on financial markets. (We will more clearly define what is included in W later.) We turn in the next section to solve the general equilibrium closed-economy model.

7.2 The Closed Economy

Equations (7.1) and (7.4) summarize the conditions that have to be satisfied for the typical firm. Using the Salop-Calvo indicator

(7.10) $z_t = E_t v_t$

where z is taken to be the wage expected elsewhere adjusted for the probability of obtaining a job, the following equations describe the economy for exogenously given real interest rates:

(7.11) $\dot{q}_t = q_t[\hat{\zeta}(E_t, y_t^w/v_t) + r_t] - [\Lambda - v_t - T(\Phi_t) + \Phi_t T'(\Phi_t)]$

(7.12) $\dot{E}_t = E_t[\Phi_t - \hat{\zeta}(E_t, y_t^w/v_t)]$

(7.13) $E_t[-1 + q_t(\hat{\zeta}_1 E_t/v_t^2 + \hat{\zeta}_2 y_t^w/v_t^2)] = 0$

where $\Phi_t = \Phi(q_t)$ and $y^w/v = [(\Lambda/v) - 1]E$. These conditions imply capital-market, product-market, and labor-market equilibrium, respectively.

GENERAL EQUILIBRIUM

To determine endogenously the term structure of real interest rates, we use the condition for equilibrium in the goods market at every moment of time. Thus, with output equal to spending, we have

(7.14) $[\Lambda - T(h_t)]E_t = C_t$

Aggregate demand here (in the absence of a government) is the sum of consumption and gross investment in new workers. Following Blanchard, we obtain for aggregate consumption demand the "consumption function"

$C_t = (\mu + \rho)[W_t + \Omega_t]$

where Ω is human wealth. In the absence of a government, we can write the value of the nonhuman wealth W as

$$W_t = Q_t = q_t E_t$$

Consumption demand thus is an increasing function of total wealth, and depends positively on q. Investment in new workers, according to (7.5) is also an increasing function of q so consumption supply is decreasing in q. Aggregate demand is brought into equality with aggregate supply through the endogenous adjustment of the term structure of interest rates.

To obtain an expression for the instantaneous rate of interest, r, we differentiate (7.14) with respect to time, and then use (7.9) to obtain, after some rearrangement,

$$(7.15) \quad r_t = \frac{\dot{E}_t}{E_t} - \frac{\Phi'T'\dot{q}_t E_t}{(\Lambda - T)E_t} + \rho + \frac{\mu(\mu + \rho)q_t E_t}{(\Lambda - T)E_t}$$

Substituting (7.15) into (7.11), we obtain

$$(7.16) \quad A_1 \dot{q}_t = A_2 + A_3 \dot{E}_t$$

where

$$A_1 = 1 + \frac{q_t E_t \Phi'T'}{E_t(\Lambda - T)}$$

$$A_2 = q_t \left[\rho + \hat{\zeta} + \frac{\mu(\mu + \rho)q_t E_t}{E_t(\Lambda - T)} \right] - [\Lambda - v_t - T + \Phi_t T']$$

$$A_3 = \frac{q_t}{E_t}$$

Further substituting for $\dot{E}$ in (7.16) from (7.12), and using the definition of A_2, we can rewrite (7.16) as

$$(7.17) \quad A_1 \dot{q}_t = q_t \left[\Phi_t + \rho + \frac{\mu(\mu + \rho)q_t E_t}{E_t(\Lambda - T)} \right] - [\Lambda - v_t - T + \Phi_t T']$$

Now, assuming that the employment rate is always strictly positive, we rewrite (7.13) as

$$(7.18) \quad q_t \left[\hat{\zeta}_1 E_t + \frac{\hat{\zeta}_2 y_t^w}{v_t} \right] = v_t$$

From (7.18), we can express v as a function of q and E, and it is easy to prove that this function has the properties

$$\frac{\partial v}{\partial q} = \frac{E\hat{\zeta}_1 + (y^w/v)\hat{\zeta}_2}{1 - q[\hat{\zeta}_2 + E\hat{\zeta}_{21} + (y^w/v)\hat{\zeta}_{22})]\partial(y^w/v)/\partial v}$$

$$\frac{\partial v}{\partial E} = \frac{q\{[\hat{\zeta}_1 + E\hat{\zeta}_{11} + (y^w/v)\hat{\zeta}_{21}] + [\hat{\zeta}_2 + E\hat{\zeta}_{12} + (y^w/v)\hat{\zeta}_{22}]\partial(y^w/v)/\partial E\}}{1 - q[\hat{\zeta}_2 + E\hat{\zeta}_{21} + (y^w/v)\hat{\zeta}_{22}]\partial(y^w/v)/\partial v}$$

With $\hat{\zeta}_{11} > 0$ and $\hat{\zeta}_{22} > 0$ by virtue of the firm's second-order condition for maximization, and making the reasonable assumption that an increase in nonwage income raises a worker's marginal propensity to quit with respect to wage prospects elsewhere, that is, $\hat{\zeta}_{12} > 0$, we have that $\partial v/\partial q > 0$ and $\partial v/\partial E > 0$.

Since $\Phi_t = \Phi(q_t)$ and $v_t = q(q_t, E_t)$, (7.17) and (7.12) give us a system of two differential equations in the two variables q and E. In steady state, $\dot{q} = \dot{E} = 0$. Along the locus where $\dot{q} = 0$, writing v_E for $\partial v/\partial E$ and so forth,

$$\frac{dq}{dE} = -\frac{v_E}{\Delta}$$

where

$$\Delta = v_q + \rho + q\Phi' + \frac{2\mu(\mu + \rho)qE}{E(\Lambda - T)} + \frac{\mu(\mu + \rho)q^2ET'\Phi'}{E(\Lambda - T)^2}$$

Along the locus where $\dot{E} = 0$,

$$\frac{dq}{dE} = \frac{\hat{\zeta}_1 + \hat{\zeta}_2\partial(y^w/v)/\partial E + \hat{\zeta}_2[\partial(y^w/v)/\partial v]v_E}{q[\Phi' - \hat{\zeta}_2(\partial(y^w/v)/\partial v)v_q]}$$

We see that the $\dot{E} = 0$ schedule is positively sloped provided the total effect of the employment rate on quitting is positive, while the $\dot{q} = 0$ schedule

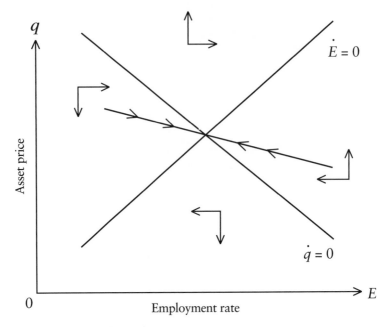

Figure 7.1 Phase diagram in the (E, q) plane

is negatively sloped. Figure 7.1 shows saddle-path stability and it displays the dynamics implied by the equations of motion in each of the four regions.

Some readers may want also a diagram that plots the real wage on the vertical axis and the employment rate on the horizontal axis. To obtain such a diagram, notice that from (7.18) we can express q as a function of v and E. Noting that $q_v\dot{v} = \dot{q} - q_E\dot{E}$, we can use (7.17) and (7.12) to plot the locus along which $\dot{v} = 0$. The slope of this locus is given by

$$\frac{dv}{dE} = \frac{-A_1 q_E E(\hat{\zeta}_1 + (\partial(y^w/v)/\partial E)\hat{\zeta}_2 - \Phi'q_E) - \psi q_E}{1 + \psi q_v + A_1 q_E E((\partial(y^w/v)/\partial v)\hat{\zeta}_2 - \Phi'q_v)}$$

where

$$\psi = \rho + \frac{2\mu(\mu + \rho)qE}{E(\Lambda - T)} + \frac{\mu(\mu + \rho)q^2 T'\Phi'E}{E(\Lambda - T)^2} + q\Phi'$$

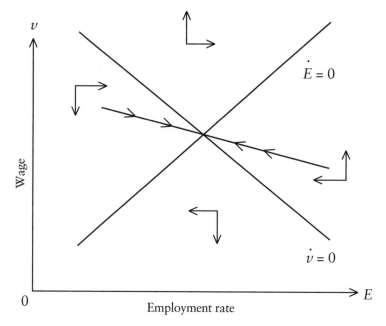

Figure 7.2 Phase diagram in the (E, v) plane: Downward-sloping stationary v locus

Along the locus where $\dot{E} = 0$ it can be shown that

$$\frac{dv}{dE} = \frac{\hat{\zeta}_1 + (\partial(y^w/v)/\partial E)\hat{\zeta}_2 - \Phi'q_E}{\Phi'q_v - (\partial(y^w/v)/\partial v)\hat{\zeta}_2}$$

The latter locus can be depicted as an upward-sloping curve and the $\dot{v} = 0$ schedule has a positive slope as well. Stability requires that the $\dot{E} = 0$ locus cuts the $\dot{v} = 0$ locus from below. Figure 7.2 depicts saddle-path stability in this case. The dynamics implied by the equations of motion in each of the four regions in Figures 7.2 and 7.3 are also displayed.

THE IMPACT OF MACROECONOMIC SHOCKS

Two main types of shocks have been studied in the macroeconomic literature, namely aggregate demand shocks and aggregate supply shocks. We first study real aggregate demand shocks, such as an increase of consumption demand arising from an exogenous increase in the rate of time preference, or more likely from a fiscal stimulus from an expansionary budgetary

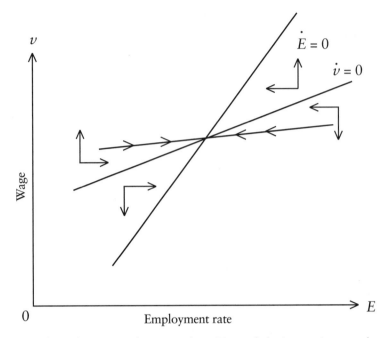

Figure 7.3 Phase diagram in the (E, v) plane: Upward-sloping stationary v locus

policy. We obtain the arresting result that expansionary fiscal policy, by raising the real rate of interest, will in fact contract employment. We discuss this result later.

Aggregate supply shocks (primarily productivity shocks) have been the main focus in the recent research in real business cycle theory. A major criticism of that literature is that the reliance on the intertemporal substitution of leisure as a propagation mechanism fails empirically to justify the large movements of employment over the course of a business cycle. Moreover, there is really no unemployment in that model, a slump being a period where workers simply want to consume more leisure. The model that we develop here provides a more plausible mechanism through which productivity shocks impact upon the rate of unemployment. We study the effects of a temporary positive productivity shock and use the model also to examine the impact of a permanent productivity improvement. We show that permanent productivity improvements leave the natural rate of unemployment invariant.

An increase in the rate of time preference. Recall that the aggregate consumption function is represented by

$$C_t = (\mu + \rho)[W_t + \Omega_t]$$

An exogenous increase in ρ, therefore, given the path of real interest rates and the corresponding q, leads to an increase in aggregate consumption demand. What is the impact of this shock on the term structure of real interest rates and aggregate unemployment? Assuming that the economy is initially at a steady state, (7.17) implies that the $\dot{q} = 0$ locus shifts downward, as in Figure 7.4. There is an immediate decline in the shadow price of a trained worker, q, and a corresponding decline in firms' investment in new workers. From (7.15), we can see that the immediate impact of the sudden rise in ρ is an increase in the instantaneous real rate of interest. Along the adjustment path BC, the instantaneous real interest rate continues to rise, giving an upward-sloping yield curve. The rise in real interest rates needed to equilibrate the goods market has the perverse effect of reducing firms' hiring of new employees, which leads to rising unemployment. There is also a decline in the real wage offered by firms. (This can be seen by noting from Figures 7.2 and 7.3 that the dynamic demand for labor shifts downward.) The economy ends up at a permanently higher rate of unemployment.

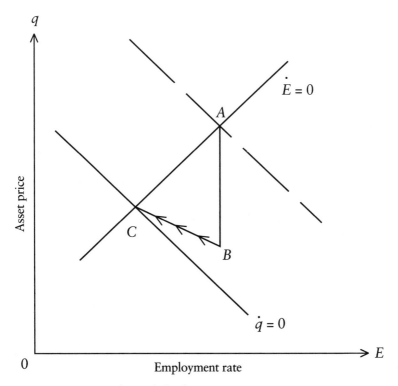

Figure 7.4 Consumption demand shocks

What happens to the path of consumption after the exogenous shock to the rate of time preference? Initially, there is an upward jump in output and consumption. The reason is that there is an upward jump in the fraction of existing employees given to production rather than to training new hires. Gradually, consumption declines as employment in the economy contracts. Per-capita consumption is permanently lower in the new steady state.

A public debt stimulus. The instantaneous government budget constraint can be written as

$$Y_t + \dot{D}_t = r_t D_t$$

assuming government spending is set equal to zero, where Y represents the lump-sum taxes and D denotes the real value of the stock of government debt, all measured in aggregate per-capita terms. We assume that the government aims at maintaining the per-capita stock of public debt constant at some level $\overline{D} > 0$, which involves levying a lump-sum tax equal to $Y_t = r_t \overline{D}$.

Nonhuman wealth is now augmented to include the stock of public debt held by the population. So we have

$$W_t = q_t E_t + \overline{D}$$

Assuming that we have initially $\overline{D} = 0$, it is easily shown that the locus along which $\dot{q} = 0$ is downward-sloping, as in Figure 7.1. Suppose that there is now a positive level of government debt, rather like a helicopter drop of government liability, so that consumers feel wealthier. The consequences are just like the case of an exogenous rise in the rate of time preference, so that Figure 7.4 again applies. There is immediately a decline in q in anticipation of higher real interest rates. This serves to discourage firms from training new workers as the marginal cost of training a new worker rises. Not surprisingly, the economy undergoes a period of retrenchment as the aggregate rate of unemployment rises.

Permanent and temporary productivity shocks. To examine the impact of productivity shocks, it turns out convenient to express $T(h)$, the opportunity cost of training per unit of the stock of employees, as $\Lambda \tau(h)$. Here, τ is interpretable as the fraction of time a trained employee devotes to training activity. Taking note of this, we can re-express (7.1) as $\tau'(h) = q/\Lambda$. The loci along which $\dot{q} = 0$ and $\dot{E} = 0$ can be expressed as

$$\frac{q_t}{\Lambda}\left[\phi_t + \rho + \frac{\mu(\mu + \rho)q_t}{(1 - \tau)\Lambda}\right] = 1 - \frac{v}{\Lambda} - \tau + \phi_t\tau'$$

$$\phi\left(\frac{q_t}{\Lambda}\right) = \hat{\zeta}\left(E_t, \frac{y_t^w}{v_t}\right)$$

respectively, where $h = \phi(q/\Lambda)$.

Now that we have a system of equations that can be expressed in terms of the following variables, q/Λ, v/Λ and E, it is straightforward to check from Figure 7.1 that a permanent productivity improvement (which raises Λ permanently) shifts both the $\dot{q} = 0$ and the $\dot{E} = 0$ locus up to the same extent so as to leave the steady-state unemployment rate invariant. It can also be checked that the real rate of interest remains unchanged. Thus a permanent shock to productivity of Harrod-neutral type discussed here is neutral for the natural rate of unemployment rate and the natural rate of interest. Further, as can be easily seen, such a shock does not disturb the equilibrium time path of the unemployment rate.

Next, let us consider a temporary productivity improvement which raises Λ temporarily. Suppose that the economy is initially at the steady state. At time t_0, the productivity parameter Λ increases but the improvement is known to last only until time t_1. At t_0, the $\dot{q} = 0$ locus shifts upward. Following our earlier argument, the $\dot{E} = 0$ schedule also shifts upward to the same extent. In selecting the dynamic path for the economy we need to take account of the fact that both loci will shift back to their original positions at t_1. Thus, we need to choose a path during the temporary improvement in Λ that brings us at t_1 to the saddle path converging to our original equilibrium. This path is shown in Figure 7.5. At t_0, there is a rise in q from point A to point B. However, q does not rise by as much as Λ rises so that q/Λ actually declines. Since it is q/Λ that matters for gross hiring, we observe that firms' investments in new workers actually contract. The economy travels from point B to point C, crossing the $\dot{q} = 0$ locus and obeying the equations of motion given by the new higher Λ regime. Along this path, the economy experiences rising unemployment. At t_1, the $\dot{q} = 0$ and $\dot{E} = 0$ loci shift back, the original equations of motion become operative, and the economy begins to return from point C to point A. Along this route, the employment rate gradually recovers to the original rate. We can again check from (7.15) that the instantaneous real interest rate falls at t_0, gradually rises to reach its peak at t_1, and then gradually declines to the original rate. The yield curve is downward-sloping at t_1.

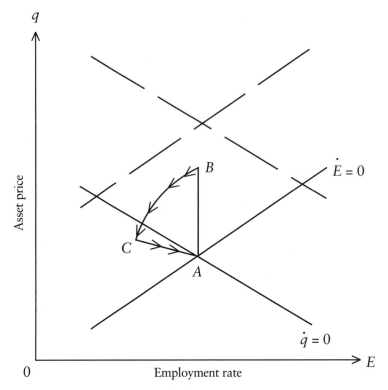

Figure 7.5 Temporary productivity shocks

The result that a temporary positive productivity shock transitorily raises unemployment can be explained as follows. A period during which workers' productivity is unusually high is one where it is more profitable for firms to direct the trained employee's time from the training activity to active production. With the higher productivity level expected to last only temporarily, firms' real wage offers also do not match the productivity increase. The result is that workers' nonwage incomes actually rise during the period of unusually high productivity, inducing higher quits. The consequence is a temporary rise in unemployment.

7.3 Commentary

The conclusion here that increased demand for the output of the consumer-good sector is contractionary—the paradox of consumption demand—runs counter both to Keynesian doctrine and to the revived neoclassical theory. In the standard Keynesian model, high expected real interest rates translate into high nominal interest rates, which stimulate employment: the increased nominal rates decrease the quantity of money demanded, thus quickening the velocity of money, which pulls up prices and thus raises the nominal demand price of labor—the money wages that employers can afford—while the money wage rates asked fail to adjust proportionately. In the standard real business cycle model, high expected real interest rates stimulate employment: workers compare the real wage today with the discounted present value of future real wages so that an increase in the real interest rate presents an incentive to work more today, less in future. This stimulates current labor supply.

The identification of booms with high expected real interest rates and slumps with low real rates, however, seems to fly in the face of the evidence of actual experience. The 1930s were not marked by depressed real interest rates; and the wartime boom of the first half of the 1940s was not characterized by high real rates. More recently, the slump in Europe in the 1980s was not accompanied by low real interest rates; on the contrary, it was a period when the real interest rates were extremely high. A virtue of the model produced here is its prediction that high real interest rates caused by exogenous aggregate demand shocks lead to higher unemployment. A temporary productivity improvement, on the other hand, leads to temporarily higher unemployment rates coinciding with lower short-term real interest rates. Thus the correlation between the real rate of interest and unemployment is contingent upon the origin of the disturbance.

It should be unnecessary to point out the possibility that, in the short term, demand-stimulating fiscal policy may lead to expansion of employment and output through the traditional Keynesian channel *before* turning into a net contractionary force via the structural, or supply-side, channels explored here. The domain of the model here runs from the infinite horizon back to some medium-term perspective observable when the monetary dust has mostly settled.

8

A Customer-Market Model

IN the modernist's vision, the enterprise economy is riddled with informational imperfections in every market, and by now more than one paradigm has been developed to describe that non-Walrasian world.[1] There are the models of incentive wages in which, though prices and wages are continuously known, certain behavior of agents cannot be continuously known or foreseen by the other parties to the transaction. There are also models in which the imperfection is the scarcity of information about prices or wages. Two prototypes in that latter line of models are the Phelps-Winter model of price-setting firms competing for customers and the Mortensen model of wage-setting firms competing for employees.[2] These latter non-Walrasian models yielded a distinctive result on market equilibrium: Provided the real rate of interest remains positive, the competition of the firms in their imperfect market medium will not wipe out all pure profit, nor drive price down to marginal cost, owing to the investment cost needed to overcome frictions in the transmission and acquisition of price information. The higher the real rate of interest, the greater will be the markup of price over marginal cost and the volume of profit. These models, however, were partial-equilibrium in nature.

This chapter takes the Phelps-Winter model of the product market, combining it with the version introduced above of the Calvo-Bowles shirking model of the labor market and the Blanchard-Yaari model of the capital market, to obtain a general-equilibrium framework with which to analyze the effects of various shocks on (the path of) the equilibrium unemployment rate.[3] This framework is particularly useful for the transparency in which it shows the effects of shocks impacting on consumer demand.[4]

The basic structure of the economy is described, and some of its implications obtained, in section 8.1. (This section recalls the main features of the Calvo-Bowles model in the version presented in section 3.2 and the Blanchard-Yaari model of intertemporal household consumption planning discussed in section 5.1, while the exposition of the Phelps-Winter model is self-contained, independent of section 4.2.) Section 8.2 introduces this basic structure into a closed economy and considers the existence and uniqueness of the general equilibrium solution. As for the effects of shocks, particular attention is paid to the equilibrium unemployment effects of increased consumer demand caused by an increased time preference or increased public indebtedness and to the unemployment effect of public expenditure. (Later, in section 12.3, this structure is imbedded instead in the small open economy, where the focus of attention is on how an exogenous increase of the external real interest rate shifts the equilibrium path of employment.) There are some concluding remarks on the findings of this chapter, though most of the commentary is left for the final chapter of Part II.

8.1 The Basic Structure: Product and Labor Markets

Production for the customer market, which is the only commercial market supplied by firms hiring labor, is carried out by a large number of atomistic firms in identical (or symmetrical) circumstances. The number of firms is a constant, a postulate which, though not valid with respect to every sort of shock, is not in the present case the serious drawback it might first seem to be.[5] The size of the labor force and the stock of customers are equal and a positive constant, both belonging to a population in a demographic stationary state. Hence the number of families, or customers, per firm, is a demographic parameter.

The characteristic of the customer market in the Phelps-Winter model, as already reviewed in Chapter 4, is the informational frictions that would impede a quick flow of customers to a firm were it to choose to post a lower price than that being charged elsewhere. A firm setting a price always below that set by the other (identically behaving) firms would only gradually drain customers from its competitors. Symmetrically, it is supposed that a firm setting a price always above that set by the others would see an equally gradual erosion of its customer stock, as customers sought alternative suppliers and required varying lengths of time to find them.[6]

It will be helpful to have some notation and definitions. Let x^i denote the stock of customers accumulated to date at the ith firm, and x denote the total number of customers per firm, a demographic constant in the closed economy.[7] The labor force per firm is also a demographic parameter, ℓ, and equal to x if there are as many customers as workers in every family. Let z^i denote the (homogeneous) output of the ith firm, and z the total output per firm. Let y^i denote the amount supplied and demanded of the consumer good per customer at the ith firm, and y the expenditure by consumers per customer. Admitting into the model the possibility that the government buys the identical product (for its own uses) from these same firms, we let its purchase be γ^h per customer, family, or household in the economy, and $\gamma^h x$ at each firm, independently of whether a firm chose to be larger or smaller than the others in terms of its own stock of customers, x^i, which no firm will have done. Then z is equal to $(y + \gamma^h)x$. The ith firm's "nominal" price in terms of the shares, or common stock, issued by the firm is denoted p^i, the average price by p. The ith firm's real price is therefore p^i/p. Finally, p^{ei}, for example, denotes the ith firm's expectation of the price at the other firms, and similarly for other variables on which it must form expectations.

Since it operates in an imperfectly informed product market, the firm works with its estimates, or expectations, of the other firms' current and future course of actions. Each firm, being atomistic, is small enough that it has only a negligible influence on the behavior of the other firms. Since all firms know this, each firm's expectations of industry, or economy, actions, such as p^{ei}, are likewise independent of its own behavior. The time path of interest rates $r^e\{t\}_{t=[0,\infty]}$ expected by the firm it also takes as given.

There cannot be general equilibrium without equilibrium in all markets. Product-market equilibrium requires that every firm and its customers have correct expectations about the actions in the aggregate, and thus per firm, in the industry. Hence, indexing the firms by i, $p = p^{ei}$ and $y = y^{ei}$ for all i. Analogously, labor-market equilibrium requires realization at each moment, from the present forward, of the expectations of every firm and its work force with regard to the labor market. Hence $v = v^{ei}$ and $1 - u = 1 - u^{ei}$ for all i. Equilibrium in the capital market entails that the post-shock path of actual interest rate, $r\{t\}_{t=[0,\infty]}$, coincides with the post-shock path of the expected interest rate, $r^e\{t\}_{t=[0,\infty]}$. In any equilibrium scenario, then, our firms correctly forecast and treat parametrically p, y, $1 - u$, v, and r.

The character of the labor market in which the firms operate must also be specified. Our firms, while collectively beneficiaries of information imperfections in the product market, are victims of imperfect information in the workplace. At each firm the members of the firm's work force—the term *employees* suggests some long-term attachment more appropriate to the quitting model, though it will slip through nonetheless—suffer randomly timed and statistically independent episodes of shirking. These episodes might take the form of a shopping errand or a personal phone call or a daydream, all of fixed and unchanging duration, say. Workers are able to shirk without certainty of being caught because monitoring is expensive and the firms cannot afford continuous monitoring. But given that the firm can monitor costlessly at times when the opportunity presents itself, workers know that an act of shirking will be detected with some positive probability. Consequently, a worker of given accumulated assets will succumb to the urge to shirk with less frequency—with a higher threshold—the greater the opportunity cost of being caught and hence dismissed. The effort rate, ε—the fraction of the workers with nose to the grindstone—is increasing in v^i, decreasing in $(1 - u)v$, and decreasing in $aR(v, 1 - u)$, as in the model of section 4.2. A firm can therefore combat the shirking propensity of its workers by offering an increased wage, raising it above the market-clearing level. As firms generally adopt the strategy of paying above-market-clearing wages, the same wage at the individual firm confers a reduced advantage—labor input and hence output costs more—so unemployment arises. The equilibrium unemployment volume is just large enough that none of the identical firms sees an advantage in offering a still-higher wage in order to further reduce shirking.

LABOR-MARKET EQUILIBRIUM

Given the wage expected to be chosen by the other firms and the unemployment rate, each firm knows that up to a point a higher wage actually lowers its cost curve, as analyzed in section 3.2. A unique cost-minimizing wage at each of the identical firms generally exists, at least over a wide range. The wage that the ith firm calculates to be cost minimizing is an increasing function of the expected employment rate and of the wage expected to be offered elsewhere, given the asset income flow—the income per unit of asset, R, multiplied by the average asset holding of its workers, a—which the firm takes to be representative of the asset holding of workers generally, employed and unemployed. At a firm in labor-market equilibrium, meaning $v = v^{e_i}$ and $1 - u = 1 - u^{e_i}$, then,

$$(8.1) \quad v^i = \tilde{v}(1 - u, v; aR) \qquad \tilde{v}_1 > 0, \tilde{v}_2 > 0, \tilde{v}_3 > 0$$

There are two more steps to reach the equilibrium wage curve. First, since a, the average holdings of firm-assets by employed persons, is taken to be the total number of shares per total number of families, each share being an ownership claim to the earnings from one customer at a firm, a must be a constant equal to 1 in the closed-economy case; the average nonwage income of employees on this account, aR, is just the income per share. Taking into account the actuarial dividend paid to annuity-holding wealth owners in Blanchard's framework, μq, this income per share may be denoted $R(v, 1 - u; q)$. Second, the equilibrium wage, if it exists, at a specified employment rate is determined by equating v^i to v for all i among the identical firms. As was shown in section 3.2, there is a range of low employment rates in which $\tilde{v}_2$ is less than one. Hence at employment rates up to some critical level $1 - \tilde{u}$, the equilibrium wage is increasing in the employment rate, given assets per worker:

(8.2) $v = V_s(1 - u; q)$ $V'_s > 0$

However, equation (8.2) comes from an exposition (Chapter 3) in which there was no public debt and public expenditure, indeed no government at all. One ought to include in the average nonwage income of employees the excess of average family pretax income on that account over the additional family tax bill needed to service the public debt. In the Blanchard world, with lump-sum taxes, the former is $(r + \mu)\beta$, and the latter is $r\beta$, where β denotes the public debt per family, a nonnegative constant here. Clearly the public debt holdings throw off a positive income net of tax, namely $\mu\beta$. It therefore increases the propensity to shirk and thus pushes up the incentive wage needed to minimize costs. When taxes are collected on expenditures or on total income, the impact of the public debt on the ratio of nonwage income to the wage rate would again be positive, and it would be stronger. The effect of balanced-budget public expenditure on employees' average nonwage income as a ratio to the wage rate depends critically on the method of taxation. Financing by lump-sum taxes reduces nonwage income net of tax (since lump-sum taxes reduce after-tax nonwage income) and thus reduces the efficiency wage needed to minimize unit costs.[8] Financing by an across-the-board proportional income tax on wage and nonwage income reduces wage rates and nonwage income equiproportionately, therefore does not disturb the shirking rate and the elasticities of the shirking-rate function, and hence does not alter the efficiency wage. We will specialize to the latter case. To keep these ideas in mind it will suffice to redefine the function V_s rather than proliferate new notation, writing

(8.2′) $v = V_s(1 - u; q, \beta)$ $V'_s > 0, \partial V_s/\partial q > 0, \partial V_s/\partial \beta > 0$

Later a result on unit costs will also be needed. Despite constant costs at the firm with respect to its own input or output, real unit cost, denoted

ς, rises with the employment rate owing to its direct impact on the shirking rate and to the indirect effect on shirking at each firm of the resulting rise in the other firms' wage.[9] If we restrict the domain to the region where total output per firm, as given by the expression

$$\Lambda\varepsilon(v, (1 - u)v, R(v, 1 - u; q, \beta))(1 - u)\ell$$

is monotone-increasing in the employment rate, equation (8.2′) notwithstanding, it follows that unit cost, though constant at the individual firm with respect to its own output, is increasing in industry, or economywide, output:

$$(8.3) \quad \varsigma = \varsigma(z, V_s(z; q, \beta)) \qquad \varsigma_1(\cdot) > 0, \ V'_s\varsigma_2(\cdot) > 0,$$
$$= \varsigma((y + \gamma^h)x; q, \beta) \qquad \varsigma'(\cdot) > 0$$

PRODUCT-MARKET EQUILIBRIUM

The other decision of the firm is the choice at each moment of the price at which to sell to its current customers—the output to "auction off," figuratively speaking, to its current customers.[10] Raising its price causes a decrease, and lowering the price an increase, in the quantity demanded by its current customers according to a per-customer demand relationship, $\eta(p^i/p, y)$, where y in this context functions as the average expenditure per family at the *other* firms.[11] Yet it is dynamic monopoly power the firms have, not the static power possessed by the textbook monopolist. Setting its price steadily very high would gradually squander a firm's stock of customers. Symmetrically, keeping its price steadily very low would forgo a surplus of revenues over costs. In contrast, with regard to sales to the government, the firm needs no price policy, as the government pays the going nominal price, p, at all firms, distributing its orders equally over the equal-sized firms.[12]

The firm thus needs a criterion to define its optimal price policy. In this model, each firm chooses the path of its real price or, equivalently, the path of its supply per customer to its consumers, to maximize the expected present discounted value of its cash flows. The maximum at the ith firm is the value of the firm, Q^i, which depends upon x^i and γ^h. In the above notation, and on the above assumptions, we have[13]

$$(8.4) \quad \max \int_0^\infty \left[\left(\frac{p_i}{p} \right) y^i x_t^i + z_G^i - \varsigma((y + \gamma^h)x)(y^i x_t^i + z_G^i) \right] e^{-\int_0^t r(u)\,du} \, dt \equiv Q_t^i$$

in which z_G^i denotes the amount produced for the government and sold at the real price of one. This maximization is subject to the differential equation giving the motion of the stock of customers of the ith firm as a function of its relative, or real, price:

$$(8.5) \qquad dx^i/dt = \chi(p^i/p)x^i \qquad \chi'(\cdot) < 0, \chi(1) = 0$$

The solution can be viewed as a time path of the price or, equivalently, as a policy giving p^i as a function of x^i, taking into account in either case the consequences for the path of x^i.

It is expedient, and perhaps rather natural in a macroeconomic context, to analyze the maximization in terms of output instead of price. Using the relation $y^i = \eta(p^i/p, y)$ and assuming that η is homogeneous of degree one in y, we obtain p^i/p as a decreasing function of y^i/y, to be written $f(y^i/y)$, $f'(\cdot) < 0$, $f(1) = 1$. In terms of output, the motion of x^i is given by

$$(8.5') \qquad dx^i/dt = g(y^i/y)x^i \qquad g(\cdot) \equiv \chi(f(\cdot)), g'(\cdot) > 0, g(1) = 0$$

The optimal y^i and z_G^i in this problem at each moment maximize the associated Hamiltonian,

$$(8.6) \qquad x^i\{y^i[f(y^i/y) - \varsigma((y + \gamma^b)x)] + q_m^i g(y^i/y)\}$$
$$+ \min(z_G^i, \gamma^b x)[1 - \varsigma(y + \gamma^b)] \equiv \mathcal{H}(y^i, z_G^i)$$

where q_m^i is the shadow price, or worth, of an additional customer, by which is meant the derivative $Q^{i\prime}(x^i)$. It fully corresponds to what is called "marginal q" in investment theory. Evidently y and z_G^i figure separably in this maximand, owing to constant costs at the individual firm, so optimal y^i maximizes the expression in the curly brace independently of its own optimal sales to the government; but the economywide sales to the government drive up unit cost. The first-order condition for optimal y^i is

$$(8.7) \qquad 0 = (q_m^i/y)g'(y^i/y) + f(y^i/y) - \varsigma((y + \gamma^b)x; q, \beta)$$
$$+ y^i f'(y^i/y)y^{-1} \equiv \mathcal{H}_{y^i}(\cdot)$$

Equating y^i to y finally delivers the condition on consumer-good supply per firm for product-market equilibrium:

$$(8.8) \qquad q_m/y = -[f(1) - \varsigma((y + \gamma^b)x; q, \beta) + f'(1)]g'(1)^{-1} \qquad f(1) = 1$$

The expression in the square brackets is the algebraic excess of marginal revenue over marginal cost, a negative quantity in customer-market models as the firm supplies more than called for by the static monopolist's formula for maximum current profit, giving up some of the maximum *current* profit for the sake of its longer-term interests.

CAPITAL-MARKET EQUILIBRIUM

As the analysis in the Phelps-Winter paper shows,[14] the first-order condition in (8.7) is joined by a necessary condition of an intertemporal nature on the motion of q_m:

(8.9) $dq_m^i/dt = [r_t - g(y^i/y_t)]q_m^i - y^i[1 - \varsigma((y_t + \gamma^h)x_t; q_t, \beta)]$

Along a path of product-market equilibrium, therefore,

(8.10) $dq_m/dt = (r_t - g^x)q_m - y[1 - \varsigma((y + \gamma^h)x; q, \beta)]$

where g^x equals zero in the closed-economy case.[15] This equation, which can be regarded as defining the firm's instantaneous rate of return to investment in its stock of assets, is an intertemporal condition of capital-market equilibrium: that the firms are correctly calculating the rate of return.

Under the assumption, made without essential loss of generality, that each firm keeps the number of its shares outstanding equal to its stock of customers, the motion of the share price, henceforth to be denoted by q_a instead of q for emphasis, is governed by a similar differential equation:

(8.11) $dq_a/dt = (r_t - g)q_a - (y + \gamma^h)[1 - \varsigma((y + \gamma^h)x; q_a, \beta)]$

where g here denotes the average rate of stock dividend, which is equal to zero, since it equals the growth rate, also zero, of the customer stock per firm appearing in equation (8.10). The instantaneous rate of interest necessarily satisfies a similar equation in which the lefthand side is instead the *expected* change of q_a. So requiring the above equation is to imply that the expected path of q_a is realized, matched by the actual path. Because firms and households are correctly forecasting the path of q_a, barring a structural shock, they are correctly forecasting the rate of return on assets that they use in arriving at the rate of interest to use in discounting future payouts and costs. This is another intertemporal condition for equilibrium—that households have got right the rate of return on their shares.

Finally, drawing upon the Blanchard-Yaari apparatus, it is argued that the economy here satisfies an Euler-type differential equation in the rate of change of consumption per customer, c. Consumption growth is governed by the excess of the interest rate over the rate of pure time preference, denoted ρ, and by the ratio of (nonhuman) wealth to consumption.[16] Here wealth per person is public debt per capita, β, plus the real price of shares, q, as there are as many shares as customers. The real price of public debt is not a variable here because it is taken to be entirely in short-term obligations, even postal savings deposits. Thus we obtain

$$(8.12) \quad dc/dt = (r - \rho)c - m(q_a + \beta) \qquad m \equiv \mu(\rho + \mu) > 0$$

Working in a backward induction, we obtain an equation giving the current level of consumption demand as a function of (nonhuman) wealth and the suitably discounted value of the stream of actual and expected wages, so-called human wealth, which may be left implicit.[17]

Customers' consumption per customer is equal to the output supplied to them per customer, y. Equating the level of consumption demand to the excess supply of output at firms obtained by subtracting the draw of the government gives the further condition,

$$(8.13) \quad (c + \gamma^b)x = \Lambda\varepsilon(v, (1 - u)v, R(v, 1 - u; q_a, \beta))(1 - u)\ell$$

In requiring here that q at each moment be at such a level as to make the path of planned consumption (its growth as well as its level) consistent with the path of output from equation (8.8), we are requiring that the market where goods are exchanged for shares (at price q)—call it the capital market—be in equilibrium. No household will find the prevailing share price different from what is expected. (In this model, a disequilibrium there would mean the market was not clearing.) It may be regarded as the condition that households be in capital-market equilibrium.

Finally, we can record the quasirent per unit of the assets in which, from a micro standpoint, the firms might be said to have invested:

$$(8.14) \quad R = [1 - \varsigma((y + \gamma^b)x; q_a, \beta)](y + \gamma^b)$$

The direct effect of increased $1 - u$, hence y, on R is evidently positive, as firms are not interested in producing at a loss, while the indirect effect via the higher wage induced by the increased y is negative.

8.2 General Equilibrium of the Closed Economy

The experienced student of dynamic systems will understand that, as described in the foregoing equations, the model here has no slow-moving variable on which all the other variables depend and which summarizes in a sufficient statistic the state, or current situation, of the economy.[18] The stationary-state solution or solutions are open to the economy at once, without any process of adjustment.

A relevant question is whether there are other solutions when it is kept in mind that the present volume limits its solutions to equilibrium paths—to paths along which expectations are being borne out, absent fresh structural change or shocks to any state variables. In general, one should be prepared for the existence of equilibrium paths, even a continuum of equilibrium paths, in addition to the stationary-state path or paths, which are the natural candidates for equilibrium solutions. Can such nonstationary paths be ruled out? In the appendix to this chapter there is a result implying that if there is just one stationary-state solution to the model, the only equilibrium path coincides with that stationary state. More generally, in the neighborhood of a stationary state there exists, in exact analogy, just one equilibrium path, namely the stationary-state path, *provided* the latter is characterized by the condition in supply-demand analysis that the demand price, if not falling, is nevertheless not rising as fast as the supply price with respect to the economy's output.[19] The equilibrium possibilities are therefore very much contingent upon the character of the stationary-state solution or solutions.

It is evident from the previous equations that any stationary-state equilibrium must satisfy the subsystem

$$(8.15) \quad r = [1 - \varsigma((y + \gamma^h)x; q_a, \beta)](y/q_m)$$

$$(8.16) \quad r = \rho + m[(q_a + \beta)/y]$$

$$(8.17) \quad r = [1 - \varsigma((y + \gamma^h)x; \beta)](y + \gamma^h)/q_a$$

$$(8.18) \quad q_m/y = -[f(1) - \varsigma((y + \gamma^h)x; \beta) + f'(1)]g'(1)^{-1}$$

It is clear that the first three equations determine the *demand price* for *shares* as a function of output, given γ^h; the interest rate is simultaneously determined. The last equation, (8.18), gives what may be called the *marginal supply price* of customers, as it indicates how high the shadow price of customers must be to elicit a given volume of total output.

It is necessary finally to relate the two asset prices. Using (8.15) and (8.17), and introducing the notation z^h for total output per household, or customer, $y + \gamma^f$, we have

$$(8.19) \quad q_a(z^h - \gamma^h) = q_m z^h$$

"Average q" is inflated relative to "marginal q" by the extra profit firms make from their government orders. Using this result in (8.16) gives

$$(8.20) \quad r = \rho + m[(q_m/y)z^h + \beta]/(z^h - \gamma^h)$$

Now equate the righthand sides of (8.20) and (8.15) to obtain

$$(8.21) \quad [1 - \varsigma(z^h x; (q_m/y)z^h, \beta)]/(q_m/y) = \rho + m[(q_m/y)z^h + \beta]/(z^h - \gamma^h)$$

We may think of this equation as providing the *marginal demand price* of customers expressed as a ratio to average customer expenditure.

The supply-price and demand-price curves are graphed for the case in which γ^h equals zero, so that marginal and average q are equal, in Figure 8.1. This graph is useful in making transparent that, as the supply-price curve originates at a point between the end points of the demand-price curve, at least one equilibrium must exist. However, it is more convenient to work in another plane.

The reduced-form demand price curve in (8.21) together with the *supply price* curve in (8.18), which using z^h becomes

$$(8.18') \quad q_m/y = -[f(1) - \varsigma(z^h x; (q_m/y)z^h, \beta) + f'(1)]g'(1)^{-1}$$

determine simultaneously the equilibrium stationary-state values of q_m/y and z^h—and hence y, that is, $z^h - \gamma^f$—if an equilibrium exists. Figure 8.2 graphs the two curves in the $(z^h, q_m/y)$ plane. How do these two curves relate?

In (8.21) an increase of q_m/y, through both of its impacts, decreases the lefthand side, which could be regarded as Wicksell's natural interest rate. At the same time it increases the righthand side, which is the interest rate required by consumers if they are not to demand more consumer-good output than is supplied. Let us now specialize for the moment to the case of small government, so to speak—to γ^f and β equal to zero or sufficiently close to give the same results. In this case the lefthand side of (8.21) is

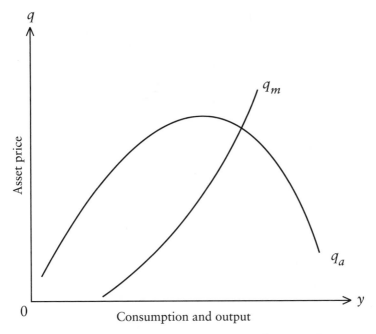

Figure 8.1 General-equilibrium output and asset price when q_m and q_a are equal

decreasing in z^b more strongly than the righthand side, since $\varsigma'(z^b) > 0$, so that z^b must decrease to restore equality between the lefthand and righthand sides. The demand price *ratio*, q_m/y, is therefore decreasing in z^b.

Continuing the analysis of Figure 8.2, we turn to the supply price relationship in (8.18′). It is clear that an increase of z^b impacts on the equation by increasing the righthand side. Hence, in view of the primary effect on the lefthand side—it would take a very large mortality rate to believe otherwise—it is natural to suppose that an increase of q_m/y requires an increase of z^b.[20] So this supply curve is taken to be upward-sloping.

Continuing with the small-government case, we may now consider the questions of the existence and uniqueness of equilibrium. From the opposite algebraic signs of the slopes, it is obvious that the stationary-state solution is unique if it exists. By the reasoning of the appendix, then, the equilibrium path is also unique and coincidental with the stationary-state path.

Existence of the stationary-state solution follows from two observations. The downward-sloping demand price curve hits the horizontal axis

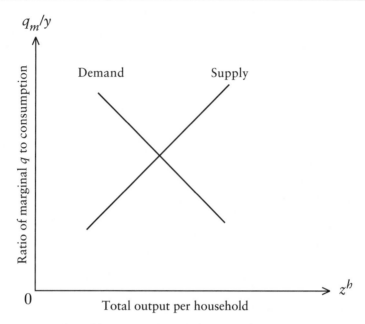

Figure 8.2 General-equilibrium output and the ratio of marginal shadow price to consumption

where $\varsigma(z^b; 0, \beta) = 1$, which corresponds to zero profit. This would be the equilibrium under conditions of classical perfect competition. The upward-sloping supply price relationship originates at the point on the horizontal axis corresponding to the static monopolist's profit-maximizing output, where marginal cost is less than price and profit is positive. The output at the latter intercept is smaller than the output at the former intercept. Furthermore, the demand price curve is bounded from above while the supply price ratio increases without bound as z^b is increased. Hence the two curves must intersect.

So in the small-government case there exists a unique equilibrium path and it is a stationary state.

In the large-government case the complication is that what is being called here the demand price curve in the $(z^b, q_m/y)$ plane may undulate on its way down to the classical perfect-competition intercept discussed above. Consequently there may be a multiplicity of stationary-state solutions corresponding to the multiple intersections of the demand price curve with the supply price curve. If, as some theorists are fond of postulating, there exists a divine hand guiding the economy to that solution exhibiting the largest output level (and highest q) up the supply price curve, this solution being the best of a bad lot, the appendix implies that our correct-expectations economy can only jump at once to this preferred stationary state, as there do not exist adjustment paths leading to it along which the economy is continuously in equilibrium. That conclusion is based on the observation that at the last and highest intersection along the supply price curve the other curve must be cutting it from above, otherwise it could not reach the horizontal z axis, which it must do. (The appendix shows that if and only if the curves intersect that way, as in the uniqueness case, the equilibrium is "saddle-point" stable, requiring a jump to the stationary path.)

COMPARATIVE (OR SENSITIVITY) ANALYSIS: DEMAND SHOCKS

Any comparative analysis of the system (8.21) and (8.18′)—the more common term *comparative statics* seems unsuitable, as one is describing how the entire equilibrium path over time differs when there is a parametric shift—must deal with the matter of how the relevant curves intersect. As argued in the previous section, if the stationary-state solution is unique the curves can intersect only the "right" way, so as to deliver a unique equilibrium path in the neighborhood of that stationary solution (namely, the stationary state itself). If there are multiple stationary-state solutions, it is only every other solution that displays the right-way intersection— only the odd-numbered intersections. What to do?

   In interpreting the comparative analyses below we may identify them with the case of uniqueness, throwing up our hands in the other case. Or, with an aim to be more general, we may take inspiration from Samuelson's widely accepted Principle of Correspondence: the principle that there is no point in doing comparative analysis if the equilibrium is unstable, for it is then unlikely to be realized and, if it was being realized before the parametric shift, unlikely to go on being realized in the face of the parametric shift.[21] In the same spirit, we may invoke what can be called the Second Principle of Correspondence: It is not possible to attach meaning to the effects of parameter shifts unless we impose the requirement that the equilibrium path studied is locally unique, not one belonging to a continuum of paths (all converging on some stationary-state solution that is "too stable," rather than saddlepoint stable). Which of these two interpretations the reader chooses is a matter of taste.

This section takes up shifts in demand for the output of the consumer-good-producing firms. In the purely demand-driven models of Keynesian theory, of course, aggregate demand is virtually the alpha and the omega of (un)employment determination.[22] In the present model aggregate demand is still the alpha. In fact this model is more "Keynesian" than Keynes's own model in that what limits the firm's output is its customers' demand, not neoclassical diminishing returns. And supply matters little![23]

In the present formulation we may identify "aggregate demand" (at a given employment rate and corresponding total output) as the righthand side of (8.20) evaluated at the initial, or preshock, value of marginal q_m, denoted by q_m^o:

$$(8.22) \quad \rho + \mu(\mu + \rho)\{[q_m^o/(z - \gamma^f)]z + \beta\}/(z - \gamma^f) \equiv \alpha$$

Any positive shock to α, brought by a positive shift of ρ or μ or β, stimulates consumer demand and thus drives up the rate of interest that must be available to savers in order that desired saving not fall short of (nor exceed) investment demand, which is zero here.[24] In what direction, however, does demand, α, operate on employment?

The foregoing results make unmistakable the surprising effects of, say, a positive shift in α. The condition for households' equilibrium in (8.5) shows that such a shift has the effect of generally *reducing* the demand price for shares and hence the worth of customers at each level of output: More precisely, the demand price curve, while keeping its former end points, draws nearer to the horizontal axis. Hence, if the demand price curve is downward-sloping in the neighborhood of its intersection with the supply price curve, the consequences are clearly a fall of both q and y. More generally, if *uniqueness* is satisfied or if the aforementioned low-debt condition is satisfied, so that the output-elasticity of the demand price (even if positive) is less than the output-elasticity of the supply price in the neighborhood of equilibrium—so that the demand curve (even if upward-sloping) cuts the supply price curve from above—the consequences are still a fall of both q and y. Thus increased demand is *contractionary* in this model—provided that, as explained at the beginning of this section, either the stationary-state solution is unique (as it must be under a zero or low debt) or we are examining the effects of a stationary-state solution in the neighborhood of which the equilibrium path is locally unique, so that in a local sense at least we have an assured determinacy of the price path.

For completeness it should be recorded that if the disturbance to α is attributable to an increase of the public debt, the increase of β has another effect through the channel of costs. The impact on the ratio of nonwage income to the wage drives up the cost-minimizing incentive wage, which in turn induces firms to economize more strongly on labor than before, cutting the supply of output as a result. That effect is not of great quantitative importance if the income on the public debt is small in relation to nonwage income in toto.[25] Neither is it very surprising. What is surprising is the effect through the interest-rate channel, on which we now comment.

Evidently a paradoxical result—and to Keynesian eyes a monstrous result—has risen up from our system despite its many Keynesian features. How did it occur? In any true Keynesian model, of course, a positive demand shift would be accompanied, as here, by an increase of the real interest rate if output is not to change; the latter is translated into an increase of the money rate of interest, which in turn fires an increase in the velocity of money, and through this monetary channel there results at least a transient increase of employment owing to rigidity or stickiness or misexpectations governing nominal wages or prices. Moneyness and nominal-price maladjustment are the essence of the matter.

In the present model, by contrast, the above monetary channel has been bypassed in the interest of focusing on the effects of aggregate demand upon the equilibrium path(s); the influence of outside Metzler-Patinkin money, if any, is neglected for simplicity. In this equilibrium context, too, increased aggregate demand imposes an increased real interest rate, achieved through a fall in the real price of shares, if output is taken as unchanged; when households try to sell some shares (for goods) at what they forecast to be an unchanged price, there is no one buying, so the real price of shares (actual and expected) drops until the capital market is reequilibrated. But in the present model it is not the case that the increase of the real interest rate that chokes off enough demand to counterbalance the autonomous shift has a positive effect on velocity and no effect on output supply, as in the Keynesian model; quite the opposite. The effect of the increased real interest rate—equivalently the drop in the real price of shares—puts the demand price below the supply price (to which it had initially been equal). On our elasticity condition, this gap can only be closed by a fall of output. This cutback in the amount of output supplied by firms is their way of attempting to reduce (from the initial level of zero) their net investment in customers, although, in a sort of paradox of competition, none of our identical firms actually succeeds in disinvesting in customers. (They only cut back more as they see that everyone is doing it.)

Of course, for this contractionary outcome to exhibit an increase of unemployment, not simply a decline of the real wage, some real-wage resistance (or else stickiness) is required.

COMPARATIVE ANALYSIS: PRODUCTIVITY AND SUPPLY SHOCKS

To study the effects of a shift in productivity or, more properly, in total factor productivity owing to, say, a technological advance or the mastering of some already existing but heretofore unutilized technology, we need to write out the system constituted by (8.21) and (8.18') in terms of the employment rate and the technical parameter Λ, which is to be shifted. To do this we use (8.13) to have z^b as a function of $1 - u$. For unit cost, ς, we write explicitly the ratio of the wage to output per worker, which is $\Lambda\varepsilon(\theta, (1 - u)\theta, 1)$, where (as in Chapter 3) θ denotes the ratio of v to R. Furthermore, we use the homogeneity property in the cost minimization problem and the first-order condition, equations (3.8') and (3.9), to find that the optimal efficiency wage is proportional to R at any given $1 - u$, the factor of proportionality being the optimal θ, and that this optimal θ is independent of the other variables of the system. In these terms the system is the following four equations,

$$(8.23) \quad \{1 - (\theta R)/[\Lambda\varepsilon(\theta, (1 - u)\theta, 1)]\}/(q_m/y)$$
$$= \rho + m[(q_m/y)z^b + \beta]/(z^b + \gamma^f)$$

$$(8.24) \quad q_m/y = -[f(1) - \varsigma(1 - u; \beta) + f'(1)]g'(1)^{-1}$$

$$(8.25) \quad z^b = \Lambda\varepsilon(\theta, (1 - u)\theta, 1)(1 - u)\ell$$

$$(8.26) \quad R = \{1 - (\theta R)/[\Lambda\varepsilon(\theta, (1 - u)\theta, 1)]\}z^b$$

in four unknowns: z^b, R, q_m/y, and $1 - u$. Attention is confined, as always, to the region where, in (8.25), z^b is increasing in $1 - u$, so that ε is not decreasing in $1 - u$ faster than $1 - u$ is increasing. To reduce notational clutter β has been suppressed from the ε function.

Now we use the third equation, (8.25), to substitute for z^b in the first two equations. Further, we use the fourth equation (upon substituting again for z^b from the third equation) to find that R always appears there as a ratio to Λ. Hence R/Λ is determined by $1 - u$, ℓ, and θ; the cost function in the first equation may then be written accordingly. The reduced system thus obtained is

(8.23′) $[1 - \varsigma(1 - u, \ell, \theta; \beta)]/(q_m/y)$

$$= \rho + m \frac{\{(q_m/y)[\Lambda\varepsilon(\theta, (1 - u)\theta, 1)(1 - u)\ell] + \beta\}}{[\Lambda\varepsilon(\theta, (1 - u)\theta, 1)(1 - u)\ell - \gamma^f]}$$

(8.24′) $q_m/y = -[f(1) - \varsigma(1 - u, \ell, \theta; \beta) + f'(1)]g'(1)^{-1}$

in which the two unknowns are q_m/y and $1 - u$.

What is the effect on $1 - u$ of an increase of the technical parameter Λ? The supply price relationship, (8.24′), is undisturbed by this shift. The demand relationship, (8.23′), *may* be shifted. Consider first the case with no public debt and no public expenditure. In this case the righthand side is unaffected. Therefore there is no effect on the equilibrium unemployment rate! Such a result could have been anticipated. The productivity shift, being Harrod-neutral, leaves the demand wage increased in proportion to Λ at an unchanged rate of interest and unchanged labor effectiveness; simultaneously, the surrogate supply wage read from the equilibrium wage curve must increase in the same proportion if, the wage having increased in proportion to Λ, nonwage income per asset at the firms has increased in the same proportion. The only consistent response is an equiproportionate increase of v and R at the initial $1 - u$. Such a response will leave the effectiveness of labor unchanged and the employment rate unchanged.

The case with positive government expenditure or public debt or both is formally different. If these parameters are truly fixed, the increase of productivity is like a decrease of public expenditure and a decrease of public debt in inverse proportion to the increase of productivity. We have already learned that the effect of such decreases would be a reduction of the real interest rate and an increase of the employment rate.

It could be complained that such an analysis overlooks the possibility that with increased productivity will come a proportional increase of public expenditure and of public debt. Then the righthand side of (8.23′) is again unaffected. But a more practical outlook would take into account that the increase of the public debt, at any rate, would surely not be immediate. Consequently the thought-experiment here is very much like a decrease of the public debt per unit of "potential output." The effect of that, to repeat, is to increase the equilibrium employment rate. It may be conceded, however, that the importance of this effect is roughly proportional to the size of the public debt to begin with. It would not be an important consideration in an economy with a public debt that was already small.

There are two related questions in which readers will surely be interested. One of these, the effect of sustained productivity growth, is best left for analysis in the framework of the two-sector model with capital. An analysis of that question using the customer-market model would not be persuasive. (In contrast, the study above of demand effects is at least highly suggestive because there is nothing about the analysis that strikes one as not generalizing to a wide class of models.)

The other question is the effect of a supply shock. Such a shock, as the term is usually or frequently understood, is not at all like a negative total factor productivity shock. The owners of some complementary resource, such as land or oil, the role of which has been excluded from the model thus far, contrive to drive up the remuneration paid to the flow supply of the service that they control. In the present model, however, there are not two classes of participants in the economy. All wealth owners work, and all labor-force participants own wealth. There is no compelling reason against supposing that these workers are also the owners of the oil or land who contract its supply to the market. In that case, the supply shock has the effect of reducing the marginal and average product of labor, since labor has less oil or land as a complementary input to work with. But nonwage income is not reduced *pari passu* with the wage rate when labor's marginal and average productivity are thus reduced, since the marginal and average productivity of the oil or the land offered to market are increased, that factor (or the supplied portion of it) having more labor to work with per unit. The effect, therefore, of an indigenous oil shock is indeed a contraction of the equilibrium employment rate. The presumption by Sachs and others that a supply shock such as a rise in the oil price drives up the world natural unemployment rate rests on good intuition. Regarding an open economy, however, further argumentation would be required to show that nonwage income will display some resilience and thereby prop up the real wage at too little a reduced level to avoid a fall of the equilibrium employment rate.

8.4 Commentary

This chapter has imbedded the customer-market apparatus in a general-equilibrium model of the closed economy. It found that a Harrod-neutral productivity shock is entirely neutral for the interest rate and the employment rate in the long run; since the stock of customers does not adjust in the closed-economy case, it being exogenously given by demography, the long run is immediate. Employment would expand at least temporarily if the public debt were an important drag on employment and the productivity rise generated a decline of the debt-output ratio.

The implications regarding demand are more unorthodox still. Instead of being the engine for a higher equilibrium employment rate, consumer demand has only the perverse effect of driving up the real interest rate and thereby causing a contraction of the supply of output—equivalently, of the derived demand for labor—which causes the employment rate to fall. A contrary model in which the effort function was homogeneous of degree zero in the firm's own wage and the general wage level, with workers' access to nonwage income playing no role, would escape the corollary that equilibrium employment is pulled down by the reduced wage. But it is far more reasonable to postulate, as here, that the effort function is homogeneous of degree zero in the more complete set of variables impinging on workers' behavior. If the wage were to fall enough to restore the amount of labor demanded to the previous preshock level, the ratio of wage to nonwage income would be reduced and there would consequently be an increased propensity to shirk at the given employment rate, making impossible a new equilibrium at that proposed configuration. Indeed, since the reduced wage actually has the effect of driving up the returns on workers' assets at a given employment rate, the reduced wage has a double effect decreasing the wage-to-nonwage-income ratio.

Appendix: *Uniqueness of the Equilibrium Path*

It is desired to show that the economy described in the text has the following property: Provided there exists only one *steady-state* equilibrium (no multiple stationary-state equilibria), as will indeed be the case if the public debt is nil or sufficiently close to it, the economy jumps at once to this state with its associated configuration of supporting real prices. In the terminology of this chapter, the economy's equilibrium (in the sense of a course in which expectations are not disappointed) is a unique path (that is the stationary-state equilibrium, of course). There is, for example, no continuum of paths converging to that stationary state that are also equilibrium paths.

The system in the text can be expressed as

(8.A1) $\quad dq/dt = rq - [1 - \varsigma(y)]$

(8.A2) $\quad r = \rho + m[(q + \beta)/y] + (dy/dt)/y$

(8.A3) $\quad y = y(q), 0 < y'(q)q/y \equiv \varepsilon(q) < 1$

Evidently the actual and expected path of q determines the other variables, r and y, so it suffices to show that the equilibrium path of q is unique.

To show that the equilibrium path of q is unique, we first note that the supply relation, (8.A3), makes $(dy/dt) = y(q)\varepsilon(q)(dq/dt)/q$. Using that equation in (8.A2) and substituting the resulting expression for r into (8.A1) reduces the above system to a single differential equation,

(8.A4) $\quad dq/dt = [1 - \varepsilon(q)]^{-1}y(q)$

$\qquad \times \{[\rho + m(q + \beta)y(q)^{-1}]qy(q)^{-1} - [1 - \varsigma(y(q))]\}$

We are interested in the stability properties of the paths of q satisfying (8.A4) in the neighborhood of the stationary-state equilibrium, hence in the sign of the derivative $d(dq/dt)/dq$ in that neighborhood. Rewrite (8.A4) as

(8.A5) $\quad dq/dt = [1 - \varepsilon(q)]^{-1}y(q)[\rho + m(q + \beta)y(q)^{-1}]$

$\qquad \times \{[qy(q)^{-1}] - [1 - \varsigma(y(q))]/[\rho + m(q + \beta)y(q)^{-1}]\}$

The expression in the curly brace of (8.A5) can be interpreted as the excess of the supply price of shares as a ratio to output over the demand price of shares as a ratio to output. Since that expression is equal to zero at the stationary state, and since $1 - \varepsilon > 0$, we have

(8.A6) $\quad \text{sign } d(dq/dt)/dq = \text{sign } d\{\cdot\}/dq$

Under the uniqueness proviso, with its implied elasticity inequality, an increase of q in the neighborhood of the stationary state increases the ratio of q to $y(q)$, the first term inside the brace, while it decreases the ratio of q to the associated output on the demand side, which is the second term inside the brace. So the expression in the brace is locally *increasing* in q. Hence the righthand side of (8.A5) and therefore $d(dq/dt)/dq$ are positive.

This implies that all the paths satisfying (8.A5) are explosive except for the stationary state satisfying it (which is unique by the initial proviso). Being explosive, according to the usual argument, they ultimately violate a nonnegativity constraint or some analogous constraint such that expectations must then be disappointed, so these cannot truly be equilibrium paths.

It can also be shown directly by differentiating the curly brace in (8.A4) with respect to q that dq/dt is increasing in q if β is zero or sufficiently small.

9

A Two-Sector Fixed-Investment Model

THIS chapter comes as the third in the triptych of "working models" of equilibrium unemployment determination—models in which we are content at this stage to derive an equilibrium incentive wage locus from intuited axioms rather than a complete micro-macro system in order to get on with the exploration of how productivity shocks and various (real) demand shocks in the goods markets alter the path of the natural rate of unemployment.

A recurring counter-Keynesian theme in the previous two chapters in the context of the closed economy was the proposition that a demand shock originating in a maintained increase in the rate of pure time preference or (in non-Ricardian cases) a maintained increase in the stock of public debt must drive up the real interest rate and drive down real asset prices for the capital market (equivalently the consumer-good market) to clear; the side effect is an induced *decline* in the real demand price of labor and, on our assumptions, an abrupt upward shift in the equilibrium path of the unemployment rate. Another finding, also confined to the closed economy, was the implication that a permanent productivity shock of Harrod-neutral type would be neutral for the equilibrium path of unemployment: the real wage and nonwage income both increase in proportion to productivity and in so doing leave unchanged the rate of interest, the real asset price, the propensity to quit or to shirk, and the unemployment rate.

The present chapter reconsiders these matters in a significantly different, yet not untraditional setting. The labor market is still marked by the problem of worker incentives, here the problem of shirking. The capital market is described essentially as before. In the product market, though, there is produced alongside the consumer good a durable capital good for productive use in cooperation with labor input. In the closed-economy case with which this chapter is concerned, this capital stock is the sole state variable of the system, the notions of functional employees and customers being put aside.[1]

In this setting, "demand" has an added dimension: Demand for the capital good, either by the government or private agents, is not the same thing as demand for the consumer good. How does a demand shock in the *capital-good industry,* in particular a maintained increase in the rate of purchase of the capital good by the government (for uses having no effects on other parameters), affect the demand for labor and thus the equilibrium path of unemployment? And how does such a shock affect the real rate of interest? If we accept as stylized fact that increased government purchases of capital goods for military purposes tend, even in a closed economy, to bring at least a transient drop of the equilibrium unemployment rate, an analysis of the employment effect of such a demand shock is clearly an acid test of the structuralist theory. If, bravely, we further accept the Penati-Mankiw-Summers contention that the real rate of interest is reduced by high wartime government expenditure, at least in the twentieth century, an analysis of the interest-rate effect of such a demand shock is also of considerable importance.

The results obtained underline a characteristic feature of the structuralist theory: the structure of demand matters for aggregate unemployment, contrary to Keynesian theory. Indeed, increased demand by the government for the *capital good* yields a transient *expansion* of employment and a transient reduction of the real rate of interest—the former a pro-Keynesian result, the latter clearly not—while increased government demand for the *consumer good* yields the counter-Keynesian outcome of employment *contraction.* Thus this structuralist theory deserves its name in another respect. The direction of any increase in demand may be crucial to the algebraic sign of its effect on aggregate employment. These findings differ fundamentally from the aggregation properties of Keynesian theory and, for that matter, from the aggregative nature of the real business cycle theory. Thus the structuralist theory places an importance on the structure of demand that is perhaps a critical feature in testing the theory and perhaps crucial for understanding some historical unemployment movements.

The analysis of productivity shocks also takes on a new element in this setting. If a permanent productivity shock of Harrod-neutral type occurs when the economy is initially in a unique equilibrium stationary state, the system cannot at once click into the new equilibrium stationary state because it will require a higher level of capital. The system will therefore shift to a path on which the capital stock and relative prices are slowly evolving toward their stationary-state targets. As a consequence, there is the strong possibility that the employment rate will at first be jarred to a different level—whether or not a larger level, as the stagnationist theorists maintained, we have to investigate—even though the model has been specified in such a way that any such effect is vanishing in the limit. In short, the effect of permanent productivity shocks is a problem in comparative dynamics, which the previous two working models managed to avoid (in the closed-economy case).

9.1 The Basic Structure

A major part of the production side is drawn from the two-sector model of production, made familiar in the work of Uzawa and of Foley and Sidrauski.[2] In this classic view of production, one sector produces the economy's consumer good and the other sector its capital good. Labor is costlessly and instantly shiftable from one use to the other. Capital is likewise instantaneously and costlessly shiftable, or reversible, between uses, no matter that it is already located and in use somewhere. Thus an enterprise may have a foot in both "sectors" and, if representative in its product mix, meet only its own capital demands. There are constant returns to scale and diminishing returns. As traditionally assumed, and as many observers accept, the consumer good is more capital-intensive at every wage-rental ratio. (Not every result depends on that specification, but some important findings do.) The population and labor force are taken to be exogenous and fixed over time. In particular, we simplify by normalizing the size of the labor force to one. In a stationary state there will be positive gross replacement investment to offset exponential shrinkage of capital at rate δ. A later section will take up "growth."

For purposes of notation, the consumer good will serve as the numeraire with which we define the real wage, v, the (instantaneous) real rate of interest, r, the real rental on capital, R, and the real price of the capital good, q. Aggregate employment, N, is the sum of the (equally able) workers employed in the consumer-good sector, N_C, and the number employed in the production of the investment good, N_I. With our normalization of the size of the labor force to unity, N also gives us the rate of employment, that is, $N = 1 - u$, where u is the rate of unemployment. The fully employed capital stock, K, is divided between the amount, K_C, used in the consumer-good-producing sector and the amount, K_I, used in the capital-good-producing sector. Output in the two sectors are denoted Z_C and Z_I, respectively.

The new wrinkle in the description of production is the incentive wage, or efficiency wage, which is used to generate positive equilibrium unemployment and generalized real-wage rigidity. The analysis goes somewhat more easily on the whole with a Calvo-Bowles-Stiglitz shirking story than with a Phelps-Stiglitz-Salop turnover (or quitting) story. The bearing of shirking on production is clear: if shirking is a continuous variable, not a binary (zero-one) variable, and we envision a continuum of Blanchard-Buiter families of differing age and accumulated wealth, no "no-shirking equilibrium" can be found; some or all employees shirk some, and the average intensity of shirking—the amount of on-the-job leisure taken per employee—finds its way into the production function.[3] Corresponding to the amount of on-the-job leisure is the amount of on-the-job effort, or attention, or diligence, which (following others) we treat as one-dimensional. Making the convenient assumption that firms have the identical distribution of employees by age and wealth, so that there is nothing special about one firm's employees, we suppose (as in the customer-market model) that the average effort of the employees at the ith firm, e^i, is given by a function that is increasing in its own wage, v^i, decreasing in the expected wage income obtained if the worker is fired from the firm where he is currently employed, z, and decreasing in workers' average non-wage income, y^w. The effort function, $\hat{e}^i$, may therefore be written

$$(9.1) \qquad \hat{e}^i = \hat{\varepsilon}(z/v^i, y^w/v^i) \qquad \hat{\varepsilon}_1 < 0; \hat{\varepsilon}_2 < 0; \hat{\varepsilon}_{11} < 0; \hat{\varepsilon}_{22} < 0; \hat{\varepsilon}_{12} < 0$$

The assumptions that $\hat{\varepsilon}_{11} < 0$ and $\hat{\varepsilon}_{22} < 0$ ensure that the second-order conditions are satisfied while $-\hat{\varepsilon}_{12} > 0$ means that the marginal effect of raising the real wage on effort (given z) declines the higher is the nonwage income.[4]

In the specification followed here, which follows naturally from past practice, the shirking rate and thus the effort of workers affects productivity simply by modifying the true labor input of which output is a function.[5] In each of the two production functions that every firm has, therefore, the labor input is the number of workers *multiplied* by their average effort indicator, $\hat{e}$. For the ith firm,

$$(9.2) \qquad Z_C^i = F_C(K_C^i, \hat{e}^i N_C^i) = \hat{e}^i N_C^i F_C(\tilde{k}_C^i, 1) = \hat{e}^i N_C^i f_C(\tilde{k}_C^i) \qquad \tilde{k}_C^i \equiv K_C^i/(\hat{e}^i N_C^i)$$

$$(9.3) \qquad Z_I^i = F_I(K_I^i, \hat{e}^i N_I^i) = \hat{e}^i N_I^i F_I(\tilde{k}_I^i, 1) = \hat{e}^i N_I^i f_I(\tilde{k}_I^i) \qquad \tilde{k}_I^i \equiv K_I^i/(\hat{e}^i N_I^i)$$

The neoclassical properties of the F functions are invoked: diminishing returns and constant returns to scale in K^i and N^i. The effort variable is the same for both the I and C branches of the firm.

The first-order conditions for an interior profit maximum with respect to the choice variables N^i, K^i, and v^i are, respectively

(9.4) $R = qf_I'(\tilde{k}_I) = f_C'(\tilde{k}_C)$

(9.5) $v = q\hat{\varepsilon}[f_I(\tilde{k}_I) - \tilde{k}_I f_I'(\tilde{k}_I)]$

       $= \hat{\varepsilon}[f_C(\tilde{k}_C) - \tilde{k}_C f_C'(\tilde{k}_C)]$

(9.6) $v = -q[f_I(\tilde{k}_I) - \tilde{k}_I f_I'(\tilde{k}_I)]\left[\hat{\varepsilon}_1 \dfrac{z}{v} + \hat{\varepsilon}_2 \dfrac{y^w}{v}\right]$

       $= [f_C(\tilde{k}_C) - \tilde{k}_C f_C'(\tilde{k}_C)]\left[\hat{\varepsilon}_1 \dfrac{z}{v} + \hat{\varepsilon}_2 \dfrac{y^w}{v}\right]$

We have here left out the i superscript based on the following argument. The behavior of firms operating at the maximum will be identical if two conditions are met: Every firm is in equilibrium, and hence has the same expectations as every other firm, and every firm assumes what has already been supposed to be the case, that it has the representative demographic cross-section of employees by age and wealth, so that its employees are exactly as shirking-prone as those elsewhere. Then

(9.7) $v^i = v$

since the other firms will have chosen identically to the ith firm.

    Equations (9.4) above state that firms choose capital to hire until the rental rate is equated to the marginal product of capital. Equations (9.5) give the firms' real demand wage, which is equated to the marginal product of labor. As factors are completely mobile between sectors, equilibrium requires that rental rates and wages are equalized across sectors. Equations (9.6) give the real supply wage, that is, the real wage required to induce optimal work effort. Using equations (9.5), we can simplify (9.6) to obtain the generalized Solow elasticity condition

(9.8) $-\left[\dfrac{\hat{\varepsilon}_1}{\hat{\varepsilon}} \dfrac{z}{v} + \dfrac{\hat{\varepsilon}_2}{\hat{\varepsilon}} \dfrac{y^w}{v}\right] = 1$

The condition states that the sum of the partial elasticities of the effort function must equal unity. For any given equilibrium value of u, if such an equilibrium u exists, v must be just high enough to bring the sum of the partial elasticities (evaluated at $v^i = v$) of effort with respect to the own wage up to the level one. A discussion is left to an endnote.[6] It follows from (9.8) and the properties of the effort function that each partial elasticity (positively defined) is less than one:

(9.9)
$$0 < -\frac{\hat{\varepsilon}_1}{\hat{\varepsilon}}\frac{z}{v}, \; -\frac{\hat{\varepsilon}_2}{\hat{\varepsilon}}\frac{y^w}{v} < 1$$

The foregoing results have further implications for labor-market equilibrium and what may be called product-market equilibrium.

Product-Market Equilibrium

With firms essentially alike except possibly for scale, the conditions in (9.4) and (9.5) have the macroeconomic implications that in the consumer-good sector the efficiency-adjusted capital-labor ratio $K_C/(eN_C)$ or $\tilde{k}_C$ is a function only of the relative price of capital, q; analogously, in the other sector the ratio $K_I/(eN_I)$ or $\tilde{k}_I$ is an increasing function of q. To prove these relationships, we define the efficiency wage–rental ratio as

(9.10)
$$\tilde{\omega} = \frac{v}{\hat{\varepsilon}R} = \frac{f_I(\tilde{k}_I) - \tilde{k}_I f_I'(\tilde{k}_I)}{f_I'(\tilde{k}_I)}$$
$$= \frac{f_C(\tilde{k}_C) - \tilde{k}_C f_C'(\tilde{k}_C)}{f_C'(\tilde{k}_C)}$$

From equations (9.10), we have

$$\tilde{k}_I = \tilde{k}_I(\tilde{\omega}) \qquad \tilde{k}_I'(\tilde{\omega}) > 0$$
$$\tilde{k}_C = \tilde{k}_C(\tilde{\omega}) \qquad \tilde{k}_C'(\tilde{\omega}) > 0$$

We obtain from equations (9.5)

(9.11)
$$q = \frac{f_C(\tilde{k}_C) - \tilde{k}_C f_C'(\tilde{k}_C)}{f_I(\tilde{k}_I) - \tilde{k}_I f_I'(\tilde{k}_I)}$$

from which we obtain a relationship between the efficiency wage–rental ratio, $v/(eR)$ or $\tilde{\omega}$, and the relative price of the capital good, q. To determine the sign of the relationship between them, we note, using (9.10) and (9.11), that

$$(9.12) \quad \frac{d\tilde{\omega}}{dq} \frac{q}{\tilde{\omega}} = \frac{(\tilde{\omega} + \tilde{k}_I)(\tilde{\omega} + \tilde{k}_C)}{\tilde{\omega}(\tilde{k}_C - \tilde{k}_I)}$$

so that an increase in the relative price of the capital good raises the efficiency wage–rental ratio under our assumption that the capital good is relatively labor-intensive. It then follows from equations (9.4) and (9.5) that R and R/q are both decreasing in q while both v/e and $v/(qe)$ are increasing in q under our assumption of relative factor intensity.

In order to derive a relationship between v^d, the real demand wage, and the relative price of capital, q, it is necessary to specify the conception of the workers' average nonwage income on which their average effort level is supposed to depend. As in the Blanchardian description of demographics and households' asset management, which is used here in modeling the capital market, the workers turn over assets as fast as they are accumulated to zero-profit insurance companies and receive in return from these companies the interest and an actuarially fair dividend; government transfers can always be added later. The income flow so conceived, y^w, will be represented here by the sum of the rental income, RK, and the actuarial dividend, μqK, as a ratio to worker population (which we have normalized to one) so $y^w = RK + \mu qK$.[7] Using this definition of nonwage income per household, we may write

$$(9.13) \quad \frac{y^w}{v} = \frac{K}{\tilde{\omega}\hat{e}} + \frac{\mu qK}{\tilde{v}\hat{e}} \qquad \tilde{v} \equiv \frac{v}{\hat{\varepsilon}}$$

where $\tilde{v}$ denotes the effort-adjusted wage. Using the Salop-Calvo indicator, $z \equiv (1 - u)v$, we may write the effort function as $\hat{\varepsilon} = \hat{\varepsilon}(1 - u, y^w/v)$. Using this with (9.13), we derive a few useful relationships between y^w/v and q, K and $1 - u$:

$$(9.14a) \quad \frac{\partial(y^w/v)}{\partial K} = \frac{(1/\tilde{\omega}) + [\mu/(\tilde{v}q^{-1})]}{\hat{\varepsilon}[1 + (y^w/v)(\hat{\varepsilon}_2/\hat{\varepsilon})]} > 0$$

$$(9.14b) \quad \frac{\partial(y^w/v)}{\partial(1 - u)} = \frac{-(y^w/v)(\hat{\varepsilon}_1/\hat{\varepsilon})}{[1 + (y^w/v)(\hat{\varepsilon}_2/\hat{\varepsilon})]} > 0$$

$$(9.14c) \quad \frac{\partial(y^w/v)}{\partial q} = \frac{-[\tilde{\omega}'K/\tilde{\omega}^2] - (\mu K/\tilde{v})[(\tilde{v}'q/\tilde{v}) - 1]}{\hat{\varepsilon}[1 + (y^w/v)(\hat{\varepsilon}_2/\hat{\varepsilon})]} < 0$$

The relationships above have made use of (9.9) and the Stolper-Samuelson relationship that a percent increase in q raises v/e by greater than one percent. To obtain a relationship between the real demand wage, v^d, and q, we make use of the relationship

$$(9.15) \quad v^d = \hat{\varepsilon}[f_C(\tilde{k}_C) - \tilde{k}_C f'_C(\tilde{k}_C)]$$

which must hold in equilibrium.[8] Differentiating the lefthand side of (9.15) with respect to q, we obtain

$$(9.16) \quad \frac{\partial v^d}{\partial q} = [f_C - \tilde{k}_C f'_C]\hat{\varepsilon}_2 \frac{\partial (y^w/v)}{\partial q} - \hat{\varepsilon}\tilde{k}_C f''_C k'_C \tilde{\omega}'$$

which says that an increase in q raises the real demand wage. It will also be useful to determine how the real demand wage depends upon the employment rate and the holding of capital stock per worker. Using again (9.15), we obtain the following relationships:

$$(9.17) \quad \frac{\partial v^d}{\partial (1 - u)} = [f_C - \tilde{k}_C f'_C]\left[\hat{\varepsilon}_1 + \hat{\varepsilon}_2 \frac{\partial (y^w/v)}{\partial (1 - u)} \right] < 0$$

$$(9.18) \quad \frac{\partial v^d}{\partial K} = [f_C - \tilde{k}_C f'_C]\hat{\varepsilon}_2 \frac{\partial (y^w/v)}{\partial K} < 0$$

The effects of the employment rate and the capital-worker ratio on the demand price of labor in (9.17) and (9.18) are immediately clear. Given K and q, an increase in $1 - u$, in reducing effort, decreases the demand wage—a new wrinkle not found in neoclassical models of two-sector economies.[9] An increase in workers' average asset holdings, K in the present case, by unambiguously increasing nonwage income, given q, and hence reducing effort, likewise decreases the demand wage at a given $1 - u$.

Under equilibrium conditions, therefore, the wage must satisfy the following demand-side relationship:

$$(9.19) \quad v = V^d(1 - u, q, K) \qquad V^d_{1-u}(\cdot) < 0, \; V^d_K(\cdot) < 0, \; V^d_q(\cdot) > 0$$

where $V^d(1 - u, q, K)$ gives the *equilibrium demand price for labor schedule* in the employment rate–real wage plane.

LABOR-MARKET EQUILIBRIUM

The equilibrium supply-side relationship can be obtained from (9.6) expressed as[10]

$$(9.20) \quad v^s = -[f_C(\tilde{k}_C) - \tilde{k}_C f'_C(\tilde{k}_C)]\left[(1-u)\hat{\varepsilon}_1 + \frac{y^w}{v}\hat{\varepsilon}_2\right]$$

This gives the *equilibrium labor supply-price schedule* showing how the supply price of labor needed for labor-market equilibrium, v^s, depends on the employment rate, given the other determinants. In the terminology used earlier, it is the labor-market equilibrium locus, also known as the wage curve and the surrogate employment supply curve.

We are interested in knowing how the real supply wage, v^s, depends upon q, $1-u$, and K, so we differentiate the lefthand side of (9.20) to obtain

$$(9.21) \quad \frac{\partial v^s}{\partial q} = [f_C - \tilde{k}_C f'_C]\hat{\varepsilon}_2 \frac{\partial(y^w/v)}{\partial q} - \hat{\varepsilon}\tilde{k}_C f''_C k'_C \tilde{\omega}'$$

$$- [f_C - \tilde{k}_C f'_C]\left[(1-u)\hat{\varepsilon}_{12} + 2\hat{\varepsilon}_2 + \left(\frac{y^w}{v}\right)\hat{\varepsilon}_{22}\right]\frac{\partial(y^w/v)}{\partial q} > 0$$

$$(9.22) \quad \frac{\partial v^s}{\partial(1-u)} = -[f_C - \tilde{k}_C f'_C]$$

$$\times \left(\hat{\varepsilon}_1 + \hat{\varepsilon}_2 \frac{\partial(y^w/v)}{\partial(1-u)} + (1-u)\left[\hat{\varepsilon}_{11} + \hat{\varepsilon}_{12}\frac{\partial(y^w/v)}{\partial(1-u)}\right]\right.$$

$$\left. + \frac{y^w}{v}\left[\hat{\varepsilon}_{21} + \hat{\varepsilon}_{22}\frac{\partial(y^w/v)}{\partial(1-u)}\right]\right) > 0$$

$$(9.23) \quad \frac{\partial v^s}{\partial K} = [f_C - \tilde{k}_C f'_C]\hat{\varepsilon}_2 \frac{\partial(y^w/v)}{\partial K}$$

$$- [f_C - \tilde{k}_C f'_C]\left[(1-u)\hat{\varepsilon}_{12} + 2\hat{\varepsilon}_2 = \left(\frac{y^w}{v}\right)\hat{\varepsilon}_{22}\right]\frac{\partial(y^w/v)}{\partial K} > 0$$

It is shown by (9.21) to (9.23) that the relationship in (9.20) makes the equilibrium labor supply price a readily understood function. Since y^w/v is a function of K and q, the supply wage, v^s, is ultimately a function of $1 - u$, K, and q—like the demand wage, v^d. The supply wage is obviously increasing in $1 - u$, given K and q. It is also clear that v^s is increasing in K since a higher K implies higher nonwage income, which in stimulating shirking requires firms to raise their wage at a given $1 - u$. To summarize, the equilibrium supply relation giving the wage required for labor-market equilibrium has the properties:

$$(9.24) \quad v = V^s(1 - u, q, K) \qquad V^s_{1-u}(\cdot) > 0, \; V^s_K(\cdot) > 0, \; V^s_q(\cdot) > 0$$

over the interval $0 < 1 - u < 1$.

Capital-Market Equilibrium

The essential asset in this economy is physical capital, unlike the two previous models. It is convenient to imagine that in their capital investments the firms rely on equity finance and that they keep the number of shares continuously equal to the number of "machines" comprising their capital stock.

In the riskless world to which the model is confined, there is an arbitrage relation between the total yield from holding the asset—the capital gain per unit of time $\dot{q}$ plus the rental R, both as a ratio to q and the instantaneous real rate of interest r:

$$(9.25) \quad \dot{q} = q(r + \delta) - R$$

This is the intertemporal equilibrium condition satisfied by households. It implies that the expected capital gain underlying the level of q (and given q the r at which households will lend) is going to be realized.

Dealing with the added unknown, the interest rate, requires bringing in the households' consumption planning. For the relationship between the interest rate and consumer behavior we draw on the same apparatus introduced into macroeconomics by Blanchard that we have already called upon in the two previous models: a demographic steady state in which nonretiring worker-consumers insure against their risk of death before running down their assets by placing their wealth with insurance companies, which in return pay policyholders an annuity reflecting the current instantaneous interest rate, r, and the common exponential mortality rate, μ. That model generates a useful proposition: the rate of growth of per-capita consumption, $\dot{c}/c$, is given by the excess of the interest rate over the rate of pure time preference, $r - \rho$, *minus*—in the non-Ricardian models of Blanchard and Buiter and Weil—a coefficient $\mu(\mu + \rho)$ multiplying the wealth-consumption ratio W/c. Hence, rearranging terms,

$$(9.26) \qquad r = \rho + \mu(\mu + \rho)\left(\frac{W}{c}\right) + \frac{\dot{c}}{c}$$

This condition too is an equilibrium condition in that it implies that the planned path of consumption, which depends upon future interest rates and incomes, is being realized—hence that expectations about future interest rates and incomes are correct.

Financial wealth here includes both the value of shares, or capital, which is qK, and the size of public debt, all of it very short-term, to be denoted by the parameter D:

$$(9.27) \qquad W = qK + D$$

It is convenient to imagine that all the debt consists of short-term obligations so that we may take its real value as given, predetermined by former deficits and surpluses or subject to a parametric shock, rather than the present discounted value of the stream of payments on long-term obligations.

There are also the following accounting relations between the private and public expenditures in each of the sectors and the output produced:

$$(9.28) \qquad C + G_C = Z_C$$

$$(9.29) \qquad \dot{K} + \delta K + q^{-1}G_I = Z_I$$

where G_C and G_I are the real value of the public expenditures in the two sectors.

9.2 The General Equilibrium Path of the Closed Economy

The first task here is to analyze how the equilibrium behavior of the supply side, in terms of the quantity of jobs offered and the supply of the two distinct products, depends upon K and q. Then the analysis turns to the way equilibrium on the demand side determines the motion of q. Finally, drawing upon the familiar classical specification of the two-sector model as a convenient example, we put together these components in the canonical phase diagram to determine the general equilibrium path of q and K, from which the behavior of the path of the employment rate may be deduced.

THE SUPPLY SIDE: JOINT EQUILIBRIUM IN THE LABOR AND PRODUCT MARKETS

The effects on the demand wage, v^d, of changes in $1 - u$, q, and K shown in (9.19) and the corresponding effects on the supply wage, v^s, shown in (9.24) together determine the corresponding effects on the equilibrium employment rate, since the latter must always change to keep v^s equal to v^d in an equilibrium scenario. In other terminology, the intersection of the product-market equilibrium locus and the labor-market equilibrium locus found in the shorthand equations (9.19) and (9.24) gives the equilibrium *point* and makes the equilibrium employment rate a function of K and q:

$$(9.30) \quad V^d(1 - u, q, K) = V^s(1 - u, q, K)$$

The lefthand demand wage is decreasing in $1 - u$, the righthand surrogate supply wage increasing in $1 - u$. Hence any intersection is unique. How does the equilibrium $1 - u$ depend upon K and q? It will be shown that the equilibrium $1 - u$ is decreasing in K, given q, and increasing in q, given K.

Equations (9.17) and (9.22) show that the real demand wage schedule is a downward-sloping curve in the Marshallian employment–real wage plane and the real supply wage schedule is an upward-sloping curve. Examining equations (9.18) and (9.23), we can see that an increase in K shifts both the schedules downward, but the real demand wage schedule shifts down by more than the real supply wage shifts down so that an increase in K lowers the employment rate, $1 - u$. Also, from (9.16) and (9.21), an increase in q shifts both the schedules upward, but the real demand wage schedule shifts up by more than the real supply wage shifts up so that an increase in q raises the rate of employment, $1 - u$.

To obtain directly the relationship between $1 - u$ and K on one hand, and $1 - u$ and q on the other, we can also work directly with the generalized Solow elasticity condition to obtain the following derivatives:

(9.31)
$$\frac{\partial(1 - u)}{\partial q} = \frac{-[(y^w/v)\hat{\varepsilon}_{22} + (1 - u)\hat{\varepsilon}_{12} + 2\hat{\varepsilon}_2] \dfrac{\partial(y^w/v)}{\partial q}}{\Delta}$$

(9.32)
$$\frac{\partial(1 - u)}{\partial K} = \frac{-[(y^w/v)\hat{\varepsilon}_{22} + (1 - u)\hat{\varepsilon}_{12} + 2\hat{\varepsilon}_2] \dfrac{\partial(y^w/v)}{\partial K}}{\Delta}$$

where

$$\Delta = [(1 - u)\hat{\varepsilon}_{11} + 2\hat{\varepsilon}_1 + (y^w/v)\hat{\varepsilon}_{21}]$$
$$+ [(1 - u)\hat{\varepsilon}_{12} + 2\hat{\varepsilon}_2 + (y^w/v)\hat{\varepsilon}_{22}]\partial(y^w/v)/\partial(1 - u)$$

Let us record these results in the summary equation,

(9.33) $N = N(K, q), \quad N_K(\cdot) < 0, \quad N_q(\cdot) > 0$

   $u = u(K, q), \quad u_K(K, q) > 0, \quad u_q(K, q) < 0$

The parallel comparative-statics question about the joint equilibrium of the labor and product markets is how the joint-equilibrium v depends upon K and q. Referring to the effects of the changes in K and q on the shifts of the real supply and real demand schedules, we note that an increase in K lowers v while an increase in q raises v. To summarize this result:

(9.34) $v = v(K, q), \quad v_K(\cdot) < 0, \quad v_q(\cdot) > 0$

The equilibrium supply side is completed with the determination of the allocation of current resources between the two sectors. The factor market conditions are

(9.35) $N_I + N_C + N_P = N = 1 - u$

(9.36) $N_C \tilde{k}_C + N_I \tilde{k}_I = \dfrac{K}{\hat{\varepsilon}}$

where N_P is the number of workers employed by the public sector. To work toward deriving two dynamic equations in terms of q and K that describe the dynamic system, we can first express the output functions as

$$(9.37) \quad Z_I = \frac{\hat{\varepsilon}[(1 - u) - N_P]\tilde{k}_C - K}{\tilde{k}_C - \tilde{k}_I} f_I(\tilde{k}_I)$$

$$(9.38) \quad Z_C = \frac{K - \hat{\varepsilon}[(1 - u) - N_P]\tilde{k}_I}{\tilde{k}_C - \tilde{k}_I} f_C(\tilde{k}_C)$$

Equation (9.37) will remind some of a paradox in models by Uzawa, Foley, and Sidrauski (and no doubt others) in somewhat different contexts: a helicopter drop of additional K will contract Z_I both absolutely and relatively to Z_C through a channel known in the trade literature as the Rybczynski effect. In the model here, an increase in K serves further to expand Z_C and contract Z_I by raising nonwage income and hence reducing both $\hat{\varepsilon}$ and $1 - u$. An increase in N_P similarly serves to expand Z_C and contract Z_I.

We can easily check that the following derivatives hold:

$$\frac{\partial Z_I}{\partial K} < 0, \quad \frac{\partial Z_C}{\partial K} > 0, \quad \frac{\partial Z_I}{\partial N_P} < 0, \quad \frac{\partial Z_C}{\partial N_P} > 0$$

Under the assumption that the production possibilities curve is concave to the origin, we also have the following derivatives:

$$\frac{\partial Z_I}{\partial q} > 0, \frac{\partial Z_C}{\partial q} < 0$$

We may summarize these implications of (9.37) and (9.38) as

$$(9.39) \quad Z_C = Z^C(q, K; N_P), \quad Z_q^C(\cdot) < 0, \quad Z_K^C > 0, \quad Z_{N_P}^C > 0$$

$$(9.40) \quad Z_I = Z^I(q, K; N_P), \quad Z_q^I > 0, \quad Z_K^I < 0, \quad Z_{N_P}^I < 0$$

It is immediately clear that the pace of capital accumulation is obtained as a function of K and q. This equation will appear below.

THE DEMAND SIDE: JOINT EQUILIBRIUM IN THE CAPITAL
AND PRODUCT MARKETS

We need finally to describe the motion of q necessary for capital equilibrium in the same reduced-form way, in terms of K and the parameters. Here we assume that the spending and other parameters, such as G_C, are, so to speak, *level parameters* in the sense that the righthand time derivative of each of them, such as $\dot{G}_C$, is equal to zero; they are subject to an initial jump (perhaps also an anticipated future jump, although the analysis of future shocks will not be undertaken here) but they are not trending up or down. Using the accounting relation (9.28) and drawing upon (9.38) we have

$$(9.41) \quad r = \rho + m\{(qK + D)/[Z^C(q, K; N_P) - G_C]\} + \dot{Z}^C/Z^C$$

$$m = \mu(\mu + \rho)$$

Now, with the help of (9.41) and (9.25), one can use (9.39), or rather the equation underlying its shorthand notation, to obtain the time derivative of Z^C in terms of the levels and time derivatives of q and K. One can use (9.40) to obtain the time derivative K in terms of the K and q levels. Then the model reduces to a pair of differential equations,

$$(9.42) \quad \dot{K} = K(q, K; G_I)$$

$$(9.43) \quad \dot{q} = Q(q, K; G_C, G_I, D)$$

Rather than attack this system straightaway, we first study as a special case the specification that was traditional in Austrian capital theory: Capital is employed alongside labor in the production of the consumer good while the capital good is produced by labor alone. Later we come back to the above system in its full generality to make some observations.

THE GENERAL-EQUILIBRIUM SOLUTION IN THE "CLASSIC" CASE

In the case studied here, to repeat, the capital good is produced without the assistance of capital. So in place of (9.37) and (9.38) we have

$$(9.44) \quad Z_I = \hat{\varepsilon}N_I = \hat{\varepsilon}[(1 - u) - N_P] - \frac{K}{\tilde{k}_C}$$

$$(9.45) \quad Z_C = \hat{\varepsilon}N_C f_C(\tilde{k}_C) = \frac{K}{\tilde{k}_C} f_C(\tilde{k}_C)$$

Clearly this "example" is really a polar case that violates in one industry the diminishing-returns conditions of the "general" case.

One implication of the model in this case may require a comment. As

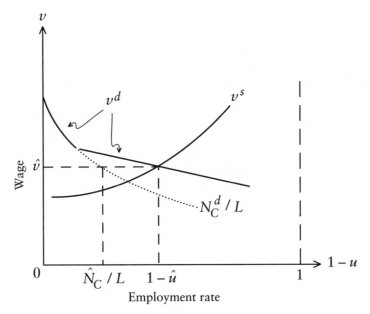

Figure 9.1 Partial-equilibrium wage and employment rate

before, in every situation such that $Z_I > 0$, price equals marginal cost; equivalently the real wage equals the real marginal productivity of labor in that industry. That condition gives the counterpart of (9.5):

$$(9.5')\quad v = \hat{\varepsilon}[f_C(\tilde{k}_C) - \tilde{k}_C f'_C(\tilde{k}_C)] = q\hat{\varepsilon}$$

In the local analysis used to establish saddle-path stability and to determine the effects of small shocks, it will be sufficient to restrict our attention to this equality condition. This is so because, despite the linearity in the constancy of costs at the level of the firm, there is a sort of increasing costs at the level of the economy owing to the behavior of effort.

Figure 9.1 illustrates the schedule of the derived demand price of aggregate labor corresponding to $(9.5')$ and the positive dependence of $\tilde{k}_C$ on $v/\hat{\varepsilon}$. At high v only the consumption-good industry generates a positive demand for labor, which is a decreasing function of $v/\hat{\varepsilon}$. At levels of v below a certain threshold, positive output levels in the capital-good industry are profitable. This threshold v corresponds to the kink in the demand-price relation. In a thoroughly neoclassical setting where $\hat{\varepsilon}$ was not present, the segment to the right of the kink would be flat; in that setting a slight downward disturbance to q would temporarily drive Z_I to zero and block marginal cost from equality with price. But in the present setting, that righthand segment is downward-sloping; hence a small downward disturbance to q from a small shock to either of the two curves has only a small downward effect on Z_I and thus does not invalidate the equality condition in (9.5′).

The other implications of the classic case for the "general" equation system, (9.1)–(9.40), are straightforward. In all these equations being carried over from the general system, wherever we find $v/\hat{\varepsilon}$ we substitute q; for $1 - u$ we substitute the supply-side semi-reduced form $1 - u(K, q)$, and for v the corresponding semi-reduced form $v(q)$. By this route we will arrive at a pair of differential equations in q and K. What is mainly gained from the classic example is the explicitness and simplicity of the output-supply functions, in which K_I is fixed at zero and K_C is given by the predetermined K.

In modeling these dynamics it is convenient to take the physical purchases of the government to be constants rather than the real values of these purchases (current real expenditure). Γ_I will denote government purchase of capital-good output in physical terms and Γ_P will denote governmental use of efficiency-adjusted labor services in the public sector; in terms of real expenditures—the famous G—these parameters satisfy

$$(9.46) \quad G_I \equiv q\Gamma_I; \quad G_P \equiv vN_P, \quad \hat{\varepsilon}N_P \equiv \Gamma_P$$

Since G_C is both the physical purchase of the consumer good as well as a real expenditure level, no new symbol is required there. The pair of differential equations summarizing the dynamics of the general equilibrium system may be written as follows in terms of K and q:

$$(9.42′) \quad \dot{K} = Z^I(q, K) - \Gamma_I - \delta K$$

$$(9.43′) \quad \left[Z_C - G_C - q\frac{\partial Z_C}{\partial q} \right]\frac{\dot{q}}{q} =$$

$$\frac{\partial Z_C}{\partial K}[Z_I - \Gamma_I - \delta K] - \left[\frac{R}{q} - \rho - \delta\right](Z_C - G_C) + m(qK + D)$$

The upper equation states that to obtain net investment we first obtain $\hat{\varepsilon}N_I$, which is given by $\hat{\varepsilon}N - \hat{\varepsilon}N_C - \hat{\varepsilon}N_P$ (the last being Γ_P), in order to get Z_I, from which we then subtract Γ_I and δK. The lower equation comes from regarding $\dot{q}/q$ as the excess of the required interest rate over the rental rate, recognizing that the former involves the rates of change of q and K, and collecting terms.

To analyze this dynamic system let us begin with stationary equilibrium. In any such stationary state,

$$(9.42'S) \quad 0 = Z^I(q, K) - \Gamma_I - \delta K$$

$$(9.43'S) \quad \left(\frac{R}{q} - \delta\right) = \rho + mq\,\frac{\tilde{k}_C}{f_C(\tilde{k}_C)}$$

It will be supposed that G_C and D are both close enough to zero that one may set them equal to zero in studying the *direction* in which q or K responds to shocks or to shifts in the other variable in these two equations. Clearly one wants to begin there—with a small government—and consider ultimately the consequences, if any, of a major enlargement of the size of the government in one dimension or another.

In this small-government case, remarkably, K drops out of (9.43′) (evaluated at the steady state) so that (9.43′S) determines the steady-state q and hence the steady-state r singlehandedly—independently of K and its determinants operating in (9.42′S).[11] The steady-state levels of r and q are determined thus: The lefthand side of (9.43′S)—the available rental rate—is unambiguously decreasing in q, while the righthand side—the required rate of return—is unambiguously increasing in q. Hence the steady-state equilibrium is unique. The equilibrium exists provided time preference does not exceed the largest possible rental rate available from the technology (*viz.*, the rate yielded as q approaches zero). This determination of the steady-state equilibrium q and r is pictured in Figure 9.2 with the downward-sloping AA curve representing the available rental rate and the upward-sloping RR curve representing the required rate. A further analysis would show the possibility that RR is downward-sloping when, contrary to the case here, G_C or D are sufficiently large.

Let us turn now to the *equilibrium path* from an arbitrary initial state in a small neighborhood of the above stationary state. The restriction that G_C and D are small enough to be neglected (as if they were equal to zero)

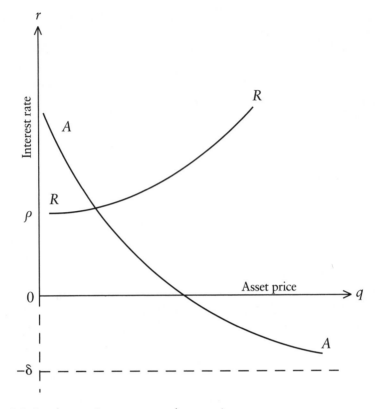

Figure 9.2 Steady-state interest rate and asset price

is maintained until notice to the contrary. The slope (dq/dK) of the locus where $\dot{K} = 0$ is given by

$$\frac{\delta - \partial Z_I/\partial K}{\partial Z_I/\partial q} > 0$$

while the slope along which $\dot{q} = 0$ is given by

$$\frac{(\partial Z_C/\partial K)[\delta - (\partial Z_I/\partial K)]}{(\partial Z_C/\partial K)(\partial Z_I/\partial q) - [(R/q) - \delta - \rho](\partial Z_C/\partial q) - Z_C[\partial(R/q)/\partial q] + mK} > 0$$

We see from the expressions giving the slopes of the two loci that they are both positively sloped. Moreover, the locus along which $\dot{K} = 0$ is steeper than the locus along which $\dot{q} = 0$. Hence we are assured of sad-dlepath stability as shown in Figure 9.3. The diagrammatics there imply that the motion of the system is described by a saddlepath that is upward-sloping and flatter than the $\dot{q} = 0$ locus. In short, there is a uniquely deter-mined perfect-foresight (or equilibrium) price of the capital good in each current situation, which is completely described by the current size of the capital stock, given the various parameters of the model; and this equilib-rium price is an *increasing* function of the current stock of capital. Hence, if the capital stock is found to be (say) below its stationary equilibrium level, so that the capital stock will be rising toward that level, the real price of the capital stock will likewise be rising.

Two comments are in order. At first this result may strike readers as counterintuitive. If an earthquake intensified the scarcity of capital, would its price not go up rather than down? Upon reflection, however, the impli-cation that the real price would drop is entirely consonant with traditional notions in capital theory: If q rose, v would be pulled up too, and the total

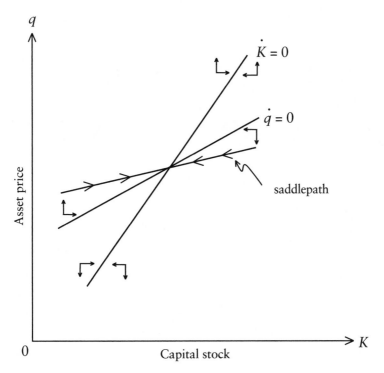

Figure 9.3 Phase diagram in the (K, q) plane

rate of return on capital, $q^{-1}[R(q) + \dot{q}]$, would be depressed, all contrary to doctrine. So the implication that q drops is orthodox.

It may also be useful to try to understand the reason for this result. If the capital stock is decreased below its stationary level, the supply of the capital-intensive good (which is the consumer good) is reduced relative to the other good (the capital good) while, if a new steady state were to start from the new situation, consumer demand (being approximately proportional to qK when D is of negligible size) and investment demand (being δK) would both be reduced in equal proportion. To reconcile demands with supplies the relative price of the consumer good has to increase, meaning that q must decrease; that "works" because a decrease of q and the elevation of the interest rate that such a decrease of q implies serve to trim the demand for the consumption good to the reduced supply. Thus it is not a triviality that a decrease of the capital stock drives down the relative price of the labor-intensive good; an intertemporal demand side is needed to deliver the result and to ensure uniqueness and stability as well.

A note on the general case. A strategy for approaching the general model looms into view. One wants to investigate the conditions under which an upward-sloping saddlepath can be deduced from the pair of differential equations in q and K describing the dynamics of the model. It is a plausible conjecture, supported by some preliminary analysis, that the saddlepath tends to be positively sloped as long as the capital-goods-producing sector is *sufficiently* more labor-intensive than the other sector. If that is right, there is a substantial interest in the implications of the classical example, just set up, for the "Keynesian questions" that give the impetus for this chapter.

COMPARATIVE STATICS — THE CLASSIC CASE

Now, returning to the classic case, in which capital is made with labor alone, we take up the effects of expenditure and productivity shocks. Attention here is restricted to expenditure shocks originating directly or indirectly in the public sector.[12]

Public-debt shocks stimulating consumer demand. Suppose there is a small increase in the stock of public debt, D, in the neighborhood of a low or nil initial level. This shock has no direct effect—no impact effect—on $\dot{K}$, only on $\dot{q}$, as shown by (9.42′) and (9.43′), respectively. Consider the lateral shift of the $\dot{q} = 0$ locus, which is the change of K needed to keep $\dot{q}$ constant at any given q. On the simplifying assumption that G_C and D are close enough to zero that the terms G_C/K and D/K can be neglected, this change is positive. Hence the shift of the schedule is rightward and thus downward.

The downward shift of the $\dot{q} = 0$ locus and the invariance of the other locus produces a downward shift of the saddlepath and the rest point on the (unshifted) $\dot{K} = 0$ locus. Hence there is a drop of q on impact, which is followed by declining K and declining q as the new rest point is approached asymptotically. The explanation for this result is that the increased demand for consumption causes an excess demand for the consumer good, which translates into a flow excess supply of assets, as households try to sell assets to one another in the capital market to finance increased consumption. Since such financing is infeasible, no increase of consumption can be realized. The effect is only to cause the price of the shares, q, to drop to the point at which the excess supply is eliminated.[13] So q is abruptly decreased, and the rate of interest—the whole yield curve, in fact—is abruptly shifted up.

The employment effect of the drop of q is, on our assumption set, contractionary. The drop of q, in shifting down the derived demand for labor schedule by more (on our assumption set) than any downward shift of the equilibrium wage curve it may cause, has a chilling effect on the amount of capital-goods output that firms are willing to supply, which in turn decreases labor demand, thus reducing employment in that sector and the economywide wage rate. The latter effect serves to boost employment in the consumer-good-producing sector, but that adjustment cannot be strong enough to overturn the contraction of jobs in the other sector since the decline of the wage on which it depends is a function of the decline in aggregate employment. Thus the decline of the real asset price that serves to eliminate the excess demand contracts aggregate employment. It is the *paradox of reduced supply of jobs from increased consumer-good demand*. Of course, it would not have come as a paradox for Hayek, for whom it was a great conviction, though he never wrote down a nonmonetary model from which such a proposition could be deduced as a theoretical result and he never effectively rebutted its ridicule by the Cambridge circus.[14]

In the present model, this contractionary effect is located entirely in the capital-good-producing industry (while in other papers there are analogous supply effects even in a one-product setting, owing to dynamic considerations operating in gaining customers and training employees). There is no very deep paradox here, though: The participants on the demand side of the consumer-good market are unable to express their excess demand, as they could finance it only by selling shares and there is no one to buy except themselves. In their efforts to sell, they only succeed in driving down the market price of assets—here capital goods (while in other models the shadow price of customers or of trained employees)—and this has contractionary effects. In the contrasting Keynesian analysis, as is well understood, the excess demand for goods is reflected to a degree in an excess supply of money, and that is eliminated by a rise of the nominal demand price of goods (which is a drop in the real value of money), which is temporarily expansionary (as long as money wages and money prices do not correctly move to their new equilibrium levels).

It should be added that there is another employment effect of increased public debt, a supply effect operating unambiguously to reinforce the contractionary effect just identified, that is not made explicit in the equations of the model. There is a direct impact of the newly created public debt on the propensity to shirk. If we think of taxes as lump-sum in nature rather than tied to taxpayers' wage earnings, it is true that the increase in interest income of households represented by the interest payment on the debt is exactly offset by a decrease in after-tax interest income representing the taxes levied to service the debt; but, for the non-Ricardian households figuring here, the new public debt adds something to annuity income and thus adds to the total income we are calling the income from wealth, y^w. (As Pigou would have said, there is a certain amenity value contributed by the increased wealth.) The net supply effect of this transfer *cum* tax is an increase in the propensity to shirk, at given q and K, and hence an upward shift in the equilibrium wage curve, as firms have to go to more costly lengths to cope with increased shirking.

The supply effect of increased public debt is doubly contractionary if we assume taxation is graduated, rather than lump-sum, and falls wholly or disproportionately on labor income. In this important case, the foregoing Pigou effect on the propensity to shirk is fortified, since financial income is inflated by the additional debt, but there is no offsetting tax on nonwage income—the worker knows enough not to attribute any part of his tax to his own financial income. Hence there is an even stronger financial cushion placed under a worker in the event of dismissal for shirking, so the propensity to shirk is pushed up more strongly in this case than in the previous one. That is not the whole of the effect. As long as a worker is earning his unchanged wage, and paying the additional tax on it attributable to the additional public debt, he bears a larger burden than his *pro rata* share since the unemployed escape paying their *pro rata* share. In summary, there is a substitution effect on top of the Pigou (or wealth) effect, which is a function of the reduction in the wage after tax absolutely and thus relatively to the before-debt-shock financial income level. It can be seen from a review of (9.8) that the after-tax wage rate is unchanged at an unchanged level of y^w and unchanged u. That implies that at given u the before-tax supply wage, which is the cost of labor for firms, is pushed up enough to leave intact the after-tax wage.[15] The final "incidence" of the tax is an increase of the before-tax wage, and a decrease of the after-tax wage, with a corollary reduction of employment.

Government purchases from the consumer-good sector. Suppose there is a small balanced-budget increase in the steady level of public expenditure on output of the consumer-good industry. By way of interpretation it should be noted that these government purchases are not reimbursements or cost-sharing for household purchases of consumer goods; they are not expenditures made on behalf of consumers. They do not substitute for nor complement the purchases made by consumers, since neither utility functions nor production functions are shifted by these government purchases. Hence the use to which the government puts the stream of output thus acquired is of no significance in the model as constructed. The output might be dumped in the sea or shot into outer space or used as a lever in foreign policy. It is not implied either that shipments by the consumer-good industry to the government have any resemblance to the consumption good. It does matter that this consumer-good sector is the sole supplier of the consumer good and the sole contractors for the particular government order under study.

Evidently G_C, like D, has no direct effect—no impact effect—on $\dot{K}$, only on $\dot{q}$, as shown by (9.42') and (9.43'), respectively. On the simplifying assumption that G_C and D are close enough to zero that the terms G_C/K and D/K can be neglected, the change in K measuring the lateral shift of the $\dot{q} = 0$ locus is positive. Hence the shift is again rightward and downward. It is intuitively clear that q would have to drop and the interest rate rise if the demand-side equations were to continue to imply a stationary q. When the government expenditure from the consumer-good industry is increased to a higher level, there is an excess demand for the consumer good, and the only means by which the excess can be eliminated is through a drop of q, which has a wealth effect in the needed direction and an interest-rate effect that also works the right way.[16]

The downward shift of the $\dot{q} = 0$ locus shifts down the saddlepath and shifts down the rest point on the (unshifted) $\dot{K} = 0$ locus. Hence there is a drop of q on impact. The increased public expenditure, in elbowing out consumers for the supply of the consumer good at the initial real wage, causes a decline of the real asset price in order to eliminate the excess demand. This initial drop is followed by declining K and declining q as the new rest point is approached asymptotically.

The employment effects of this drop of q are the same as those identified in the discussion of a consumption shock. The drop of q, in shifting down the derived demand for labor schedule by more (on our assumption set) than any downward shift of the equilibrium wage curve it may cause, has the net effect of contracting the employment rate. Here too, as in the previous section, the participants on the demand side of the consumer-good market are unable to express their excess demand, as they could finance it only by selling shares and there is no one to buy except themselves. In their efforts to sell they only succeed in driving down the market price of assets—here capital goods (while in other models the shadow price of customers or of trained employees)—and this has the contractionary employment and output effect uncovered by formal analysis. Ultimately, therefore, households *do* succeed in saving less (out of their reduced after-tax incomes) but only through the mechanism that reduces income, and this tends to increase consumption only insofar as it lowers the propensity to shirk or lowers the real wage, thus lowering the "efficient-adjusted" wage.

It is instructive to add that there is another employment effect of increased G_C, one deriving from the impact of the increased tax burden of financing the newly instituted public expenditure on the propensity to shirk. If again we think of taxes as lump-sum in nature rather than tied to taxpayers' wage earnings, this increase in tax bills represents a decrease of the after-tax interest income of households and thus in their after-tax income from wealth. The effect of that, taken alone, is a decrease in the propensity to shirk, at given q and K, and hence a *downward* shift in the equilibrium wage curve, which is expansionary. It is therefore theoretically possible in this case that the net effect of the public expenditure is *expansionary,* not contractionary as provisionally found above. This finding suggests that the consequences for employment of a shock to private demand for the output of the consumer-good-producing sector may depend on whether the shock is an increase of the *public debt* or is instead an increase of *government purchases.* In either case the asset price must fall and interest rates rise in response to the excess demand created, with the side effect tending to contract employment; but the former shock has an impact through the increased wealth on the propensity to shirk that is contractionary, even with lump-sum taxation, while impact of the latter shock through that mechanism is to reduce wealth and is, therefore, expansionary.

The case of a graduated tax on *wage* income leads to quite a different conclusion, however. Here the tax increase poses no decrease in after-tax income from wealth, hence no wealth or income effect tending to lower the propensity to shirk and to lower the supply wage to firms on that account. Furthermore, the increase in the tax rate on the wage introduces a substitution effect tending to raise the propensity to shirk and thus raise the wage to the firm that is required for labor-market equilibrium at a given employment rate and income from wealth. In the *graduated* wage tax case, therefore, the tax effect is *contractionary*—the supply wage is pushed up—and thus it reinforces the contractionary effect arriving from the channel of the asset price.

Finally, in the case of a graduated tax on expenditure or on income across the board, the tax increase, in hitting after-tax wages and after-tax nonwage income equally, is neutral for the supply wage.

The interested reader having some experience with the use of phase diagrams will readily confirm that the *anticipation* of a *future* increase of government demand for the output of the consumer-good sector will cause an immediate drop of q, though not so large a drop as when the increased government demand is immediate. (This result does not seem to depend upon bringing in the graduation of taxation.)

Government purchases from the capital-good sector.   Next consider an increase in the steady level of government expenditure on output produced in the capital-good sector. If the capital good is the trucks, say, with which to transport the consumer good, pasta, it is not implied that the government is stepping up its purchase of the identical truck. It may have ordered tanks, the only restriction being that the firms in the capital-good industry use the same production function except possibly for a multiplicative constant. (If a tank costs twice as much as a truck, we can think of the government order in units of half-tanks or pairs of trucks.)

Such an increase of Γ_I has direct effects in both (9.42′) and (9.43′) and thus the curves in Figure 9.3. The lateral shift of the $\dot{K} = 0$ locus is the change in the K needed to keep $\dot{K}$ constant at given q. This change is negative. Hence, this shift is leftward and upward. The explanation is that some private investment is crowded out by the increased public expenditure in the capital-good industry, so that for $\dot{K}$ to be unchanged in the face of that crowding out an increase of q would be needed in order to stimulate an increase in output matching the increase in government demand.

The lateral shift of the $\dot{q} = 0$ locus, making the simplifying assumption that G_C and D are negligible, is also negative. Hence, this shift is likewise leftward and upward. In reducing the growth rate of the capital stock (at any given q) through the crowding-out impact, the public expenditure also implies (at given q) a slowdown in the growth rate of consumption-good supply, which will have to be matched by an equal reduction in the rate of growth of consumption in the Euler-type equation of the Blanchard-Yaari system (see (9.26)). That prospective deceleration of consumption implies a drop of the rate of interest, which in turn implies through (9.25) an increase in the current level of q if $\dot{q} = 0$.

It can be observed from (9.43′S) and Figure 9.2 that the new steady-state q remains unchanged. The implication is that the two shifts are equal. The two loci shift to the left in tandem. It follows immediately that the stationary-equilibrium level of q is unchanged by this public-expenditure shock in the capital-good industry—upon the simplifying assumption that G_C and D are zero or close enough to zero that little error is introduced by ignoring them in the above calculations. The new steady-state K is, however, lower.

The near-term consequences of the public-expenditure shock are another story. The equal leftward shifts must shift leftward the saddlepath equally as well. This leftward, and hence upward, shift of the saddlepath implies an upward jump of q at any given K. The consequences are an upward jump of the current equilibrium real wage and level of employment. The equilibrium unemployment rate is shifted down by the real shock in the capital-good industry. Thereupon, with the "crowding out" (which is perhaps not the best term) of investment expenditures, a steady decline of the capital stock is set in motion, which brings about a concomitant decline of the real price of capital. As q returns asymptotically to its old stationary-equilibrium level, the real wage and the equilibrium unemployment rate likewise revert gradually to their preshock stationary levels. (The equilibrium steady-state unemployment rate is unaffected, therefore.) Readers might benefit from mapping this scenario onto a diagram like that in Figure 9.3.

There is another observation to be made that may be of very great importance. In the monetary models of employment begun by Keynes, a fiscal stimulus such as an increase of public expenditure of any kind is expansionary for employment only if it drives up the nominal rate of interest, for that is the mechanism by which the fiscal stimulus raises the velocity of money and thus the level of employment. It was therefore a troubling finding of Penati and Mankiw-Summers that the wartime periods in the United States in the twentieth century were times of low real interest rates rather than high real rates. With this finding it became impossible for Keynesian theory to attribute the bulge of employment during the wars to the stimulus of increased government expenditure. For that matter, the nonmonetary models proposed in the early 1980s by Robert Barro and by Robert Hall, also work through a positive real interest effect: increased government expenditure is regarded as driving up the real interest rate, which is in turn postulated to have a positive Hicks-Lucas-Rapping effect on the supply of labor. So the evidence on wartime real interest rates was a setback for that embryonic nonmonetary theory as well.

Happily for the structuralist model here, the mechanism by which increased public expenditure in the capital-good industry expands employment does not require an increase of the real interest rate, and indeed the model implies that the real interest rate *falls* as a result of that fiscal shock. This is immediately deducible from the rise of q, which reduces the rental rate, $R(q)/q$, and which, being recognized as vanishing under the hypothesis of correct expectations, also reduces the expected rate of capital gain (by introducing the expectation of falling q). Of course, the subject of wartime expenditure in a context in which the end of the war is unknown cries out for a probabilistic treatment.

Bringing in lump-sum taxation, it will now be clear, would only reinforce the expansion shown by the employment rate and actually introduce a permanent component to that expansion. But recognizing that taxation is primarily graduated and based on wage income introduces a contractionary effect opposing the expansionary effect through the asset price. This contractionary effect, recall, is the consequence of the need to provide the right after-tax wage-to-income-from-wealth ratio for labor-market equilibrium at a given employment rate. It is clear, then, that an increase of the tax rate from, say, 50 percent to 75 percent would require a doubling of the wage to firms to restore the aforementioned ratio to its right level; the labor-demand effect of the increased public expenditure on capital-good-sector output financed by that tax-rate increase, assuming for the sake of argument that it succeeded in raising revenue, would have to be phenomenal to offset that cost effect. But the demand-side effect of the capital-sector public expenditure might overcome the effect of the tax rate if it were only a move from a zero tax rate to a one percent tax rate. The model thus prepares us for the possibility of either outcome at low tax rates, while the implied effect on the real interest rate is unambiguously negative and the effect on the real wage unambiguously positive.

It may be verified by the reader that the *anticipation* of a *future* increase of government purchasing from the capital-goods sector likewise causes immediately a positive jump of q, though not as large as if the increase in demand were immediate. Thereupon q will be rising further, reaching a

peak when the increased public expenditure begins, and then falling back
to its original level.

Government employment.   Consider lastly the effect of an increase in
the sustained level of purchase of efficiency-adjusted labor services by the
public sector. An increase of Γ_P, like an increase of Γ_I, has a direct effect
upon the $\dot{K} = 0$ locus, as the use of (9.44) in (9.42') shows, and a direct
effect upon the $\dot{q} = 0$ locus, as can be seen from the use of (9.44) in (9.43').
The lateral shift of the former locus is leftward. The reason is that the
increase in public-sector employment contracts the excess supply of labor
to the capital-good-producing industry at specified q (hence v) and L, the
labor force, and thus contracts the supply of investment goods (net of depreciation) to the private sector at specified q and K, given L, the labor
force.

The lateral shift of the $\dot{q} = 0$ locus, making once more the simplifying
assumption that G_C and D are negligible, is likewise leftward. The channel
is largely the same as that through which an increase of Γ_I produces a
leftward shift. As before, the shifts of these two curves calculated above
are clearly identical. So the effects of an increase of Γ_P are similar to those
of an increase of Γ_I. The stationary-equilibrium path is unaffected by the
increase in government expenditure but the saddlepath is shifted up, so
that q must jump up at the current level of K, which causes the real wage
and employment to jump up as well.

This finding is perhaps obvious to readers who have come as far as the
analysis of an increase of expenditure on the capital good. But those working through the series of previous models will have found there that increased government employment is shown to be contractionary. It elbows
out only consumer demand—there is no capital good of the physical kind
traditionally studied—and the rise of the interest rate thereby entailed has
contractionary effects through the supply of output. So it is instructive to
have an example in which government employment is expansionary for
aggregate employment: If the data will not give support to the hypothesis
that government employment is contractionary, it is useful to know that
the structuralist theory does not really entail that bold and radical hypothesis.

It must be noted, however, that the above implication that increased
government employment expands aggregate employment (and the corollary that it decreases the real interest rate) has been obtained on the assumption, born of casual empirical observation, that the public sector is
extremely labor-intensive. What if the government uses capital alongside
labor to operate the public sector? Let us suppose that the government
leases capital from the private financial intermediaries—for example, the

companies in the business of supplying Blanchard-type life insurance to households. Then to answer the question we need to examine the equation for $\hat{\epsilon}N_I$ underlying (9.42′) to allow for governmental employment of capital K_P alongside its hiring of labor N_P:

$$\hat{\epsilon}N_I = \hat{\epsilon}[(1 - u)L - N_P] - \hat{\epsilon}N_C$$

$$= \hat{\epsilon}[(1 - u)L - N_P] - \frac{[K - K_P]}{\tilde{k}_C}$$

$$= \hat{\epsilon}(1 - u)L - \frac{K}{\tilde{k}_C} - \hat{\epsilon}K_P\left[\left(\frac{N_P}{K_P}\right) - \left(\frac{N_C}{K_C}\right)\right]$$

Apparently the hiring of capital by the public sector has an effect on the supply of investment and thus upon q and aggregate employment that is *opposite* to that of the hiring of labor. The diversion of privately owned capital to the public sector is, from this point of view, akin to the destruction of capital by an earthquake or other natural disaster; we noted earlier that earthquakes depress q and thereby contract aggregate employment. It can be seen at once that governmental operation of the public sector enters negatively in the righthand side, as in the simple case where no capital was required by the government, if and onl if $(N_P/K_P) > (N_C/K_C)$. So this is the condition for the activity level of the public sector to be expansionary for aggregate employment (and, as a corollary, to be interest-rate-reducing). Of course, it seems not to be the case empirically that the public sector is as capital-intensive as the more capital-intensive of the two private sectors of the economy.[17]

Suppose instead that the government capital represents its investment of some of the output it purchased earlier from the capital-good industry. Capital used by the government that is owned by the government is not to be netted from the total stock of capital in the calculation of $\hat{\epsilon}N_I$ because such owned capital does not divert capital from the consumer-good industry. The relevant "labor-intensiveness" of the public sector is measured in terms of the ratio of labor to privately owned capital. If the government were to own all the capital it uses, the effect on aggregate employment of the public sector would be the same as if that sector used the same labor with no capital at all. Thus, if this reasoning is right, the assumption in the equations that the government produces without capital, while seeming at first to be seriously restrictive, is almost innocuous since, as an empirical matter, the great bulk of the capital used by the government is under public ownership.

Note finally that insofar as the government's production is financed by graduated taxation of wage income there is a contractionary effect transmitted by the impact on the after-tax wage rate to households.

Technological advances.[18]   The other category of shock is the so-called productivity shock. A change in productivity due to a disturbance to the capital stock has already been studied, and more on that question will come up indirectly again. The effects of a change in productivity caused by an "oil shock"—a disturbance to its availability or (more naturally in an open-economy setting) its real price—were briefly considered in a previous model, and that question does not need to be reexamined in the present setting. However, the effect of changes in so-called total factor productivity owing to technological advances needs a careful examination.

A tradition in the neoclassical economics of growth, even since Solow and Uzawa, has been to postulate that technological advances are always and entirely Harrod-neutral: at an unchanged ratio of income (in consumer-good units, say) to capital (in its natural units, say), the interest rate or (more accurately) capital's unit rental (in consumer-good units) would be found also not to have changed, despite the technological advance, so that relative shares were then also unchanged. In contrast, Hicks neutrality looks at an unchanged capital-labor ratio, and what may be called Solow neutrality holds constant the income-to-labor ratio. The concept arises because along so-called golden-age path, in which the income-to-capital ratio is unchanging over time and likewise relative shares, technological change is clearly Harrod-neutral; if some or all technical advances are not Harrod-neutral, the economy cannot exhibit golden-age growth. In this brief section our attention will be confined to Harrod neutrality, even though that hypothesis is perhaps significantly amiss as an empirical matter.[19] In order that there exist a golden-age growth path for *all* values of the parameters governing consumer demand, or the supply of saving, it is further necessary that technical advances be Harrod-neutral for *all* income-to-capital ratios. When progress is, in that sense, everywhere Harrod-neutral there are then two possibilities in a two-sector model, of which the leading one is that progress is *labor-augmenting* in each of the two sectors' production functions.[20] Here we will go farther by supposing that labor augmentation is always equal in the two sectors. Letting Λ denote the common labor augmentation prevailing at the current time, and suppressing the time subscript, we have

$$(9.47) \quad Z_C = F_C(K_C, \hat{\varepsilon}\Lambda N_C)$$

$$(9.48) \quad Z_I = F_I(K_I, \hat{\varepsilon}\Lambda N_I)$$

Our attention will be confined, despite the general formulation in (9.47)–(9.48), to the classic case. The sole feature of the context that is crucial, however, is the property that the saddlepath makes q an increasing function of the state variable K, all parameters being held constant.

The effect of the "level." Consider first the effect of a one-time shift, or break, in the "level" of the labor augmentation. Thus Λ jumps to a higher level. It will be supposed here that Λ is always expected to remain at its current level. More generally, we may suppose that the expected *rate of technical progress*, as measured by the proportionate rate $(\lambda(s))$ at which Λ is expected to be changing at any moment in the future (s), is *invariant* to the level it has currently attained. (Later we study shocks to the steady rate of labor augmentation.)

The key to understanding the effects of such a shift was found in the recent analysis of the neoclassical real model of the "business cycle" by King, Plosser, and Rebelo.[21] *If* it were the case, which it will never be in fact, that the capital stock increased immediately in the *same proportion* as Λ, the effect under certain simplifying assumptions would be an immediate increase of output and the real wage in the same proportion while there would be no jump at all in the (unit) rental on capital, the asset price, q, and the rate of interest. Thus, at given employment, N, wage income and the aggregate rent on capital would increase in proportion to K and to Λ, and so would total income and financial wealth, qK. With the ratio of wage to income from wealth and the wage-wealth ratio unchanged (and likewise the rate of interest), the propensity to shirk would be the same as before and, crucially, so would the unemployment rate for labor-market equilibrium implied by the industry-wide first-order condition, (9.8). By way of interpretation, one may say that the optimal "incentive wage" at the unchanged unemployment rate has risen *in proportion to the income from wealth* and hence in proportion to the demand wage.

A formal analysis proceeds by defining some new variables that have been normalized by Λ, namely: v/Λ, $(v/\Lambda)/e$, $K_C/(\hat{e}\Lambda N_C)$, Z_C/Λ, and so forth. Certain relative prices figuring in the relationships between quantities of goods, q and r to be specific, remain unnormalized. In terms of this new set of variables the solution path is unaffected by the equiproportionate increase of K and Λ.

The key observation is that an increase of Λ, the current K unchanged, *does* affect the solution in terms of this new set of variables. Such a shock decreases the initial value of the variable K/Λ. The same analysis in King, Plosser, and Rebelo implies that the consequences for the variables v/Λ, $(v/\Lambda)/e$, $K_C/(\hat{e}\Lambda N_C)$, Z_C/Λ, . . . , q, r, are exactly like the effect on the *original* variables of a decrease in the initial K, with Λ unchanged.

The consequences of such a capital-stock shock in the *classic case* studied at length must be analyzed with the aid of the phase diagram. The upward slope of the saddle-path in Figure 9.3 implies that there is an immediate drop in q. Let us discuss the effects as if the shock were literally a drop of K. Although net investment must be increased as a ratio to capital, to bring about convergence to the steady state corresponding to the elevated level of labor augmentation, absolute gross investment is reduced. Hence there is a drop in the derived demand price of labor. But there may also be a drop in the income from wealth: directly from the reduction in capital, which decreases the aggregate rentals on capital, and indirectly from the induced reduction of q, which may operate to reduce annuity income more than it raises interest income through its effect of reducing the real wage. Such a drop in the income from wealth would cause a drop in the "supply wage"—the wage needed for labor-market equilibrium. Provided the drop of the "demand wage" exceeds the drop of the supply wage (if indeed it drops), the consequence of the shock will be a temporary *contraction* of employment. There is also the theoretical possibility that the consequence will be instead a temporary *expansion* of employment in relation to the path that would otherwise have been taken.

Another interesting benchmark case is the *one-sector* case in which the factor intensities of the two sectors are identical for all wage-rental ratios confronting the firms. Here too the derived demand price of labor schedule drops with a decrease of the initial capital stock, since the demand price involves the marginal productivity of labor and that is an increasing function of the capital stock, given the employment rate and the labor force. However, there is again the possibility that the wage needed for labor-market equilibrium—the supply wage—also shifts down. Hence, in the one-sector case also we find the theoretical possibility of an expansion or a contraction of employment in the early phase of the adjustment to the decreased capital stock.

The effect of the "rate of change."   The second question is the effect of the steady *rate* of labor-augmenting technical progress. This constant will be denoted, not untraditionally, by λ. As always unless expressly noted, a shift of this parameter is to be understood as a change *not previously anticipated*. Yet, upon its occurrence, it is fully recognized by all agents and, as implied by the equilibrium nature of the scenarios we are examining, correctly built into expectations. Hence the subsequent technical progress is *henceforth anticipated*.

If λ is increased, the steady-state (or, more accurately, the steady-growth) equilibrium will shift from one with a growth rate higher by the increase in λ. There is an equal increase in the rate of growth of the stock of capital, consumption, wealth, income from wealth, the wage bill, and the wage. With regard to certain ratios and relative prices, it may be noted that there is an increase in the steady-state rate of interest.

The effects of the increase in λ may again be studied with the use of a phase diagram analogous to that in Figure 9.3. The modification is the substitution of the variable K/Λ for the unnormalized K. Of course, Λ is going to behave like $e^{\lambda t}$. The resulting phase diagram resembles that in Figure 9.3 with the *normalized* capital stock on the horizontal axis. When λ increases, there is no immediate effect on the variable K/Λ, of course, since neither the initial K nor Λ jumps. The curve showing the locus of points along which K/Λ, or $K/e^{\lambda t}$, is constant does shift, however. It can be shown that this curve shifts up and to the left. This is as might be expected since stationarity of the normalized capital stock in the face of the increased rate of technical progress requires an increased rate of growth of K, hence an increase in q or a decrease of K to shift resources over to capital building. The net effect on the $\dot{q} = 0$ locus is nil. Therefore the new steady-state q is reduced and the saddlepath is shifted down.[22] It follows that q drops abruptly at the moment of the increase in λ. This is intuitively reasonable since we might well expect that rate of interest to jump up as well as the level and growth rate of consumption. The near-term effect on employment of the drop in q is *contractionary*. The steady-state K/Λ is reduced, and the steady-state q is also unambiguously lower, even lower than the post-impact q since the subsequent decline in K/Λ operates to pull q down.

There is, however, a complication not so far brought into the analysis. With the real wage expected now to be growing rapidly, a worker will sacrifice more than before if, risking an act of shirking, he is dismissed and thus has to spend time in the unemployment pool.[23] On this account, therefore, there is an additional impetus to shirk with reduced frequency, and that is expansionary. But, on the other hand, the increase of the rate of interest brought about by the faster rate of progress causes the expected value of the real penalty for being dismissed to be discounted more heavily. On this account, there is more reason to shirk than before. These two forces tend roughly to cancel, however, since the rate of interest is pulled by approximately as much as the rate of growth of the wage, an approximation that is exact in the new steady state. We can proceed as if this channel is not operative in steady state.

The effect of capital augmentation.   Although the foregoing analysis touches the traditional bases it is far from comprehensive. There can be *capital augmentation* as well as labor augmentation. A brief discussion for the classic case follows.

Since the stylized facts of economic growth have usually included constancy of relative shares and of the ratio of capital to national income, there is a fairly compelling case for the hypothesis that technical progress tends on average to be Harrod-neutral. In a one-sector model such neutrality requires that factor augmentation be purely labor-augmenting. In a two-sector model, however, there could be Hicks-neutral technical progress in the consumer-good sector—capital augmentation matching labor augmentation. At first blush, such a development would seem to threaten the ever-increasing importance of the consumer-good sector, which is the more capital-intensive, so that capital's share would always be increasing. But there will nevertheless exist a sort of balanced-growth state in which the relative price of the capital good is steadily rising at a rate equal to the rate of growth of the factor-augmentation factor (common to both factors) in the consumer-good sector.

Even if no capital augmentation were compatible with the invariance of shares at an invariant rate of interest, the facts of economic growth do not present a pattern of rigidity in either relative shares or the rate of interest. There could have been occasional episodes of capital augmentation that produced a one-time disturbance to the relationship between the rate of interest and relative shares.[24]

How does an increase in the level of augmentation disturb things? Looking at the steady-state equations before contemplation of technical change, particularly (9.43'S), we see that such a technical change would increase the rental at given q, thus increasing the lefthand side, and increase the consumer-good-output-to-capital ratio at given q, thus decreasing the righthand side, with the result that q is increased and also y^w. The immediate effect of the capital augmentation is likewise to increase the marginal product of capital and thus shift up the prospective stream of rentals on capital, which drives up q and y^w. It is not obvious that the implication for the employment rate is any less ambiguous than the implication of an episode of labor augmentation. It may be left as a question for further research.

9.3 Commentary

This chapter has extended the structuralist theory of natural unemployment and natural interest—the largely nonmonetary theory founded on hypotheses of some sort of real-wage rigidity or else real-wage stickiness, and much enriched by the idea that the supply of jobs (or the derived demand for labor) shifts with changes in interest rates and certain real asset prices—to a model of production patterned as closely as possible on the traditional two-sector model of capital and growth. The resulting dynamic system behaves nicely, being saddlepath stable and simply analyzable with the usual phase diagram in the (K, q) plane.

A basic finding of some earlier papers in this structuralist line by the present author, by now a theme of some years, concerns the real wage and employment effects of increased public expenditure on output of firms producing the consumer good (or goods). An unanticipated increase of G_C, in driving up (the term structure of) real interest rates, causes the real price of the capital good (and the price of shares) to jump down, thus making both the natural rate of employment and the real wage jump *down*. This is the dark side of the structuralist doctrine. The surprise of the present chapter is the set of results regarding the effects of public expenditure elsewhere in the economy. An unanticipated increase of G_I, the level of public expenditure on the output of the capital-good industry, causes the real asset price to jump up and (surprisingly) the real rates of interest to drop, thus making employment and the real wage jump *up*. An unanticipated increase in G_P, the expenditure on production by the public sector itself, has identical effects apart from scale.

Some of these results may be quite helpful for understanding the large events experienced over the past century. Notable among these is the finding that increased expenditure on the output of the capital-goods-making firms, such as the increased purchase of military ships and planes in wartime, acts to expand employment while actually reducing the instantaneous real rate of interest—both effects vanishing asymptotically. Until now the only extant explanation of the curious wartime pattern—high employment and low real interest—was the interesting idea of Mankiw: the prospect of an impoverishing war drives capital used in the domestic sector, such as garage space and pickup trucks, into the commercial sector, where it drives down the marginal product of capital; this effect and the impoverishment could, singly or in combination, induce an increase in the amount of labor supplied at the same time.[25]

The results are also of some doctrinal interest as well. The Keynes of the early 1930s was an advocate of public works—pyramid building—as the best or at any rate the second-best way of pulling up employment in the midst of Britain's devastating slump.[26] Later, in the *General Theory,* there were no more references to such expenditures as a particularly appropriate or efficacious remedy; the whole emphasis of that book was on *ag-*

gregate demand, to which each dollar of government spending supposedly contributed equally, or so his interpreters explained. The Keynesians pointed to the improved performance of those countries that opted for big public-spending programs as evidence of the correctness of the Keynesian analysis. More than anything else this experience must have ensured the triumph of the Keynesian system over the great many doubters.

The leading challenger was Hayek, who argued that increased consumption spending would be contractionary, not expansionary.[27] But Hayek blundered into overgeneralizing, mistakenly believing or giving the impression that what was true of fiscal stimulus to consumption was true of all fiscal stimuli. He should have claimed the association of recovery with capital-goods purchases and public employment, where it was observed, as just as favorable to his own position as that of Keynes.

Finally, some caveats and suggestions for further research: One's understanding of the present model is not complete until the reverse assumption about comparative factor intensiveness is studied. In this connection, even the one-sector model will repay some study. Second, the open-economy variation on the model must be studied before drawing up empirical hypotheses on the basis of the structuralist theory, as will be done in Chapter 13.

10

Synthesis of the Single-Economy Theory

THIS chapter begins with an exploration of how the three foregoing closed-economy models, each with a single and distinct asset, can be combined to form a multi-asset model. This loose synthesis, or union, of the elementary models is presented in the first section below. The purpose is only to make clear what it means to speak of the union of the three models, or of the theory as a whole. The purpose is not to undertake an analysis of the omnibus model, which would produce little value added over the findings obtained from the elementary models.

The next section goes on with the substantive business of the chapter. The aim here is to draw from the three elementary models the main theses (or, at any rate, most of the main theses) on the consequences of various parameter shifts and state shocks for the level and subsequent course of economic activity—particularly those propositions that hold true of the multi-asset omnibus model. In fact, barring errors, these theses seem to be supported by one or more of the elementary models and contradicted by none of them.

As was emphasized in the Preface, the theory here is a particular representative of structuralist theory, not the totality of structuralist models. In the interest of completeness, and because they are of substantive interest in their own right, whatever their empirical importance is judged finally to be, a number of other non-monetary mechanisms, which have been championed by others, are discussed in the appendix to this chapter.

10.1 The Closed-Economy Models Integrated

The modern theorizing of the past dozen years or so offers a variety of conceptions of the mechanisms determining unemployment and real wages.[1] The models developed here seize upon a few mechanisms believed to be endemic to all economies—problems of incentives and market frictions. The hope is that, collectively, they describe what may come to be regarded as the paradigm case, or core model, of the modern theory. As a sort of review we may consider a synthesis of their distinctive features.[2]

The three elementary models all contain a labor-market mechanism of the incentive-wage type. Thus they share the characteristic that the real wage, though flexible in one sense, has an equilibrium (i.e., consistent-expectations) level that does not clear the labor market, owing to one or another problem created by deficiencies of information. The consequences of these labor-market mechanisms can be summarized by an equation giving the current real wage, v, needed for labor-market equilibrium (i.e., for correct expectations of the general wage). In the closed economies modeled here, that equilibrium wage-curve equation takes the form

$$(10.1) \quad v = V_s(1 - u; \mathbf{\Pi}; \mathbf{x}, \mathbf{q}, \{r\}; \mathbf{Y}) \qquad V_s'(1 - u; \ldots) \geq 0$$

where $\mathbf{\Pi}$ is the vector of shift parameters, such as the productivity parameters; $\mathbf{x}$ is the vector of state variables representing the per-worker size of the capital stock, the customer stock, and the stock of assets held by firms in the form of employees having the needed firm-specific training; $\mathbf{q}$ the vector of real asset prices, r the instantaneous real rate of interest, and $\{r\}$ the associated yield curve at the current time, and $\mathbf{Y}$ represents the prevailing set of social policies reflected in tax and welfare legislation.[3]

The second block in these models is a parallel description of the condition for equilibrium in the product market (meaning correct expectations about the price level relative to the price of normalized shares). Given that firms are in product-market equilibrium, the real demand price of labor is derivable and is typically a nonincreasing function of the employment rate, $1 - u$, given the various parameters (hence the production functions) and the relevant stocks and corresponding real asset prices:

$$(10.2) \quad v = V_d(1 - u; \mathbf{\Pi}; \mathbf{x}, \mathbf{q}, r; \mathbf{Y} \ldots) \qquad V_d'(1 - u; \ldots) \leq 0$$

The role of interest here is part Austrian in inspiration, part modern.

The intersection of these two relationships determines the joint-equilibrium v and $1 - u$ as functions of $\mathbf{q}$, $\{r\}$, $\mathbf{x}$, and the various givens:

$$V_d(1 - u; \mathbf{\Pi}; \mathbf{x}, \mathbf{q}, r; \mathbf{Y} \ldots) = V_s(1 - u; \mathbf{\Pi}; \mathbf{x}, \mathbf{q}, \{r\}; \mathbf{Y})$$

Thus the general-equilibrium (macro)economics of the natural rate of unemployment involves certain real prices and real interest rates as well as
various stocks which are the state variables of the system.

Completing the general-equilibrium system requires capital-market
equilibrium in order to determine equilibrium asset prices and interest
rates. For there to be no discrepancy between the gross flow demand for
assets and the gross flow supply—for households to be in expectational
equilibrium in the capital market—consumer-good supply must be equal
to consumer demand. The former is a determinable function C^s of the asset
prices, the various stocks, and public purchases of that good, G^C. Under
the Blanchard-Yaari setup, the latter is a function C^d of the stocks of the
various assets, their real prices, and certain parameters. Then

$$(10.3) \quad C^s(\mathbf{q}, \mathbf{x}; G^C) = C^d(H, \Sigma qx + D; \rho, \mu)$$

where H denotes "human wealth", D (here a parameter) represents the
real public debt and the present value of other government entitlement
payments net of taxes, ρ is the rate of time preference, and μ is the mortality
rate. Equivalently, consumption demand satisfies a familiar Euler-type differential equation; upon substituting consumption supply for consumption
demand, we have

$$(10.3') \quad r = \rho + \{\mu(\rho + \mu)(\Sigma qx + D) + [dC^s(\mathbf{q}, \mathbf{x})/dt]\}/C^s(\mathbf{q}, \mathbf{x}; G^C)$$

For full equilibrium consumers need correct expectations of their future
income stream and its present discounted value, hence future interest rates.
Capital-market equilibrium requires in addition the intertemporal conditions that, for each asset, the financial rate of return, shown on the lefthand
side of the equation below, be equal to the rate of interest required by
households:

$$(10.4) \quad q^{-1}[R(\mathbf{q}, \mathbf{x}) + dq/dt] = r$$

The six-equation system comprised of (10.1), (10.2), (10.3) or its alter-
nate (10.3'), and the three equations in (10.4), one for each q, constitute
a subsystem determining the current level of the three qs, r, u, and v, taking
as *given* the next period's three qs as well as the predetermined $\mathbf{x}$. The
right solution—the one we want—is the one obtained from the restriction
that the path of each q must converge asymptotically to the stationary-
state value corresponding to the stationary-state $\mathbf{x}$.

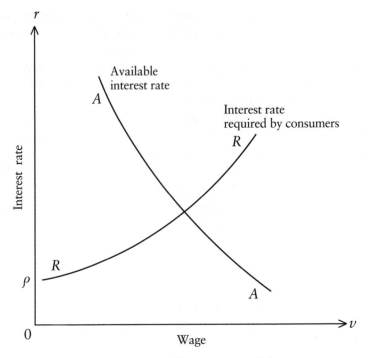

Figure 10.1 Steady-state wage rate and determination of the interest rate

The system is closed with the three stock-accumulation relationships:[4]

$$(10.5) \quad dx/dt = \Psi(\mathbf{q}, \mathbf{x}; G^l)$$

The full system thus has nine equations. We may think of the right solution as determining the three qs, r, u, v, and the three dx/dts as a function of the levels of the three xs by the method of undetermined coefficients.

To capture informational imperfections in the capital market generating credit and equity rationing and hence so-called balance-sheet effects, a consideration touched on in Chapter 5, would require some major recasting but would not apparently reshape the theory out of recognition.

The difficult task of extending this sort of system to the small open economy and, even more formidable, the interactions of large open economies, is left for Part III.

The spirit of the synthesized model can be expressed by Figure 10.1. This diagram depicts the determination of the multi-asset model's *station-*

ary state in the wage–interest rate plane, (v, r). It may call to mind Figure 9.4 in the (q, r) plane, where q is the real price of physical capital; but in the model underlying that diagram q is monotone-increasing in v/e, not necessarily in v alone; further, Figure 10.1, being based on an integration of all three models, involves all three assets. In using this construction, it should be remembered that many parameter shifts of interest impact on both curves, not just one.

10.2 The Structuralist Theses

The foregoing chapters have developed a number of propositions on just how this or that change in the structure of the economy disturbs the path of the equilibrium rate of unemployment (along with the paths of the interest rate, the growth rate, assets at domestic firms, and national wealth). The shocks that were taken up for study may well be the thought-experiments that would first come to mind among most macroeconomists. In any case, most of these shocks could have been chosen for their possible importance at one time or another in understanding postwar history.

The shocks studied may be grouped into three categories. First, there are the usual shocks to productivity—an oil shock or a shock to the level of the technology—and to the rate of technical progress. The size of the labor force, a parameter in our models, clearly belongs here, and so does the size of the existing capital shock, a predetermined state variable subject to accidents. Second, there are shocks to tax rates and certain fiscal entitlements that affect the propensities to quit and shirk and hence the height to which incentive wage rates are pushed up. Third, there are expenditure shocks, including disturbances to private expenditure induced by shocks to the public debt. These will be taken up in order.

SHOCKS TO STOCKS AND PRODUCTIVITY

In the turnover/quitting model of equilibrium unemployment (Chapter 7), in which *employees* are the vessel for a firm's investment, a sudden, one-time technical advance that is purely labor-augmenting, hence Harrod-neutral, was found to be neutral in a sense for the equilibrium path of the unemployment rate and of the rate of interest: There would be neutrality in the closed economy *if* there somehow occurs an equal proportionate increase in the public debt; in the open economy there would be neutrality *if* overseas asset holdings increased in the same proportion as well. Then the worth, or shadow price, of a new recruit and the wage paid to employees would increase in proportion to the increased productivity level, leaving firms' optimal recruiting program unchanged. In the first of the two shirking/supervision models of equilibrium unemployment (Chapter 8), in which a firm invests in attracting and keeping *customers* from the other firms, the implications were similar. The main interest in this neutrality proposition by itself is the implication that (unanticipated) productivity advances do not imply successive reductions of the equilibrium unemployment rate, which would be contrary to the stylized fact of trendlessness in the unemployment rate. Various corollaries are also of interest, however. The expectation of a future labor-augmenting technical advance drives up the shadow prices of the assets in anticipation of their increased levels when the advance arrives, and the effect of this is heightened recruiting of employees and intensified competition for customers, both of which generate a transitory rise of employment.

The plot thickens with the appearance of investment by firms in the physical *capital stock*. It is an old idea in business-cycle analysis that when the capital stock somehow gets ahead of itself, a correction is required; an episode of lower-than-average employment ensues. It also seems to be a rather widespread assumption in macroeconomic histories that over a period in which a closed economy, such as the world economy, was "growing into" advances of knowledge a higher-than-average employment rate would be the tendency. The Keynesian models of Hicks and Hansen ingeniously formalized those theses, though in the neo-Keynesian revision, Samuelson and Tobin objected that these employment effects would occur only if the monetary authorities needlessly failed to match investment demand to full-employment saving. Does the structuralist equilibrium theory developed here provide its own theoretical support for these traditional Keynesian positions? Does it at least represent these hypotheses as not implausible theoretical possibilities? Or does it instead ally itself with the nontraditional conclusion of Harrod and some other Keynesian dissidents that increases of the capital stock warrant an increase of employment, not a decrease, and perhaps support the modern-day "Luddites" who believe that technical advances destroy more jobs than they create?

It turns out that in the closed-economy model containing capital, the one in Chapter 9, either *both* popular propositions are true—increases of the capital are contractionary *and* increases in the technology level (of a certain type) are expansionary—or both are *false*. The reason is that all the models studied here have built into them a number of homogeneity properties ensuring that it is the *ratios* of various state variables and pa-

rameters to one another, not the absolute levels, that are determining for
the equilibrium path of the unemployment rate and the interest rate. In
particular, a positive technological shock that is Harrod-neutral in its factor-saving, thus leaving relative factor shares unchanged if and when the
rate of interest is found at its original level, would be *neutral* for the equilibrium path of the *unemployment rate* and the interest rate *if* accompanied
(through some extraordinary accident) by shocks of the right magnitude
to certain stock variables or state variables: In a closed economy these
conditions include the requirement that the capital stock somehow should
increase *proportionally* to the technology level (as measured by the cumulative labor augmentation common to all the economy's production functions). The conditions also include the requirement that public debt and
all public expenditures, if positive, should likewise increase in proportion
to the technology level.[5] Since in the long run, following a Harrod-neutral
technical advance, physical capital would actually tend to increase in the
same proportion as the technology level provided that the *public debt* did
the *same,* such a technical advance can be said to be *neutral for long-run
unemployment,* thanks to the homogeneities built into the models: If there
is no actual, or historical, association between increases in the world technology and world public debt as a ratio to the technology level (or in real
wage units), then the model implies no association between the technology
level and the equilibrium steady-state world rate of unemployment.

What of the short run, though, in which we have to reckon on the
initial invariance of the stock of capital and the stock of public debt?[6] The
following recapitulation of the analysis of Chapter 9 abstracts from the
effects channeled through the public-sector variables by taking these variables to be zero.

Shocks to the level of labor augmentation or to the capital stock.   Consider the consequences of the predeterminacy of the initial capital stock,
K, in the face of a supposed jump of economywide labor augmentation,
Λ. Recall that we are discussing a *closed* economy here, hence effectively
a model of a homogeneous world economy. The impact of the jump in
the technology index is a drop in K/Λ. But this drop in the normalized
capital stock and the change in q that it induces are entirely transient, since
the new equilibrium steady state will exhibit the same K/Λ and q as before.
Among the effects there is a drop of the effort-adjusted efficiency wage,
$v/(e\Lambda)$, and hence a corresponding upward jump in the rental, R, and a
downward jump of q. The effects of the drop in K/Λ upon q and in turn
on $v/(e\Lambda)$ and u are exactly those that would occur if the shock was a

decrease of K rather than an *increase* of Λ. Thus the question at issue is equivalent to the question: What are the consequences of a sudden change in the capital stock?

What is the effect of an *increase*, say, of K? There are *two* employment effects: the indirect one via q and the direct one obtained by holding q constant. It was seen to be impossible to show that one channel necessarily overcomes the other. But we can illuminate the matter.

In increasing q, if that were the sole channel, an increase of K would operate to *expand* employment through a mechanism that is crucial for some questions: The increase in q may operate to shift up the demand wage, v^d, which in the two-sector model is the v solving equation (9.17′):

$$(10.6) \quad v = e(1, 1 - u, y^w(q, k; \mu)/v)\Lambda q \qquad y^w = [R(q) + \mu q]k, \, k \equiv K/L$$

In a very *extreme* case the increase in q would increase y^w on balance and do so in *proportion* to q, in which case v^d would increase in proportion to q—a case that can be interpreted as corresponding to a very high μ; in all less extreme cases the lesser rise of income from wealth would mean that the increase in q would have a negative impact on the ratio y^w/v, thus a feedback effect inducing increased effort, and hence cause a larger-than-proportional increase of the demand wage. In this same extreme case, the "incentive" wage (or "supply wage"), defined as the solution to equation (9.8′a),

$$(10.7) \quad 1 = e_1(1, (1 - u), y^w/v)/e(1, (1 - u), y^w/v)$$

being proportional to y^w, would also increase in proportion to q; in the less extreme cases, the supply wage would increase less than proportionally to q. In the extreme case, then, the *indirect* effect on employment through the increased q would fail to be significant, and the *direct* (constant-q) effect of the increase of K, in increasing income from wealth, would decide the matter: Taken alone, it pulls down the demand wage (by dampening employees' effort) while driving up the supply wage (by enriching workers and thus boosting nonwage income), so the employment rate must drop to a level re-equating the demand wage to the supply wage. In this extreme case, therefore, the net effect of the increase of K and associated increase of q would be *contractionary* for the employment rate.[7] But in the non-extreme cases, the associated increase of q induces an increase in the ratio of the demand wage to the supply wage; that introduces a reverse effect, hence the possibility that the net effect is *expansionary* on balance.[8] In any case, expansionary or contractionary, the net effect on employment is transient under the premises maintained here.[9]

Such a predominance of the direct effect over the indirect effect, in implying an increase of the capital-to-technology ratio to be *contractionary* on balance,would lend a (nonmonetary) hand to the old Keynes-Hansen position. Yet the theoretical model here is too rich, in a sense, to force that implication. The door is left open to the possibility that the capital-to-labor-augmentation ratio is an *expansionary* influence on employment. Both possibilities seem to be compatible with considerations of existence, uniqueness, and stability. Yet we are not at the end of the story.[10]

If the public-sector parameters are initially positive, the labor augmentation has the effect of diminishing their effect on the rate of employment—as if these parameters had been scaled uniformly down without any change of labor augmentation. What would be the effect of that? Since it was found that the public debt is contractionary, the effect of that scaling back is accordingly expansionary. If there are public expenditures being made that are expansionary, on the other hand, their scaling back would be contractionary, of course. But such contractionary effects might be offset by the expansionary effects of public-sector expansion to take advantage of the increase of productivity and real income.

Finally, to anticipate Part III: the case of the small open economy is fundamentally different in a crucial respect, namely the determination of the rate of interest. There the indirect effect via q does not apply.[11]

Effects of the rate of technical progress. The consequences of a constant rate of technological progress of the labor-augmenting type for the equilibrium path of employment differ considerably from those of a change in the level of augmentation. The ambiguity shifts from the short run to the long run. Readers are again reminded that the subject is the closed economy, hence the world as a whole, not a small country within the world economy.

Under a faster rate of steady and anticipated labor-augmenting progress, the steady-growth state is one with a higher real rate of interest and hence a lower q. Let us compare two histories, suitably constructed, at the moment when they have the same level of technology: The faster-growth one will exhibit the lower K, hence the lower wage. How the employment rates in the two steady-growth states compare is a matter of these effects on K and q. If we take the direct effect of the reduced K to be decisive over the decrease in q, which can be regarded as the indirect effect of the reduced K, then sustained and anticipated economywide labor-augmenting progress is implied to be *expansionary* for employment, on balance, in the *long run.* If the indirect effect outweighs the direct effect, which remains an important possibility, there is implied to be a *long-run contraction* of employment. In any case, there is no presumption of long-run neutrality, unlike the case of a one-time shift in the technology level.

What of the short run, however? The unanticipated appearance of a sustained and henceforth expected labor-augmenting progress at a faster rate causes an immediate drop in q, hence an immediate *drop* of employment. If the direct effect of K outweighs the indirect effect, the subsequent downward adjustment of K/Λ is expansionary, and ultimately employment may be greater than originally. If the indirect effect is dominant, the sequel is one of further contraction.

This conclusion needs some caveats and comments, three of which must be mentioned here. One of these cautions is that a sudden *decrease* of the steady rate of labor-augmenting progress will *not* necessarily generate an immediate increase of q, and thus a transient boom in employment, *if* it is known that the public debt will commence to increase in order to finance for a while the same path of government transfers and expenditures as were programmed under the previous fast-progress milieu. Further, the government may intervene with fiscal stimuli to raise the real prices of assets.[12] Finally, the implications of the model regarding the rate of technical progress are not very robust to large changes in the parameter representing the consumption-elasticity of the marginal utility of current-period consumption, which, following standard developments, is taken to be equal to minus one in the models here.

SHOCKS TO THE STRUCTURE OF TAXATION AND ENTITLEMENTS

There is rather little explicit analysis of shifts in these parameters in the foregoing chapters, but that is only because, with some reflection, the answers are quite obvious. That does not mean that in every case they are the conventional answers, however. Indeed, the implications of the three models for the question of tax structure are among the most exciting products these models offer.

Value-added and expenditure taxes vs. wage taxes.   It is clear that an across-the-board increase of tax rates on consumer expenditure or the production of consumer goods, since it leaves intact the marginal physical productivity of labor in the schedule sense, would leave unchanged the demand price for labor in terms of money if the nominal price to consumers rose to cover the tax.[13] It is also clear that, under such a price increase, the money wage necessary for labor-market equilibrium at a given unemployment rate would also be unchanged, since the equilibrium incentive wage (in terms of money) is indexed simply by average nonwage income (in terms of money) and the latter is not increased by the upward push of prices, which merely covers the tax. If the tax revenue raised by our closed economy—the world economy—is used to fend off some threat of disease or other threat, the shock resembles an adverse technological shock: Abstracting from capital, the world will carry on with reduced real wage rates and real unearned incomes—that is, the purchasing power of wage rates and nonwage income over the consumer good after payment of the tax are reduced—yet with unchanged employment. (Some qualification is needed if there is some public debt outstanding that is indexed to the price level.)[14] The fact that taxes were proportional, hence graduated, not lump sum, does not matter; consumer taxes are equally neutral for employment. Upon bringing capital into the analysis, we encounter the issues raised by the prospect of downward adjustment of the capital stock in response to the unfavorable shock. If instead we imagine the revenue to be used to finance lump-sum transfer payments to the citizenry in such a way as to compensate each individual for the additional tax burden suffered, the net effect is totally neutral. For practical purposes, therefore, one may think of expenditure taxes as essentially neutral per se, while any resource-absorbing public expenditure that they are used to finance may itself have some nonneutral effect through effects on investment in employees and in physical capital.

How different are the dreaded taxes on payrolls! Taxes on income that exclude unearned income are essentially the same case. Such taxation represents an important change in the structure of the economy. Here, if firms think to raise money prices so that the after-tax money marginal product of labor remains undiminished, nonwage income in terms of money will thereby be increased, since not all business proceeds were factor payments to labor; some were paid to the shareowners. Hence the equilibrium incentive wage corresponding to the initial unemployment rate will be pushed up. The end result is a decline of employment, a rise in the product wage to firms, and a decline in the real wage to households. To put all this in other terms: Although firms can afford to pay labor the same wage deflated by factor cost as before, the demand wage in terms of consumer goods inclusive of tax is reduced; since nonwage income in real terms is not reduced in the same proportion, the supply-side wage—the equilibrium incentive wage—does not fall in proportion to the demand wage; hence the employment rate must fall as a consequence.

The structure of entitlements clearly has enormous potential for distortionary effects, favorable or unfavorable, as well. The bearing of the theory here for the incidence of unemployment compensation demands a discussion even though it is not introduced formally in our three models exactly as they appear in the present volume.[15]

Entitlements. What of the argument that the availability of unemployment compensation encourages shirking, thus driving up the incentive wage, reducing the amount of labor firms can afford to hire, and hence raising the equilibrium path of the unemployment rate? It is quite clear that if workers knew that upon dismissal from their jobs they would be supported by the government at the same level offered by their wages, no amount of unemployment and elevation of industry wages would make any dent on the propensity to shirk, and the equilibrium unemployment rate would be enormous (if such an equilibrium existed at all). However, a premise of the argument that is often left inexplicit requires that the employee caught shirking and dismissed is nonetheless deemed eligible for the unemployment compensation. Overt cases of dereliction of duty are certainly disqualifying in many parts of the world. Yet there is a possible counter to this objection. If a worker knows that being often observed not working may mean an increased likelihood of being chosen for layoff in the event that some labor shedding is required by slower promotion, this prospect of layoff will exert a stronger disciplinary force on the worker the lower or more short-lived the rate of unemployment compensation.[16]

It may also be argued that unemployment compensation encourages quitting. Of course, eligibility of employees for unemployment compensation upon voluntarily deciding to quit must also be a rarity in the empirical world. It could be argued, however, that an employee wishing to quit can behave in ways that make him a candidate for involuntary layoff, so that an increased probability of job separation with full unemployment compensation is the result. Knowing that all employees will jockey for selection among the layoffs, the employer will respond with increased wages as an incentive. Then unemployment compensation works against the firms' attempts to combat quitting, and the equilibrium incentive wage is thereby pushed up.

It may well be that these influences on equilibrium unemployment are dwarfed by the aggregate budget of the welfare system. The larger the payments of nonwage income to those not in the labor force, the stronger are the incentives of a person to opt for a length of time outside the labor force, with the support of the welfare system under various contingencies, as an alternative to holding onto a job. Thus both the propensity to quit and to shirk may be aggravated by the operation of the welfare system.

This observation goes beyond the analysis offered in the foregoing chapters, however.

Throughout this section on taxation and entitlements, it will be seen, the crucial indicator is the effect of the shock on nonwage income, in the present or with some probability in the future, taken as a ratio to wage income per employed worker.

SHOCKS TO EXPENDITURES

In this book the theory of equilibrium unemployment determination developed here has been termed *structuralist* in several standard meanings of the term. Of course, as the theory abstracts from the transient and thus "cyclical" influences of incorrect expectations, the path of unemployment isolated by the model gives the volume of equilibrium unemployment—but that is somewhat short of genuinely structural unemployment.[17] Closer to the mark is the point that the theory sees unemployment as, at bottom, a by-product of the "structure" of the labor market and the employment relationship between firm and worker, particularly informational or organizational imperfections there. There are, furthermore, two other ways in which the theory is structuralist: Being nonmonetary in its essentials, it treats unemployment as the outcome of the configuration of *real* demands and supplies—the "structure" of the economy in some sense—rather than the supply of money in relation to the sticky price or nominal wage level, which we do not generally think of as a part of the structure (at least not the deep structure) of an economy. Finally, in this theory the "structure," or composition, of demands for goods in relation to supplies makes a difference for employment: *Where* an increase of demand is directed—and, for that matter, an increase of supply—can be crucial even to the *sign* of its employment effect. In contrast, the monetary models aggregate demands, and real business cycle theory too has been steadfastly aggregative.

The expenditure shocks considered in the previous three chapters were shocks to consumer demand, the result of an increase of time preference or an increase of the public debt, and shocks to the various types of public expenditures.[18]

Time preference.   Determining the effect of an increase in the rate of pure time preference is an exercise falling into a rather special category since no direct way of observing that parameter exists. It is of pedagogical value, however, and it cannot be devoid of substantive interest since there are sometimes periods in which there is circumstantial evidence of increased or decreased time preference or else something akin to it, such as the sense that certain risks have arisen.

An increase in the time-preference parameter has the obvious impact of increasing consumption demand. The immediate consequence of that can be described as an upward shift in the path of the rate of interest required to match the path of consumer demand to the pre-shock path of consumer-good supply. Equivalently, the immediate effect is an excess demand for the consumer good, as consumers try to switch from future to present consumption. Viewed either way, the result in a *closed* economy is a drop of the price of the real asset—trained employees, customers, or capital goods. (Note that this result does not require excluding "Ricardian equivalence.") Aggregate employment falls and the real wage is driven down in the same process. This finding on employment is reinforced by the impact through another channel that was not modeled: The increased time preference means that households will discount more heavily the subsequent stream of current utility that would be lost in the event they quit or are caught shirking. This will have the effect of driving up the supply wage, the incentive wage that employers must choose to minimize unit cost. The effect of that increase in costs is a further reduction of employment, this effect being accompanied by a rise of the wage.

Public debt.   The creation of a public debt through a brief period of tax cuts, say, was repeatedly found to be contractionary in the closed economy. A figurative helicopter drop of additional government bills or postal-savings deposits has the impact of stimulating private consumption demand. Of course, that would not have been the case under the assumption set called Ricardian, which would not render debt capable of any wealth effects. This wealth effect on consumer demand creates an excess demand in the market for the consumer good, hence an excess supply in the capital market. Equilibration requires a drop of the real asset price, which in turn has the side effect of inducing an actual contraction of the supply of some or all kinds of output, hence a contraction in the derived demand for labor, at a given real wage. An immediate increase of the real interest rate and an upward shift of the entire yield curve is also implied. In this respect, obviously, the theory runs directly counter to the spirit of Keynesian theory. In that theory, the increase of consumption demand serves to drive up the money interest rate as a by-product of its crowding out some private investment expenditure, and the rise in the money interest rate releases holdings of cash balances, speeding the velocity of money and thus driving employment to a higher level.

Various public expenditures.   In the first two models, public expenditures were also contractionary through this anti-Keynesian mechanism, thanks again to the non-Ricardian aspects of the setting. In the model based on investment in physical capital, though, new modeling vistas opened up. It became necessary to distinguish public expenditure on output produced by the capital-good-producing sector from expenditures on output from the consumer-good-producing sector. A real-life example of the latter would be the hiring of hotel rooms or passenger cars in the conduct of government business, such as national defense, disease control, or any other public good.[19]

In the two-sector physical-capital model it is still the case that a steady expenditure by the government on output produced by the *consumer-good sector* has a contractionary effect through the asset price/real interest mechanism. On the other hand, the implied tax burden on wealth owners could operate through the wealth mechanism driving the supply wage to reduce the propensity to shirk, thus to expand employment. But if taxation falls predominantly on wage income, the wealth mechanism acting on the propensity to shirk gives way to a substitution effect operating to increase shirking and thus to contract employment; then the contractionary effect of the asset mechanism is reinforced.

As a qualification, it should be mentioned that increased government spending arising from entitlement programs presumably fail to be contractionary through the interest rate–asset price mechanism. The reason is that the receipt of such benefits by a household ends with its death, just as the taxes do; the entitlement is not transferable and hence salable to the next generation, unlike public debt. Hence there is no presumption that entitlement spending creates an excess demand for the output of the consumer-good sector. The contractionary effect of the entitlement spending through the increased tax rates on labor income are the same as in the previous case, though.

It was discovered, however, that a permanent public expenditure taking the form of purchase of output produced by the *capital-good sector* sets in motion the asset-price mechanism in reverse, and is consequently expansionary on this count. The excess demand for the output in that sector requires an *increase* of the real asset price, in this model the relative price of the capital good. The side effect of that rise in the real price of the capital good is an *increase* in the derived demand for labor, an increase originating in the capital-good sector, where there is an inducement to supply more output at a given real wage. It is true, however, that under a wage-based tax system there would be a countervailing effect in the direction of contraction from the higher tax rates on wages.

Public expenditure taking the form of public employment for the purpose of government production also has an expansionary effect through its positive impact on the derived demand for labor, which operates to pull up the wage and the employment rate. That relative-price mechanism is in essence the one familiar to foreign-trade and general-equilibrium theory specialists—the government has added to the demand for the relatively labor-intensive good—though it is transplanted here to an intertemporal setting of some complexity. Again there is the qualification that the higher tax rates on labor income will operate to produce a contractionary employment effect on that count. Undoubtedly there is a certain nonlinearity here, for when tax rates are already high the necessary increase of rates needed to finance a small additional amount of public employment will be quite large and hence possibly decisive for the net effect on employment.[20]

REFLECTIONS ON THE COUNTER- AND PRO-KEYNESIAN CONCLUSIONS

It is evident that several of the more important predictions of the structuralist theory developed here, particularly with regard to the employment effects of various shocks, are in direct opposition to the doctrine drawn from Keynesian theory, if by that theory we mean for present purposes the Keynes-Hicks IS-LM framework joined to a price/wage-supply block that constrains unemployment sooner or later to gravitate toward an essentially *constant* natural rate of unemployment in the long run. Both the near-term and the far-term effects of shocks may be compared.

Keynesians regard demand shocks as neutral in the long run, supply shocks as nonneutral for output in the long run. But all shocks are neutral for the unemployment rate in the long run. In contrast, the structuralist models here portray few shocks as neutral. Two central exceptions are the labor-augmentation factor and the size of the population, its demographic distribution unchanged. A shock to the initial stock of capital is also neutral for the long run, of course, but that is because the shock dissipates as the excess or deficiency of the capital stock is worked off. In the structuralist theory here, the supply factors presumed to be of major secular importance, population increases and Harrod-neutral progress, are ultimately neutral, while all other shocks, including demand shifts, are nonneutral for the unemployment rate—a marked departure from Keynesian doctrine.

As for the short run, the structuralist position runs counter to the Keynesian position in some important areas. The contrast is clearly drawn on the functioning of the propensity to consume, the public debt, kinds of public expenditure impacting on the demand for the output of the consumer-goods industries. Keynesian doctrine sees these as operating through a mechanism producing an expansionary effect in the closed economy. (In the small open economy, this expansionary effect is largely or wholly "exported.") The structuralist models here find these forces all to operate through a mechanism exerting a contractionary influence. (In a small open economy this contractionary effect is similarly exported, and a competitiveness mechanism may operate that delivers an expansionary effect.) Central to this contrast is the operation of the real-interest mechanism in the structuralist theory, in place of the money-interest-rate mechanism in Keynesian theory. In both theories, "the interest rate" is driven up. But in the latter theory it is the nominal rate that increases, which creates an excess supply of money, thus increases the velocity of money and hence thrusts the economy up the sloping LM curve of the Keynes-Hicks model to a higher level of employment. In the structuralist theory, it is the real rate being driven up, which drives down the real demand wage. (In the open economy, the real interest rate is given by the world rate, so these interest-rate effects on employment are exported.) Of course, the tax-rate impact of the increased debt service or the increased public spending can be expected to exert a separate contractionary effect.

If the structuralist models went only this far, their relation to Keynesian doctrine would be reminiscent of the contest between Keynes and Hayek around 1930: Keynes advocating increased public spending, having in mind public-works programs, Hayek opposing public spending, having in mind government programs that reduce the supply of saving. In the structuralist theory developed here, we found that increased public expenditure in the capital-good sector, for aircraft and other equipment or for structures, and public hiring of workers would exert expansionary effects, as in Keynesian doctrine.[21] (Ironically, Hayek could have been attacked on his own grounds with the argument that fiscal stimuli, if properly structured, would succeed in increasing aggregate employment by lowering the rate of interest.)

In its conclusions, then, the structuralist theory developed here does not stand 180 degrees to Keynes. It runs *counter* to Keynesian doctrine and sides with Hayek in some of its central theses—particularly those regarding the demand for consumer goods (nondurables, to be precise) and the effect of the rate of interest on the supply of output—while it *concurs* with Keynes and seemingly contradicts Hayek at other important points—on public employment and capital-goods purchases. As shown in the following appendix, some dissident elaborations of structuralist theory manage to reach much more widely pro-Keynesian conclusions.

Still it could be said, however little value it would have to say it, that
in one respect the structuralist theory *builds on* Hayek by bringing out
the essentially nonmonetary nature of his argument, which he regularly
obscured, and making good the failure to draw the necessary distinctions
among types of spending (there are ways in which the theory bears the
influence of Keynes too, of course). The debt to Hayek is perhaps ominous.
Hayek lost the debate, it will be remembered. So it would seem that to
build a theory that parallels Hayek at any point is to flirt with disaster. It
is possible, however, that victory in the debate was handed to Keynes for
a mistaken reason. By the time of the second world war, the Keynesians
were able to point to the improved performance of those countries, such
as Germany and Italy, that engaged in big public-spending programs, to
the doleful experience of those that did not, and to the pickup of employment in the countries that went to war, as evidence of the correctness of
the Keynesian analysis. But this was not evidence from an experiment with
consumption stimulus, the quintessential Keynesian experiment. It was evidence on the effects of increasing public-sector demand for capital goods
and labor. This particular evidence, at any rate, had no power to reject
Hayek over Keynes.

Of course, times were very different then. Expectations of inflation
were relatively low; market agents had little prior experience with large
fluctuations in money wage and price levels; and investment was typically
so low during the Depression that there would have been little of it to
crowd out had the Keynesian experiment of consumption stimulus been
tried. Hayek may very well have had a smaller *share* of the truth then
than did Keynes. In any case, the experience of the Depression needs to
be restudied with alternative interpretations, structuralist theory being a
strong candidate.

But is it not apparent that consumer confidence is a factor driving employment? The experience of the early 1990s should be enough to convince
us of that. Whatever the forces behind the recent data, it is crucial to recognize that increased demand for consumer durables is very much like business demand for producer durables: it raises the real price of the durables
and thus lowers interest rates, quite unlike the effect of an increase in consumer demand for nondurables.[22]

Thus some exciting questions have arisen that, after the many decades
since the *General Theory*, can be investigated without the overzealousness
of the early years. It seems that the empirical status of Keynesian theory
is now due for a major reassessment. No one should be very sure how that
assessment will finally turn out.

Appendix: Other Structuralist Models

Before concluding that a large part of structuralist theory is inherently counter-Keynesian over an important area, we must recognize that along-side the models here there coexist some other models having an equal claim to the structuralist mantle that deliver some quite different conclusions.

The user-cost mechanism.   An old but usually neglected channel running from the product market to employment brings into operation the factor called *user cost*. There are seventeen references to it in Keynes's *General Theory*. User cost in his sense, as here, is not a cost to users but the cost of use. It is the value of the productive power of the plant and equipment that is lost in the process of using that capital in the production of the current output.[23]

Keynes, after complaining that Marshall and Pigou had acknowledged the phenomenon but had not seen the applicability of it, went on to promote it as "one of the links between the present and the future," alongside what he called the "marginal efficiency of capital."[24]

> In the case of raw materials the necessity of allowing for user cost is obvi-ous—if a ton of copper is used up today it cannot be used tomorrow, and the value which the copper would have for the purposes of tomorrow must clearly be reckoned as a part of marginal cost. But the fact has been over-looked that copper is only an extreme case of what occurs whenever capital equipment is used to produce . . . The use of capital brings nearer the date at which replacement is necessary.[25]

Yet one does not readily find in Keynes's musings on user cost any sugges-tion of how it might figure in the way that this or that shock disturbs output and employment.

An important role for user cost in output and employment determina-tion was developed as long ago as 1970, in a paper by Taubman and Wil-kinson.[26] The proposition there, translated to the present nonmonetary context, is that an unforseen demand shock producing a jump in the rela-tive price of some output and the expectation of a gradual return, if cou-pled with a fixed instantaneous real rate of interest (or one expected to fall at most less quickly than the rate of decline of the price), so that the product rate of interest is unambiguously increased at all terms, short and long, makes optimal an immediate increase in the utilization of the existing capital stock—a sort of speeding up of the machinery at the sacrifice of some future capital services—in order to supply increased output. "When prices rise but are expected to fall, it becomes possible to 'borrow' output from the future and sell it at the higher price" (p. 417). By the same logic, and referring now to the case of relative prices that are not (and perhaps never can be) disturbed, an upward shift of the real yield curve would make it possible to "borrow" output from the future at a reduced discounted cost and sell it at the unchanged price. In both cases, the effect is to *raise* the derived demand for labor, since the increased flow of capital services will make profitable an accompanying increase in the flow of labor services.

Moving to general equilibrium, it is clear that a consumption-demand shock—an increase of time preference, of the public debt, or of public expenditure in the consumer-good-producing sector—in driving up the real rate of interest would have an *expansionary* effect on the demand wage through the *user-cost* channel; the end effect in the sort of models employed here is certainly an increase in the employment rate. In later work that focuses instead on a technical advance requiring for its implementation the construction of new capital goods, a purely neoclassical model is studied in which the effect is likewise to *raise* the derived demand for labor and induce an intratemporal substitution of consumption for leisure[27]—hence "an expansionary effect of investment shocks on employment."[28]

Certainly these findings inject a complication into the situation. Stimuli to the demand for consumer goods, particularly nondurables, are contractionary in some structuralist models, expansionary in others. But it would be a mistake to conclude that the user-cost models reestablish the Keynesian effects of expenditure shocks. For if the increase of real interest rates brought by expenditure shocks that actually raise rates of interest operates to expand employment, then by the same logic the decrease of rates brought by expenditure shocks that in fact reduce rates of interest—our capital-good and public-employment expenditures—operates to contract employment. Would-be rescuers of the Keynesian theses cannot have it both ways.

How important should we expect the user-cost channel to be? The paucity and obscurity of the literature on the user-cost channel should not tempt us into portraying it as having earlier failed a plausibility test administered by the watchful profession whenever a new idea comes along. But note that the user-cost mechanism leads to an implication that is sharply at odds with conventional impressions. It implies that the consumer or investment expenditure shock, in driving up the real rate of interest, drives *up* the real wage. What has made this theoretically possible is the "borrowing" of output from the future in response to the inducements of the present. This interesting aspect of the user-cost mechanism ought to be made one of the objects for scrutiny in the last part of this monograph, which weighs the empirical evidence for and against the structuralist models developed here.

Mineral costs.   It is an obvious corollary of user-cost theory that an increase of the real rate of interest decreases the supply price at which owners of minerals will be willing to extract deposits for sale to enterprises requiring minerals in their production processes. The marginal cost of production is the sum of the factor cost outlays and the discounted value of the opportunity to sell in the future instead of in the present.

A general-equilibrium model containing a mineral-extraction sector instead of a capital-good-producing sector will certainly have the property that an expenditure shock driving up the real interest rate drives down the price of the mineral, thus decreasing marginal costs in the consumer-good sector and expanding employment there, while it contracts employment in the mineral-producing sector. In a closed economy, if wages occupy a larger share of revenues in the mineral-producing sector than in the other, the effect on aggregate employment will be contractionary; that would accord with the thesis resting on the three models studied in this volume. However, the opposite conclusion would follow if the comparative factor intensities were reversed. In an open economy dependent on imported minerals, however, a rise of the external rate of interest would exert an expansionary influence on employment through its effect in reducing the cost of the imported mineral.

Assessing the importance of this channel is, again, an empirical question. Here too it should be noticed that the dissenting structuralist argument for expecting an expansionary outcome implies as a corollary that the real wage is increased—pulled up by the same rise in the derived demand for labor that drives up the employment rate. So the implication is that the higher real interest rate is accompanied by an increase of the real wage, not a decrease.

Cartel markups.   A recent paper by Rotemberg and Woodford[29] injects the Rotemberg-Saloner theory of cartel markups into a macroeconomic model in order to restudy the consequences of certain expenditure shocks and technological shocks. In this theory, a rise of the real interest rate, let us say a transient one in keeping with their methodology, heightens the temptation of the members of the cartel to cheat or otherwise violate the cartel's price agreement, implicit or explicit. The reason is that the benefits of staying in the cartel are largely in the future, which now must be discounted more heavily. This effect in turn induces the members of the cartel to *moderate* their markup in order to block that temptation and thus hold the cartel together.

In the authors' general-equilibrium setting of a closed economy, the impact of a transient addition to expenditure, for example, a temporary military expenditure on "output," is a jump of the rate of interest (which is mirrored by a drop in the market value of the cartel resulting from the jeopardy that the shock has placed it in). The consequent drop in the markup has the side effect of *raising* the derived demand for labor and thus pulling up the employment rate. The employment story appears to be 180 degrees to that told by the consumer-market model of markups. In the natural extension to the small open economy, the interest rate would be incapable of being driven up, the shadow price of staying in the cartel incapable of being pushed down; there might be an expansionary effect through the real exchange rate, just as in the customer-market story of the small open economy.

Once again, the importance of this model relative to the customer-market model is an empirical question. And as before, there is the interesting implication that the cartel model predicts the wage to be pulled up by an increase of the real rate of interest arising from an expenditure shock, while the customer-market model (and the other two models developed here) has the real wage being pushed down.

It should not really surprise us that there is more heterogeneity in the implications of structuralist models than is pleasing or convenient. The truth is that the other schools of thought also have their anomalous cases, their exceptions. There tends to develop a tacit agreement by writers and readers to put those exceptions to one side in the interest of simplicity, in order to get on with the business of development and evaluation, which all sides want.[30] The policy here will be the same. For this volume, the "structuralist doctrine" will be conceived as the conclusions emerging from the three structuralist models advanced and analyzed in this volume—not others' structuralist models. In the end, of course, the data will play an important role in deciding what the structuralist doctrine is most usefully held to be.

III

SMALL AND LARGE OPEN ECONOMIES: WORKING MODELS

11

International Linkages through Investment in Employees

THE three chapters constituting the main body of Part III set out models of the small open economy and the two-country world corresponding to the three sorts of assets introduced in Part II—the trained employee, the customer, and fixed capital. Again there is a concluding chapter that pulls together the findings. The difference between these models is that the small open economy, in the traditional terminology, has only a negligible effect on the world real rate of interest; it can take the external interest rate as given. The second category of models examine the interactions between two countries, neither one small.

A number of questions arise about the small open economy. How would such an economy, if it resembled any of those we have been studying, be affected by external shocks—to the world real interest rate, to world real incomes, and so forth. How would the effect of internal shocks be modified by the openness to the rest of the world? Of course, an external shock occurring uniformly in a homogeneous "rest of the world" will have the same effects there as it would if that region were closed, provided the small country is negligible for the larger region in all respects. The effects on the home countries of shocks, external and internal, bear studying, however.

The two-country models contribute analysis of the *intermediate* case in which the region experiencing, say, a private or public shock to demand in the consumer-good-producing sector is neither so gigantic that the domestic effects are analyzable as if it were closed nor so small that its effect abroad is negligible. We want to show that the interest-raising expenditure shocks in one country can be big enough to have an appreciable contractionary effect in the other country (as seen to be the case when the former country is gigantic) while at the same time the country where the shock originates can be small enough that the employment effect it experiences is expansionary (as seen to be the case when this country is small). To this end our attention will be confined to the case in which the two countries are of more or less equal size.

The two-country models serve another function. It is ultimately important to have the full set of equations representing the rest of the world in place of the one or two parameters found in small-open-economy analyses. The reason is that disturbances to the external rate of interest or to income abroad may reflect an underlying parameter shift having an impact on two or more variables simultaneously. Owing to the complexity of these models, little should be expected in the way of explicit and rigorous analysis. The material here is merely a first look, the few results being easy targets of opportunity.

This chapter will take up the two models of the open economy, small and large, that are based on the investment-in-employees model introduced in Chapter 7. The incentive problem that this model places at center stage, the problem of employee turnover, can be considered an important consideration in understanding natural-rate determination. In large countries without obstacles to intranational migration, especially, the turnover problem is an essential factor in determining equilibrium unemployment.

The usefulness of the model in that respect, however, does not make the model very helpful in understanding all episodes of increased or decreased equilibrium unemployment experienced in the global economy.[1] The purpose of this modest chapter is as much to set down the ways in which the model fails to be rich enough to rely on in studying two-country interactions as it is to see that the model does indeed shed some light on some questions.

11.1 A Small-Open-Economy Model of Investment in Employees

The equations that describe the small open economy which treats the world rate of interest $\{r_t\}_{t=[0,\infty]}$ as given in the world capital market can be summarized by equations (7.9) and (7.11)–(7.13), where per-capita non-human wealth (in the absence of a government) is now augmented to include the holding of foreign assets:

$$W = qE + F$$

where F is the per-capita holding of foreign assets and where, for simplicity, we assume that domestic firms are owned entirely by domestic residents.[2] Nonwage income, y^w, must now also be augmented to $E[\Lambda - v]$ $+ rF$. The change in foreign assets is given by

$$\frac{dF}{dt} = rF + \Lambda E - ET(h; \Lambda) - C$$

With two state variables, E and F, the treatment of the dynamic behavior of the small open economy is difficult. We simplify the analysis by assuming that parameters are such that the economy is initially neither a net creditor nor debtor with respect to the rest of the world. In steady state, $\dot{q} = \dot{E} = \dot{F} = 0$. We have the relationships[3]

$$\frac{dq}{dE} = \frac{\hat{\zeta}_1 + \hat{\zeta}_2 \partial(y^w/v)/\partial E + \hat{\zeta}_2[\partial(y^w/v)/\partial v]v_E}{q[\Phi' - v_q(\partial(y^w/v)/\partial v)\hat{\zeta}_2]}$$

along the locus where $\dot{E} = 0$, and along the locus where $\dot{q} = 0$ we have

$$\frac{dq}{dE} = \frac{-\{q[\hat{\zeta}_1 + (\partial(y^w/v)/\partial E)\hat{\zeta}_2] + v_E[1 + q(\partial(y^w/v)/\partial v)\hat{\zeta}_2]\}}{r + v_q[1 + q(\partial(y^w/v)/\partial v)\hat{\zeta}_2]}$$

The $\dot{E} = 0$ schedule is presumably positively sloped, as in Chapter 7, while the $\dot{q} = 0$ schedule may have either a negative or positive slope. A sufficient condition for saddle-path stability is that $-q\hat{\zeta}_2\partial(y^w/v)/\partial v < 1$. The condition amounts to requiring that the wealth effect on quitting be not too large. Then the phase diagram describing the small open economy has qualitatively the same features as Figure 7.1.

As an exercise, let us examine the impact of an unanticipated permanent increase in the world real interest rate when the economy is initially at rest. Equation (7.11) implies that the $\dot{q} = 0$ locus shifts downward. There is an immediate decline in the shadow price of a trained worker, q, it being a forward-looking variable. Consequently, there is an immediate drop in the number of new hires at each firm, which leads to increasing unemployment. With the decline in firms' investment in new workers and the decline in consumption demand resulting from the decline in asset prices, the economy runs a current-account surplus.

As another exercise, suppose that the small open economy experiences a permanent productivity shock. Equations (7.11) and (7.12) imply that the $\dot{q} = 0$ and $\dot{E} = 0$ curves shift up equally since F is initially nil. Hence q jumps in equal proportion to Λ. The consequences are unchanged hiring and net foreign investments, hence constancy of E and F at their initial (old rest-point) levels.

A temporary positive productivity shock shifts up the $\dot{q} = 0$ and $\dot{E} = 0$ schedules temporarily. However, q does not rise by as much as Λ rises, so that investment in new workers declines. Since the productivity improvement is expected to last only temporarily, the level of consumption does not rise by much. The result is that the economy experiences a current-account surplus during the period of unusually high productivity.

11.2 A Two-Country Model of Investment in Employees

Each of the intermediate-size countries in the two-country world here[4] are described by the equations for the small open economy in section 11.1 with the key differences that the rate of interest is now a variable, not a parameter, and that the net creditor-debtor position and current-account balance of one country must be counterbalanced by an equal and opposite state of affairs in the other.

Two restrictions are placed on the model. First, the two countries exhibit initially identical tastes and technologies. Accordingly, the countries are initially not in a net debtor or net creditor position. Second, the two countries are initially of equal size in every respect.

A highly useful simplification is also introduced. In the full statement of the model, there is for each country a relation between the quit rate and the employment rate that is indexed by the shadow price of employees and the net claims accumulated against the other country, and there is a relation between the hiring rate and the shadow price (given productivity), which together imply that a jump of q disturbs the excess of hiring over quitting and thus generates a *gradual* adjustment of the employment rate. Here the analysis leaps ahead to a *medium run* in which this adjustment is taken to be virtually complete and the movement of the employment rate is only that due to the current movement of the slow-moving state variable in the system—the claims by the nationals of one country against those of the other. In this medium-run analysis the employment rate is treated as if it were a jump variable as much as the wage rate.

The two countries are denoted A and B. Having in mind the Fitoussi-Phelps thesis on the 1980s slump in Europe and elsewhere, according to which an upward disturbance to the world interest rate originated in expenditure shocks in America, we will think of country A as America and country B as an amalgam of Britain, the European Continent, and the former British commonwealth.[5]

The above simplification of the "medium run" yields the static employment rate equations,

(11.1a) $0 = \Phi(q_A/\Lambda_A) - \zeta(1, 1 - u_A, y_A^w/v_A; \Lambda_A)$

(11.1b) $0 = \Phi(q_B/\Lambda_B) - \zeta(1, 1 - u_B, y_B^w/v_B; \Lambda_B)$

Here, as before, y^w in each of the countries is implicitly determined by[6]

(11.2a) $y_A^w/\Lambda_A = [1 - (v_A/\Lambda_A)](1 - u_A) + r(D_A - F_B)/\Lambda_A$

(11.2b) $y_B^w/\Lambda_B = [1 - (v_B/\Lambda_B)](1 - u_B) + r(D_B + F_B)/\Lambda_B$

with

(11.3) $F_A = -F_B$

Of course the net foreign claim of country B, F_B, though initially equal to zero, will gradually turn positive or negative following any asymmetric kind of shock.[7]

Upon substituting the y^w definition into the above employment rate equation for each country, we obtain for each country a sort of employment demand function: this employment-rate function makes $1 - u$ increasing in q, through its impact on the hiring rate, while it is decreasing in the country's F and increasing in its v, through their consequences for y^w/v, which impacts on the quit rate. Equivalently, these latter equations define demand-wage relations,

(11.4a) $v_A^d = V^d(1 - u; q_A, \Lambda_A, D_A - F_B)$

(11.4b) $v_B^d = V^d(1 - u; q_B, \Lambda_B, D_B + F_B)$

which are homogeneous of degree one in the three quantities after the semicolon: the shadow price of employees, national productivity, and national wealth.

The incentive-wage condition for cost minimization,

(11.5a) $q_A[\zeta_1(1 - u_A) + \zeta_2(y_A^w/v_A)] = v_A$

(11.5b) $q_B[\zeta_1(1 - u_B) + \zeta_2(y_B^w/v_B)] = v_B$

delivers supply-wage functions making a country's v^s increasing in its q, $1 - u$, and its F:

$$(11.6a) \quad v_A^s = V^s(1 - u_A; q_A, \Lambda_A, D_A - F_B)$$

$$(11.6b) \quad v_B^s = V^s(1 - u_B; q_B, \Lambda_B, D_B - F_B)$$

As before, the supply wage, like the demand wage, is homogeneous of degree one in the arguments after the semicolon.

Equating the demand wage in (11.4) to the supply wage in (11.6) in each country yields reduced-form relationships making $1 - u$ and v functions of q, Λ, and F. The employment equations may be written as follows:

(11.7a)
$$0 = \Phi(q_A/\Lambda_A)$$
$$- \zeta\left(1, 1 - u_A, \frac{\{\Lambda_A[1 - V^s(1 - u_A; q_A, \Lambda_A, D_A - F_B)](1 - u_A) + r(D_A + F_A)\}}{V^s(1 - u_A; q_A, \Lambda_A, D_A - F_B)}\right)$$

(11.7b)
$$0 = \Phi(q_B/\Lambda_B)$$
$$- \zeta\left(1, 1 - u_B, \frac{\{\Lambda_B[1 - V^s(1 - u_B; q_B, \Lambda_B, D_B + F_B)](1 - u_B) + r(D_B + F_B)\}}{V^s(1 - u_B; q_B, \Lambda_B, D_B + F_B)}\right)$$

Denote the solutions for the employment rates by the functions $n(q_A, \Lambda_A, D_A - F_B)$ and $n(q_B, \Lambda_B, D_B + F_B)$, respectively, where the influence of r is negligible, since the case under study exhibits approximately zero levels of public debt and foreign claims in both countries. That is,

$$(11.7a') \quad 1 - u_A = n(q_A, \Lambda_A, D_A - F_B)$$

$$(11.7b') \quad 1 - u_B = n(q_B, \Lambda_B, D_B + F_B)$$

In these terms the reduced-form wage equations may be written as:

$$(11.8a) \quad q_A[\zeta_1 n(q_A, \Lambda_A, D_A - F_B) + \zeta_2(y_A^w/v_A)] = v_A$$

$$(11.8b) \quad q_B[\zeta_1 n(q_B, \Lambda_B, D_B + F_B) + \zeta_2(y_B^w/v_B)] = v_B$$

where the y^w/v ratios involve only Λ/v and the ratio $(D + F)/v$.[8] These reduced form wage functions will be denoted $v_A(q_A, \Lambda_A, D_A - F_B)$ and $v_B(q_B, \Lambda_B, D_B + F_B)$.

What are the properties of these reduced-form solutions for $1 - u$ and v? Since both the demand wage in (11.4) and the supply wage in (11.6) in each country are homogeneous of degree one in that country's q, Λ, and $D + F$, and we are taking the latter quantity to be close or equal to zero, it is immediately clear that v is homogeneous of degree one in q and Λ in each country. Hence $1 - u$ is homogeneous of degree zero in q and Λ in each country. What remains to be studied is the effects of q and Λ when taken alone. It follows that we may regard each country's $1 - u$ and v as functions of its normalized variables, q/Λ and $(D + F)/\Lambda$, and the world real rate of interest.

How do each country's q/Λ and $(D + F)/\Lambda$ influence its $1 - u$ and v? In the present exposition we merely take it for granted that the demand-wage curve is steeper than the (upward-sloping) supply-wage curve in the quasi-Marshallian $(1 - u, v)$ plane. It then follows that an increase of q/Λ, in pulling to the right the demand-wage (or employment-demand) curve while pushing up and thus to the left the supply-wage curve, causes an increase of $1 - u$ along with an increase of v/Λ. Hence, an increase of Λ *alone* produces a decrease of $1 - u$ and a decrease of v as well. Similarly, an increase of D, in pulling leftward the employment-demand curve and pushing upward the supply-wage curve, decreases both $1 - u$ and v.

The other structural equations of the model are not altered. Upon substituting the above results for the wage and the employment rate, the differential equations for q/Λ become

(11.9a) $d(q_A/\Lambda_A)/dt$

$$= (q_A/\Lambda_A)[r + \zeta(1, n(q_A/\Lambda_A, 1, (D_A - F_B)/\Lambda_A), y_A^w/v_A; \Lambda_A)]$$

$$- [1 - v_A(q_A/\Lambda_A, 1, (D_A - F_B)/\Lambda_A) - \tau(\Phi(q_A/\Lambda_A)) + \Phi\tau'(\Phi)]$$

(11.9b) $d(q_B/\Lambda_B)/dt$

$$= (q_B/\Lambda_B)[r + \zeta(1, n(q_B/\Lambda_B, 1, (D_B + F_B)/\Lambda_B), y_B^w/v_B; \Lambda_B)]$$

$$- [1 - v_B(q_B/\Lambda_B, 1, (D_B + F_B)/\Lambda_B) - \tau(\Phi(q_B/\Lambda_B)) + \Phi\tau'(\Phi)]$$

The differential equations for foreign assets are

(11.10a) $dF_A/dt = rF_A + \Lambda_A n(q_A, \Lambda_A, D_A - F_B)[1 - \tau(\Phi(q_A/\Lambda_A))]L_A - C_A$

(11.10b) $dF_B/dt = rF_B + \Lambda_B n(q_B, \Lambda_B, D_B + F_B)[1 - \tau(\Phi(q_B/\Lambda_B))]L_B - C_B$

Global consumption supply is the sum of the national supplies, obtained by summing C_A and C_B in the two equations in (11.10) and using the relation $F_A = -F_B$. Hence global consumption supply satisfies

$$(11.11) \quad C_A + C_B = \Lambda_A n(q_A/\Lambda_A, 1, (D_A - F_B)/\Lambda_A)[1 - \tau(\Phi(q_A/\Lambda_A))]L_A$$
$$+ \Lambda_B n(q_B/\Lambda_B, 1, (D_B + F_B)/\Lambda_B)[1 - \tau(\Phi(q_B/\Lambda_B))]L_B$$

where τ is the fraction of employees breaking in new hirees. Consumption demands in the two countries satisfy the differential equations

$$(11.12a) \; dC_A/dt = (r - \rho)C_A$$
$$- \mu(\mu + \rho)[q_A n(q_A/\Lambda_A, 1, (D_A - F_B)/\Lambda_A) + D_A - F_B]$$

$$(11.12b) \; dC_B/dt = (r - \rho)C_B$$
$$- \mu(\mu + \rho)[q_B n(q_B/\Lambda_B, 1, (D_B + F_B)/\Lambda_B) + D_B + F_B]$$

Adding the equations in (11.12) gives a differential equation in global consumption demand,

$$(11.13) \quad d(C_A + C_B)/dt$$
$$= (r - \rho)(C_A + C_B)$$
$$- \mu(\mu + \rho)[q_A n(q_A/\Lambda_A, 1, (D_A - F_B)/\Lambda_A) + D_A - F_B]$$
$$- \mu(\mu + \rho)[q_A n(q_A/\Lambda_A, 1, (D_A - F_B)/\Lambda_A) + D_A - F_B]$$

By substituting the time derivative of the amount of global output supplied to consumers in (11.11) for the time derivative of the amount demanded on the lefthand side of (11.13), and substituting analogously for the level appearing on the righthand side, we obtain a condition on the world real interest rate,

$$(11.14) \quad r = \rho + \Upsilon(d(q_A/\Lambda_A)/dt, \; d(q_B/\Lambda_B)/dt, \; q_A/\Lambda_A, \; q_B/\Lambda_B)$$

where the symmetry of the employment functions has been used to show that the rate of change of F_B does not impact upon the rate of change of global employment.

The resulting reduced-form system consists of three equations: a differential equation in F_B and a pair of differential equations making the time-

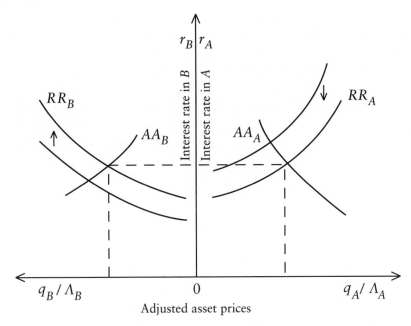

Figure 11.1 Determination of the steady-state world real interest rate, national asset prices, and net foreign asset positions

rate of change of each country's q/Λ a function of the level of its own q/Λ and (through the world real interest rate) that of the other country's. It should be recalled that D_A and D_B are shift parameters. From the initial conditions and the motion of the system in terms of these three variables, one can obtain the motion of the employment rate and the wage in each country.

The equilibrium steady state and comparative analysis. The analysis of the steady state can be organized around Figure 11.1. An essential point is that, given its parameters and its net foreign claim, F_B/Λ, country B's steady-state q_B/Λ_B and its steady-state interest rate, say r_B, are both determined. The same F_B and country A's parameters similarly determine its steady-state q_A/Λ_A and its interest rate, r_A. But we require interest rate parity, $r_A = r_B$. Hence there must be an adjustment of F_B to reconcile the two steady-state interest rates. The equilibrium steady state is attainable when and only when the net foreign claim has made the whole of this adjustment. An increase of F_B, in increasing the wealth of residents in B, boosts the rate of interest required by them in any steady state, thus shifting up RR_B, while the available rate of return in a steady state, represented by the companion curve AA_B, is not shifted. In country A the effect of the increase of F_B is just the reverse. Thus an increase of F_B serves as the instrument by which an excess of the steady-state r_A over r_B is erased.

In algebraic terms, we have the steady-state relationships

$$(11.15) \quad r_A = \rho + \mu(\mu + \rho)[q_A n(q_A/\Lambda_A, 1, (D_A - F_B)/\Lambda_A) + D_A - F_B]$$

$$(11.16) \quad r_A = \frac{[1 - v_A(q_A/\Lambda_A, 1, (D_A - F_B)/\Lambda_A) - \tau(\Phi(q_A/\Lambda_A)) + \Phi\tau'(\Phi)]}{(q_A/\Lambda_A)}$$
$$- \zeta(1, n(q_A/\Lambda_A, 1, (D_A - F_B)/\Lambda_A), y_A^w/v_A; \Lambda_A)$$

$$(11.17) \quad r_B = \rho + \mu(\mu + \rho)[q_B n(q_B/\Lambda_B, 1, (D_B + F_B)/\Lambda_B) + D_B + F_B]$$

$$(11.18) \quad r_B = \frac{[1 - v_B(q_B/\Lambda_B, 1, (D_B + F_B)/\Lambda_B) - \tau(\Phi(q_B/\Lambda_B)) + \Phi\tau'(\Phi)]}{(q_B/\Lambda_B)}$$
$$- \zeta(1, n(q_B/\Lambda_B, 1, (D_B + F_B)/\Lambda_B), y_A^w/v_A; \Lambda_B)$$

$$(11.19) \quad r_A = r_B$$

It is unambiguous, at least for small levels of the public debt, that the righthand side of the first and third equations, which give each country's required rate of interest, is increasing in the country's own q. Regarding the second and fourth equations, it is also unambiguous that an increase in a country's q pulls down the available rate of return both by decreasing the quasi-rent per employee (since v is increased) in the numerator of the first term on the righthand side and by increasing the denominator in the same term; and since increased q also increases $n(\cdot)$, the quit rate is increased, which subtracts further from the rate of return to investing in a new employee. So in each country its q and r are uniquely determined. It is then obvious that if, say, r_A exceeds r_B at some historical F_B that can be regarded as small, then an increase of F_B does the trick of increasing r_B by increasing net wealth among residents of country B and by decreasing the net wealth of the residents in country A.

The long-run effects of certain shocks are now evident. Consider an increase of D_A, due to a temporary tax cut and thus a temporary deficit in the government budget. This shock pushes up the required interest rate curve RR_A and thus drives up the steady-state r_A. It follows that if the global economy was initially in its equilibrium steady state before the shock, the new equilibrium steady state corresponds to an increase of F_B. It follows that r is higher while q is decreased in both countries. As a result, employment is decreased in both countries. If taxation falls primarily on wage income, there is in the country of origin an additional contractionary effect flowing from the further reduction of the after-tax wage as a ratio to nonwage income resulting if the higher tax rates to service the increased debt fall relatively heavily on labor income.

The near-term effects of such a shock take us back to the reduced-form dynamic system consisting of the aforementioned triple of differential equations. A casual inspection of that system strongly suggests that it exhibits saddlepath stability.[9] While abstaining from a formal analysis of that system, we may nevertheless deduce that the only way the global economy can generate this transfer of net wealth from country A to country B is through an upward jump of C_A. It is obvious that the impact is a jump of the world real interest rate, more precisely a jump up of the yield curve. The result is a drop of q in each country, which has the effect of decreasing employment in *both* countries. Global consumption is down, though cushioned by a reduction in the fraction of time that employees spend training new hires. In country B, of course, steady-state consumption is increased as a response to the improved rate of interest; the whole of the increase (and more) is ultimately provided by the interest on the net foreign claim accumulated against A.

Another exercise that is particularly interesting is to study an increase in productivity in, say, country B. It is at once clear that if the global economy was initially in an equilibrium steady state with both D_B and F_B equal to zero, the sole effect on the new equilibrium steady state is an increase of q in proportion to Λ, so that v is increased in the same proportion and there is no effect on $1 - u_B$ and r_B. Once that steady state is approximated, therefore, there is no effect felt in country A. The world real rate of interest is unaffected. More than that: there seems to be no impediment to an immediate jump of q and v by the requisite amounts to place country B at once in its new equilibrium steady state.

The situation is quite different, however, if country B was initially a net foreign creditor, so that initially F_B is positive. Then, in a manner of speaking, country B wants to accumulate *more* in the way of net foreign claims as befits its new productivity, and if it were a small open economy it would proceed at once gradually to do that. But when country B is large, as here, it cannot accumulate more claims abroad without driving down the real rate of interest—by creating an excess supply in the world goods market. That is also sufficient to achieve net foreign investment, for in country A there will be an upward jump of q_A, causing its residents to feel richer and thus to fill in the excess supply with more consumer demand of theirs. The side effect of this process on country A, evidently, is an upward jump of employment and the wage. With time, though, the boom subsides, with the rate of interest and the wage returning in the direction of their original levels. To what new equilibrium steady state will the global economy head? The new steady state will display a reduced wealth level in country A and hence a fall of its supply wage. Therefore r must be lower than it was originally, in country A as well as B, and q will be greater, hence v too. It follows that country A will enjoy permanently higher employment, because of higher wages and lower wealth, but still it may have to pay a price in future consumption for the additional present consumption it accepted early on in response to the productivity gain overseas. In country B, as well, the tendency will be for higher employment in the long run, since wealth is unable to increase in equal proportion to productivity.

11.3 Commentary

The results that are perhaps the most interesting were the product of idle curiosity rather than an agenda. It was found that a technological improvement in a country causing an increase in its productivity there has no effect on its international competitiveness—the wage jumps at once precisely to offset the impact of the shock—in a special, but not unnatural or unrepresentative case: that in which the country is neither a net foreign creditor nor a debtor. If, however, the country is, say, a net creditor, the productivity improvement causes it, speaking somewhat figuratively, to want to add to its share of overseas assets, hence to run an increased current-account surplus for some length of time.

The major motivation for this chapter has instead been an interest in the generalizability of the Fitoussi-Phelps argument: There is a broad range of expenditure shocks in a large region or country that, in raising interest rates there, contract employment elsewhere while nevertheless managing to expand employment in the region or country of the shock.

The small open economy carries us part of the way along the Fitoussi-Phelps argument, with its implication that an increase of the external real rate of interest spells a contraction of employment domestically. But such a model by its nature is incapable of explaining what is happening abroad as a result of the same underlying shock. The model did have some interesting results to offer on the effects of productivity shocks.

The two-country model, though attractive in several respects, is insufficiently rich to underpin the Fitoussi-Phelps contention that ordinary fiscal shocks, in particular an increase in the public-debt shock or in government purchases, are capable of driving up employment in the country of origin while exerting a contractionary influence abroad. In the present model, a positive shock to public debt or to public expenditure on output tends to contract (or expand) employment in both countries from the start.

There seem to be two recipes for obtaining an "asymmetric" employment effect. One is to look at particular expenditure shocks, such as a national subsidy to investment in new employees (or, in fixed-capital models, a fixed-investment tax credit). Then the world real rate of interest is driven up, pulling down activity abroad, yet in the country of origin a stimulus to employment is felt on balance, thanks to the direct impact of the subsidy.[10]

The other route is a rather different model in which the real exchange rate, rather than being tied down by the law of one price, is a variable. That opens up the possibility that garden-variety expenditure shocks will have asymmetric effects on employment in the two countries.

12

International Linkages through Investment in Customers

THE implications of the structuralist approach for a world of open economies linked by a perfect international financial market and a frictional world market in goods now need to be explored.

A customer-market model of the small open economy is taken up in the first section, 12.1. This is one of two such models, that in which virtually all customers of domestic firms, other than the domestic government, are foreigners—to be referred to as model F. A simplified version of the opposite model, having the property that, in the relevant neighborhood, all customers are nationals—which may be called model N—is briefly set out in Chapter 14. The present model F has the methodological advantage that it is capable of being modeled under the restriction of perfect foresight, or rational expectations, a postulate that would make model N analytically intractable.

The chapter goes on in section 12.2 to construct and analyze a two-country extension of the customer-market model, one with strong resemblances to that in Chapter 8. This is the world inhabited by Fitoussi and Phelps, and the main question for analysis here is the same motivating that earlier work. In having a look at the two-country model, we are particularly interested to learn whether its implications parallel the finding in Fitoussi-Phelps that demand stimulus is—or may be—*expansionary* in the country of origin while *contractionary* for the other country. The answer is not immediately derivable from analysis of the Fitoussi-Phelps two-country customer-market model (the first of their three models), since the reasoning there, at points couched in monetary terms, left it unclear whether nonmonetary channels would have sufficed to generate the conclusions reached.

Thus this second section can be seen as a report on the extent to which the Fitoussi-Phelps thesis on the 1980s slump in Europe—high imported real interest rates did it—is robust to the exclusion of monetary mechanisms or, to put it better, to the neutrality of money. However, the analysis here is also a step that would have been inevitable anyway in exploring the implications of the structuralist theory for the workings of the international economy.[1] And there is some attention to productivity shocks as well as expenditure shocks.

12.1 A Small Open Economy

The objective of this section is to sketch the behavior of an economy that has the "basic structure" of section 8.1 but in which the firms are subject to international competition in the global customer market.[2] The model here is confined to the small open economy, meaning one too small to affect perceptibly the *world* real interest rate—the real interest rate in terms of the good supplied by foreign firms at their price. That modeling decision leaves open how the economy relates to the world goods market.

The problem of modeling the goods market suggests two modeling tactics to choose between. In one polar case, all the relevant customers of national firms—firms that produce only with national labor—are nationals, and foreign firms—the firms that produce only with foreign labor—have succeeded, as we look in on the economy, in capturing a share of the nation's customers. (There is no third type of firm producing with a mix of nationals and foreigners.) Although the small open economy is too small to affect perceptibly the world real rate of interest, by definition, disturbances to the demand of its national customers will certainly be felt by national firms, and so will the exchange rate and the real interest rate in terms of the good supplied by national firms and their price. At the other modeling pole, customers are cosmopolitan, exhibiting no tendency to follow the flag, and national customers are too few to have a perceptible effect on the demand for the output of national firms. They export essentially all their output, nationals being a negligible fraction of their stock of customers. The *former* case has the drawback that it presents the analyst with two state variables whose dynamics are to be studied: first, the market share, say, the fraction of national customers belonging to national firms and, second, the accumulated wealth of those national customers on which the demand of national firms depends.[3] The limitation of the *latter* case is that it excludes any perceptible effect of changes in national consumer demand on the national economy. But it does permit an analysis of the effects of a change in foreign demand. The effects of the world real interest rate and of national productivity can also be easily seen. Hence this chapter selects the latter model.

The features of the product market here are rooted in the same Phelps-Winter model with the difference that the customers are essentially all foreigners, as are the competing firms. As before, the firms' respective products, though not identical in every respect, such as location, are essentially perfect substitutes in the sense that a price differential would not be indefinitely sustainable: if a firm tried to maintain its price forever above that of the others in the world market (by some nonvanishing differential) it would gradually lose its entire stock of customers—its market share—to the other firms (to the numerous overseas firms and negligibly to its compatriot competitors). Yet, owing to frictions in the transmission of information, a firm that charges less than the "going" price will not instantaneously gain the whole market, and owing to the costs of gathering information about alternative suppliers, a firm that unexpectedly charges more than the going price will not instantaneously or abruptly lose all its market share.

In the case here, a national firm's customers are an apparently homogeneous lot of overseas consumers, nationals being a negligible share of the world market. At every moment, then, the firm has to set a price for these homogeneous buyers. This price we will think of as the firm's relative price in the world market, the representative firm in the world market always having a price equal to one. Thus the identical firms in the nation set a real price, p, defined in terms of the representative overseas firm's supplies. In the open economy, then, the average real price set by national firms may differ from one. (But a difference cannot last except vanishingly.)

The dynamics of the customer stock at a national firm are represented by the same differential equation introduced in equation (8.5). For the average stock of cosmopolitan customers at national firms the same equation applies:

$$(12.1) \quad dx/dt = g(p)x \qquad g'(p) < 0, g''(p) < 0, g(1) = 0$$

where g denotes the growth-rate function, the argument of which is now the relative price. Again, by choice of units, the average *world* price, p^*, is an implicit constant here, set equal to one, it being the numeraire with which to measure a firm's real price and real wage in world terms—in terms of its purchasing power over the predominantly foreign-produced goods being consumed by nationals.

At each moment, a firm's output, z, is planned to meet exactly the amount demanded by its current stock of customers at its current price, $D(p; y^*)$, per customer. Here y^* can be thought of as real income (in units of the goods supplied by foreign firms, which are the numeraire good) per customer, which is exogenous since virtually all customers are foreign and our country is too small to affect their real incomes. The output demanded per firm, then, is

(12.2) $z = D(p; y^*)x$ $D'(p) < 0, 0 < D''(p) < 2D'(p)^2(1/D(p))$,

$$D(p) = 0 \text{ at large } p$$

It should be commented that it would be tempting to interpret y^* as a demand-shift parameter, where $D_{y^*}(p; y^*) > 0$, indicating the state of the demand, essentially foreign demand, for the outputs of the country's firms. The danger in this interpretation is that, as the closed-economy model implied, a general increase of goods demand by consumers in the rest of the world—here virtually the whole world—may actually contract the incomes with which they can import more goods. Interpreting this as a demand shift is possible if there is something country-specific about the distinctiveness of the goods supplied at domestic firms, but that veers away from the spirit of the model in which the law of one price gradually tends to hold again following a shock that has disturbed prices.

As specified in section 8.1, the firm exhibits constant unit real cost, equal to the minimized value of $v_i/\Lambda\varepsilon(v^i/y^w, (1 - u)v/y^w, 1)$, where y^w corresponds in the present context to $aR(v^*, 1 - u^*)$, the returns on the workers' cosmopolitan assets of a per worker. Given a, then ς is an increasing function of the employment rate. The latter can just as well be regarded as a function of productivity-adjusted output, z/Λ, by virtue of the reduced-form relation $z = \Lambda\varepsilon(1 - u; a)(1 - u)\ell$. Equating output to amount demanded, we have for unit cost

(12.3) $\varsigma = \varsigma(D(p; y^*)x\Lambda^{-1}; a)$

As mentioned earlier, it is desired to keep the dimensionality of the model down to a single state variable, x, the representative national firm's stock of cosmopolitan customers. Consequently, we will first analyze the system while holding constant the flow of income on the assets owned by workers and then return to that loose end before concluding the analysis.

At each moment the firm's optimal pricing policy must maximize (from that moment forward) the present value of the expected future stream of quasi-rent, or real "cash" flow, resulting from its policy and the informational frictions in the market. Hence the individual firm maximizes the indefinite *integral* of discounted real cash flow,

(12.4) $[p^i - \varsigma(D(p, y^*)x/\Lambda; a)]D(p^i, y^*)x^i e^{-r^*t} \equiv F(p^i, x^i; p, x)$

subject to the constraints

(12.5) $dx^i/dt = g(p^i)x^i \equiv G(p^i, x^i)$ and $x^i(0) = x_o^i$

The optimal path of the firm's price has the property that at each moment it maximizes the current Hamiltonian,

(12.6) $F(p^i, x^i) + q^i G(p^i, x^i) \equiv \mathcal{H}(p^i, x^i)$

The first-order and second-order conditions are

(12.7) $0 = F_{p^i} + q^i G_{p^i}$

(12.8) $F_{p^i p^i} + (-F_{p^i}/G_{p^i}) G_{p^i p^i} < 0$

and q^i, the shadow price of customers, obeys the relation

(12.9) $dq^i/dt = r^* q^i - (F_{x^i} + q G_{x^i})$

It should be remarked that all the "prices" in this maximization are being expressed in terms of the supplies of the representative foreign firm, so the real rate of interest here is likewise the world rate, not the national rate; the latter would be lower than the world rate by the amount of the "real inflation," $(1/p)\,dp/dt$, or, equivalently, the rate of real exchange-rate appreciation.

GENERAL EQUILIBRUM DYNAMICS

Let us simplify notation by using p to denote the p^i chosen by the ith firm and indeed every one of the identical firms in the nation, and use $\tilde{p}$ to denote the price level commonly expected to be set and actually set by the *other* firms.

To describe equilibrium we differentiate totally the first-order condi-

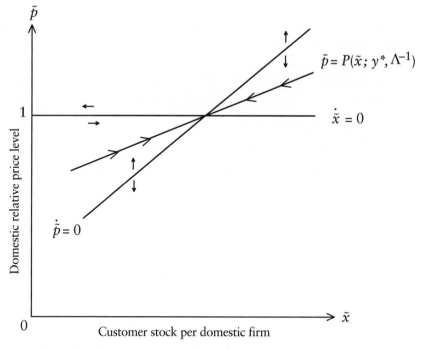

Figure 12.1 Phase diagram in the $(\tilde{x}, \tilde{p})$ plane: The small open economy

tion, $q = -F_p/G_p$, evaluating it at $x = \tilde{x}$ and $p = \tilde{p}$, as we are studying only equilibrium paths. The result is

$$(12.10) \quad \dot{q} = (-1/G_p)\{[F_{pp} + F_{p\tilde{p}} - (F_p/G_p)G_{pp}]\dot{\tilde{p}}$$
$$+ [F_{px} + F_{p\tilde{x}} - (F_p/G_p)G_{px}]\dot{\tilde{x}}\}$$

Using (12.10) and (12.7) in (12.9) then gives

$$(12.11) \quad \dot{\tilde{p}} = \frac{r^*F_p + (F_xG_p - F_pG_x) - (F_{px} + F_{p\tilde{x}} - (F_p/G_p)G_{px})G}{F_{pp} + F_{p\tilde{p}} - (F_p/G_p)G_{pp}}$$

The character of the contour of points $(\tilde{x}, \tilde{p})$ along which the real price level is stationary, which is illustrated in Figure 12.1, is quite similar to the corresponding contour obtained in the Phelps-Winter model where increasing cost is internal to the firm, not external. Here the external cost effect of increased x at other firms makes $H_{p\tilde{x}} > 0$, just as the internal cost effect made the analogous $H_{px} > 0$ in the fixed-wage model (which evidently has in mind a small Marshallian industry).

To close the general-equilibrium dynamic system, we need only to reuse at the macro (small-country) level the differential equation for the growth of customers previously used to describe the growth or decay of the customer stock at any individual firm in the economy. Hence

(12.12) $\dot{\tilde{x}} = g(p)\tilde{x}$

To study the motion of the economy under conditions of general equilibrium (that is, correct expectations), the standard phase diagram in Figure 12.1 may be used. The locus of points on which $\dot{p}$ equals zero, obtained from (12.11), is an upward-sloping curve. The locus of points on which $\dot{\tilde{x}}$ equals zero, given by (12.12), is the horizontal line. This system is saddle-path stable and generates the uniquely determined price–customer stock relationship shown by the curve labeled $\tilde{p} = P(\tilde{x}; y^*, \Lambda^{-1})$. This relationship uses the fact that, starting from an identical situation, the stock of customers of all the firms in the country will remain equal.

The diagram in Figure 12.1 shows that, given a stable environment with respect to foreign demand, national costs, and so forth, the economy gravitates asymptotically toward a unique steady state corresponding to that environment. This will be sometimes referred to as the rest point, or *RP*. A leading feature of this rest point is that the real price level equals the foreign level of one. If a shock occurs when the economy is initially at the rest point, the real price is at once driven away from one. Accordingly, the customer stock, which is our starring state variable, must grow or decline, whichever is appropriate, to the point where the real price is once again at its sustainable level.[4]

COMPARATIVE STATICS

We now consider the effects of shocks to three parameters. The first is y^*, the real income enjoyed in the global customer base. The second will be Λ^{-1}, an increase of which represents a (positive) cost shock, in particular, Harrod-neutral regress. The third shift parameter of interest is r^*, an increase of which causes national firms to discount the future more heavily. The focus will be on the effects of these disturbances over the near term, leaving to the interested reader the question of long-term effects. The analysis will be confined to small disturbances upon the economy when initially in a state of rest—that is, at the rest point, *RP*. The analysis will also remove the unnecessary overmarks.

A positive y* shock. An increase of y^* shifts up the *P* curve, thus causing the real national price level to jump up, if and only if it shifts up the $\dot{p} = 0$ curve. It is left to an endnote to argue that this upward shift does occur and that it is deducible from that shift that output and employment must have increased to support it.[5] The following algebra reaches the same conclusion: Write

$$(12.13) \quad dz/dy^* = D_{y^*} + (d\tilde{p}/dy^*)D_{\tilde{p}} = D_{y^*} + [(d\tilde{p}/d\varsigma)\varsigma'(z)(dz/dy^*)]D_{\tilde{p}}$$

Then

$$(12.14) \quad dz/dy^* = D_{y^*}/\{1 - D_{\tilde{p}}[(d\tilde{p}/d\varsigma)\varsigma'(z)]\} > 0$$

$$(12.15) \quad d\tilde{p}/dy^* = (d\tilde{p}/d\varsigma)\varsigma'(z)D_{y^*} > 0$$

The rise of price, which is unambiguous, merely dampens the rise of output. So output and the real price of output move up hand in hand. The real wage—the wage in terms of the consumption of the cosmopolitan nationals—must increase.[6]

We may look beyond the short run. The increase in the real price charged by the firms of our country, which resulted from the increase of the employment rate as all firms expanded output to take advantage of the temporarily improved terms at which they found they could sell, sets in motion an erosion in their customer stocks. The aggregate stock must go on falling to the point where the real price is no longer elevated above the internationally competitive level of one. At that point, which is reached only asymptotically, employment will have slid back to its original level, and so will have the real wage. This surprising invariance of steady-state employment and real wage to the demand per customer is a result of the fact that although, in the constant-cost case adopted here, the supply price of the *individual* firm is independent of the amount demanded per customer, the "industry" supply price (even at a constant real wage) is an increasing function of output (and more strongly increasing when account is taken of the increasing real supply wage corresponding to the given real nonwage income of workers). If the frictions in product markets could be overcome in a day, say, it would be obvious to us that the nation's firms would immediately shed enough "customers" to go on producing the accustomed total output at the accustomed real price of one, with no change in the real wage or employment resulting from this inconsequential disturbance.

It is now clear that for the purposes of this exercise we can neglect *a* altogether, as there is nothing about this shock that impels a change in households' asset accumulations.

Government purchases of output by the firms. Another important kind of shock should be recognized, an increase in government demand for the firms' output. At the initial rate of employment, this expenditure creates an excess demand. It can be argued that the following outcome is theoretically possible and, indeed, the presumptive outcome: The firms will expand total employment, while at the same time charging a higher price to their customers in response to the higher marginal cost at higher output—a real appreciation. The appreciation will not be so great as to crowd out private demand equal to the increase in public demand; at the much more elevated real price corresponding to that full crowding out, a marginal increase of production and sales to customers (from the hypothetically reduced base in terms of sales to private customers) would be more attractive than it would have been before (at the higher base and lower price). Relative to this hypothetical full-crowding-out position, with its sharp real appreciation to clear the market, the firms proceed to *increase their supply of output in order to moderate that appreciation and thus dampen the cutbacks to their customers and the consequent erosion of their customer base* (by foreign competitors in the overseas markets where they compete).

The incidence of the government diversion of output falls in part on customers in the form of a higher price, which represents a real appreciation for the home country. It seems certain to fall in part on the firms, in the sense that they will accept a lower markup of price over marginal cost, the latter rising by more than the former; but this proposition is not worth attempting to prove.

The conclusion that employment expands is rather important as it indicates that what is true of the whole—namely, the paradox that increased demand for output of the consumer-good sector may lead to a reduced amount of it being produced—may not be true of any part taken alone, and conversely. Each country may hope to increase its output by acting alone through measures to stimulate demand for domestic firms' output, but as all countries do so, the consequence, according to the paradox, is a worldwide contraction of employment.

This last proposition, on the potentially expansionary effect of increased domestic demand, other things equal, is made reasonably rigorous, though at the cost of invoking static expectations, in terms of model N, the theoretical setting in which all customers are nationals. That model is briefly set forth at the beginning of the commentary in Chapter 14.

A negative productivity shock.   A positive cost shock, more precisely an increase of Λ^{-1}, has an easily understood effect on output. Let us begin by again considering the effect on the $\dot{p} = 0$ curve in Figure 12.1. The derivative can be shown to be positive.[7] Hence the $\dot{p} = 0$ curve shifts up, pulling up with it the saddlepath schedule, which gives the firms' price corresponding to the given stock of customers. It follows that the amount of output demanded falls. Reduced output is implied.

What about employment? There is an employment-contracting effect from the rise in the real price, but this must be set against the employment-expanding effect of the increase in employment needed to produce any given level of output. Clearly, employment will fall on balance if and only if the increase in the price that the firm would require to go on employing the same number as before exceeds the increase in the output "demand price" of its (given) customers that would be displayed if the reduced output producible by an unchanged number of employees were to be auctioned off to them. Since the Phelps-Winter firms operate somewhere on the *inelastic* portion of their demand curves or not far from it, unlike the textbook monopolist (whose customers are prisoners forever), there appears to be the strong possibility that the short-run effect of the cost increase is actually an *increase* of employment.[8] (A Harrod-neutral technical advance causes an initial drop in employment.)

In some sort of medium run in which the customer stock has adjusted, customers having drifted away as a result of the high price charged by domestic firms, employment must approach a medium-run steady state that is below the original one. The explanation is simply that, as $\tilde{p}$ approaches p^* ($= 1$) again, the real wage must reach a level below its original one; the firm will not absorb the whole increase of unit costs. It follows from the positive slope of the equilibrium locus that the reduced real wage will be accompanied by reduced employment.

If it were the case that the nonwage income of workers fell in proportion to the reduced real wage in this medium-run steady state, there would, owing to the postulated homogeneity of the effort function, be no corollary fall of employment. Since the return on workers' existing holdings of assets hold up in the medium run, only a negligible portion being invested domestically, the productivity shock in reducing the wage rate also reduces the key wage-to-nonwage income ratio. But ultimately, following dissaving, nonwage income will decline equiproportionately. Ultimately, therefore, the rest point will exhibit the same employment but reduced wage income and nonwage income in equal proportion.

A positive shock to r*. The deleterious effect on the equilibrium employment rate of higher real interest rates has already been discovered in the closed-economy analysis. The mechanism stands in sharper relief when the increase of the real interest rate is exogenous and pure, unaccompanied by a simultaneous movement of some national parameter (such as increased time preference or increased public-debt holdings).

An increase of $r*$ can be seen to shift up the $\dot{p} = 0$ locus. Of course the other curve, the $\dot{x} = 0$ locus, is undisturbed. It follows that the saddlepath shifts up. The consequence is an immediate increase in the real price level and thus an abrupt drop in the output demanded and produced. There is also the onset of a gradual decline in the stock of customers at the national firms. The decline of the customer stock has two opposing effects on employment: In lowering the real price charged by firms it helps to restore the amount demanded per customer, but only at the cost of reducing total demand at any given price (by reducing the number of buyers). The latter effect tends to outweigh the former, causing the employment rate to fall further after its initial drop.

There is, however, a fallacy of composition lurking here that we had better avoid falling into. If the increase of the world real interest rate is an effect of a worldwide increase of consumption demand, spontaneous or induced by public transfers to households, not all countries can witness an increase in the relative price charged by their firms. The representative country is fated to have a relative price equal to one, no matter what common shock it and the others experience. Nevertheless it *is* necessary to work through a number of *ceteris paribus* thought-experiments if we are to graduate to the level of two-country models. The concluding section will indicate the right way to understand and put together the various results of this chapter.[9]

12.2 A Two-Country Model of Investment in Customers

The rather cursory examination in section 12.1 of the small open economy operating in a worldwide customer market argued that an increase of government demand or of home-consumer demand for the output of domestic firms, in causing a steep real appreciation as long as total output fails to be increased, would induce those firms to increase a little their supply of output in order to moderate that appreciation and thus dampen the cutbacks to their private customers and thus the consequent erosion of their customer base by foreign competitors (in the overseas markets where they compete). Thus employment in the small open economy is boosted, at least over the near term—though evidently not in an open economy so large as to be virtually closed.

What, however, is the effect of the shock on employment abroad? The obvious guess is that the upward effect of the demand increase on the domestic real interest rate would be transmitted abroad, causing real interest rates to rise there as well; and as we also saw from the examination of the small open economy in section 12.1, shocks abroad that drive up the real interest rate overseas thereby contract employment at home by emboldening firms to raise their markups and thus to curtail their demand for labor.

If a very large open economy would suffer a contraction from its public expenditure, it being approximately a closed economy, while the small open economy experiences an expansion, the question is whether in a world of two equal-size and otherwise similar countries such a fiscal stimulus will be expansionary for the country undertaking it.[10]

The closed-country customer-market model in Chapter 8 was constructed from certain known building blocks, including the Phelps-Winter treatment of the firm operating in frictional competition in the product market. Recast in the notation to be used here, that one-country model reduces to a system, shown below, of three equations in the price of shares, q, consumption per customer, y, and the real interest rate, r.

(12.16) $dq/dt = rq - [1 - \varsigma(y)]y$ $\varsigma(y) > 0,$

(12.17) $dy/dt = y\{r - \rho - m[(q + \beta)/y]\}$ $m > 0, \rho \geq 0,$

(12.18) $q = Q(y),$ $Q'(y)y/Q(y) > 1$

The first of these is a Fisherine differential equation determining the appreciation of the real value of shares as a function of interest and cash flow per customer, where $\varsigma(y)$ denotes real unit labor cost. Behind this equation is the premise of constant costs at the level of the firm and increasing cost at the industry level, owing to the positive slope of the equilibrium real wage–employment rate locus derived from a Calvo-Bowles shirking model. The second, arising from Blanchard-Yaari consumption dynamics, is a differential equation in consumption per customer involving the real value of the outstanding shares plus public debt per household and thus per customer, $q + \beta$. The parameter m is compounded of the time prefer- ence rate, ρ, and the age-independent death rate. Finally there is a timeless relationship on the supply side between y and q that comes from the Phelps-Winter firm's static maximization each moment of the appropriate Hamiltonian function, which involves the real shadow price of customers and current cash flow; but the shadow price can be treated as equal to the real price of shares (by keeping the number of shares equal to the number of customers). This equation gives the supply price, or required price, of customers—equivalently, of shares—needed to induce firms to supply the expenditure per customer specified; it recognizes that a higher expenditure, in entailing higher employment, necessitates a higher real wage in the econ- omy as a whole.

This three-equation system of the one-country model is in turn reduc- ible to a single differential equation in q, or equivalently in y, in which there are no state variables the evolution of which would move q over time. It can be shown that, under the hypothesis of "perfect foresight" over the remaining future, q simply jumps at once to the steady-state value corresponding to the given parameters. See the appendix to Chapter 8.

THE FULL DYNAMIC MODEL

The two-country generalization is contained in the system of equations in Table 12.1. In all, there are eleven equations in eleven variables in that two-country model.

There is now a subsystem for each of the countries. Together these subsystems contain eight equations, not six as might have been expected, because of two consequences of international competition. Country A has nationals—equal in number to x_A—of whom x_{BA} are currently customers at firms in B, leaving $x_{AA} = 1 - x_{BA}$ as customers of home firms. As a result, there is a differential equation for consumption per customer abroad, c_{BA}, as well as a similar equation for consumption per customer at home, c_{AA}. The second consequence is that it is appropriate to distinguish between the values, q_{BA} and q_{AA} respectively, of the two types of customer, national and foreign, found in B since they have different demands arising from their generally different real incomes. It may be supposed, only for clarity, that the firms in B actually issue the two types of shares, impute the corre- sponding earnings on each of the shares correctly, and make stock divi- dends or buybacks so as to keep the number of shares of each type equal to the number of its customers of that type. That feature provides an intuitive explanation of why the interest rate in the equation for the valuation of

Table 12.1   The proper two-country generalization

(1) $dq_{AA}/dt = (r_A - g_{AA})q_{AA} - \{1 - \varsigma(y_{AA}(x_A - x_{BA}))\}y_{AA}$

(2) $dy_{AA}/dt = (r_A - \rho_A)y_{AA} - m_A\{[q_{AA}(x_A - x_{BA})$

$$+ eq_{BA}x_{BA} + eq_{BB}s_{BBA}](1/x_A) + \beta_A\}$$

(3) $q_{AA} = Q^A(y_{AA}, y_{AA}(x_A - x_{BA}), e)$

(4a) $dq_{BA}/dt = (r_B - g_{BA})q_{BA} - \{1 - \varsigma(y_{BB}x_B + y_{BA}x_{BA})\}y_{BA}$

(4b) $dq_{BB}/dt = (r_B - g_{BB})q_{BB} - \{1 - \varsigma(y_{BB}x_B + y_{BA}x_{BA})\}y_{BB}$

(5a) $dy_{BA}/dt = (r_B - \rho_A)y_{BA} - m_A\{[(1/e)q_{AA}(x_A - x_{BA})$

$$+ q_{BA}x_{BA} + q_{BB}s_{BBA}](1/x_A) + (1/e)\beta_A\}$$

(5b) $dy_{BB}/dt = (r_B - \rho_B)y_{BB} - m_B\{[q_{BB}(x_B - s_{BBA})](1/x_B) + \beta_B\}$

(6) $\dfrac{q_{BB}x_B + q_{BA}x_{BA}}{x_B + x_{BA}} = Q^B\left[\dfrac{y_{BB}x_B + y_{BA}x_{BA}}{x_B + x_{BA}}, y_{BB}x_B + y_{BA}x_{BA}, e\right]$

(7) $r_A = r_B + (de/dt)/e$

(8) $(dx_{BA}/dt)/x_{BA} = g_{BA}(e)$ $g_{BA}(1) = 0, g'_{BA}(e) < 0$

(9) $ds_{BBA}/dt = \{1 - \varsigma(y_{BB}x_B + y_{BA}x_{BA})\}(x_{BA} + s_{BBA}) - y_{BA}x_{BA}$

each type of customer and the corresponding share, which is a claim to the income stream that the type of customer generates, appears net of the rate of growth, g, of the stock of customers; for if the stock is growing, share owners are receiving *pro rata* capital gains. Note finally that each firm in B, being unable to distinguish and discriminate between them, is supposed to set the same real price for both types of customers; so the weighted-average amount supplied per total number of customers is functionally related to the weighted-average share price.

Then we have the familiar arbitrage equation in the two real interest rates, where e denotes the real exchange rate (American definition);[11] the Phelps-Winter differential equation governing the motion of x_{BA}; and finally a differential equation governing the accumulation of shares in B-firms by wealth owners in A. The portfolio preferences here are lexicographic: Public debt of one's own country is the first choice, then the shares of firms in one's own country, then the shares corresponding to compatriot customers overseas, and lastly the shares representing claims to the earnings from the domestic customers of the B-firms. A is a net creditor country, B a net debtor, so A has wealth left over to hold some shares in B firms. Let s_{BBA} denote the number of domestic customers of B-firms whose shares are held by nationals of A. It is supposed that, at the initial moment, s_{BBA} is positive, though perhaps small. It is clear that in steady states x_{BA} is positive if and only if s_{BBA} is positive, because ownership merely of the earnings from B's foreign customers would not suffice to pay the import bill of those customers; it would pay only the profits but not the wages generated by sales to those customers.

It may need to be remarked that, as in the closed-economy chapter, the shares of a country serve as the numeraire in terms of which to measure the "money" prices of goods and labor. The nominal exchange rate is then the amount of A-money needed to buy one unit of B-money. Multiplying this nominal price of foreign exchange by the nominal price level in B gives the price of goods supplied by B-firms in terms of A-money; then dividing by the nominal price of A-goods in A-money gives the real exchange rate. This real exchange rate is denoted by e.

One other comment. A strength of the customer-market view of product markets, with its emphasis on incomplete information, is that it rationalizes two-way trade in the same product. But as modeled here the battlefront between the two warring camps of firms, those of A and those of B, is found either in the territory of one camp or the other—A's territory in the present case. (The motive was simply to avoid adding to the number of state variables in the dynamic system, which has been held to two.) This asymmetry in market penetration is unattractive but, I believe, not a critical drawback. One can assume, if one likes (and as will be done in the discussion of the "short run"), that the initial attachment of A-customers to B-firms is arbitrarily small.

A SIMPLIFIED VERSION OF THE TWO-COUNTRY MODEL

Although the above model may be the theoretically appropriate extension to two countries of the one-country model summarized earlier, for purposes of analyzing the near-term response of the system to shocks a simplified version of the model is sorely needed. The simplification is the elimination of the two classes of stock in country B, corresponding to the division of customers there between foreign and domestic. In country B there is

Table 12.2 The simplified two-country model

$$(1) \quad dq_A/dt = [r_A - g_A(e)]q_A - \{1 - \varsigma(y_{AA}(x_A - x_{BA}))\}y_{AA}$$

$$(2) \quad (dy_{AA}/dt)/y_{AA} = r_A - \rho_A - m_A\{[q_A(x_A - x_{BA})$$
$$+ eq_B s_{BA}](1/x_A) + \beta_A\}(1/y_{AA})$$

$$(3) \quad q_A = Q^A(y_{AA}, y_{AA}(x_A - x_{AB}), e) \quad Q_1^A > 0, Q_2^A < 0, Q_3^A > 0$$

$$(4) \quad dq_B/dt = [r_B - g_A(e)]q_B$$
$$- \{1 - \varsigma(y_{BB}x_B + y_{BA}x_{BA})\}\frac{y_{BB}x_B + y_{BA}x_{BA}}{x_B + x_{AB}}$$

$$(5a) \quad (dy_{BA}/dt)/y_{BA} = r_B - \rho_A - m_A\{[(1/e)q_A(x_A - x_{BA})$$
$$+ q_B s_{BA}](1/x_A) + (1/e)\beta_B\}(1/y_{AB})$$

$$(5b) \quad (dy_{BB}/dt)/y_{BB} = r_B - \rho_B - m_B\{q_B(x_B + x_{BA} - s_{BA})(1/x_B) + \beta_B\}(1/y_{BB})$$

$$(6) \quad q_B = Q^B((y_{BB}x_B + y_{BA}x_{BA})/(x_B + x_{AB}), y_{BB}x_B + y_{BA}x_{BA}, e)$$
$$Q_1^B > 0, Q_2^B < 0, Q_3^B < 0$$

$$(7) \quad r_A = r_B + (de/dt)/e$$

$$(8) \quad dx_{BA}/dt = g_{BA}(e)x_{BA} \quad g_{BA}(1) = 0, g'_{BA}(e) < 0$$

$$(9) \quad ds_{BA}/dt = \{1 - \varsigma(y_{BB}x_B + y_{BA}x_{BA})\}\frac{y_{BB}x_B + y_{BA}x_{BA}}{x_B + x_{BA}}s_{BA} - y_{BA}x_{BA}$$
$$\text{where } -g_A(e)(x_A - x_{BA}) = g_{BA}(e)x_{BA} = g_B(e)(x_B + x_{BA})$$

now one class of shares, with price q_B and growth rate g_B, which is a claim to the average earnings per customer from the representative mixture of foreign and domestic customers. This ten-equation model is in Table 12.2. Readers are invited to have a brief look at this simplified system.

EMPLOYMENT AND INTEREST IN THE NEAR AND FAR TERM
This section will analyze the determination of employment and interest in the model both in the near-term equilibrium evolution and in the equilibrium steady state that is presumed to be approached in the far-term future.

Table 12.3 The "short-run" under static expectations

(1') $r = \{[1 - \varsigma(y_{AA}x_{AA})]y_{AA}/Q_A(y_{AA}, e; x_{AA})\} + g_A(e)$

(2') $y_{AA}x_{AA} = x_{AA}m_A[Q^A(y_{AA}, e) + eQ^B(y_{BB}, y_{BA}, e)s_{BA}x_A^{-1} + \beta_A]/(r - \rho_A)$

(4') $r = \dfrac{[1 - \varsigma(y_{BB}x_B + y_{BA}x_{BA})][(y_{BB}x_B + y_{BA}x_{BA})/(x_B + x_{BA})]}{Q_B(y_{BB}, y_{BA}, e)} + g_B(e)$

(5') $y_{BB}x_B + y_{BA}x_{BA} = x_B m_B[Q^B(y_{BB}, y_{BA}, e)(x_B - s_{BA})x_B^{-1} + \beta_A]/(r - \rho_A)$

$\qquad\qquad\qquad + x_{BA}m_A[(1/e)Q^A(y_{AA}, e)$

$\qquad\qquad\qquad\qquad + Q^B(\cdot)s_{BA}x_A^{-1} + (1/e)\beta_A]/(r - \rho_B)$

The "short run" under static expectations. Were one to adopt the hypothesis of perfect foresight over the remaining future, after any shock that may have just occurred, the analytical task would be to solve for the functions that show how the jumpy co-state variables—the q's, e, and the rest—depend upon the (henceforth time-independent) parameters, such as β_A, and the two state variables of the system, which move gradually, x_{BA} and s_{BA}. Once in hand, the results indicate how under perfect foresight the path of q_B and that of the other variables would jump with, say, a step increase in the parameter β_A, which we may interpret as a helicopter drop of public debt onto the citizenry by the government of A. One takes into account not only the effect on q_B of the adjustment of x_{BA} and s_{BA} that is set in motion, but also implicitly how the anticipation of that adjustment modifies the initial jump of q_B. Unfortunately the present model appears to be somewhat too dense in interrelationships to make it feasible to calculate these results within a reasonable period of time. In part as a compromise, and in part because it may be that markets underestimate the speed with which the prices will be driven by the adjustment of the state variables, it may be acceptable instead to analyze the short-run effects of disturbances under the hypothesis of *static* expectations regarding e and the q in each country. In this "short run" the customer stocks are taken as given.

Under static expectations, the short-run behavior of the simplified model reduces to the static model shown in Table 12.3. The expected rate of change of the real exchange rate is always nil, so the real rate of interest in one country, which is defined in term of goods supplied by the firms of that country, must equal the real interest rate in the other country to satisfy the arbitrage equation (7) in Table 12.2; so there is a common world real interest rate, r. The expected rates of change of the two share prices are likewise nil, so equation (1) and its counterpart (4), also in Table 12.2, become static equations in the real interest rate; these are (1') and (4') in Table 12.3. It can also be shown that if the expected rate of change of the real wage and of the unemployment rate are nil, the resulting consumption function for each type of customer is identical to the steady-state relationship obtained by setting the rate of change of consumption equal to zero in equations (2), (5a), and (5b) in Table 12.2; the result is (2') and (5') in Table 12.3. Note that it is not supposed that the expected growth rate of the customer stocks is always nil; it would contradict the logic of the model to assume that producers believed fate would freeze their customer stocks regardless of their actions.

Equation (1') of the short-run system derives from the static version of (1) and the equation in (3), which shows how the shadow price of customers required to elicit a specified output depends upon the quantity of that output. Equation (4') is obtained in the corresponding way. The equations (1') and (4') are analogous to the Hicksian IS curve in that they give the rate of interest that firms are willing to pay, which IS curves do.[12] Furthermore, the curve of the equation is downward-sloping in the output–interest rate, or (Z, r), plane, as IS curves can be (and are usually assumed to be), and hence quite unlike Hicks's necessarily upward-sloping LM curve. The explanation of that negative slope is that an increase of, say, Z_A increases the q_A required to induce firms to supply more output to their customers; and since the supply of output is inelastic with respect to q, as indicated in the closed-economy model, a doubling of Z_A, even if it doubled profits in the numerator of the righthand side of (1'), would more than double q_A in the denominator and thus lower the rate of return on the share price; so r must fall on this account. In addition, with a rising industry supply curve because of the higher real wage and higher shirking at greater levels of employment, the numerator will less than double with a doubling of output and so r_A must fall on this account as well.

Consider now the other pair of equations in the short-run system. Equation (2'), to take first the simpler of the pair, gives the level of consumption expenditure on domestic product of A as a function of $r_A - \rho_A$ and the wealth of domestic customers (who are all nationals); but here again (3) is used to express wealth as a function of consumers' expenditures at the firms, so share wealth drops out. We may say, as the aforementioned "IS-LM" paper did, that this curve, not (1'), is the true analogue of the LM curve, since it gives the rate of interest "required" by wealth owners—required, to be more accurate, if consumers are planning a consumption path that is flat to a good approximation. (Yet in one respect this equation and its counterpart for country A are analogous to Hicks's IS equations: These equations indicate how high the real interest rate must be to trim consumption demand and hence, in the model here, aggregate demand to the level that would be provided by the specified level of domestic production, after netting out the amounts of output to be purchased by the government and by firms, from which we have abstracted here.) Note an important difference, though: It is these required-interest equations that shift up with an increase of local public debt, not the other equations.

Which way do these latter two equations slope? If $m_A = 0$, so we are in the so-called Ricardian case, the corresponding interest rate—the rate read off the curve—is simply the rate of pure time preference, ρ_B, so the curve is flat, meaning parallel to the output axis. Here we are excluding the Ricardian case, however.

Under our non-Ricardian stipulation that $m_A > 0$ and $m_B > 0$, (2′) makes the rate of interest an increasing function of consumption expenditure and hence the level of output—provided that the level of public debt is not too far above zero. The reason is that, according to the Blanchard formula, the steady-state interest rate is an increasing function of the wealth-consumption ratio while the latter, more precisely the ratio of real-share wealth to consumption, is an increasing—repeat, *increasing*—function of the level of consumption expenditure by virtue of the fact that the share price must rise more than proportionately with output to induce firms to supply increased output, according to equation (3) in Table 12.2. Hence the curve of (2′) has a positive slope, provided the debt is not too large.[13] It is true that the case for an upward slope is somewhat weaker in B where some of the domestic shares are held by foreigners. However, nothing would be lost by admitting a downward slope provided that the curve does not slope downward more strongly than the companion curve corresponding to (1′).

Thus the system described in Table 12.3 consists of four equations in e, r, and the respective output levels in the two countries. To forestall or terminate confusion I will refer to (1′) and (4′) as the expected-return equations, for which ER may serve as an abbreviation, and we will refer to (2′) and (5′) as the required-return, or RR, equations.

Figure 12.2 graphs the four equations of the short-run system in a pair of back-to-back diagrams in the interest rate–employment plane— in "IS-LM space." In his two-country Keynesian model Robert Mundell used the

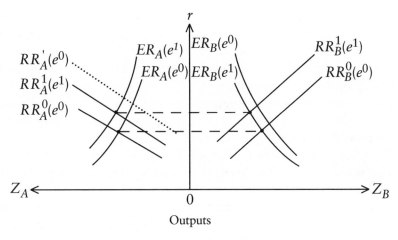

Figure 12.2 The two-country customer-market short run

same apparatus. It offers us a clear view of the differences between the monetary approach represented by the Mundell-Fleming model and the real approach taken here.[14] The downward-sloping curves ER_A and ER_B correspond to (1′) and (4′), respectively, and the upward-sloping curves RR_A and RR_B refer to (2′) and (5′), respectively.

An alert reader will have noticed that A's RR_A curve makes the interest rate depend on the other country's output level, Z_B, not just its own output, through the supply-price effect of Z_B on the price of shares in B held by A-nationals who are customers in A. Even in B, where nationals do not hold foreign shares, foreign customers hold such shares, so the interest rate in B depends upon foreign output, Z_A. To simplify the discussion and to avoid muddying the results of the analysis with effects that are presumably small in fact between large trading areas, I will take x_{BA} and s_{BA} to be arbitrarily small. As a result of this simplification all the terms in total wealth that involve multiplication by e or $1/e$ are taken to be negligible. The sole disadvantage of this procedure, it appears, is that the initial effects of a fiscal stimulus cannot include an initial widening of the trade deficit of appreciable magnitude; such a widening will take time to develop.

Nevertheless the real exchange rate, e, is still a variable being held constant in the construction of any pair of RR curves since e figures in the supply-price functions Q^A and Q^B appearing in the underlying equations, (2′) and (5′). Also, e affects the customer-stock growth rates figuring in the ER curves, so there too a shift of e will shift the curves.

The exchange rate is determined as follows. For a given e, at least any *e* in the relevant range, we may assume there will be an intersection of the two curves in the righthand panel, the (r, Z_B) plane, and an intersection of the two curves in the lefthand panel, the (r, Z_A) plane. The solution value of the variable *e* is determined by the condition that it be at such a level as to make the intersections occur at the same value of *r*. (This is not the equilibrium exchange rate since expectations in that regard are fundamentally "off.") The effect of a change in the exchange rate on the intersections will be analyzed below.

The effects of an increase of public debt in A. Let us now study the consequences of fiscal stimulus in *A* for employment, consumption, etc., in *A* and in *B*. We take up here a helicopter drop, so to speak, of public debt that is rained down on the citizenry of *A* and financed by a balanced-budget increase of lump-sum taxes. This is a stylized way of representing a burst of deficits due to a temporary tax cut. In applications to the unemployment pattern that developed in the 1980s, one would want to identify *A* as "America" and *B* as "Britain"/Europe. (Of course, there are any number of honorary members of the latter group, such as Sweden and Norway, Australia and New Zealand, Canada, and some portions of Latin America and Africa; some other countries were predominantly influenced by other external shocks or internal forces, and so do not fit the model well or fit it for different reasons.)

A step increase in β_A impacts only on one curve, the RR_A curve; a propagation mechanism is involved in the determination of the general-equilibrium effects. The impact is an upward shift of that RR curve, hence a rise of the "required" interest rate in *A* at the initial level of Z_A. This shift juxtaposed against the unchanged ER_A curve implies a positive impact on the interest rate in *A*, taking the exchange as given. A corollary that is paradoxical for Keynesian thinking is the corresponding negative impact on output in *A*, given the exchange rate. This much is just the result obtained from closed-economy models of the customer-market economy: the higher real interest rate discourages firms from investing so intensively in future customers, and the consequent jump of the desired markup has the side effect of contracting employment until the desired markup and the real wage associated with the prevailing employment level are again consistent.

In *B* the increase of β_A does not produce a shift of the curves, given *e*, so there is no impact on the interest rate there. In view of the positive impact on the interest rate in *A*, absent a change of *e*, an incipient disparity between the interest rates in the two countries in favor of *A* is created.

To restore interest-rate parity, it will be argued, a real depreciation of the exchange rate is necessary in *B*: that is, *e* must fall; equivalently, there must be a real appreciation in A. What are the mechanisms and what are the side effects on employment in the two countries? In the stripped-down model this real appreciation in A operates to correct the interest-rate disparity through two mechanisms.

First, an appreciation in A operates to reduce the markup that firms in A will require at a given output, in view of the consequences of appreciation for their competitiveness; that means that the output that they are willing to supply at a given customer shadow price (and a given real wage) is increased; equivalently, the shadow price of customers, q_A, that is required (at a given real wage) to induce them to supply a given output is reduced.[15] With q_A down and hence real wealth down at any given output level in A, it follows that the required real interest rate in A at each output level is reduced; RR_A shifts back down. Yet the implied decline of the share price tends to raise the expected return; so on this account ER_A shifts up. (A similar analysis of the response in B gives mirror-opposite results, of course.) The latter effect by itself exacerbates the interest-rate disparity, raising further the interest rate in A and lowering it in B.

If, in addition, it were the case that A nationals held appreciable quantities of shares in B firms, the real appreciation in A would have the further effect of reducing real wealth of nationals in A who are customers in A; thus the appreciation would operate just like a decrease of β_A, shifting down the RR curve in A, so it would act to moderate the rise of the interest rate in A. Similarly, holdings by B-nationals of shares in A-firms would appreciate, which would operate like an increase of β_B: it shifts up the RR curve in B, thus causing a rise of the interest rate there. Hence the rise of e would tend on this account also to restore interest-rate equality. It does the same through its effect on the wealth of the foreign customers of A-firms.

A second set of effects are the following: An appreciation in A, by reducing the competitiveness of A firms, acts to reduce the algebraic growth rate of the stock of customers in A—from zero if the world economy was initially in its steady-state equilibrium to some negative growth rate, as domestic customers began to drift overseas upon locating cheaper supplies there. In B, therefore, the effect of this real-exchange-rate response is a rise in the growth rate of the customer stock there—from zero initially to some positive growth rate. On this account, therefore, ER_A in Figure 12.1 shifts down, lowering the initially elevated interest rate in A, and ER_B shifts up, raising the (lower) interest rate prevailing in B.

One conclusion concerns the effect of the increased debt in A on the world real interest rate. In the present model, the world interest rate can be seen to increase if and only if the real appreciation removes the interest-rate disparity at least in part by raising the interest rate in B, not simply by driving the interest rate back down in A. It has just been seen that there is a positive effect on r in B operating through RR_B and two mutually opposing effects operating through ER_B. It follows that r in B rises if and only if the net ER_B effect on r, if negative, does not swamp the RR_B effect. This will certainly be the case if the growth rate of the stock of customers is sufficiently insensitive to real appreciation.

Henceforth it will be assumed that the upward RR shift in B (brought by appreciation in A) is decisive for the interest-rate response there, and similarly in A: the unambiguous upward shift of RR in B leaves the interest rate up on balance in B, notwithstanding the strong possibility that the net shift of the ER curve in B is downward (because the rise in the prospective customer-growth-rate effect is not strong enough to predominate).

Some more novel conclusions concern employment in the two countries. Consider the effect of the appreciation in A on country B. The upward shift of the RR curve in B contracts employment there, and if indeed ER in B moves down on balance (because the customer-growth-rate effect is not strong), there is a further contractionary effect. Thus the fiscal stimulus in A operates to contract employment in B unless the customer-growth-rate effect is so strong as to offset the other two effects. After Fitoussi-Phelps this result is no longer stupefying. In the customer-market model of that volume too, the real depreciation in B tends to contract the supply of output in B by tempting firms to exploit the increased protection from foreign competition by raising their markups. In the present model, one of the effects is precisely parallel: the required q for the supply of any given output in B is increased by the real appreciation in A, which shifts down the rate of return given by the ER_B curve, thus contracting employment. Here, it also shifts up the RR_B, further contracting output. (The effect on the ER_B from the prospect of a higher growth rate operates in the opposite direction, pulling up employment, but, again, we take this consideration to be nondecisive.)

With regard to the effect in A, there is a strong theoretical possibility that the supply effect of the real appreciation in A is sufficiently expansionary for employment to overcome the initial (contractionary) employment impact of the increase of the public debt there. At a geometrical level the explanation resides in the fact that the consequent reduction in the real shadow price of customers needed to induce a given level of output operates to shift outward the ER curve in A (assuming the customer-growth-rate effect is small) as it shifts outward the RR curve. It is clear that if country *B* were so large that appreciation in *A* must drive the interest rate in *A* back to its original level—so *A* was described by the small-country case—the new equilibrium point in *A* would have to be at the same, old interest rate on an *outward-shifted ER* curve, hence to show an *increased* employment rate.[16] At the other extreme, we learned earlier that if the country were so large as to be virtually closed, the employment rate would be *decreased*. The implication is that employment in *A* will actually *expand* in the near term if *A* is *not too large* in relation to the rest of the world, here country *B*. Whether for an employment expansion it is sufficient that *A* is equal in size to *B* is beyond the scope of the present analysis.

This theoretical possibility—output increased at home, decreased abroad—has, I believe, the following explanation: On the one hand, in both countries the higher interest rate drives firms to discount the future more heavily, hence to sacrifice less present cash flow via moderation of their markup in the interest of gaining future customers, which is equivalent to offering a reduced real wage for the same level of production; and since the workers require, so to speak, an unchanged real wage for an unchanged level of employment, as the optimal incentives to combat shirking, the result is a reduction of employment to the point where the two real wages are reconciled. But on the other hand, the real exchange-rate appreciation in country *A*, the origin of the fiscal stimulus, introduces an asymmetry further discouraging supply in country *B* but actually encouraging supply in country *A*. This latter effect is the one operating through the peculiar supply curve that makes the amount of output supplied an increasing function of the shadow price of customers weighted by how easily they are gained or lost. (In all this we should not forget that we found also a demand effect of the appreciation that was seen to work in the opposite direction, lowering expectations of customer growth in *A* and thus lowering the expected-return curve, thus also lowering the demand price for customers, and thus moving the economy downward and leftward along the aforementioned supply curve.) If this analysis is right, it is an empirical question whether the net employment effect of the appreciation needed to equalize interest rates will be big enough to offset the contractionary impact on employment of the increased public debt.

Potentially, therefore, the results are similar to those reached in the Fitoussi-Phelps analysis of a customer-market setting as well as in the two other models studied there. That analysis implied that fiscal stimulus in *A* was expansionary there, in stark contrast to the effect in *B*. The Fitoussi-Phelps models have an easier time generating an expansionary effect in the country where the fiscal stimulus originates because they allow some degree of short-run monetary nonneutrality, so the higher nominal interest rates resulting from the fiscal stimulus, in quickening the velocity of money, have an expansionary effect.

Note in passing that the appreciation in A will set in motion a gradual outflow of customers from A to B. But it would be a *non sequitur* to conclude that the future will similarly witness an ongoing (though ever diminishing) attrition of market share in A. If wealth owners in A, laden with the newfound windfall of wealth, sooner or later begin selling off some of their shares in B-firms to wealth owners in B, the steady-state import bill of A that can be financed by foreign income will tend to erode; so one expects that in the *long run* firms in A will gain, not lose, market share, as more customers are repatriated to A-firms. To check this conjecture let us proceed to the analysis of the long run.

The steady state under perfect foresight. There exists, generally speaking, an equilibrium (that is, a correct-expectations) stationary-state solution to the model, and it will be taken for granted that the economy approaches that steady-state equilibrium after the initial shock. What are the salient features of the steady state and how will the new one differ from the old?

Since the rate of change of x_{BA} equals zero in this steady state it follows from equation (9) of Table 12.2 that $e = 1$ in this state. Also $r_A = r_B$. Since the rates of change of y_{BA} and y_{AA} are both zero and $e = 1$, it follows from equations (2) and (5a) that $y_{BA} = y_{BB}$; if that equality were not to hold the customer allocation would still be in flux, hence the steady state would not be in place. With these solutions the remaining system reduces to five equations in r, Z_A, Z_B, x_{BA}, and s_{BA}.

This system, labeled the Equilibrium Steady State, can also be analyzed with the aid of back-to-back diagrams of the IS-LM type in the (Z_A, r) and (Z_B, r) planes. See Figure 12.3. The equations underlying this system can be found in the endnotes.[17] The four curves generated by these four equations are generally indexed by x_{BA} and s_{BA}. We may think of x_{BA} as provisionally given here and employ s_{BA} to shift up or down the righthand intersection, the real interest rate as determined in B, so as to achieve interest-rate equalization. This leads to conceiving a companion diagram in the (s_{BA}, x_{BA}) plane in which there is a required s_{BA} for each given x_{BA}. In the same diagram, not drawn, we can graph the relationship that shows how x_{BA} depends on s_{BA} through equation (10). These two curves thus simultaneously determine the steady-state x_{BA} and s_{BA}.

It is now clear how the equilibrium steady state is disturbed by the increase of the public debt we have been studying. The consequence in

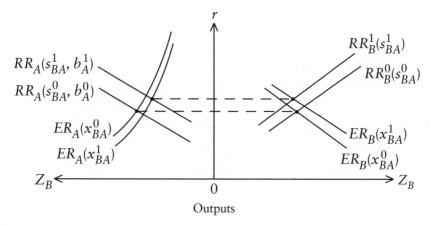

Figure 12.3 The two-country customer-market steady state

Figure 12.3 is an upward shift of the steady-state RR curve in the (Z_A, r) plane. To restore equality of the interest rates it is necessary, given x_{BA}, to have a decrease of s_{BA}, which functions in B rather like a tit-for-tat increase of β_B and in A like a rollback of some of the increase of β_A. The steady-state RR curve is thus shifted down in A and up in B. The equalization must therefore occur at a higher world real interest rate than the rate prevailing in the equilibrium steady state before the shock.

A steady-state result of the fiscal shock, then, is a leftward shift of the curve giving s_{BA} as a function of x_{BA} in the (s_{BA}, x_{BA}) plane. The other curve in this plane, the one giving x_{BA} as a function of s_{BA}, is unambiguously upward-sloping. Hence the leftward shift of the former curve implies a downward and leftward movement of the intersection of the two curves, and thus a final decline of s_{BA}, *mutatis mutandis*, which pulls x_{BA} down with it—if and only if the former curve is downward-sloping or, if not, is steeper than the latter curve. This seems to be the relevant empirical case.

I believe the following propositions can be shown, though I cannot give the full argument here, as it would require a more detailed version of the model. First, there is a rise in the steady-state world real interest rate by virtue of the fact that the increase in the public debt in A ultimately drives up the required interest rate curve, RR, in both countries. As a result both countries are moved up their "IS" curves—up their negatively sloped ER curves. Second, although this conclusion is less theoretically certain, owing to the possibility that the ER curves themselves may move in response to the redistribution of market shares, there results a contraction of output in *both* countries in the steady state. If, as assumed, there is in the end a net reflux of customers from B back to A, and if such a reallocation lowers the interest rate in A and raises it in B, the rise of the world interest rate will be moderated and s_{BA} will have to decrease less than would otherwise have been required to restore interest-rate equality.

There seems to be no visible escape from the conclusion that in the equilibrium steady state, employment is decreased in *both* countries by the increased debt in A. For if it is granted that the world real interest rate is increased in the steady state, it will be readily agreed that the real wage in both countries must be reduced in the new steady state. But a lower real wage unaccompanied by a proportional reduction of nonwage income can only mean a downward and therefore leftward movement along the equilibrium real wage–employment locus arising from the incentive-wage theory of labor-market unemployment equilibrium used here—hence a contraction of steady-state employment.

12.3 Commentary

The customer-market apparatus was first imbedded in a model of the small open economy—a rather special model created to avoid analytical impediments when we are still building strength for the final ascent. This is model F, the special feature of which is that all or virtually all of the customers of the domestic firms reside overseas. Subsequently, a two-country model was presented in which initially the producers in one country possess at least the domestic customers and battle the competitors in the other country for a share of its customers.

The analysis of model F showed that a positive productivity shock, productivity being unchanged overseas, would have a positive effect on *production*, as firms took advantage of their increased competitiveness to establish a price advantage and thus produce and sell more output. But producing any given level of output now requires a lower level of employment, so the net effect on employment is not at first clear. It may be argued, however, that the former boost to employment is outweighed by the latter effect, so employment drops. This effect is ultimately vanishing, though. It would also have been interesting to see what a small-open-economy model of the customer-market type implied about the effect of a one-time, unanticipated increase in the (henceforth anticipated) rate of growth of productivity.

These models were created primarily to obtain a more realistic conception of the effects of expenditure shocks. It was necessary to have models enriched with frictions or nontradabilities in one or more of the product markets in order to let expenditures "bite" on real exchange rates.

Model *F* is instructive in showing that, given the interest rate in the rest of the world, increased demand for *domestic* output, either *export* demand or *government* demand, generates a real appreciation and an increased supply of total output and jobs in our country. Increased demand for *foreign* output causes a real depreciation and a decreased supply of output and jobs. Keynesian results without Keynes and his monetary apparatus!

The effect on such an open economy of a *general* increase of demand by consumers *worldwide,* including the demand from overseas customers, given their income, is a somewhat different matter. The closed-economy model immediately implies that, since the countries in the world constitute a closed economy, the world will suffer a *decline* of real income and employment as a result of the increased real interest rate that the increased consumer demand entails. The decline of real incomes overseas means that the overseas consumers who are customers at the national firms—and in model *F* that is essentially all of the national firms' customers—will be buying *less* output, just like the customers of foreign competitors. If all economies have the same structural architecture, no real depreciation results in any country, only the fall of output shared by all countries.

A message of the model is that no amount of money-wage/money-price and exchange-rate flexibility is sufficient to insulate the economy from fluctuations in the world economy, particularly world income. Stability of a nation's employment in the face of these demand disturbances would require a *real* wage "flexibility" that is precluded by the incentive-wage model of labor-market equilibrium. The power to neutralize demand disturbances that Friedman imputed to free fluctuation of the exchange rate is impaired by its supply effects.

The purpose of the model of *two large* economies was to try to show the possibility that higher demand for domestic output would *expand* home output and *contract* output abroad. This outcome seems to be possible. But the model is not very hospitable to the rigorous analysis needed to resolve many of the questions that one has about the behavior of this kind of theoretical economy! Why bother with the customer-market model if it is so resistant to analysis? It is true that in this volume there are already other models capturing the interaction of countries through the world capital market and the price that it determines, the world rate of interest. Only empirical research will tell which of these models or, more likely, which blend of these models is the most pertinent description for the explanatory purposes at hand. Of these various sorts of models, the customer-market kind of model is possibly the most "ornery" and inelegant. Yet it may be wondered whether it is possible to understand events over a medium-term horizon without recognizing the informational frictions that impede adjustments in the product market and without taking carefully into account their myriad system effects.

13

International Linkages through Investment in Fixed Capital

THE third member of our family of provisional models of economic activity is the two-sector model of investment in fixed capital. With two other open-economy models already on our plate the question arises whether, in the analysis of international interactions, this third model adds value. Three reasons for paying particular attention to that model in the two-country context suggest themselves.

A rather important reason for having the two-sector model among our tools in studying two-country interactions is that it is useful to have a model with a nontradable sector alongside a tradable sector; such a model can generate temporary real appreciations and depreciations, which are observed in actual data, and do so without appealing to the modernist construct of temporary informational frictions presented by customer markets. The classic two-sector model emerging from Austrian capital theory can be conveniently converted to serve as a two-sector model of the tradable/nontradable type by the simple device of supposing that the capital-good-producing sector, say, is nontradable while the other sector is taken to be tradable.

Another reason for studying the fixed-capital model in the international setting is that fixed capital is out there, after all, and in recognition of its presence data on its movements have for some time been available. Moreover, there have often been sharp disturbances to the distribution of the capital stock around the world, owing to wars and other shocks. We can hardly afford not to have some grasp, therefore, of the international effects of changes in national capital stocks.

The last, but not least, reason for including the fixed-capital model here is the importance of being able to study fiscal stimuli to fixed-capital investment. It was the Fitoussi-Phelps thesis that fiscal stimulus over the period

1981 to 1986 in the United States, by impacting on the real rate of return there, operated through the world capital market to force up real interest rates and contract aggregate employment in Europe (and to a degree in other continents as well). In the model with fixed investment, the mechanism produced a crowding-out of investment in Europe, hence a slump in the nontradable capital-goods industries there, and in this way a fall of aggregate employment. If the sole fiscal stimulus was a string of deficits generating an increase in the American public debt, the objection could be raised that a similar contraction of employment in the United States was implied by that model; the latter implication was counterfactual, and the model seemed on this count to fail to solve the problem of explaining the American boom amidst slump overseas. To meet that objection it was argued in Fitoussi and Phelps that various structural fiscal stimuli—an investment tax credit and accelerated depreciation allowances are the leading examples—were important components of the fiscal-stimulus package in the United States, and these components did not have the implication that investment and capital-goods output, which were identical under nontradability, would fall in the United States while falling in Europe. Since, as an empirical matter, investment tax credits and accelerated depreciation allowances have often appeared to be of importance in American history and they have applied only to investment in fixed capital, not investment in employees and in customers, an adequate toolbox of models must contain the fixed-capital model.

We are interested, then, in the effects at home and abroad of the enactment by one of the countries in the two-country model of such structural fiscal stimuli. The corresponding consequences of an increase in one of the countries in particular kinds of public expenditure are also very much worth studying. Further, one would like to understand the implications of the model for the effects of a change in a country's labor force or in its capital stock (accompanied by a specified change in its wealth) on employment levels in the home and foreign countries. It will not be possible here to pursue these questions with a rigorous analysis, but by putting the various known pieces together one can draw some important conclusions on the question.

13.1 The Small Open Economy

The exercise here is to examine how a small open economy with a structure like the economy just studied, save for its openness, is affected by external and internal shocks. We restrict ourselves to a few of the more crucial questions: What is the effect of an increase in the (stationary) level of the world real interest rate? What is the effect of an increase in the domestic marginal efficiency of capital? The analysis is again confined to the "classic" case.[1]

The open-economy version of the model, since it focuses on physical capital rather than the dynamics of customer markets, portrays the consumer good as tradable on a perfect goods market under conditions of pure competition. The extension to neoclassical monopolistic competition would be of some benefit but not worth the cost at this early stage. Extension to the case in which there are some nontradable consumer goods alongside tradables would also be useful but does not seem critical for the propositions to be developed.

The key additions to the structure of the model appear to be two: First, the capital good is nontradable. To avoid results that would be seriously misleading, such as the finding of real-wage equalization and various corollaries flowing from that finding, it is crucial to have at least one capital good that is nontradable, and since it is convenient to have just one capital good it is required that this one capital good be nontradable. It may be conjectured that rather little would come from adding a capital good that is costlessly tradable in a perfect capital-goods market. Second, there is a perfect world capital market ensuring equality of the home country's real interest rate, defined (as elsewhere) in terms of the consumer good, and the real interest rate in the rest of the world, to be denoted r^*. Since there is a single consumer good in the world of this model, and the real interest rate is equalized across all regions and countries, one can speak unambiguously of a "world real interest rate" and it is thus natural to refer to the external rate (and for that matter the internal rate as well) as the "world rate." Of course, the small open economy by definition is too small to affect this rate, so the interest rate facing the country is parametric. For simplicity, the external interest rate will be taken to be stationary over time, though subject to a one-time shock. Letting r^* denote the fixed-world-rate parameter, then, we have the equation,

$$(13.1) \quad r = r^* \equiv \text{constant} > 0$$

It is true that the above is not a complete description of the environment for *all* purposes. But it is adequate for the questions we will address here. Hence we will proceed with it.

The other equations of the model are as follows. We retain the arbitrage condition, which remains expressible in terms of the domestic interest rate:

(13.2) $\dot{q} = q(r + \delta) - R(q)$

The capital-accumulation equation is, at one level, also unchanged:

(13.3) $\dot{K} = Z^I(q, K) - \Gamma_I - \delta K$

However, the determination of u and y^w have to be adapted to the new surroundings. For the latter we introduce the real value of overseas asset holdings, F, the insurance income from which is $(r^* + \mu)F$. Then

(13.4) $y^w = (r + \mu)qK + (r^* + \mu)F$

and

(13.5) $W = qK + F + D$

The reduced-form equation for the unemployment rate then becomes

(13.6) $u = U(q, K, F)$

where the function U is taken to be decreasing in q, increasing in K, and increasing in F. The differential equation governing consumption growth becomes

(13.7) $\dot{C}/C = r - \rho - \mu(\mu + \rho)[(qK + F + D)/C]$

where C is related to the surplus on current account, $\dot{F}$, by the following accounting relationship:

(13.8) $\dot{F} = Z_C - G_C + (r^* + \mu)F - C$

This completes the dynamic system.

The steady state.   We may obtain a feel for this system by considering first its equilibrium stationary state. In any stationary state, of course, all rates of change are equal to zero. To study this state it is convenient to introduce f to denote the ratio F/K, and to regard D, G_C, and Γ_I as constant ratios to K. These constants will be denoted Δ, γ_C, and γ_I, respectively. In these terms, the stationary equilibrium can be described by the following system:

(13.9) $r = r^*$

(13.10) $r = (1/q)R(q) - \delta$

(13.11)
$$r = \rho + \mu(\mu + \rho) \frac{q + f + \Delta}{f_C(\tilde{k}_C)\tilde{k}_C^{-1} + (r^* + \mu)f - \gamma_C} \qquad \gamma_C \equiv G_C/K$$

(13.12) $f = F/\kappa(q, F; \Gamma_I, r^* + \mu)$

where the function κ represents the solution for K of the equation based on (9.42'S) giving Z_I and its development (see page 125)

(13.13) $\hat{\epsilon}(1 - u)L - \Gamma_P - (K/\tilde{k}_C) = \delta K + \gamma_I K \qquad \gamma_I \equiv \Gamma_I/K$

upon substituting for $1 - u$ from (13.6). Thus (13.12) and (13.6) make f some function of q and F, given r^* and various other parameters. In keeping with our specification of the closed-economy model, it will be assumed regarding (13.13) that here too an increase of q increases K through the same mechanism: increased q raises the lefthand side by increasing effort-adjusted employment and increasing efficiency-adjusted employees allocated to the capital-good-producing branch, while an increase of K serves to increase the righthand side faster than the lefthand side.[2] Then an increase of F, since it has an income effect reducing $\hat{\epsilon}$ and driving up u in the process, thus decreasing the lefthand side, operates to decrease K. Hence f in (13.12) is a decreasing function of q and, what is important here, an unambiguously increasing function of F.

This system is illustrated by the diagram in the (q, r) plane in Figure 13.1. As in its closed-economy counterpart, the curve of the equation giving the available rate of return on asset holdings, equation (13.10), is labeled AR and is downward-sloping. Opening the economy has not modified this curve. The curve of the equation giving the domestic interest rate that at a given f is required by savers, equation (13.11), is again labeled RR and it is upward-sloping, since $f_C/\tilde{k}_C$ is decreasing in q. This curve is obviously modified with the opening up of the economy by the addition of a term proportional to f. The dashed curve represents what RR would be if f were equal to zero. In the case illustrated by Figure 13.1, the result

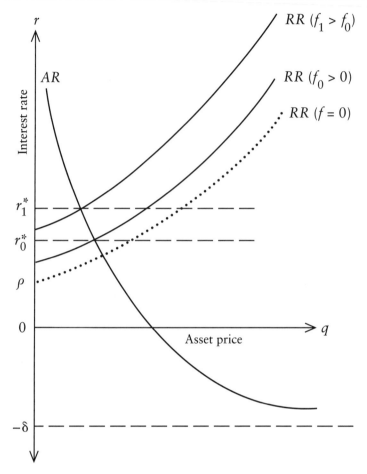

Figure 13.1 Determination of net foreign assets in the steady state

would be a domestic interest rate smaller than the external interest rate r^*. In this case the solution for the steady state requires a *positive* value of f, since that serves to drive up the RR curve, provided that r^* is not so large relative to q that consumption is boosted more than wealth is by a small increase of f—a case too bizarre to admit into the analysis.[3] In the non-Ricardian world where wealth matters for consumption plans, the increase of overseas wealth drives up the steady-state required rate of interest at a given q in order to align it with the world rate.

  Three comparative-statics exercises will perhaps suffice to capture the workings of the economy in steady state. Consider first an increase of r^*. The effect is to bring about an increase of f in order to satisfy the condition of interest-rate parity. With f higher at every given q in the relevant neighborhood than before, F must also be increased at given q. The corollary effect of this increase in r is a decrease of q, which by (13.12) operates to increase F some more. Two side effects of this decrease of q are a decrease in the demand for labor, and an increase of wealth, $qK + F$, so that the income from wealth is up on both counts, which decreases effort. Both of these side effects operate to decrease the steady-state employment rate. This conclusion is independent of the effect on the steady-state capital stock. But it is deducible that K is decreased. For if q is down and F is up, the effect on K is unambiguously negative by (13.13).

Consider next a public-debt shock. There can be no change in steady-state r and q, since r^* has not changed nor has AR shifted. Since the increase of Δ shifts up the RR curve, it must be that F decreases by enough to shift it back to where it was. Evidently there is an efflux mechanism working here to drive down F. If F decreased by exactly the amount of the increase of the public debt, D, so that K did not change, equation (13.8) would imply that consumption fell, and (13.11) would say that wealth fell in the same proportion, which is a contradiction. The solution must show a drop of consumption and wealth in equal proportion, with a decrease of K alongside the decrease of F.

Finally consider the following sort of productivity shock: an equiproportionate amount of labor augmentation in both sectors. It is a simple exercise to show that the effect is a proportional increase of K and F and the wage, v, while there is no effect on q and of course r. It is true that for this result it is necessary to assume that the public debt and the various public expenditures, where positive, all increase in the same proportion. This is not the sterile result it might seem at first to be. It points to the conclusion that a productivity increase sooner or later induces a period of current-account surplus that finally leaves the country with an increased steady-state level of assets overseas. By contrast, the monetary models of the classroom, which are typically static, are apt to prove that the rate of interest is driven up by the good productivity shock, causing a real appreciation and throwing the balance of trade and the current account into deficit.

The "short run."   What can we say of the immediate effects of such shocks? A rigorous analysis patently requires study of the differential-equation system presented above, with its two state variables and two co-state, or jump, variables. Such an analysis would impose costs threatening to go well beyond the benefits. Let us content ourselves with a few observations that may suffice for most purposes. As always, the analysis is couched in terms of initial conditions corresponding to the pre-shock steady state.

(Interested readers can see how to translate the propositions presented to other initial settings.)

The immediate effects of a positive shock to the external real interest rate include an immediate drop of q. That conclusion is reinforced by the demonstration above that even in the long run q remains lower than it was before the shock. Some of the ramifications of this immediate drop of q are clear enough. Output and employment in the capital-goods sector are immediately cut. Although the real wage will be reduced in turn (because the equilibrium wage curve in a diagram like Figure 10.1 is upward-sloping) and that adjustment will lead to a cushioning increase of employment in the consumption good/export sector, this feedback effect can only serve to moderate the drop in aggregate employment that the real wage reduction reflects. Meanwhile, consumption abruptly drops directly in response to the increased rate of interest and indirectly through the induced drop of wealth (via q), so the balance of trade (which must have been initially negative if the initial F was positive, and zero if the initial F was zero) is improved, the current account swings into surplus, and F commences to grow. The entire medium-term outlook is for recovery of wealth and finally growth to a higher level than before, with the result that the growth rate of consumption will tend to be decreasing back toward its steady-state value (zero). At the same time, the capital stock will be steadily falling, as its production remains short of depreciation. But in the small open economy, q cannot be an increasing function of K, which would imply that the shrinking of the capital stock would pull q down further following its initial drop. The reason is that if q leveled out at a lower level, the algebraic-capital-gain term would then turn from negative to zero while the rental rate, $R(q)/q$, would also then be higher than earlier, while, by hypothesis, the new real interest rate r^* is not further increasing—it is only at a new and higher plateau; in this phase, therefore, q must actually be recovering, the decline of the capital-gain term just offsetting the rise of the rental rate so as to leave the overall yield continuously equal to the new but unchanging r^*. It is not to be expected, though, that both of the state variables proceed monotonically to a soft landing. A new development begins if q recovers sufficiently that K ceases to go on declining while F is still rising *or* we find F having reached its steady-state value while K is still declining. From then on, we can expect some oscillatory behavior as K and F cycle around their new steady-state values. However, rather little importance attaches, it would seem, to the details of the post–medium term approach to the rest point of the dynamic system.

Consider finally a positive shock to the public debt in a fiscal regime of essentially balanced budgets. The impact is a jump of consumption demand followed by steadily declining consumption, since the growth rate of optimal consumption is actually reduced by increased wealth. Moreover, the Pigou effect of the increased wealth on the propensity to shirk and the tax-rate effect of the debt service both operate to drive up the wage curve describing labor-market equilibrium, which raises costs and thus decreases the supply of both consumer-good output and capital-goods output. The balance of trade is thus worsened, and the current account thrown into deficit, while net investment, which was zero, turns negative. The medium-term outlook is therefore for wealth to be falling from its newly elevated level and the capital stock to be declining. With wealth on its way back down and finally to a new low, q, though initially driven up from the cost side, will be declining back to its original level; the prospective rate of capital loss moderates as the rental rate recovers. This cost-side improvement serves to attenuate and finally to arrest the decline of K, and the decrease of wealth ultimately drives consumption to a sufficiently lower level to arrest the decline of F.

Other shocks are of considerable interest, of course. But this is not the last opportunity to consider them. Something can be left for discussion in the context of two-country models.

13.2 A Two-Country Model of Fixed-Capital Investment

An investment tax credit can be incorporated into the model[4] by requiring the output volume of capital goods to equate its marginal cost to the sum of price, q, and the size of the tax credit, say ι. Then the demand wage in a country with such a tax credit is given by a revised version of equation (9.17′)

$$(13.14) \quad v = \varepsilon(1, 1 - u, y^w(q, k, f; \mu)/v)\Lambda(q + \iota)$$

where, as in the small open economy of Chapter 9,

$$(13.15) \quad y^w = [(1/q)R(q; \iota) - \delta + \mu]q(K/L) + (r^* + \mu)(F/L)$$
$$\equiv y^w(q, F/L, k, f)$$

The measurement of net foreign assets, F, will be taken up shortly. Equation (13.15), it will be noted, leaves aside the public debt, D, which we shall take as small and unchanged here.[5]

The positive impact in (13.14) of the tax credit on the demand wage, in interaction with the supply-wage equation, operates to increase employment and output in the capital-good-producing sector, and hence the pace of capital accumulation, at a given q; at the same time, employment in the consumer-good-making sector is decreased in response to the higher wage (at given q) brought about by the tax credit in the other sector. Let us regard the aggregate unemployment rate in any country as a derived function of that country's own state variables, K and F, and one of its co-state variables, q; the other country's situation can matter only through the rate of interest, the direct (or impact) effect of which is negligible since the former country starts without a net creditor position and the indirect effect of which is reflected in the former country's q. Hence

(13.16) $\quad u = U(q, k, f; \iota)$

Then equation (9.39′) describing both the open economy and closed economy is revised as follows:

(13.17) $$\dot{K} = Z^I(q, K, F; \Gamma_P, \iota) - \Gamma_I - \delta K$$

$$Z^I(q, K, F; \iota) \equiv \Lambda[\varepsilon(1, 1 - U(q, k, f; \iota), y^w(q, k, f)/v(q))$$

$$\times (1 - U(q, k, f; \iota))L - n_C(q + \iota)K - \Gamma_P]$$

The differential equations in q and in C are also affected through the increase in the wage (at given q) caused by the tax credit: the supply of output of the consumer good is consequently contracted, which pushes up the required rate of return, and the rental on capital is consequently decreased, which lowers the available rate of return.

(13.18) $\quad r = \rho + \mu(\mu + \rho)(qK + F + D)/[o_C(q; \iota)K] + \dot{C}/C$

(13.19) $\quad r = \dot{q}/q - (1/q)R(q; \iota) - \delta$

where o_C is the output-capital ratio in the consumer-good sector. For both reasons, the introduction of an investment tax credit causes q, interpreted as the price of existing capital assets, abruptly to drop. The price including the subsidy or tax credit that is received for production of newly made, or currently produced, capital goods is surely increased on balance, though.

As in the small open economy, C in each country is related to the surplus on current account, $\dot{F}$, by the accounting relationship,

(13.20) $\quad \dot{F} = o_C(q)K - G_C + (r + \mu)F - C$

It will be convenient to conceive of F, the net creditor position of the country under examination, as taking the form of net holdings of foreign debt. For in that case, if D is interpreted as indexed short-term debt, so that the real value of the existing debt is insensitive to asset revaluations and interest-rate changes, then F is similarly insensitive to such disturbances. The analysis here is confined to special initial conditions in which F is at first zero in both countries; hence each country has no net holdings of foreign debt. After a shock, that will change as some country's F grows positive, the other's negative (since it is the mirror image). Hence positive public debt levels are implied. Nevertheless it will be assumed that these debt levels are small enough that we can regard them as zero throughout the analysis with little error.

One view of the structure of the two-country model is therefore the following. A pair of differential equations gives the motion of the capital stocks in countries A and B. Another pair of differential equations gives the rate of change of each country's q. A third pair of differential equations gives the rate of change of consumption in each of the countries. In the last pair of differential equations the pace of accumulation of net foreign claims in country B, F_B, is set equal to overseas interest less the excess of consumption by residents in B over domestic production of the consumption good (which is to say imports). At the same time, this accumulation, being the decumulation of net foreign assets in A, is equal to A's net overseas interest less the excess of its residents' consumption over its domestic production of the consumption good (that is, its imports). Finally, the two real interest rates must equal one another by virtue of the law of one price in the world consumption market. This system is

$$(13.21a) \quad \dot{K}_A = Z^I(q_A, K_A, F_B; \iota) - \Gamma_I - \delta K_A$$

$$(13.21b) \quad \dot{K}_B = Z^I(q_B, K_B, F_B) - \Gamma_I - \delta K_B$$

$$(13.22a) \quad \dot{q}_A = q_A(r_A + \delta) - R(q_A; \iota_A)$$

$$(13.22b) \quad \dot{q}_B = q_B(r_B + \delta) - R(q_B)$$

$$(13.23a) \quad \dot{C}_A = (r_A - \rho)C_A - \mu(\mu + \rho)(q_A K_A - F_B + D_A)$$

$$(13.23b) \quad \dot{C}_B = (r_B - \rho)C_B - \mu(\mu + \rho)(q_B K_B + F_B + D_B)$$

$$(13.24a) \quad -\dot{F}_B = -r_A F_B + o_C^A(q_B)K_B - C_A$$

(13.24*b*) $\dot{F}_B = r_B F_B + o_C^B(q_B) K_B - C_B$

(13.25) $r_B = r_A$

There are nine variables in this nine-equation system.

By adding the last two equations one could obtain the implication that

(13.24*c*) $C_A + C_B = o_C^A(q_A; \iota) K_A + o_C^B(q_B) K_B$

In other words, the global supply of the consumer good is the sum of the national supplies in *A* and *B*. Further, by adding the previous pair of equations (13.23*a*) and (13.23*b*) one could obtain

(13.24*d*) $\dot{C}_A + \dot{C}_B = (r - \rho)(C_A + C_B)$

$$- \mu(\mu + \rho)(q_A K_A + D_A + q_B K_B + D_B)$$

where *r* is the world real rate of interest. The time-rate of change of world consumption demand, this equation shows, is the sum of the corresponding time-rates of change in *A* and *B*. Of course, (13.24*c*) and (13.24*d*) are not independent equations, and hence they are not part of the already complete dynamic system represented by the previous nine equations. Yet they may serve as a distinct perspective on the system. From this pair of equations, upon differentiating (13.24*c*) with respect to time, one could proceed to obtain *r* as a function of the rates of growth of the capital stocks, even to reduce the relationships to the growth of the world capital stock under special assumptions.

Some Informal Two-Country Equilibrium Analysis

Let us look now at the steady-state relationships. For country *A*, the tax-credit country, these can be represented by the following trio of equations in which steady-state consumption has been solved out:

(13.26) $0 = Z^I(q_A, K_A, F_B; \iota) - \Gamma_I^A - \delta K_A$

(13.27) $r_A = \rho + \mu(\mu + \rho) \dfrac{q_A - (F_B + D_A)/K_A}{o_C(q_A; \iota) - r_A(F_B/K_B)}$

(13.28) $r_A = (1/q_A) R(q_A; \iota) - \delta$

For country B there is the corresponding subsystem,

(13.29) $0 = Z^I(q_B, K_B, F_B) - \Gamma_I^B - \delta K_B$

(13.30) $$r_B = \rho + \mu(\mu + \rho) \frac{q_B + (F_B + D_B)/K_B}{o_C(q_B) + r_A(F_B/K_B)}$$

(13.31) $r_B = (1/q_B)R(q_B) - \delta$

This seven-variable system is closed with $r_B = r_A$.

The analysis of this system is broadly similar to the analysis found in the two previous chapters. The algebraic net creditor position of one of the countries, say F_B, is the variable the adjustment of which serves to equalize the two steady-state interest rates determined in the three-equation subsystems.

In the subsystem pertaining to B the first equation, (13.29), may be solved to obtain K_B as a function of q_B and F_B. Then (13.30) and (13.31) may be solved to obtain r_B and q_B; these are functions of F_B and r_A, but for the latter we may substitute r_B, to which it must be equal, so the solution for r_B and q_B is obtained as a function of F_B alone. Clearly it is possible by a similar procedure to obtain the solution for r_A and q_A as a function of F_B.

For the model to work in the intuitive way it is necessary that an increase of F_B has the effect of pushing up r_B while pulling down r_A. It tends to do that by increasing wealth in B, which pushes up the required interest rate given in (13.30); the supply of consumption is also increased, which works in the opposite direction to reduce the required interest rate, but since consumption can be taken to exceed profits, the proportionate effect on the denominator is less than that on the numerator, so the net effect on the required rate is positive. (In addition, the increase of wealth in B has an adverse effect on the supply of capital-goods output through employees' effort rate, and because it increases the steady-state debt-capital ratio there is a further increase of the required rate of interest in B.) It seems reasonable to suppose that the model behaves in this desired way.

Figure 13.2 provides the back-to-back diagrams for illustrating how the net creditor position of country B may play the role of reconciling the two steady-state national interest rates.

What happens in the short run, at given capital stocks and net creditor position, to reconcile interest rates? The answer can only be the jump of the *rates of change* of the asset prices in the two countries, which impact

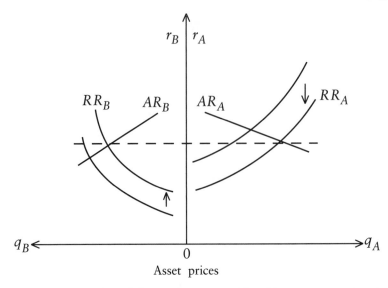

Figure 13.2 Determination of the steady-state world real interest rate and national asset prices

on the overall rates of return available, and the *rates of change* of wealth (capital nationally owned) in the two countries, which governs the rate of change of consumption and hence the required rates of interest. In view of the huge dimensionality of the dynamic model—three state variables and six co-state variables—a formal analysis demonstrating saddlepath stability or rather the conditions under which that stability will obtain is well beyond the ambitions of the informal analysis ventured here. Yet, despite the impediments to a formal analysis, some reasonable inferences about the course of adjustment to a shock can be pieced together from the implications of the steady-state analysis and the structure of the dynamic system.

Effect of increased public purchases of labor services or capital goods. Let us first consider the effect of the unanticipated introduction of a permanent balanced-budget program of public expenditures in country A for increased public-sector employment in that economy. A balanced-budget program of public expenditure for output of the capital-goods-producing sector was found in Chapter 9 to disturb the closed economy similarly, owing to the same factor-proportions considerations, so the analysis here applies equally to government purchases from the capital-goods-producing sector.

Throughout the analysis both countries are taken to be initially neither a net debtor nor a net creditor. Indeed, no resident in either country holds any shares of firms operating in the other country. In the immediately following formal analysis it is also assumed that taxation is lump-sum; it will be clear enough how distortionary taxation affects the results.

With regard to the ultimate, or asymptotic, consequences of the expenditure program, it can be seen from the steady-state equations pertaining to A that there is just one channel of influence, and this one can be neglected if we take the initial public-debt level to be small: As (13.26) shows, the redirection of capital-goods output to meet government demand in A has the effect of decreasing the steady-state level of the (nontradable) capital stock purchased and accumulated in A, and this in turn increases the force of the public-debt term in the required-interest-rate equation (13.27), hence raising the required rate of interest schedule in the (q_A, r_A) plane of Figure 13.2. Henceforth we neglect this channel of influence on the ground that it is unlikely to be of decisive importance as an empirical matter.

On this proviso that the steady-state interest rate in A shows no impact of the expenditure program there, the steady-state capital-goods price and steady-state wage must likewise be unaffected. (The implication is that the belt-tightening decrease in consumer demand, at the initial asset price, implied by the fiscal burden of the expenditure program is finally matched by the contraction of consumer-good supply in A, at the initial asset price, as the crowding-out of private investment causes an erosion of the consumer-good sector's capital stock; thus the excess supply of the consumer good is corrected at the initial asset price. To a satisfactory approximation, one may say that the workers released, along with the workers laid off as replacement investment falls off, move over to meet the needs of the expenditure program.)[6] Since there are no shifts of the curves in Figure 13.1 that cannot be neglected in the case under study, the consequences for the long-run creditor positions must likewise be negligible; that is, there is essentially no change in F_A and F_B from their initial levels of zero. If A initially runs a current-account surplus it must later run an offsetting current-account deficit.

What, under the present scenario, are the short-run consequences of the introduction of the expenditure program? There seems to be no chance that a formal analysis would prove illuminating, other than to formalize insights that may as well be put forward informally. In any case, let us engage in some informal thinking about the question to see what insights occur.

We learned from the study of the closed-economy two-sector model, in Chapter 9, that the near-term effect of the increased public expenditure (on labor or on the production of the labor-intensive sector), starting from a steady state, is a *drop* of the instantaneous real rate of interest—to be more exact, a pivoting of the yield curve around an unchanged perpetuity asymptote—and an accompanying upward jump in the real price of the capital good, to be followed by a gradual decline toward its unchanged steady-state value. The jump in the capital-goods price is a result of the drop of the interest rate, which is in turn an effect of the fiscal burden imposed by the expenditure program, which operates to curtail consumer demand (at the initial level of employment) and thus to increase the supply of saving. A consequence of the jump in the price of output in the capital-goods sector is a similar upward jump of employment in the capital-goods-producing sector; that is followed by a similar vanishing of the elevation shown by employment. Thus employment precisely mirrors the behavior of the asset price in this thought-experiment.

In the present two-country setting, the tendency for the interest rate to drop in A causes the common interest rate in *both* countries to drop.[7] This effect is also transient, just as in the closed-economy case. With the drop of r_A there is an upward jump of q_A in tandem with the upward jump of q_B. The jump in q_A is mirrored by an upward jump of employment in B. Thus the particular kind of public-expenditure program we are studying here, a fiscal program that *lowers* the world real rate of interest, operates as the *structuralist locomotive* by which employment in *all* countries is pulled up in unison.

The other effects pertain to consumption and the current account. With the interest rate driven down in B and the asset price driven up, consumption demand will jump up in B while consumption supply is reduced by the wage increase caused by the real price rise in the capital-good sector. This is part of the adjustment of the world to the excess supply of the consumer good that is the impact-effect of the burdensome expenditure program in A, the other part of the adjustment being the decreases in the supply of the consumer good induced by the increase of wage rates in both countries. The implication is that there is a jump of the current account from exact balance to *deficit* in B, in A a jump to surplus. It might therefore seem at first that, asymptotically, the residents of country A end up with an increase of wealth, in the form of a stock of net foreign assets, and a corresponding increase of consumption financed by the income from the foreign assets; but the implications of the steady-state relationships tell us that no change in the steady-state net creditor/debtor positions is possible, since the expenditure program has no impact on the pair of curves in each country determining the national steady-state interest rate. It follows that the period of current-account deficit in B gives way to a period of current-account surplus; it would be no surprise if further oscillations followed. It must be that net foreign assets are not neutral for the current-account deficit (surplus): Once the interest rate has returned or approximated to its original value, the accumulated net creditor position in A must then be producing a current-account deficit in A, as the real income from the overseas asset accumulation from surpluses in the past induces an additional import demand that exceeds that real foreign asset income, thanks to the "wealth effect" of those assets (for which the non-Ricardian nature of the households modeled is necessary though not quite sufficient); correspondingly, a current-account *surplus* is being run in B. Thus net foreign assets gravitate back to their original levels.

Effects of an investment tax credit.   Let us then consider the effect of the unanticipated introduction of a permanent investment tax credit in country A, whose public debt is held constant. It should be borne in mind that throughout the analysis both countries are taken to be initially neither a net debtor nor a net creditor.

With regard to the *steady-state* consequences of the tax credit, there are three channels of influence, and the first to be discussed of these can be neglected if we take the initial public-debt levels to be small: From (13.26) it follows that the investment tax credit in A has the effect of increasing the steady-state level of the capital stock accumulated in A, and this in turn reduces the force of the public-debt term in the required-interest-rate equation (13.27), hence lowering the required rate of interest schedule in the (q_A, r_A) plane of Figure 13.2. Henceforth we neglect this channel of influence on the ground that it is unlikely to be of decisive importance as an empirical matter.

The other two influences work in opposite directions. On the one hand the tax credit contracts the supply of the consumer good forthcoming at a given q_A; that is to say, $o_C(q_A; \iota)$ is decreased. Hence the required real interest rate schedule is pushed up, driving up r_A and driving down q_A. On the other hand, the tax credit reduces the rental on capital earned at a given q_A; that is, $R(q_A; \iota)$ is decreased. The impact of this is to pull down the available rate-of-return curve in Figure 13.2. One implication is unambiguous: the steady-state q_A is reduced. The implication for r_A depends on details open for specification. In the interesting case (which we have generally excluded) of so-called Ricardian equivalence there is no effect on the interest rate, of course, but that is not a useful point of reference here. An inspection of equations (13.27) and (13.28) indicates that if the output-capital ratio and the marginal product of capital in the consumer-good sector are decreased in equal proportion, as would be true under the Cobb-

Douglas production function, then, in view of the constants in these two equations, the available rate of return would fall more in proportionate terms than the required rate of interest would rise; so there is some presumption that the steady-state rate of interest in A would be reduced by the tax credit. That may seem counterintuitive, but it must be remembered that an effect of the tax credit in the present two-sector model, in which the capital-good-producing sector is comparatively (in our example, entirely) labor-intensive, is to drive up the wage.

If indeed the steady-state interest rate is driven down in A, the consequences for the creditor positions must be, on our assumption (above) about the effect of net assets on a country's steady-state interest rate, the accumulation of net foreign assets by country A—that is, an *increase* of F_A into the positive range and a *decrease* of F_B from its initial level of zero to a negative level. Evidently the decrease in the world interest rate induces residents of B sooner or later to run a current-account deficit, as consumption demand fails to fall as much as consumption supply (if it falls at all), for a sufficiently long time to accumulate a net debtor position—though this is ultimately vanishing, as a trade surplus develops to service the indebtedness to foreign lenders. Of course, if instead the steady-state interest rate in A is driven up by the tax credit there, the effects on net creditor positions are reversed.

What, pursuing the scenario under discussion, are the *short-run* consequences of the introduction of the tax credit? Again there is a direct impact of the credit on the real wage, operating to contract consumption supply, and a direct impact operating to contract existing rentals on capital. Further, there is the immediate expectation of the reduced level of q_A in the far future. For both these reasons it may be concluded that there is an abrupt drop of q_A in the present. How does this drop compare with the reduction in the steady-state level? It may be reasoned that q_A overshoots its final reduced level, since the subsequent growth of the capital stock tends to pull it up. Hence there is the possibility that even if r_A is reduced asymptotically, because R_A/q_A is reduced on balance, the ratio R_A/q_A is actually increased in the short run. Further, there is a stream of capital gains in prospect, which also operates to produce an upward jump of r_A. If all this is correct and not misleading, it is theoretically possible for the near-term effect of the tax credit on the short-term interest rates to be positive. The contention here, then, is that an investment tax credit may operate like a one-time jump in the level of the technology in causing an initial lift to interest rates which is gradually eroded (and in the present case actually reversed to a degree) as the capital stock is increased.

In the event of such an upward jump of the (short-term) interest rate in A, followed by a decline and ultimately some net decrease from the old steady-state level, it seems to be theoretically possible that the asset price in country B will likewise drop in sympathy with the drop in A. The only doubt on that score arises from the implication of the steady-state analysis that F_B is ultimately decreased, from which it follows that q_B is ultimately increased.

Suffice it to say that the findings here regarding the consequences of an investment tax credit have produced some surprises, and that more than the usual amount of caution should be shown in relying on the above results and surmises.

13.3 Commentary

This chapter has been short enough that little purpose would be served by summarizing the results and claims arrived at. Some brief reflections on this chapter may be useful, however.

The two-country two-sector model has posed some questions taking us into territory that is not widely known, possibly quite unknown. Since a formal analysis of the whole trajectory is ruled out by the rather large dimensionality of the dynamic system, the theoretical correctness of the conclusions drawn from the model is subject to more than the usual risks of analytical error. The propositions obtained are in one or two respects somewhat unanticipated: The proposition that an investment tax credit tends sooner or later to lower the real interest rate, and thus ultimately (if not immediately) to be *expansionary* overseas, is the leading example; the proposition that increased public-sector employment is *expansionary* at home and overseas *both* is another example. Yet it would be premature to judge the empirical plausibility of these findings without long consideration. For one thing, the analysis leading to these conclusions abstracts from the effect of the increase of distortionary tax rates that is typically required to raise the additional revenue to finance the tax credit or the enlargement of the public sector.

It might be best to finish with a general conclusion to be drawn from the two-country two-sector model. This is the conclusion that the structure of demands and supplies matters. Whether a domestic demand shock, for example, is expansionary at home, and if so whether it is also expansionary abroad or instead contractionary for the rest of the world, is not independent of the direction, or object, of the increased demand.

14

Synthesis of the Global-Economy Theory

IT will be worthwhile to try to see where we have arrived following the exercises with the trio of basic models in the two open-economy settings of Part III. The intention is not to summarize the findings but rather to select the propositions that give hope of being particularly useful in understanding long-term macroeconomic fluctuations.

In what may be called the monetary approach to unemployment fluctuation, even real shocks—real demand shocks and supply shocks—depend for their effect upon a monetary mechanism: the interest elasticity of the demand for money and the laggard or wayward behavior of money wages or money prices. That approach has proved a durable part of Keynes's legacy, accepted in most monetarist, New Classical, and New Keynesian models and so well assimilated into the thinking of practitioners that it is hardly ever made explicit in their discussions. This theoretical slant has given powerful support to the thesis that fiscal stimulus in a country not only expands domestic employment, at least in the near term; much of that expansionary effect spills overseas if the economy is open, exchange rates free, and finance internationally mobile.[1] The proposition has been popularized with the image of the locomotive powering a whole train and with the New England saying, "a rising tide lifts all boats." Econometric analyses have tended to confirm such expansionary effects over a one- or two-year horizon. Yet empirical research has not yet spoken clearly about the medium-term and longer effects of consumer-led and government stimuli to "aggregate demand."

It is true that in just the past decade a *real* theory of the "business cycle" that is *neoclassical* in character—more accurately, neo-neoclassical—has been refined that might conceivably serve in place of the monetary approach. Yet that neoclassical theory has the shortcoming that its premises exclude the existence of involuntary unemployment in either of the two existing senses of that term (Keynes's and the job-rationing notion); for the most part it contents itself with explaining booms and slumps as movements of the labor force instead of unemployment. If one were to interpret the neoclassical models as suggestive of the results that would be obtained in general-equilibrium models with involuntary unemployment, the finding would have to be the same. The neoclassical theory has thus far failed to show it can plausibly account for the peculiar features of the 1980s slump in much of the world any better than it could account for the depression of the 1930s.[2] One of its central tenets, that high real interest rates serve as a mechanism channeling positive demand shocks into *high* employment, seems to be opposite to what is needed to explain the association between the slump in Europe and the rise of overseas real interest rates. The need for another line of nonmonetary models is indicated.

The contrasting structuralist line of nonmonetary models developed in this volume seeks to explain low-frequency employment fluctuations by appeal to a supply-wage apparatus characterized, on the one hand, by the notion of an equilibrium real-wage-setting locus (the modernist surrogate for the labor supply curve) and, on the other hand, by a demand-wage mechanism activated by wealth, real interest rates, and real exchange rates, *inter alia.*

What are the consequences of various real aggregate-demand shocks from the point of view of the structuralist theory? As was seen in Part II, the results from *closed-economy* models uniformly show that *fiscal stimulus* to consumption demand is *contractionary* for employment, in sharp contrast to Keynesian doctrine. The intuitive explanation is that the consequent shift of consumption demand serves only to drive up real interest rates, not to elicit increased output from producers of consumer goods. In models with capital goods, the resulting fall in the real prices of the capital assets produced by the investment-goods-producing sector has a chilling effect on the willingness of firms there to produce them, causing an immediate drop of employment there and thus in aggregate employment; in customer-market models, the resulting fall of share prices encourages firms to attempt to raise their markups, and the implied fall in the real wage offered (when unchanged employment requires an unchanged real wage) actually contracts output and employment throughout the economy.[3] It was also seen that in the two-sector closed-economy model the accumulation of *additional capital* could stimulate the demand-price of labor by more than enough to offset the push that increased wealth gives to the required wage, hence *expanding* employment, which is again contrary to Keynesian doctrine; or it could produce the opposite net result.

In Part III we have looked into what the structuralist theory sketched here appears to say with regard to the international transmission of shocks. The question regarding the effects of shocks is the relation of the emerging structuralist doctrine to Keynesian doctrine. Does structuralist doctrine, particularly regarding shocks to consumption demand and consumption supply (capital shocks), tend to be the mirror-opposite of Keynesian doctrine?

- Is it the case that those fiscal stimuli and other expenditure shocks in a country or region that operate to raise real interest rates there have the effect of contracting employment abroad? If so, do they also contract employment in the country of origin, or may it gain some employment at the expense of the other countries?

- What of the effects of a supply shift in one country? If the accumulation of wealth and thus additional capital in a closed economy operates to expand employment, is it further the case that an equal increment of capital and domestic wealth in one open economy will expand employment in that country? In the rest of the world?

It was a theme of Fitoussi and Phelps in 1986 and 1988 that *some* shocks in a country are expansionary in the home country despite the accompanying rise of the domestic interest rate while having a contractionary effect abroad. But the arguments there appealed to a mixture of nonmonetary and monetary channels, and it was left unclear whether it would be possible to reconstruct the thesis on a purely nonmonetary basis. The main objective of the preceding investigation of the open-economy extensions of our three working models has been to explore the extent to which the Fitoussi-Phelps thesis can be reconstructed out of the materials of these nonmonetary models.

This chapter offers two sections that may be helpful to one in attempting to assimilate the more important mechanisms and implications studied in Chapters 11–13. Section 14.1 offers the other small-open-economy model mentioned in Chapter 12, that designated model N, in which, initially at least and for all shocks operating in the necessary direction, all customers of domestic firms are nationals. Although containing some formal contrasts with model F in section 12.2, this model does constitute something of a summary model for Part III since it does manage to incorporate two assets, fixed capital and customers. Section 14.2 then offers a commentary on what has been learned in Part III.

14.1 The Other Small Open Economy

Modeling the small open economy brings in as a parameter the overseas real interest rate, r^*; invoking interest parity between this interest rate and the domestic real interest rate presents a new equation with which to determine a new variable, the real exchange rate, e. The open-economy versions of the models also require introducing the country's algebraic net creditor position, as measured, say, by the holdings by domestic residents of equity shares to fixed capital, employees, and customers located overseas; the new equation introduces a new state variable, the national stock of net foreign assets, F. Further, in customer-market models there is the country's stock of overseas customers (which model N fixes at zero) and the country's stock of domestic customers (which model F fixes at zero). This introduces another state variable, x, the domestic firms' customer stock as a ratio to the labor force.

One of the lessons from the small-open-economy versions of the structuralist models is that those positive domestic expenditure shocks that would tend to drive up the interest rate in a closed economy and, through the interest-rate channel, would have a contractionary effect on the closed economy's employment rate will, if such a shock is confined to one or only a few small open economies, *fail* to have a contractionary effect on *domestic* employment, thanks to the invariance of the world real interest rate to country-specific shocks that are in proportion to the country's small size. In the customer-market model of the small open economy, there is an *expansionary* effect on domestic employment because the real appreciation necessary to reestablish interest-rate parity serves to deter firms from holding their output constant in the hope of taking the entire gain in the form of an increased price relative to that of foreign competitors; that is, the firms accommodate to some limited degree the increased demand in order to reduce the rate at which the foreign competitors will proceed to take customers away. Somewhat analogously, a drop in the capital stock—especially if accompanied by a drop of wealth, as the capital turns out to be domestically owned—may actually cause domestic employment to expand in the short run; the firms again opt to dampen the rate at which they lose customers by moderating the part of their cost increase they pass along to customers.

Section 12.1 established both propositions in the intertemporal-equilib-

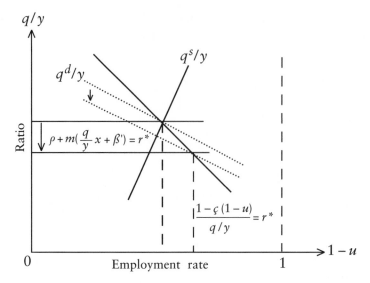

Figure 14.1 The asset-price-to-consumption ratio and employment in the open economy: The effect of an internal debt shock

rium analysis of model *F* of the customer-market type, in which only a negligible fraction of the customers of domestic firms are nationals. For the sake of greater realism, however, we now take up model *N*, in which all the customers of domestic firms are nationals.

The following discussion of model *N* of the customer-market type, which will center on Figure 14.1, adopts the premise of static expectations (instead of correct expectations) for the sake of analytical tractability. To begin with, we hold capital aside. The equations behind the curves there are as follows.

The employment-output ratio at the *i*th firm is given by a function that reflects shirking, $\phi(1 - u, v^i/y^w, v/y^w)$, where y^w denotes net-of-lump-sum-tax nonwage income per worker.[4] Hence the *i*th firm's constant unit cost, ς, is given by $(v/\Lambda)\phi(1 - u, v^i/y^w, v/y^w)$.

Then the identical firms in minimizing their costs satisfy Solow's elasticity condition,

(14.1) $v = -[\phi_2(\cdot)/y^w\phi(\cdot)]^{-1}$

whence, for labor-market equilibrium,

(14.2) $v \equiv y^w\theta(1 - u)$

Using that relationship in the Okun's-law relation between output and employment, and again in the accounting relation between wage outlays and nonwage income, thus obtaining

(14.3) $yx\phi(1 - u, \theta(1 - u), \theta(1 - u)) = (1 - u)\Lambda$

(14.4) $y^w + y^w\theta(1 - u) \cdot \phi(1 - u, \theta(1 - u), \theta(1 - u))yx = yx$

implies that y^w is a reduced-form function of $1 - u$ alone:

(14.5) $$y^w = \frac{(1 - u)/\phi(1 - u, \theta(1 - u), \theta(1 - u))}{1 + (1 - u)\theta(1 - u)}$$

$$\equiv \Psi(1 - u)\Lambda$$

Hence

(14.6) $v = \Psi(1 - u)\Lambda\theta(1 - u)$

(14.7) $\varsigma = \Psi(1 - u)\theta(1 - u)\phi(1 - u, \theta(1 - u), \theta(1 - u)) \equiv \varsigma(1 - u)$

It is important to require that "industry cost" be rising with "industry employment," in our case the economywide employment.

In these terms what may be called the rate-of-return curve of Figure 14.1 depicts the equation

(14.8) $[1 - \varsigma(1 - u)](q/y)^{-1} = r^*$

where r^* is the foreign-real-interest-rate parameter.

The rate-of-interest curve depicts the equation

(14.9) $\rho + \mu(\mu + \rho)[(q/y)x + \beta'] = r^*$

where β' denotes the ratio of public-debt holdings (of nationals) to consumption (of nationals).

Equating the lefthand sides of equations (14.8) and (14.9) yields the "demand" curve of Figure 14.1,

(14.10) $1 - \varsigma(1 - u) = (q/y)\{\rho + \mu(\mu + \rho)[(q/y)x + \beta']\}$

Finally, the "supply" curve of Figure 14.1 comes from maximization by each domestic firm with respect to its supply of the consumer good per customer, y^i, of a Hamiltonian function, which, in terms of foreign goods, is

$$(14.11) \quad \mathcal{H}^i \equiv x^i\{[p(y^i/y)P - v^i P\phi(1 - u, v^i/y^w, v/y^w)]y^i$$
$$+ q^i P\delta[1 - p(y^i/y)P/P^*]\} \qquad \delta > 0$$

Here δ is the Phelps-Winter parameter measuring the responsiveness of customer flow to a hypothetical price differential; $p(y^i/y)$ denotes the firm's demand price relative to that of other *domestic* firms, $p(1) = 1$, $p'(\cdot) < 0$; P denotes the real price of the other domestic firms relative to *foreign* firms; and P^* $(= 1)$ denotes the real price charge by foreign firms in all countries of operation.

The first-order condition at the identical domestic firms and the stipulation of equilibrium give the equation of the "supply" curve,

$$(14.12) \quad 0 = p'(1) + 1 - \varsigma(1 - u) - (q/y)\delta p'(1)(P/P^*)$$

An implicit assumption is that $p'(1)$ is independent of y. Not surprisingly, $\varsigma'(1 - u) > 0$ is required for the positive slope of the "supply" curve in the $(1 - u, q/y)$ plane.

Readers can see how if, as in the case illustrated, a positive domestic expenditure shock, such as a debt shock, should drive down the demand-price curve, moving down its intersection with the rate-of-return curve, there has to be a real appreciation—an increase of P/P^*—just sufficient to shift the supply-price schedule downward and rightward so as again to pass through the other curves' intersection, which constitutes the solution. The domestic debt shock is therefore expansionary for domestic employment.

Incorporating physical capital as a factor of production requires three basic changes in the model above. In the expanded model to be described, only domestically produced output (no foreign-made output) can be used for domestic investment.

First, output becomes equal to the sum of consumption, investment, and the costs of adjusting the capital stock. Thus, changes in investment demand constitute changes in the demand for output. This adds new terms to equation (14.4). Investment demand becomes—in a new equation—a function of a q-type variable which is the present discounted value of the prospective marginal value products of capital. The latter is equal to the sum of the marginal physical product, the reduction in adjustment costs, and the value of the new customers attracted by a fall in the relative price of the firm's output, minus depreciation.

Second, the marginal product of labor becomes a function of the stock of capital and employment at the level of the firm. This affects the Okun's-law relation—equation (14.3)—since marginal costs will now be increasing at the firm level.

Third, since marginal costs are now increasing in output at the firm level, the price of shares is no longer equal to marginal q for customer but to average q. Average q can be calculated as the present discounted value of firms' net cash inflow, which is equal to output minus the wage bill and the costs of investment (including adjustment costs). Equation (14.8) must be replaced, first with an equation for marginal q containing increasing marginal costs and, second, with an equation for average q. Average q will then also appear in equations (14.9) and (14.10).

A sudden jump in the stock of capital will have the following effects. Since the domestic profitability of investment did not increase, the stock of capital will be too large. Thus investment will fall. However, the larger capital stock will raise the dividend—because less labor is needed for the same output level or more output can be produced by the same use of labor—and hence the price of shares will go up. This will increase consumption demand until the capital stock has fallen back to its initial value, at which time investment will also have reached its initial value. The supply of output will initially be higher and, assuming that the increase in consumption demand is not much larger than the decrease in investment demand, the rate of interest will have to fall to make the demand for and supply of output equal again. The fall in the domestic rate of interest makes the real exchange rate depreciate immediately and then gradually appreciate—thus maintaining uncovered interest rate parity. Thus as the stock of capital gradually comes back down, the real exchange rate appreciates and the domestic interest rate rises, all toward their initial level.

Employment will be affected by these changes. The rise in the stock of capital increases the demand wage directly. (In this model all customers are nationals, so their demand will rise with capital.) The fall in the interest rate does the same by raising the shadow price of customers and thus lowering markups. The exchange-rate depreciation, however, causes markups to increase and lowers the demand wage. The rise in wealth (due both to the fall in the real interest rate and to the initial increase in the stock of capital), by reducing labor effort, reduces the demand wage. The net impact of these four effects on the demand wage is uncertain. Lastly, the reduced effort impacts positively on the supply wage—shifting up the wage locus in equation (14.1).

14.2 A Selection of Implications

The overseas real interest rate.   All three treatments of the small open economy in Part III show unmistakably that an increase in overseas real interest rates resulting from a shock abroad—thus a rise in world real rates, the country under study being too small to affect real rates in terms of an overseas numeraire good—operates by itself to *contract* employment in the small economy. Despite much misimpression to the contrary, this result is *not* also an implication of *Keynesian* theory. In Keynesian models of freely fluctuating rates, the rise of the overseas real interest rates represents also an increase of the *nominal* interest rate to which the domestic nominal rate must be equal, leaving aside possible expectations of future currency appreciation or depreciation following the initial adjustment of currency values; and this elevation of nominal interest rates operates to quicken the velocity of money and thus to make possible the increase of output and employment; an abrupt nominal depreciation serves to clear the goods market, permitting the additional output to be sold through increased exports or switching from imports.[5]

The small open-economy models also show that, in general, the demand shock or the capital shock that is the cause of the rise in the world real interest rate is, in general, *expansionary* for employment in the country of origin. But only a large country would be capable of causing a large and sustained rise of the world real interest rate. Hence a two-large-country model may be the natural vehicle for pursuing the question of asymmetric effects from one-country shocks.

Expenditure effects at home and abroad.   The two-country settings of Part III permit us to address the other part of the expenditure question: Does the country or region producing the expenditure shock itself suffer also a contraction in employment—one of its own doing—or may it actually gain an expansion of its employment at the expense of the rest of the world?

The two-country setting in section 11.2, in which firms in each of the countries invest in the indoctrination of new employees, was not fertile ground for finding opposing internal and external employment effects of demand shocks. That model approximates too closely to a perfectly aggregative model exhibiting the law of one price across countries to give wide scope for asymmetric employment effects of national demand shocks. An increased demand by the government of a country for (world) output drives up the (world) real interest rate, and the effects of that are distributed neutrally between the two countries. (Bringing to bear the emerging net debtor position, thus the decline of wealth, that follows as consumers refuse to contract consumption by the whole of the increase in taxes would tilt the long-run results toward a greater reduction of employment overseas; bringing in the effect of the additional tax distortions in the country increasing its public expenditure would suggest that employment would fall more there than abroad, not less.)

The dynamics of the investment-in-employees model, however, earn it a place in the portfolio of structuralist models. For illustration, consider an increase in the demand by the government in one of the countries for public-sector employment, an immediate impact of which is an instantaneous drop in unemployment.[6] A result, in turn, is increased turnover rates at private firms in that country, hence an emerging excess demand in the global consumer-good market and a rising rate of interest as firms in that country allow their work force to decline. Thus the real asset price of trained employees drops abroad as well as at home. Hence there is a drop in private hiring in both countries—employment abroad falling from an unchanged initial position while employment in the home country is falling from its initially boosted position. (As net foreign assets and thus wealth fall in the home country as a result of the balanced-budget public expenditure, there will be a tendency on this account for domestic employment to remain increased in comparison with the overseas rate; however, the increased tax rate on wage income to finance the increased public expenditure clearly operates in the offsetting direction.)

The two-country customer-market setting of section 12.2 is a considerably richer mine for finding opposite domestic and foreign employment effects from demand shocks. There, shocks that are asymmetrical as between the two countries may very well have qualitatively different effects on the willingness of firms in the two countries to compete for customers.

This customer-market model gives considerable support to the thesis that an increase in domestic demand[7] operates—through one central mechanism at least—to raise domestic employment, temporarily at any rate, while reducing employment abroad. The gist of the argument from one slant is the following. Consider an increase of public expenditure on the output of domestic firms[8] or an increase of public-sector employment. If, contrary to our conclusion, the increase of domestic demand were *not* accompanied by an increase of domestic employment—the trial solution to look at—firms' real prices in international terms would have to be raised to trim the amount of output demanded by private customers by the whole amount of the shock. (One could trace the real appreciation to the shock's causing an incipient disparity of real interest rates between the two countries, which the restoration of goods-market clearing serves to eliminate.) But this situation cannot be the starting point of the new equilibrium path. At that trial-solution point, the increase of the real price in international terms—since it is unaccompanied by any change of the required product wage at the existing employment rate, nonwage income in terms of product being unchanged—raises the sensitivity of customer inflow to an increase of output; provided the interest rate has been left approximately unchanged, as would be true of a *small* open economy, domestic firms will step up their output and employment in response, tempering the (trial-solution-level) markup of prices over wages and thus moderating the real appreciation. The corresponding real depreciation in the other country implied by the same trial solution presents firms there with a different incentive: The shelter of the real depreciation through the rise of real prices by their overseas counterparts would induce them to cut back their output and employment, thus to raise their markups.

From another slant, one can explain that the shock has a positive impact on employment (at the initial exchange rate) in the country of origin and although the real interest rate is also pulled up the net effect is expansionary, since the dampening real-interest effect through "supply" is divided between home and abroad. In the other country, the shock is the upward push on the real interest rate from overseas, and the effect is unambiguously contractionary. Of course, if the country that is the site of the shock is truly small, the contraction of overseas employment will be of negligible size as will the rise of the world real interest rate, by definition. If instead that country is relatively gigantic, the rise of the world real interest rate, while reinforcing contraction overseas, will more than offset the relative price effect, causing employment to contract there as well—precisely as if it were a closed economy.[9]

All this would be extremely difficult, if not impossible, to show with rigor and generality. Yet the intuitions behind it are simple enough. When incipient interest-rate disparities are created, and real appreciation/depreciation results, there are effects on the firms' equilibrium output supplies, hence their equilibrium derived demands for labor. These supply effects are in stark contrast to the demand effects of (nominal) appreciation that are the focus of Keynesian doctrine. Hence it is not surprising that the predictions of the two theories for the effects of national expenditure shocks in a global economy are apt to be radically different. It may be acknowledged, however, that illustrative cases have been systematically chosen to heighten the importance of the transmission channel on which interest centers and thus to downplay the potential importance of other channels reminiscent of the Keynesian ones. Only thorough empirical investigation will determine, if anything can, whether it is plausible to abstract from so much of the standard monetary theorizing.

The structuralist doctrine evolving here is further elaborated in the two-country two-sector model of Chapter 13, in which the asset is fixed capital. One thought-experiment is an increase in the demand by one country for the consumer good, which is internationally tradable in a perfect market. In the case of the small open economy, a spontaneous increase in private consumption demand seems to have no immediate impact. The increased consumer demand simply spills out of the country into the world market, generating a drop in the algebraic current-account surplus. In the case of a large open economy, with the consumption demand shock scaled up accordingly, the effect is a jump of the common real rate of interest in the two countries. The impact in both countries is a decline of employment.

Labor-intensive expenditures. Of particular interest, then, are the implications of a shock to the demand in a country for relatively labor-intensive goods. It may be hypothesized that government military expenditures, in falling largely on the capital-goods sector, are comparatively labor-intensive if, as assumed in the model, the capital-goods-producing sector is more labor-intensive than the consumer-good-producing sector. What is even clearer, however, is that government hiring of labor to staff the public sector is comparatively labor-intensive, provided that such workers have lower capital requirements than workers in the two private sectors.

The impact of an increase in a country in its labor-intensive public expenditures—say an increase in government demand for the output of the capital-goods sector—in the small-open-economy setting falls on the real demand wage, which is pulled up and lifts employment along with it. In the two-sector setting, the impact in the country that is the site of the shock is a rise of the relative price of the capital good, a fall of the rental, and thus a fall in the real rate of interest. The immediate effect overseas is to lower the rate of interest and hence to raise the real price of the (nontradable) capital good produced there. The implication is that employment is increased in both countries. A rather important part of Keynesian doctrine has been replicated, though its domain is much narrowed as it applies to public spending with the right factor-using slant.

Capital and wealth.   Consider an increase of wealth and capital in one of the countries. The open-economy customer-market model in section 12.1 portrayed capital and employment as rivals. A different conclusion seems to be implied in the fixed-capital model, owing to the absence of customer markets and the role of the two-sector formulation. The rate of interest is lowered. But there is little similarity beyond that. It appears to be theoretically possible that employment in the country of the shock is increased, not decreased as suggested by the customer-market view. In any case, employment abroad would be increased.

If physical capital is imbedded into the customer-market setting along the lines sketched in section 14.1, a positive shock to capital and wealth would, at the existing employment rate, generate a real-interest-rate disparity and thus lead to a real depreciation, contrary to the two-sector model with a frictionless world market for consumer goods instead of a customer market. Through this mechanism the shock may very well contract employment in the country of origin while it expands employment abroad.

Taxes and tariffs.   Although tax and tariff rates received little formal analysis, their effects become clear after reflection. Taxation of labor is contractionary for the open economy as well as the closed economy. Taxation of expenditure and value-added taxation are benign.

Strikingly, the introduction of import tariffs is seen in the structuralist perspective to be contractionary—just the opposite from the implication of most Keynesian models. The protection against imports, actual or merely potential, in dulling the sensitivity of customer outflow to a cutback of supply, emboldens domestic firms to cut back their production and employment. Since a real appreciation results, there is a further effect if domestic firms have overseas customers as well as national ones: the increased nonwage income of all nationals measured in terms of competitors' goods in overseas markets, in driving up wage costs similarly measured, will reduce the competitiveness of the firms in those overseas markets, thus shrinking exports. The wisdom that competing with the outside world makes a country strong is not a senseless belief.

IV

MICROTHEORETIC FORMULATIONS, MODERN AND NEOCLASSICAL

15

Interest and Wealth in the Microeconomics of the Incentive Wage and Equilibrium Unemployment

EVIDENTLY the structuralist approach to the determination of the volume of involuntary unemployment differs from the monetary approach in scope and methods.[1] The approaches use the common notion of a non-market-clearing equilibrium path, shaped by evolving real factors, in opposing ways.[2] The monetary approach sees high unemployment as a deviation of the actual unemployment-rate path above the equilibrium unemployment-rate path, while the structuralist approach sees it as a temporary or permanent elevation of the equilibrium path itself. The structuralist premise is that the monetary approach, though still an indispensable perspective on high-frequency fluctuations, cannot plausibly explain the long swings in the unemployment rate. To understand the protracted world boom from the late 1940s to the late 1960s, the nearly global recession of the 1970s, and the 1980s depression over much of the world, we need models showing how shifts in real supplies and demands disturb the equilibrium unemployment path.

An important branch in the family of structuralist models, the one developed in this volume, portrays the current real wage as a free variable at each moment, not a predetermined one.[3] In the models here, the corresponding equilibrium path of the unemployment rate will either be currently approaching or it will jump to a level determined by the interaction of the labor-market equilibrium block and the product-market equilibrium block of the model.[4] (In models having a stock of capital or a variable stock of customers this target, or natural, unemployment will also be moving in general.) It may help in laying the ground for the present chapter, at the price of some repetition of Chapter 3, to review the main elements.

The labor-market equilibrium condition generates a relationship, called here the equilibrium wage locus, giving the wage rate required for labor-market equilibrium as a function of the rate of unemployment.[5] Letting N denote employment, L the labor force, and $1 - u \equiv N/L$ the employment rate, we may write this relationship as $v = V_s(1 - u; L, \ldots)$, with $\infty > V'_s(1 - u) \geq 0$. If this curve is flat, we have a rigid real wage. If upward-sloping, it still expresses a kind of real-wage rigidity.[6] More than one conception of the labor market, and particularly its non-neoclassical feature, has been found to support such a relationship. The same visions of the labor market that arose in the original conceptualizing of the natural rate of unemployment—the turnover-training model and later the supervision model, both implying use of an "incentive wage" above market-clearing levels to discourage or deter quitting or shirking—turned out, upon suitable restrictions, to generate an upward-sloping equilibrium wage locus. Two early attempts at proto-general-equilibrium models in this vein were made by Salop, based on turnover, and by Shapiro and Stiglitz, based on supervision.[7] Labor-market models of union bargaining, which are an addition to the natural-rate catalog, and models of insider-outsider phenomena, which depart somewhat from standard natural-rate doctrine in their hysteresis feature, also produced a type of equilibrium wage locus.[8] This chapter, though, is oriented toward the older incentive-wage theories, which have been workhorses for the foregoing models.

From the conditions for product-market equilibrium is derived the other locus: the derived labor demand locus (in the employment rate–wage plane) giving the labor demanded at a given wage as a ratio to the fixed labor force—equivalently, the real labor demand price locus giving the demand price of labor as a function of the employment rate. The product-market block of a number of models imply the real demand price of labor to be a nonincreasing function of the level of employment, given the various parameters (such as production functions) and various real asset prices set in the capital market—including the real exchange rate in the open-economy case. This relationship may be denoted $v = V_d(1 - u; L, \ldots)$, $V'_d(1 - u) \leq 0$. A procession of suggestions has been advanced as to the important sources of shifts in the derived demand for labor going well beyond neoclassical aggregative models.

The intersection of the demand price function with the equilibrium wage locus gives the unemployment rate and real wage toward which the equilibrium path of these variables will be heading or to which it will jump. Shocks operate to move this equilibrium by disturbing one or both of the loci. Observations of prolonged high unemployment in the 1970s and rising unemployment in the early 1980s stimulated various hypotheses: a spontaneous and unexplained upward shift of the wage locus;[9] an energy-cost shock causing a downward shift of the labor demand price locus;[10] in Europe and some other continents, an external real-interest shock causing a downward shift of labor demand price by depressing various real asset prices—the real price of capital goods, of experienced employees, physical capital, and the real exchange rate;[11] in the world economy as a whole, a positive shock to demand in consumer-good industries—induced by increased public debt, say—causing a rise of the world interest rate, which has the above effects on derived labor demand.[12] The mechanism behind this last hypothesis is this: A negative shift in the supply of output of the consumer-good-producing firms or a positive shift in the corresponding demand, whether the extra demand comes from the government or from households, creates an excess demand in that market as the firms are unwilling to supply more in the absence of a decline of the real wage; elimination of the excess demand requires the real-interest-yield curve to shift up and hence the various real asset prices to drop; paradoxically, these real-price effects cause aggregate employment to contract if, in the model at hand, the real demand price for labor is an increasing function of the real asset price. Yet government purchases from the capital-goods sector have the opposite effects.[13] Other structuralist propositions refer to tax rates and subsidies.[14]

These attractions of the structuralist approach notwithstanding, the microfoundations underpinning the various structuralist models' specifications of the quitting and shirking behavior behind the wage-setting locus have to be regarded as scrappy, for they rest on austerely narrow examples that are frequently inadequate to the question asked of the model. The short history of these models may be recalled.

The Phelps-Stiglitz-Salop turnover models of wage-setting told the story of employees on the east coast with randomly timed and variable urges to go west and west-coast employees to move east. At the equilibrium wage corresponding to any given employment level, each firm is paying the "incentive wage" that balances turnover costs against the wage bill to minimize total cost. The 1968 paper by the present author took the quit rate at the ith firm to be a function of the unemployment rate and its *relative* wage, v^i/v. Adopting such a *ratio* formulation, Salop built on it a general-equilibrium model in which the endogenous natural rate is *invariant* to a productivity-boosting Harrod-neutral technological shock. (The wage locus is upward-sloping, but both the wage locus and the derived labor demand curve shift up in equal proportion when productivity is shocked.) So this formulation, in Salop's hands, does *not deliver* the result that a permanent oil shock shifts up the natural unemployment rate.[15]

The Calvo-Bowles-Shapiro-Stiglitz line of shirking models—now usually called the efficiency-wage model—presented another story. Calvo simply postulated a shirking-rate function making the average rate of shirking a function of the *difference* between the firm's own wage and the employment-rate-weighted wage elsewhere, $v^i - (1 - u)v$. This *difference* formulation, besides producing a sloping equilibrium wage locus, implied that a permanent and positive productivity shock would have a positive effect on the equilibrium employment rate.[16] The Shapiro-Stiglitz paper directed its attention to the slope of the wage-setting locus, showed it to be upward-sloping in the theoretical setting specified, and made it clear that a permanent productivity improvement raising the demand curve for labor would move the equilibrium point to one with a reduced natural unemployment rate as well as a higher wage.[17] But this formulation clearly *delivers too much*: secular technical progress driving the real wage ever upward is implied to put the unemployment rate on a decreasing trend.

Thus the accustomed models of unemployment based on incentive-wage theory run into difficulties. If cumulative productivity growth implies a cumulative rise of employment—an ever-shirking unemployment rate—the theory flies in the face of evidence that unemployment was trendless for 150 years, until the past two decades. Moreover, with such an implication, as Lawrence Summers has pointed out, secular progress could be relied upon to bail out the economy from any slump as soon as it had pushed the real wage to its pre-slump level—contrary to the empirical impressions of most observers.

The solution to this problem in the present work is to dynamize the formulation of shirking and quitting decisions by introducing saving, wealth, and interest-type income. In the model of shirking constructed below, it will be shown that increases in wage rates serve to decrease the propensity to shirk, which could be shown in a broader model to increase the employment rate; at the same time, though, increases in workers' wealth levels, given wage rates and interest rates, work in the reverse direction, operating to increase their propensity to shirk. Hence, though capital accumulation and technological gains are steadily pulling on labor demand, and thereby working to pull an economy out of a slump, the upward trend imparted to real wealth by the same secular progress works the opposite way by pushing up the incentive wage. Slumps are not implied to be swept away by ongoing progress. Second, it will be shown that, under a familiar class of utility functions, the propensity to shirk at a given flat real interest rate is a function—an increasing function—only of the ratio of the wage rate to wealth. It is clear that this zero-degree homogeneity of shirking in wage rate and wealth, when combined with constant labor-augmenting technical progress, permits an equilibrium of steady growth in which the unemployment rate is *unvarying* through time. So an implied unemployment trend is averted. Finally, a computer simulation will be reported showing that, under the utility restriction adopted, an increase of the flat interest rate stimulates the propensity to shirk. So increased interest rates are doubly contractionary, contracting the demand wage while pushing up the incentive wage.

15.1 An Intertemporal Utility Analysis of Shirking, Wages, and Wealth

This is an intertemporal model, in which both households and firms are forward-looking. To make room for moral hazard to rear up its head, and also to permit escape from Ricardian equivalence, the model must not be reducible to the behavior of a single agent with an infinite time horizon. To make it possible for wealth to shift the shirking demand curve (and thus shift the equilibrium incentive wage locus), the model must incorporate saving, dissaving, and an asset market. To minimize complexity, the incentive problem is formulated as a shirking problem rather than a quitting problem. The Yaari-Blanchard demographic setup is maintained until, for the last hard-won results, we are driven to the Ramsey-Weil fiction of a stationary or steadily growing population of deathless Ricardo-Barro dynasties. The subsection below lays out the elements of the model of key importance for this paper. The subsequent section models the behavior of households and sets forth the results obtained.

Key elements of the dynamic model. The focus here is on the choices that have to be made by worker-savers. Agents are born into the labor force and remain there for life, independently of real prices and wealth. A worker who is an employee will keep his job until death or until the firm catches him at a moment when he is shirking; an employee caught shirking is immediately dismissed, expelled into the pool of the unemployed. A worker who is unemployed waits until the continuous, random drawing for newly open positions picks his name or number. These worker-savers also accumulate and decumulate real wealth. Wealth here will generally refer to the *real value* of private holdings of equity shares and any public debt. If the government has created some public debt, these government securities are perfect substitutes for shares, and hence bear the same rate of return. Thus a worker, whether in the employed state or the unemployed state, must continuously be choosing his rate of consumption and thus his saving or dissaving, which is done in the form of share accumulation or decumulation.[18] In addition, a worker as long as he is employed must continuously be choosing the rate, or frequency, with which he shirks; in any small period of time in which this "rate" is unchanged, the shirking is to be interpreted as a series of equally spaced intervals of equal length during which the worker is on the phone with a friend or away from his work station or perhaps simply looking away from the monitor or meters at his work place—and hence not in those subintervals performing actual work.

At places where we would like to think about the whole general-equilibrium picture, the simplest point of reference exhibiting at least some of the structuralist ideas is the customer-market economy, whose only real asset is its stock of customers and which is closed to the rest of the world, so the customer stock is fixed. The derived market demand for labor is a decreasing function of the real wage and has to be indexed by the real price of this asset, to be denoted q, of which labor demand is an increasing function. The equity shares of the firms outstanding may be thought of as being backed by customers—one customer for every one share, without loss of generality.

The model of shirking and saving here is first placed in the demographic setting used by Blanchard to model personal saving. There we find a demographic stationary state with births exactly equal to deaths at each moment. Later we go to the limiting Ramsey-Weil case of a zero mortality rate.[19]

So there are three sorts of stochastic events in the lifetime of persons living in this world: detection of shirking and summary ejection into the unemployment pool, call-up from the unemployment pool into a job, and—in the Blanchard-Yaari case—death.

In this demographic setup, the death rate, μ, is independent of age and time—so all workers have the same remaining life expectancy (which is infinite in the zero-mortality-rate case of Ramsey and Weil). All agents have identical utility functions and the same abilities as well. A worker, meaning a labor-force participant, can be completely characterized by his real wealth, w, and his employment status, which is either jobless, indicated by 0, or employed, indicated by 1. There is an economywide wage, v, equal across firms, as I take them to be identical, and equal across a firm's employees, as I assume a nondiscriminatory wage policy by every firm (perhaps required by law). A firm, knowing the workers are all equally able and not being permitted to obtain or (if obtained) to use wealth or unemployment history to estimate their propensity to shirk, which depends on their wealth, pays all its employees the same wage. As firms are identical, the wage paid is equal across firms at each moment along an equilibrium path.[20]

We will limit ourselves to equilibrium scenarios of a sort: the agents have correct expectations conditional on their assumption that the prevailing parameters are not going to change; that is, the agents have theoretically correct conditional expectations about the (paths of the) distributions of the prices and actions on which their behavior depends. (This is different from and a little less restrictive than the rational-expectations postulate, but we need not digress here.) We also want to design the model in such a way as to ensure, for given parameters, the existence and uniqueness of a stochastic stationary state that is *deterministic* in various *aggregates* and *averages* such as the real wage, v, and the real interest rate, r. In this stationary-state equilibrium each worker expects a fixed v and r over the infinite future. What is *stochastic* is the microeconomic (or ultra-micro) description in terms of who happens to be observed shirking by the firm's detector, who happens to be called up in the random drawing determining the dismissed employee's replacement from the pool of unemployed workers, and accordingly who is saving and who is dissaving.

With regard to rest of the model, it needs to be said that each firm responds to the shirking by raising its real wage. In its calculation of the optimal wage, when figuring the shirking rate it will suffer at each wage, the firm assumes the wealth of its employees is the average level in the population and that its shirking experience will correspond to that wealth level. The industry wage, v, must rise and with it the unemployment rate, u, until the point is reached at which the individual firm does not want any longer to pay a wage above the industry wage. Note also that the demand function for labor is indexed by q, the real asset price, which is in turn determined by the condition that it equilibrate the product market. In this stationary state, the employed are generally buying assets from the unemployed while the average number of shares held by the unemployed tends to be stabilized by the excess of the shares of those entering the unemployment pool over the shares of those exiting from that pool (who on average have not lately or ever been employed).

THE DYNAMIC MODEL OF HOUSEHOLD BEHAVIOR

Let us now describe more formally the decision problems of the worker-savers. The employed worker chooses the rate at which he "shirks"—or, the intensity of his on-the-job leisure—at such a level as to balance the "utility" of the respite from work against the "utility" advantage of remaining an employee at the firm over waiting in the unemployment pool to be randomly called to employment. The return function denoting a worker's optimized discounted lifetime utility, g, must satisfy Bellman's principle of optimality, so that over a small time interval h from the current moment the employed worker's expected lifetime utility must satisfy as an approximation

$$(15.1) \quad g(w; 1) = \max_{(c_1, l)} \{U(c, l)h + (1 - \mu h - \rho h)[(1 - \phi lh)g(w + \dot{w}_1 h; 1)$$

$$+ \phi lhg(w + \dot{w}_1 h; 0)]\}$$

Here $U(c_1, l)$ is shorthand for $U(c_1, l; 1)$, which is the worker's current instantaneous rate of utility while in the employed state, denoted state 1; c_1 is the current rate of consumption; l stands for the "rate" of on-the-job leisure, or the "intensity" of shirking at the current moment; μ is the instantaneous force of mortality (the death rate), a constant independent of age and time; ρ is rho, the rate of pure time preference or utility discount rate; ϕl is the exponential attrition rate of employees who choose to shirk with intensity l—that is, ϕlh is the probability of being caught shirking over the tiny interval h—so ϕ reflects the intensity with which firms seek to detect their employees' shirking, which is the same across the identical firms; $g(w, 0)$ is the expected liftetime utility of an optimizing worker with wealth w who finds himself currently in the unemployed state (in state 0); and the return function on the lefthand side of the functional equation gives the analogous expected lifetime utility for an optimizing worker with wealth w who is employed (in state 1). Here the speed of wealth accumulation, $\dot{w}_1$, is given by

$$(15.2) \quad \dot{w}_1 = v + r^* w - c_1 \qquad r^* \equiv r + \mu$$

It should be noted that w is qs, the real price of shares times the number held. Although an individual cannot "jump" his wealth by his own saving or dissaving, a macroeconomic shock could cause w to drop by abruptly decreasing q.

The unemployed worker chooses only the rate of consumption, knowing the rate of escape from the pool, **a**. Over a similar small time interval h the expected lifetime utility of the unemployed work must satisfy the analogous approximation

(15.3) $g(w; 0) = \max\limits_{c_0} \{U(c_0; 0)h + (1 - \mu h - \rho h)$

$\times [(1 - ah)g(w + \dot{w}_0 h; 0) + ahg(w + \dot{w}_0 h; 1)]\}$

where the rate of saving of the unemployed worker, $\dot{w}_0$, is

(15.4) $\dot{w}_0 = r^*w - c_0$

Using the bag of tricks originating in Bellman's *Dynamic Programming*, one arrives at the following optimality conditions:

(15.5) $U(c_1, l) + g_w(w; 1)(v + r^*w - c_1)$

$= \phi l[g(w; 1) - g(w; 0)] + (\mu + \rho)g(w; 1)$

(15.6) $U_{c_1}(c_1, l) = g_w(w; 1)$

(15.7) $U(c_0; 0) + g_w(w; 0)(r^*w - c_0)$

$= -a[g(w; 1) - g(w; 0)] + (\mu + \rho)g(w, 0)$

(15.8) $U_{c_0}(c_0) = g_w(w; 0)$

(15.9) $U_l(c, l; 1) = \phi[g(w; 1) - g(w; 0)]$

Upon substituting the conditions in (15.6) and (15.8), which equate the marginal utility of consumption to the marginal utility of wealth, we have conditions on the optimal rates of consumption resembling the familiar Ramsey-Meade optimal-saving condition:

(15.10) $U(c_1, l) + U_{c_1}(c_1, l)(v + r^*w - c_1)$

$= \phi l[g(w; 1) - g(w; 0)] + (\mu + \rho)g(w; 1)$

(15.11) $U(c_0) + U_{c_0}(c_0)(r^*w - c_0)$

$= -a[g(w; 1) - g(w; 0)] + (\mu + \rho)g(w, 0)$

The foregoing conditions are suggestive. If the utility advantage of employment over being unemployed waiting for employment—the g differential on the righthand side of (15.9)—is decreasing in w, owing essentially to diminishing marginal utility, then, by (15.9), l must be increasing in w at least in the separable case where l is independent of c and more generally if l and c are complements (so that the increased consumption induced by increased wealth by itself operates to increase the marginal utility of leisure, thus further increasing the need when w is increased for increased l to reduce the marginal utility of leisure). Second, if the utility advantage of employment is increasing in v, l must be decreasing in v in the aforementioned separable case. If indeed l is increasing in w and decreasing in v it is plausible to think that there exists a specification of the utility function generating a shape of the function $g(w; 1; v, \ldots)$ such that, if v and w both increase by the same percentage amount at unchanged r, there will be no change in l. Third, if the above utility advantage is decreasing in r (as well as in w), l must be increasing in r (as well as in w). These observations are too iffy to be useful by themselves, however. We now must dig deeper for self-standing, operational results of a comparative-statics nature.

ANALYSES OF THE DYNAMIC MODEL

This section begins its investigation of the determination of the rate of shirking with an examination of the wealth effect and proceeds to show how a familiar specification of the utility function delivers restrictive implications with regard to wealth and the wage rate. The last subsection tackles the question of the effect of the rate of interest.

Wealth effects. It would be good to begin the analysis by obtaining some results of a comparative-statics nature without special restrictions on the utility functions before proceeding to the restriction that is required for balanced growth without a trend in the rate of shirking (and hence, by virtue of the optimal wage choice of firms, without a trend in the path of the equilibrium unemployment rate). We can obtain results of some generality with regard to the effect of increased wealth.

The total differential of (15.9) with respect to w is

$$(15.12) \quad U_{ll}(c_1, l)\,dl + U_{lc_1}(c_1, l)\,dc_1 = \phi[g_w(w; 1) - g_w(w; 0)]\,dw$$

Owing to the strict concavity of the utility functions and the linearity of the budget constraints, the unknown g functions are strictly concave in wealth, w. Of course, that does not prove that the individual with wage income at present has a lower marginal utility of wealth than he would have if he immediately became unemployed, since wage income is not like extra wealth: (1) wage income is distributed over the future with a stochastic duration, and (2) the employed individual will optimally take less leisure than he would take if unemployed. Nevertheless, such a conclusion can be argued if we appeal to the basic analysis of behavior in the face of contingent states. The unambiguous gain from having the job, albeit one of stochastic duration, must be reflected in the lower marginal utility of consumption one has when in the employed state than when in the unemployed state. (This lower marginal utility does not mean that consumption itself will be higher in the employed status; consumption would actually be lower if the decrease in leisure during employment (greater leisure is impossible since leisure during unemployment is at the upper bound) decreases the marginal utility of consumption—decreases the appetite for consumption—so much that consumption must be decreased to prevent the marginal utility of consumption from dropping too much.) The individual would like to have an actuarially fair insurance contract enabling him always to consume his permanent income with an adjustment for reduced leisure when on the job in such a way as to have equalized marginal utility of consumption across these states; but there will be no one willing to write such insurance in view of the moral hazard that the insuree would then have no incentive or a reduced incentive not to get caught shirking— his rate of utility might fall little if at all. So, with or without an increase of present consumption in response, there is an immediate decrease of the marginal utility of consumption when a job is acquired. By (15.6), then, there is a corresponding drop in the marginal utility of wealth when an individual becomes employed; though *total* expected utility is higher on the current wealth, w, its marginal utility is lower.

Since the marginal utility of wealth must be lower for the worker who has a job than for persons with the same wealth who currently lack a job, the righthand side of (15.12) is negative. So increased wealth induces a decrease of the marginal utility of on-the-job leisure (as well as a decrease of the marginal utility of consumption) via the total of its leisure and consumption effects.

In the separable case, this decrease in the marginal utility of on-the-job leisure with increased wealth can only be achieved by an increase of on-the-job leisure. In the complements case, any increase of consumption by itself would increase the marginal utility of leisure with the consequence that leisure would be increased by more than in the former case. But it has to be shown that consumption does indeed increase with wealth in the complements case! The substitutes case also has to be considered. The total differential of (15.6) with respect to w is

$$(15.13) \quad U_{c_1 l}(c_1, l)dl + U_{c_1 c_1}(c_1, l)dc_1 = g_{ww}(w; 1)dw$$

Equations (15.12) and (15.13) constitute a pair of equations in the consumption and leisure responses from which we can at least characterize the response of the employed person's consumption to an increase of wealth. The solutions are

$$(15.14) \quad dc_1/dw = J^{-1}U_{ll}\{g_{ww}(w; 1) - (U_{c_1 l}/U_{ll})\phi[g_w(w; 1) - g_w(w; 0)]\}$$

$$(15.15) \quad dl/dw = J^{-1}U_{c_1 c_1}\{\phi[g_w(w; 1) - g_w(w; 0)] - (U_{lc_1}/U_{c_1 c_1})g_{ww}(w; 1)\}$$

$$\text{where } J = U_{c_1 c_1}U_{ll} - (U_{c_1 l})^2 > 0$$

Equation (15.14) makes it obvious in the complements case, $U_{lc_1} > 0$, that consumption of the employed person is indeed increasing in wealth. Equation (15.15) shows again that in the same case the demand for on-the-job leisure is also increasing in wealth. But in the substitutes case, $U_{lc_1} < 0$, the presumptive wealth effect seems to be threatened by high substitutability—by a cross-partial derivative far less than zero. But with the restriction of the utility function below, there will be a more promising opportunity to examine the wealth effects.

Let us state loosely what has been learned. Demand for consumption and for shirking (on-the-job leisure) are not generally independent of wealth. Over a broad range—complementarity, independence, or not too much substitutability between on-the-job leisure and consumption—consumption and shirking both increase with wealth, given the rate of interest and the wage rate.

The utility specification for homogeneity in wage and wealth. We want to consider the implications of the specification

$$(15.16a) \quad U(c_1, l) = (n + 1)^{-1}c_1^{n+1}Y(l) \qquad 0 < l < 1$$

$$(15.16b) \quad U(c_0) = (n + 1)^{-1}c_0^{n+1}$$

where $Y(l) > 0$ and $Y(l) = 1$.

The corresponding marginal utilities are

$$(15.17a) \quad U_{c_1}(c_1, l) = c_1^n Y(l) \ (> 0) \qquad U_l(c_1, l) = (n + 1)^{-1} c_1^{n+1} Y(l) > 0$$

$$(15.17b) \quad U_{c_0}(c_0) = c_0^n \ (> 0)$$

The parameter n is the elasticity of marginal utility of consumption with respect to consumption, and has sometimes been understood (incorrectly) as the coefficient of relative risk aversion. There are two cases. For a bounded U, favored by Ramsey, $n + 1 < 0$; and corresponding to this case $Y'(l) < 0$ in order to have a positive U_l. In this case, U is actually negative, increasing with consumption toward its bliss level of zero as consumption goes to infinity; accordingly, the values of the return functions will likewise be negative. The other case is the opposite one in which both $n + 1$ and $Y'(l)$ are positive instead of negative.

A third case is the logarithmic one,

$$(15.16a') \quad U(c_1, l) = \log c_1 + Y(l) \qquad Y'(l) > 0$$

$$(15.16b') \quad U(c_0) = \log c_0$$

but we will not stop to treat it.

If we differentiate with respect to time the Ramsey-Meade conditions found in (15.10) and (15.11), we obtain two Euler-type equations in the proportionate rate of growth of the marginal utilities of c_1 and c_0, respectively. (These may be left implicit.) They differ from the usual Euler equations for household consumption in containing considerations of shirking detection and unemployment call-up.[21] Upon substituting the specification in (15.16) we have the following Euler-type equations for c_1 and c_0, respectively:

$$(15.18a) \quad -n(dc_1/dt)/c_1 + [Y'(l)\,l/Y(l)](dl/dt)/l$$
$$= r^* - (\rho + \mu) - \phi l + (c_0/c_1)^n (1/Y(l))\phi l$$

$$(15.18b) \quad -n(dc_0/dt)/c_0 = r^* - (\rho + \mu) - \mathbf{a} + (c_1/c_0)^n Y(l)\mathbf{a}$$

Only the proportionate rates of growth of the two consumption rates and their ratio figure here, not their absolute levels. So if the level of the real wage and the initial level of real wealth, v and w respectively, doubles, say, with no accompanying change in the rate of interest, then every individual would optimally switch to a path of consumption twice as high *if* this shift of the wage and wealth paths does not induce a change in the path of on-the-job leisure (which would mean not only a change in l in (15.18) but also an induced change in the unemployment rate and the separation rate, hence in **a**).

Now we will show that if initial wealth and the wage both double and the paths of the two consumption rates double as well, the optimal path of on-the-job leisure will in fact not be altered. We can use to this end the optimal on-the-job leisure condition in (15.9), with the differential lifetime utility on the righthand side, upon substituting for the unknown return functions there from the optimal consumption conditions in (15.5) and (15.7), and also substituting for the unknown marginal-utility-of-wealth terms from the conditions in (15.6) and (15.8) to obtain

(15.19) $\quad g(w; 1) - g(w; 0) =$

$$(\rho + \phi l + \mathbf{a})^{-1}\{U(c_1, l) + U_{c_1}(c_1, l)(v + r^*w - c_1)$$

$$- [U(c_0) + U_{c_0}(c_0)(r^*w - c_0)]\}$$

Using (15.19) in (15.9) and further using our utility specification in (15.16) finally yields

(15.20) $\quad (n + 1)^{-1}c_1^{n+1}Y'(l) =$

$$\phi(\rho + \phi l + \mathbf{a})^{-1}\{(n + 1)^{-1}c_1^{n+1}Y(l) + c_1^{n+1}Y(l)(v + r^*w - c_1)/c_1$$

$$- [(n + 1)^{-1}c_0^{n+1} + c_0^{n+1}(r^*w - c_0)/c_0]\}$$

Upon multiplying and dividing by c_1^{n+1} the expression in the square brackets it is clear that c_1^{n+1} factors out from the equation, leaving income terms as a ratio to consumption, the ratio between the two consumption rates, and the demand for on-the-job leisure. Hence doubling initial wealth, the wage, and the paths of the two consumption rates will not alter the optimal path of on-the-job leisure, as was to be proved.

To restate the argument, if paths $\{l\}$, $\{c_1\}$, and $\{c_0\}$ were feasible, and satisfied both the transversality condition and the Euler-like conditions when wage and initial wealth were (v°, w°), then, upon an equiproportionate increase of wage and wealth, the flat path of the real rate of interest being held constant, there will be a new program in which the two consumptions are increased in the same proportion and leisure is unchanged and which has the properties that the Euler-type equations are again satisfied as well as feasibility and the transversality condition. So if a solution to the choice problem exists and is unique, then when wealth and wages go up equiproportionately the unique response is a proportional increase of both consumption rates and no change in shirking.

To sum up the homogeneity results of this subsection: The demand for leisure is homogeneous of degree zero, and the consumption demands homogeneous of degree one, in the wage and initial wealth; only the ratio of wage to wealth matters, given the interest rate. Hence, if over the set of preferences where it is unambiguous that leisure is an *increasing* function of initial wealth we add the utility specification in (15.16) so that the homogeneity propositions apply, it follows immediately that over the same set the demand for on-the-job leisure is a *decreasing* function of the wage rate. This is a proposition about the effect of the economywide wage; it is not the obvious finding that the analogous proposition about the effect of the individual firm's wage would be.

It might be noted that since, in the event the wage and initial wealth both increase by 1 percent, both consumptions increase by the same percentage and leisure does not change, the expected value of the rate of utility will be increased by $n + 1$ percent at each point in the future. So it is clear that the value of the return functions is likewise increased by $n + 1$ percent.

Asset-price and interest-rate effects in the Ramsey/Weil case. To explore the effect of an increase in the interest rate reflected in turn by a decrease of the asset price, let us specialize the model to make it more amenable to analysis. The mortality rate is set equal to zero. This case originates in the specification of the problem of optimum national saving that was the principal focus in the classic 1928 paper by Ramsey.[22] (Of course, his was a somewhat different context from the one here.) To ensure the existence of an optimal path in the special case of zero pure time preference, Ramsey also postulated a bounded utility function. Combined with our isoelastic utility specification, this requires $n < -1$. Weil added overlapping growth of infinite-lived dynastic families, which is neglected here.

E will denote the positive elasticity, $-n$, introduced in (15.16). Further, I have taken advantage of the homogeneity property that with an unchanged wealth-wage ratio the value of the g functions increase like v^{1-E} with increased v. Hence letting z denote the wealth-wage ratio,

$$(15.21) \quad g(w, v; 1) = v^{1-E} f(z; 1) \qquad E > 1$$

$$\text{where } f(z; 1) \equiv g(z, 1; 1) \text{ and } z \equiv w/v$$

Upon denoting by $F(z)$ the differential between the f functions of employed and the unemployed persons having the same z, and denoting by b_1 the consumption-wage ratio corresponding to the employed status, the equations (15.10) and (15.9) become

$$(15.22) \quad (1 - E)^{-1}b_1^{1-E}Y(l) + b_1^{-E}Y(l)(1 + rz - b_1) = l\phi F(z) + \rho f(z, 1)$$

$$(15.23) \quad (1 - E)^{-1}b_1^{1-E}Y'(l) = \phi F(z)$$

$$\text{where } F(z) \equiv f(z; 1) - f(z; 0) \text{ and } b \equiv c_1/v$$

This is the system in the two variables, b_1 and l, to be used here.

To begin we may investigate the response of on-the-job leisure demand to an increase of the wealth-wage ratio. The total differentials with respect to z, making use of (15.23) in the calculations with (15.22), comprise the system

$$(15.24) \quad -Eb_1^{-E-1}Y(l)(1 + rz - b_1)db_1 + b_1^{-E}Y'(l)(1 + rz - b_1)dl$$
$$= [l\phi F_z(z) - b_1^{-E}Y(l)(r - \rho)]dz$$

$$(15.25) \quad b_1^{-E}Y'(l)db_1 + (1 - E)^{-1}b_1^{1-E}Y''(l)dl = [\phi F_z(z)]dz$$

The solution for the response of on-the-job leisure is

$$(15.26) \quad dl/dz = J^{-1}\{b_1^{-E}Y(l)(r - \rho)b_1^{-E}Y'(l) - \phi F_z b_1^{-E}Y(l)[(lY'(l)/Y(l))$$
$$- (-E)(1 + rz - b_1)/b_1]\}$$
$$\text{where } J \equiv (1 - rz - b_1)[U_{c_1c_1}U_{ll} - (U_{lc_1})^2] > 0$$

The saving-consumption ratio, $(1 + rz - b_1)/b_1$, figures on the righthand side. But from (15.9) and (15.10) we also have, when $\mu = 0$,

$$(15.27) \quad (1 - E)^{-1}c_1^{1-E}Y(l) + c_1^{-E}Y(l)(v + rw - c_1)$$
$$- l(1 - E)^{-1}c_1^{1-E}Y'(l) = \rho f(z, 1)$$

or, upon rearranging terms,

(15.28) $(v + rw - c_1)/c_1 = (1 - E)^{-1}\{-1 + (lY'(l)/Y(l))$

$$+ [\rho f(z, 1)/c_1^{-E}Y(l)]\}$$

With $E > 1$ to make the rate of utility bounded from above, as here, the saving-consumption ratio is positive—recall that $f(z, 1)$, like $U(\cdot)$, is everywhere negative—and the ratio is large enough to ensure that the expression on the righthand side of (15.26) in square brackets, which becomes $\{E - lY'(l)/Y(l) - E[\rho f(z, 1)/c_1^{-E}Y(l)]\}(E - 1)^{-1}$, is unambiguously positive. Hence the righthand side of (15.26) is likewise positive. So the demand for on-the-job leisure increases with increased wealth.

We come now to the last of the three questions motivating this paper, which concerns the effect on the propensity to shirk (and thus on the size of the incentive wage required to minimize costs) of the real price of the asset, q, and the effect of the interest rate. The need for answers to this is acute because previous analysis of a series of "working models" in which the shirking or quitting function is rather *ad hoc* has repeatedly found that a consumption demand shock such as an increase of time preference, in driving up real interest rates and thus inducing a drop in the real price of the model's real asset (customers, operational employees, durable goods), causes the derived demand for labor to drop. The effect on the employment rate through this channel—through the "demand wage"—is contractionary. The tentative conclusion reached, thus, is that the demand stimulus is a drag on employment. But the question arises: is it theoretically possible that the rise of the interest rate, r, and the associated fall of the real asset price, q, operate to reduce employees' demand for shirking and, moreover, to do so by so much as to reduce the cost-minimizing "incentive wage" that firms pay by enough to offset or more than offset the reduction in the demand wage? That is, may the higher interest rate so reduce the propensity to shirk that the surrogate "supply wage" required by incentive considerations drops so as to accommodate or more than accommodate the reduced demand price for labor? I will argue in the negative.

The following discussion abstracts from the impact of an increase of time preference on the propensity to shirk. This direct effect of the intertemporal taste change apparently can only work in favor of the desired result since an increase in present-mindedness implies an increased willingness to substitute present on-the-job leisure for future on-the-job leisure, just as it implies an increased willingness to substitute present consumption for future consumption. There are, then, two considerations: the relevant

income or wealth effect, if any, and the pure effect of the interest rate
(given the income from wealth).

Nonwage income as the driving force, given the interest rate.   In the
"Ramsey" case set out above, what matters for the amount of on-the-
job leisure demanded—and thus how it will respond to increased r and
decreased q—is not wealth but rather the *income* from wealth. Disre-
garding for the moment the consequences of the rate of interest on the
demand for leisure through any other channels, the employees' propensity
to shirk will drop, and hence the firm's optimal incentive wage will drop,
if and only if the time-preference shock driving up r and driving down q
causes a drop in the *nonwage income* of the employees—this income being
rw, or rqa, for an employee holding assets in the amount a whose real
price is q. At the initial v, this income is not decreased by the rise of the
interest rate: shares go on earning the same income as before—only their
price is reduced to provide the rate of return to match the increased rate
of interest. Hence there is no income/wealth effect operating to reduce the
propensity to shirk at the initial wage, which would in turn cause a reduction of the cost-minimizing incentive wage, or efficiency wage, and thus
operate in the direction of accommodating the downward disturbance of
labor's demand price. (The pure interest-rate effect aside, the optimal incentive wage locus as a function of the employment rate is not shifted, on
our assumptions, provided that nonwage income is always calculated using
the incentive wage rather than the demand wage, which the analyst is free
to do.)

The drop in wealth, qa, induced by the time-preference shock cannot
induce a drop in the propensity to shirk (hence an accommodating drop
in the supply wage) because, in the Ramsey/Weil zero-mortality case,
workers care about the stream of income from wealth, rqa, not the market
value of the assets as such, qa. The model with or without utility discounting might just as well be reformulated with the income from wealth,
say y^w, as the state variable, defined by rw, instead of w. The same first-
order conditions in (15.9), (15.10) and (15.11) are obtained, with the sole
difference that the expected values of lifetime utility for the employed and
unemployed statuses are represented as a function of y^w, not w.

The pure effect of the interest rate, given nonwage income.   If the interest rate mattered for household behavior only via rz, the whole analysis
would need to go no further. The chain of consequences from the demand
shock driving q down and r up would be only that stemming from the
impact on the demand wage. However, there is no reason to think that
the interest rate has no direct effect.

Conjectures abound on the question of just how the demand for on-the-job leisure depends on the rate of interest, given nonwage income, in the sort of intertemporal model studied here. One of the more persuasive is the conjecture that the penalty on shirking—the differential in the lifetime expected utility prospect of the employed person and that of his unemployed brother with identical wealth—is decreased by an increase of the rate of interest. Given that the two persons have a given positive nonwage income, which is identical, their different prospects with regard to lifetime wage income dwindle into insignificance as we go on increasing the interest rate in steps without bound. (It is only if the interest rate were going to be high just for a few days that a person would be keen to be employed, so that he might save virtually all his wage income over those days.) But a way to prove this conjecture in the continuous-time infinite-horizon model under study here has not been hit upon.

It is reasonable to hope that numerical simulations will exhibit a systematic effect from a higher interest rate, and a number of simulations have been carried out to verify the presence of this hypothesized effect. For this purpose it was necessary to work with a discrete-time version of the model, of course. It was also decided to restrict the study to the case, studied in the previous section, in which the absolute elasticity of the marginal utility of consumption is greater than one, so that the rate of utility approaches the "bliss" level as the rate of consumption goes to infinity. Several questions were studied, of which two were deemed basic.

A basic exercise was to check that, in the infinite-horizon case, current consumption demand is indeed homogeneous of degree one, and on-the-job leisure demand homogeneous of degree zero, in the wage rate and the current nonwage income of the worker. That was as much a check on the model as anything else, since analytic results to that effect were obtained for the continuous-time version.

The crucial exercise was to shock the interest factor, $1 + r$, while assuming that the price of the asset drops such that nonwage income is initially unchanged, since the assumed wage rate is unchanged and likewise the assumed employment rate. Fortunately it was found in every case that the effect was to *increase* the demand for on-the-job leisure. That is, the propensity to shirk at given wage rate and nonwage income is stimulated by an increase of the interest rate, given the time-preference rate and the other parameters. A fairly wide range of the parameter space was explored, and there was never any deviation from this result. The effect was found to be weaker the higher the ratio of the wage rate to nonwage income, as could have been anticipated.

The simulations were carried out by Alexander Reyfman, then a Columbia College student, whose report is included below as an appendix.

15.3 Commentary

The intertemporal microeconomics of saving and shirking in the presence of imperfect monitoring is, as we have seen, not an analytically convenient subject. Yet the diamonds we hoped to mine were finally extracted: the homogeneity in wealth and wage rate, given the interest rate; the inhibitory effect of the wage on shirking, given wealth and the interest rate; and the tendency of a higher interest rate to encourage shirking by reducing the present discounted value of the wages an employee forgoes when caught shirking.

These findings, though not at all general, come as a relief to anyone concerned with macroeconomic modeling. Although proofs remain for future research, the macroeconomic implications of the foregoing results in now-standard models are pretty clear: The homogeneity result enables balanced growth, with trendlessness in the unemployment rate, and restricts a labor-augmenting permanent productivity shock to have only a vanishing effect on the unemployment rate. The role wealth is shown to have makes it a strategic factor in the transitory effects of a permanent productivity shock: the implied drop in the real price of capital (as a capital-destructive catastrophe would do), in reducing wealth (in value terms) and reducing (at least relative to the wage rate) the total income from wealth (as the reduced price lowers the income-like flow of actuarial insurance dividends), lowers the propensity to shirk and thus lowers the wage-setting locus, thus leading to a temporary bulge of the employment rate. The positive effect of increased interest rates on shirking, which suggests that similar results can be obtained in quitting models, shores up a weak spot in the argument that those demand shocks that raise real interest rates are contractionary for equilibrium activity through their depressing effect on asset prices: not only does derived labor demand drop, but the equilibrium wage-setting locus shifts up and thus adds to the total contractionary effect.

The problem to be met in carrying out the necessary macroeconomic extension is to pin down the distribution of asset holdings over the population of workers, employed and unemployed, in any stationary state. Such an analysis can be expected to permit us to shore up the last weak point in the argument: to show that not only does each individual respond to demand and productivity shocks as was conjectured when the quantity of assets held by the individual is given, but in addition a system-effect redistribution of asset holdings is not such as to overturn the *ceteris paribus* tendency. Only when that last step is successfully taken will the micro propositions become macro propositions as well.

Appendix: *Computing Numerical Approximations of the Equilibrium Solutions to the Stochastic Dynamic Model of Consumption and Shirking*

BY ALEXANDER REYFMAN

The main text of this chapter develops a model of household consumption and "shirking," or on-the-job leisure, decisions. The economy is made up of identical firms and workers who are identical except for wealth. The workers derive utility from consumption and on-the-job leisure.

In the discrete-time version of the model set up here for purposes of computation, an individual worker for the duration of any period is either employed and receiving the economywide wage or unemployed and running down his savings. In the employed state a worker must decide how much to consume and how much to shirk, knowing that if he gets caught by the firm he will be fired, the dismissal to take effect starting with the next period. The employer pays the wage at the end of the period. In the unemployed state, a worker must decide how much to consume knowing that in every period he has some chance of being hired again at the economywide wage. The chance of being fired is the same from period to period, as the workers are in a macroeconomically deterministic stationary state in which the identities of the persons changing places in the unemployment pool constitute the micro stochastic element. Hiring takes place at the beginning of a period. The worker chooses his consumption and the rate at which he shirks over the period so as to maximize the expected value of lifetime utility, which is equal to current-period utility plus the expected sum of discounted future utilities.

$$(15.A1) \quad g_N(w; \sigma) = \max E[U_N(c, l) + \alpha \sum_{i=N-1}^{0} U_i(c, l)]$$

$$\text{where } 0 < c < w \text{ and } 0 < l < 1$$

Here, E is the expected-value operator. The periods are numbered in reverse, so N is the number of periods remaining. The expectation under optimum performance, $g_N(w; \sigma)$ is a function of the current wealth and employment status ($\sigma = 1$, employed; $\sigma = 0$, unemployed); U is the utility function of consumption, c, and on-the-job leisure, l; α is the discount factor; and v/β is the beginning-of-the-period value of the wage the individual will receive at the *end* of the period. β represents the interest factor in the economy, $1 + r \equiv \beta > 1$. By Bellman's principle of optimality, we can write

$$(15.A2) \quad g(w_N; 1) = \max\{U(c_N, l) + \alpha[(1 - \theta l(1 - \mathbf{a}))$$
$$\times g(\beta[w_N - c_N + \beta^{-1}v_N] + \beta^{-1}v_{N-1}; 1)$$
$$+ \theta l(1 - \mathbf{a})g(\beta[w_N - c_N + \beta^{-1}v_N]; 0)]\}$$
$$g(w_N; 0) = \max\{U(c_N, l) + \alpha[\mathbf{a}g(\beta[w_N - c_N] + \beta^{-1}v_{N-1}; 1)$$
$$+ (1 - \mathbf{a})g(\beta[w_N - c_N]; 0)]\}$$

where θ is the intensity of on-the-job leisure detection practiced by the firms and $\mathbf{a}$ is the probability of being rehired during any one period. Here, w is the start-of-period wealth, excluding any current-period paycheck, the present value of which is v. After formulating the model in this manner we can proceed with examining some of its predictions.

The variable under scrutiny is the shirking rate, l. How is it affected by parameter changes? We want a utility function that delivers the following implications: A larger initial wealth and a larger wage would both result in a higher consumption. A larger initial wealth would tend to increase l, while a larger v would tend to decrease it. If both the wage and initial wealth were increased proportionally, the model should produce a homogeneous result: consumption rises by the same proportion while the shirking rate remains unchanged. We want to show that such a function exists and study what it implies for the effect of a rise in β on l.

It is reasonable to require that the utility function have positive first derivatives, negative second derivatives, and an upper bound. One function that displays these properties is

$$(15.A3) \quad \frac{c^{1-E}}{1 - E} \Psi(l)$$

where E denotes the elasticity of marginal utility of consumption with respect to consumption and is greater than one. The range of $\Psi(l)$ is between

1 and 1/2, while $0 \leq l \leq 1$. So, the higher l is the more $\Psi(l)$ shifts $(c^{1-E})/$ $(1 - E)$ upward. Another important restriction on $\Psi(l)$ is that $\Psi'(l) = -\infty$ at $l = 0$ and $\Psi'(l) = 0$ at $l = 1$, as well as having $\Psi''(l) \leq 0$. These restrictions guarantee a well-behaved and reasonable $\Psi(l)$. Specifically, a shirking rate of 1 will be chosen only when $g(w_N; 1) = g(w_N; 0)$, which logically should be never; a shirking rate of 0 will also never be chosen, because at 0 the marginal utility of l is infinite. One simple function that fits the bill is the lower left quarter of an ellipse that is tangent to the y axis at 1, to the line $y = 1/2$ at 1, and centered at (1, 1).

$$(15.A4) \quad \Psi(l) = 1.0 - 0.5 \sqrt{1 - (1 - l)^2}$$

The explicit form of the functions for optimum consumption and rate of shirking proved to be unobtainable. Therefore, the alternative of computer approximations had to be adopted. Moreover, since only qualitative effects were of interest, exact functional answers could be forgone. The recursive nature of dynamic models lends itself ideally to computer manipulation.

The overall approach to working with this particular model lies in reversing the temporal sequence of events. First, we must calculate $g(w_N; 1)$ and $g(w_N; 0)$ for the trivial case in which a worker has one period left to go ($N = 1$) and then use the results to find $N = 2, 3, 4$, and so on. The case $N = 1$ is trivial insofar as it depends only on w_1. The loop is summarized in Table 15.1. Generally, ten loops, or periods, were sufficient to approximate the infinite-period solution.

While the basic case of $w_N = v$, where v is the wage (usually $v = 1.0$ for simplicity), was the one of particular interest, during each loop it was necessary to solve $g(w_N; \sigma)$ for a range of w_N's, specifically $w_N = (1/2)v$ to $w_N = (3/2)v$. The reason for this stems from the method employed to find the optimum c and l. The method, called the "golden-section" algorithm, is simply an efficient guessing procedure for finding a maximum of a function.[23] An initial guess at the true maximum is made and then quickly improved to the tolerance (significant-digit resolution) of the computer. In the process of deriving the optimum c, $g(w_N; \sigma)$ must be calculated several times, each time with a different w_{N-1}. Each trial c_N results in a different w_N and, consequently, in a different value of g_{N-1}. Therefore, beginning with $N = 1$, $g(w_1; \sigma)$'s were computed for the range of w_1's. Then, during the calculation of $N = 2$, the trial w_2 is used to produce the $g(w_2 + \beta^{-1}v_2; 1)$ and $g(w_2; 0)$ values, which are in turn used in the derivation of the

Table 15.1   The algorithm used

Step 1.   Calculate $g(w_1; \sigma)$ for $\dfrac{1}{2} v \le w_1 \le \dfrac{3}{2} v$.

Step 2.   Perform the next four steps ten times.

Step 3.   Calculate $A + \dfrac{B}{w_{N-1}}$ approximations for $g(w_{N-1}; \sigma)$.

Step 4.   Go through all the w_N's in the range, using steps approximately one-twentieth the size of v.

Step 5.   For each w_N, using the golden-section method, find the optimum c_N and l_N.

Step 6.   Go back to step 3.

---

trial value of g_2. With this reverse-view procedure the optimum c_N's were derived.

The reader might have noticed that this procedure is not completely feasible. The values of $g(w_{N-1}; \sigma)$ are computed only for $(1/2)v \le w_N \le (3/2)v$, while $w_{N-1} + \beta^{-1}v_{N-1}$ is outside the range of w_{N-1}'s for very small and very big values of c_N. This stumbling block is overcome by approximating the $g(w_N; \sigma)$ functions with hyperbolas of the form

(15.A5) $$A + \frac{B}{w_N}$$

The fit between the approximations and the actual values is remarkably close for nonextreme values of the parameters. In particular, with $E > 2$ and $\beta > 2$ this approximation quickly fails. Trial values of w_N are used in the approximating equations to produce values of $g(w_N; \sigma)$.

At this point it might seem that the critical variable l has been neglected. Actually, it is possible to express l as a function of c, thereby significantly simplifying the problem. By taking the derivative of equation (15.A2) with respect to l one arrives at

(15.A6) $\dfrac{\partial g(w_N; 1)}{\partial l} = U'(c_N; l) + \alpha\theta(1 - a)[g(w_{N-1}; 0) - g(w_{N-1}; 1)]$

Upon using the specification in (15.A3) for $U(c, l)$ we get

(15.A7) $\dfrac{\partial g(w_N; 1)}{\partial l} = \dfrac{c^{1-E}}{1 - E}\Psi'(l) + \alpha\theta(1 - a)[g(w_{N-1}; 0) - g(w_{N-1}; 0)]$

Using equation (15.A4) for $\Psi(l)$ and noting that at the maximum $\partial g/\partial l = 0$ we can rewrite (15.A7) into the form

(15.A8)
$$l = 1.0 \sqrt{\left(1.0 + 4\left\{\dfrac{-(1 - E)\alpha\theta(1 - a)[g(w_{N-1}; 0) - g(w_{N-1}; 1)]}{c^{1-E}}\right\}^2\right)}$$

Equation (15.A8) depends on c_N, which is the object of the golden-section algorithm, and the values of $g(w_{N-1}; \sigma)$, which are calculated using the hyperbolic approximations of $g(w_{N-1}; \sigma)$. Note that (15.A8) equals to 1 only when the lifetime utilities from the employed and the unemployed cases are equal; also, it is never equal to 0. The equations used to find $g(w_N; \sigma)$ were

(15.A9a) $g(w_N; 1) = \dfrac{c^{1-E}}{1 - E}\left[1.0 - \dfrac{1}{2} - \sqrt{(1.0 - (l - 1.0)^2)}\right]$
$+ \alpha[(1.0 - (\theta l(1 - a))g(w_{N-1}; 1))$
$+ (\theta l(1 - a)g(w_{N-1}; 0))]$

(15.A9b) $g(w_N; 0) = \dfrac{c^{1-E}}{1 - E}0.5 + \alpha[(ag(w_{N-1}; 1)) + (1 - a)g(w_{N-1}; 0)]$

When the golden-section algorithm produces an optimum c_N, the optimum l_N readily follows. (It might be commented that running this program on an IBM PS/2 Model 50 Z with an Intel 286 and without a math co-processor takes several hours. All of the math functions used came from a standard Borland Turbo C library.)

Armed with this program, we can begin studying the effects of parame-

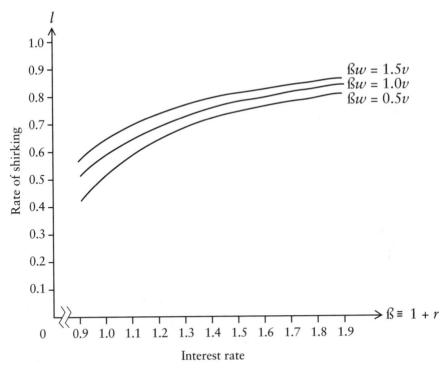

Figure 15.1 The effect of the interest rate on the rate of shirking (given $E = 1.5$)

ter changes mentioned above. The first question concerns the homogeneic nature of the model. If initial wealth and wage are both increased proportionally, what happens to optimum c and l? By running the above program for different values of initial wealth and wage, we can convince ourselves that the model indeed agrees with the predictions: c goes up by the same proportion, while l remains unchanged. The second question, which did not have an associated intuition-based prediction, concerns the effect of an increase in the interest rate (an increase in β) on l. This problem has one additional complication. We are interested only in the effect of a change in β and not in wealth. Therefore, βw must remain constant. In order to solve this problem a setup similar to the one used to answer the first question needs to be slightly modified. For every loop with a new value of β the initial wealth is decreased so as to hold their product constant. The results are depicted graphically in Figure 15.1.

The method of working with a stochastic, dynamic, infinite-period model described in this paper is not without flaws. The most important one concerns the somewhat arbitrary nature of the approximating functions used in the calculations. An alternative not attempted in the course of this work consists of using successively smaller ranges for w_N centered at v. For example, for period $N = 1$ the range of w_N could be 1.0×10^{-10} to 1.0×10^{10}. With each step the range would decrease by a factor of ten at each end. No longer would $w_{N-1} + \beta^{-1}v_{N-1}$ be outside the range of w_{N-1}'s. This "pyramid" approach would involve the same amount of calculations, inasmuch as the number of points computed would remain constant while the intervals between them would decrease with each period. During the calculation of the $N + 1$ period, linear interpolations between the values of period g_N may be used.

Another, less serious, shortcoming involves the accuracy of the $g(w_N; \sigma)$ results. In order to refine further the value of $g(w_N; \sigma)$ arrived at after ten loops, the result can be cycled through the equation

$$(15.A10a) \quad g(w; 1) = \max\{U(c, l) + \alpha[(1 - \theta l)(1 - a)g(w; 1)$$
$$+ \theta l(1 - a)g(w; 0)]\}$$

$$(15.A10b) \quad g(w; 0) = \max\{U(c, l) + \alpha[ag(w; 1) + (1 - a)g(w; 0)]\}$$

using the optimum values of c and l until the value converges to the tolerance of the computer. This would guarantee that the result really approximates the infinite-period case.

Finally, the last flaw concerns the golden-section method. It is quite likely that there exist other, more efficient (and more elegant) ways of finding the maximums of $g(w_N; \sigma)$, such as, for example, the parabolic-interpolation method.[24] However, the golden-section method was sufficiently powerful for the computationally simple problems examined in the course of this work.

16

Structural Shifts and Economic Activity in Neoclassical Theory

THE effects of fiscal policy on employment, investment, and the real rate of interest is a central issue in macroeconomics. The complexity of the analysis, arising from the impact of fiscal policy on both current and future prices, has created the need to study these effects in the context of intertemporal general-equilibrium models. A number of authors identified with the so-called real business cycle school have used the standard vehicle in that tradition, the neoclassical one-sector model, to analyze the dynamic effects of fiscal policy. Some of these papers are explicitly concerned with fluctuations in employment.[1] Others have primarily focused on consumption and the capital stock by assuming an inelastic labor supply.[2]

This literature has concentrated on the effects of a permanent increase in public expenditure. According to this analysis, the implied decline in resources available for consumption and investment reduces consumption demand and increases labor supply, as both consumption and leisure are normal goods. At each point in time the impact on labor supply raises the current real rate of interest and lowers the current real wage; these latter price changes have substitution effects that may amplify or dampen the resulting rise of employment, while the income effects cancel; the upward shift of the real-interest-rate path operates to reduce the present value of human wealth, which tends to amplify the increase of labor supply. With labor demand at first undisturbed, it follows that consumption declines and employment increases. Although these short-run results are obtained with Ricardian equivalence, they carry over to the case of finitely-lived agents with no bequest motive.

This chapter will analyze the dynamic effects of fiscal policy in a neo-classical two-sector economy. Its technology is that studied by Uzawa, in which the sector producing the consumption good is more capital-intensive than the sector producing the investment good.[3] It adopts the treatment by Blanchard of finitely-lived agents with no bequest motive, in part in order that public debt will also have real effects, which we wish to explore.[4] With these two seemingly innocuous extensions, several results emerge that differ significantly from the present doctrine of neoclassical business cycle theory.[5]

It will be shown that an increased national debt contracts employment while it drives up the real rate of interest. Increased public expenditure in either good expands employment, but not in the same way and thus with otherwise contrasting effects. Higher government purchases of the consumer good, which is relatively capital-intensive, push up employment while raising the real interest rate and reducing the real wage through their positive impact on labor supply. Higher government purchases of the capital good reduce the real interest rate and raise the real wage; there is a positive impact on labor demand as well as labor supply.

The latter decline of the real rate of interest is consistent with the famous Penati-Barro observation that the rate of interest typically declines during wartime periods if such periods are marked by unusually large government demands on the vehicle, aircraft, and metal-working industries of the capital-goods-producing sector.[6] To account for this phenomenon, it has been suggested by Mankiw that if agents, along with a nondurable good, enjoy the services of a durable good that can be instantaneously turned into productive capital, then higher government purchases reduce the demand for both goods and drive some of the durable good into productive use, thus lowering the rate of interest despite the fact that capital as a whole is crowded out.[7] But Mankiw's model lacks an endogenous labor supply. Had he included it, his view could be sustained in the present context only if the induced increase in labor supply does not outweigh the induced increase in the supply of capital to the commercial sector, thus to reverse the decline in the rate of interest.

Another important feature of the model is that it does not lead to the empirically implausible conclusion of the neoclassical one-sector model that higher employment must be accompanied by a lower real wage. The two-sector neoclassical model we study here implies that higher employment is accompanied by a *higher* real wage *if* the driving force is increased public expenditures in the capital-good-producing sector but it is accompanied by a lower real wage in the other case. The former result—the rise in the real wage—is consistent with the observation that during the last world war, when capital-goods purchases were high, wage rates were driven above trend.

Thus, in putting forward a less aggregative, more structuralist, version of the neoclassical theory, the present analysis serves to rescue the real business cycle school from some of its worst embarrassments. But the main motive has been to investigate whether and how the implications of a more structuralist neoclassical model differ from those of the *modern* equilibrium theory advanced in the present volume. It is now clear that, in one respect, the conclusions reached with the two-sector neoclassical model here stand in sharp contrast to those obtained with the two-sector model constructed along modern instead of neoclassical lines in Chapter 9.[8] The implications of the various kinds of public expenditure for the rate of interest are the same, and the mechanism is broadly similar despite the different kind of wage determination. But it was found in the modern model that higher government purchases of output from the *consumer-good-producing* sector lead to a *contraction* of employment. With respect to employment, there is agreement only with respect to government purchases of capital goods, being relatively labor-intensive, and of the services of labor itself.

Finally, this chapter studies the implications of labor-augmenting technical progress that is equiproportionate in the two sectors. It is found that an unanticipated and permanent increase in the *rate* of technical progress of the labor-augmenting sort is *contractionary* in the short run. In contrast, an unanticipated and permanent upward shift in the *level* of the labor-augmenting technology is found to be *expansionary* in the short run.

Here too there are potential contrasts of the neoclassical with the modern. It was argued in the context of the modern two-sector model in Chapter 9 that it *could* be that a sudden helicopter drop of capital is *expansionary* over the near-term future; but then it is a corollary that a sudden and permanent increase in the *level* of the technology is *contractionary* in the short run. (On the other hand, as a purely theoretical matter it could equally be that the truth is the other way around.) In the neoclassical model, such a technological gain would be expansionary via a jump in labor supply. However, both models suggest that the sudden prospect of increased technological pregressiveness, in inducing an upward revision of consumption plans and thus driving up the real yield curve, operates to depress asset prices and through that channel to reduce employment.

The chapter is organized as follows. In the first section the agents' maximization problem is described and solved. The next section briefly discusses the effects of an increase in the national debt and an increase in government purchases in a one-sector model. In Section 16.3 the two-sector model is described and solved. We go on to study the effects of an increase in the national debt; the effects of an increase in government purchases of the consumption good; and the effects of an increase in government purchases of the capital good. Finally, we introduce technical progress and study the effects of a rise in the level as well as the rate of growth of technical progress. Most of the algebra is relegated to a long appendix.

16.1 The Agents' Problem

Agents derive utility from consumption of a nonstorable good and leisure. Following Blanchard, it is assumed that agents have finite lives and they face an instantaneous probability of death μ which is constant throughout their life. Given the large number of agents in the economy, life insurance can be offered without risk by insurance companies, which are assumed to operate in a competitive environment making zero profits. Thus an agent with wealth w will pay w to the insurance company if he dies and receives μw per unit time as long as he does not die.

Let $c(s, t)$ denote consumption at time t of an agent born at time s, $l(s, t)$ labor supply, $w(s, t)$ nonhuman wealth, $h(s, t)$ human wealth, and $\tau(s, t)$ lump-sum taxes. Also let $v(t)$ be the real wage, $r(t)$ the real rate of interest, δ the rate of depreciation of the capital stock, ρ the rate of time preference, and $\overline{H}$ total available time. The agent maximizes

$$(16.1) \quad \int_t^\infty [\log c(s, \lambda) + \log(\overline{H} - l(s, \lambda))] e^{(\rho+\mu)(t-\lambda)} d\lambda$$

subject to

$$(16.2) \quad \frac{dw(s, t)}{dt} = [r(t) + \mu]w(s, t) + l(s, t)v(t) - \tau(s, t) - c(s, t)$$

and a transversality condition preventing agents from going infinitely into debt.

The solution to the agent's problem is given by

$$(16.3) \quad c(s, t) = (\rho + \mu)(w(s, t) + h(s, t))$$

$$(16.4) \quad \frac{\overline{H} - l(s, t)}{c(s, t)} = \frac{1}{v(t)}$$

so that

$$(16.5) \quad \overline{H} - l(s, t) = \frac{(\rho + \mu)(w(s, t) + h(s, t))}{v(t)}$$

where human wealth is given by

$$(16.6) \quad h(s, t) = \int_t^\infty [l(s, \lambda) v(\lambda) - \tau(s, \lambda)] e^{-\int_t^\lambda [r(\zeta) + \mu] d\zeta} d\lambda$$

Hence consumption is a linear function of total wealth and leisure is a linear function of total wealth divided by the real wage. In particular, current consumption depends positively on the current and future real wage. Current labor supply depends positively on the current real wage and negatively on future real wages, that is, the substitution effect dominates the income effect. Current consumption is not affected by the current (instantaneous) rate of interest but depends negatively on future rates of interest because future labor income is discounted more heavily so that human wealth declines. Finally, current labor supply is not affected by the current (instantaneous) rate of interest but depends positively on future rates of interest, as future labor income is more heavily discounted so that human wealth declines.

Normalizing the population to one, dropping the time index t and denoting aggregate variables by capital letters, we obtain

$$(16.7) \quad C = (\mu + \rho)(H + W)$$

$$(16.8) \quad \frac{\overline{H} - L}{C} = \frac{1}{v}$$

so that

$$(16.9) \quad \overline{H} - L = \frac{(\mu + \rho)(H + W)}{v}$$

The dynamics are given by

(16.10) $\dot{H} = (r + \mu)H - Lv + T$

(16.11) $\dot{W} = rW + Lv - T - C$

(16.12) $\dot{C} = (r - \rho)C - \mu(\mu + \rho)W$

Two points are in order with regard to the distinction between individual and aggregate variables. First, individual consumption evolves according to $\dot{c} = (r - \rho)c$, so if $r = \rho$ individual consumption is constant over a lifetime but aggregate consumption will be falling if W is positive, as each generation enjoys a successively lower level of consumption. Second, consider a steady state with $r > \rho$. In such a steady state, aggregate consumption and employment are constant but individual consumption is rising and individual hours of work are falling. The individual, by working longer hours and by consuming less, is able to accumulate wealth during the earlier part of his life; this enables him to increase his consumption as well as his leisure later in life.[9]

We now turn to the production side. We first study an example of a one-sector economy and then an example of a two-sector economy.

16.2 The Implied One-Sector Case

The single good is produced by a standard constant-returns-to-scale (CRS) production function,

(16.13) $Y = F(K, L)$ $F_L > 0, F_K > 0, F_{LL} < 0, F_{KK} < 0, F_{LK} > 0$

Capital accumulation is given by

(16.14) $\dot{K} = F(K, L) - \delta K - C - G$

where G is government purchases that are used to provide a public good, which is assumed not to affect the marginal utility of consumption and leisure.

Letting D be the stock of government debt, the government dynamic budget constraint is

(16.15) $\dot{D} = rD + G - T$

It will be assumed that the government operates under a balanced budget at all times by raising enough taxes. This admittedly unrealistic assumption prevents the analysis of temporary deficits but simplifies the model considerably, as the dynamics of the economy are reduced from a system of three to a system of two dynamic equations.

Since the wage is a function of the capital-labor ratio, the first-order condition (16.8) implies that employment can be expressed as a function of consumption and capital:

$$(16.16) \quad L = L(C, K) \qquad \frac{\partial L}{\partial C} < 0, \frac{\partial L}{\partial K} > 0$$

Given the level of the capital stock, a rise in consumption reduces the marginal utility of consumption so employment has to fall in order for the marginal utility of leisure to fall and the real wage to rise. Given the level of consumption, a higher level of the capital stock drives up the real wage so employment increases.

The rate of interest is a function of the capital-labor ratio and is thus also a function of consumption and capital. The dynamics of the economy are therefore described by two differential equations in C and K:

$$(16.17) \quad \dot{C} = (r(K/L(C, K)) - \rho)C - \mu(\mu + \rho)(D + K)$$

$$\dot{K} = F(K, L(C, K)) - \delta K - C - G$$

Here $D + K$ is the nonhuman wealth, W, in this economy.

The linear approximation of the system around the steady state with zero government debt and expenditure, and assuming that the production function is locally Cobb-Douglas, is discussed in the appendix. In this steady state $r > \rho$ so the interest rate is above the Golden Rule rate of interest, which is zero since there is no population growth. Here we summarize with the aid of the phase diagrams in Figures 16.1 and 16.2.

The $\dot{K} = 0$ locus is upward-sloping, as illustrated in Figure 16.1: an increase in K increases output by $F_K - \delta$ and stimulates employment, which further increases output by $F_L L_K$; so in order for net investment to remain constant, consumption has to rise. The $\dot{C} = 0$ locus is downward-sloping if the mortality rate μ is not too high. Then, the effect of K by way of the first term in the $\dot{C}$ equation, which involves the rate of interest, is stronger than the effect by way of the second term, which describes the effect of the level of nonhuman wealth on $\dot{C}$: given C, a rise in K increases nonhu-

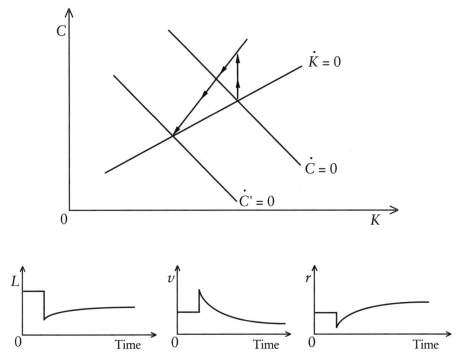

Figure 16.1 Increase of public debt in the one-sector economy

man wealth but operates on $\dot{C}$ mainly by stimulating L, driving up the real wage and driving down the rate of interest so $\dot{C}$ becomes negative; in order for the rate of interest to increase, consumption has to fall so that the marginal utility of consumption increases, which in turn requires a rise in the marginal utility of leisure through a rise in employment. This rise in employment brings about the necessary rise in the rate of interest. A more detailed discussion of this is presented in the appendix, where it is also shown that if the $\dot{C} = 0$ locus is downward-sloping the economy has a unique saddlepath around the steady state, as shown in Figure 16.1.

We now turn to the study of two fiscal policy experiments, namely a permanent increase in the level of government debt and a permanent increase of government purchases.

First consider an unanticipated increase of government debt, which is transferred equally to all agents. Taxes equal to the interest payments on the debt are levied to balance the budget thereafter. It is shown in the appendix that the $\dot{C} = 0$ locus shifts down while the $\dot{K} = 0$ locus is unaf-

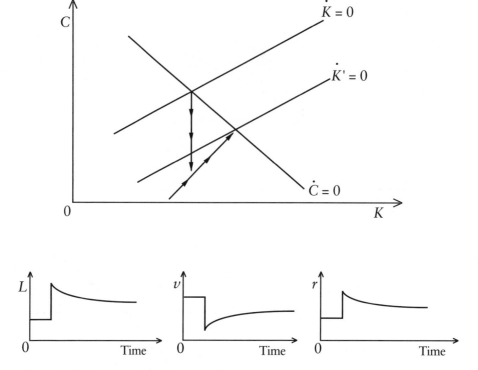

Figure 16.2 Increase of public expenditure in the one-sector economy

fected (see Figure 16.1). Agents' cash flow increases by rD and they pay rD more taxes as well. But agents now receive μD more from Blanchard's insurance companies, so they will want to increase consumption and reduce labor supply since both consumption and leisure are normal goods. Consumption immediately increases and employment falls. The higher capital-labor ratio is supported by a lower rate of interest and a higher real wage, which somewhat dampens the decrease in labor supply. Subsequently, the economy converges to a new steady state with lower capital stock and lower employment. The new steady-state wage is lower and the interest rate is higher.[10]

Next, consider an unanticipated permanent increase in government purchases financed by higher taxes so as to balance the budget in all periods. It is shown in the appendix that the $\dot{C} = 0$ locus remains unaffected while the $\dot{K} = 0$ locus shifts down (see Figure 16.2). Higher taxes imply a fall in income and therefore consumption falls and employment increases. The lower capital-labor ratio is supported by a higher interest rate and a lower real wage, which somewhat dampens the increase in employment. Investment is stimulated by the higher employment expenditure despite the fact that the interest rate increases. Subsequently, consumption and the capital stock increase and converge to a new steady state with lower consumption and higher capital stock compared with the initial steady state.

Since K is rising along the adjustment path, for a given wage rate the supply of labor is falling, owing to a positive wealth effect, and the demand for labor is rising, because the productivity of labor is increasing. We show that a sufficient condition for L to decline along the adjustment path is that the share of capital in total output is small enough that the rise in labor demand produced by the rise of capital is less than the fall in labor supply produced by the rise of wealth.[11] (The elasticity of the marginal product of labor with respect to capital is an increasing function of capital's share.) The rate of interest overshoots its new, higher, long-run value and then declines, and the wage undershoots its new, lower, long-run value and then increases.

Contrary to the conventional view that public expenditure crowds out investment through a rise in the rate of interest, the neoclassical one-sector model predicts that investment is actually crowded in despite the rise in the rate of interest. As soon as the government increases its purchases, agents go through a period of relatively long hours of work, high saving rates and high investment, all of which are later somewhat reduced as the economy settles down to a new steady state. Thus the folklore of real business cycle theory now finding its way into the intermediate textbooks in macroeconomics, which views the interest rate rise (on which the increase in labor supply is said to depend) as a concomitant of an assumed crowding out, actually misunderstands the basis on which its characteristic conclusions from its characteristic models may correctly be argued.

16.3 The Two-Sector Case

In the classic two-sector model, studied by Uzawa and Foley and Sidrauski, one sector produces the capital good and the other sector produces the consumption good. Labor and capital can freely move from one sector to the other so the real wage and the real return to capital are equalized in the two sectors. There are constant returns to scale and diminishing returns, and the consumption good is more capital-intensive than the capital good at every wage-rental ratio. It will be assumed here that the capital good can be produced without capital, and in particular that the output of the capital good is a linear function of the labor employed in the capital-good sector. This unrealistic formulation clearly takes the capital-intensity assumption to its extreme but simplifies the analysis considerably.

The amount of the consumption good supplied is given by

$$(16.18) \quad C = F(K, L_C) - G_C \qquad F_L > 0, F_K > 0, F_{LL} < 0, F_{KK} < 0, F_{LK} > 0$$

where L_C is labor employed in the consumption-good sector and G_C are government purchases of the consumption good.

Capital accumulation is given by

$$(16.19) \quad \dot{K} = \omega L_I - \delta K - G_I$$

where L_I is labor employed in the capital (investment) good sector, ω is a positive constant, and G_I are government purchases of the investment good. Both G_C and G_I are used to provide some public good which does not affect the marginal utility of consumption and leisure.

Labor can move costlessly between sectors so real wages are equalized among sectors. Let the consumption good be the numeraire and denote the price of the capital good by q. Then real wages satisfy

$$(16.20) \quad v = F_L(K, L_C) = \omega q$$

The rental of capital is given by

$$(16.21) \quad R(q) = F_K - q\delta$$

and the rate of interest obeys the arbitrage condition

$$(16.22) \quad r = \frac{F_K}{q} - \delta + \frac{\dot{q}}{q} = \frac{R + \dot{q}}{q}$$

Finally, total employment is the sum of the employment in the two sectors

$$(16.23) \quad L = L_C + L_I$$

The government dynamic budget constraint is

(16.24) $\dot{D} = rD + G_C + qG_I - T$

Again it will be assumed that the government finances interest payments and future purchases by taxes continuously over the entire future.

Equation (16.20) can be used to express L_C as a function of q and K:

(16.25) $L_C = L_C(q, K) \qquad \dfrac{\partial L_C}{\partial q} < 0, \dfrac{\partial L_C}{\partial K} > 0$

Given K, a rise in q implies that v, the reward to the factor used intensively in the consumer-good sector, rises so the amount of labor demanded falls. Given q and thus v, the capital labor ratio in the consumer goods sector is determined so an increase in K is matched by an equiproportionate rise in employment.

Equation (16.18) with the aid of (16.25) can be used to express C as a function of q, K, and G_C:

(16.26) $C = C(q, K; G_C) \qquad C_1 < 0, C_2 > 0, C_3 < 0$

Given K, a rise in q implies a rise in v so labor demand falls and thus the output of the consumption good falls. Given q, a rise in K leads to an equiproportionate rise in employment, so total output expands. Finally, a rise in G_C reduces the supply available for consumption.

The first-order condition (16.8) together with (16.26) implies that L can be expressed as a function of q, K, and G_C:

(16.27) $L = L(q, K; G_C) \qquad L_1 > 0, L_2 < 0, L_3 > 0$

Given K, a rise in q implies a rise in the real wage and thus an increase in the amount of labor supplied and thus an increase in employment. Given q, a rise in K leads to lower labor supply through a positive wealth effect. Finally, given q and K, the resulting impoverishment due to an increase in G_C causes an increase in labor supply and thus employment.

Employment in the capital-good sector L_I is the difference between L and L_C and so L_I is also a function of q, K, and G_C. Upon substitution of r from the $\dot{C}$ equation (16.12) into (16.22) and after collecting terms in $\dot{q}$ and $\dot{K}$, we obtain the following pair of differential equations:

(16.28)
$$\dot{q} = \frac{\left[\rho + \mu(\mu + \rho)\dfrac{qK + D}{F - G_C}\right]q - (F_K - q\delta) + \dfrac{Fq}{KC}\dot{K}}{1 - \dfrac{F_L^2}{F_{LL}(F - G_C)}}$$

$$\dot{K} = \omega L_I(q, K; G_C) - \delta K - G_I$$

Defining

(16.29)
$$\Phi(q, K; G_C, G_I, D) \equiv \left[\rho + \mu(\mu + \rho)\frac{qK + D}{F - G_C}\right]q - (F_K - q\delta)$$

$$\Psi(q, K; G_C, G_I, D) \equiv \omega L_I(q, K; G_C) - \delta K - G_I$$

the system (16.28) becomes

(16.30)
$$\dot{q} = \frac{\Phi(q, K; G_C, D) + \dfrac{Fq}{KC}\Psi(q, K; G_C, G_I)}{1 - \dfrac{F_L^2}{F_{LL}(F - G_C)}}$$

$$\dot{K} = \Psi(q, K; G_C, G_I)$$

We choose to conduct the analysis around the steady state that obtains when D, G_C, and G_I are zero and assume that the production function of the consumption good is locally Cobb-Douglas with γ being the labor share. Noting that the denominator of the $\dot{q} = 0$ equation evaluated at the steady state is simply $1/(1 - \gamma)$, where γ is the share of labor in total output, the first-order Taylor expansion of the system around the steady state is

(16.31)
$$\begin{pmatrix}\dot{q}\\\dot{K}\end{pmatrix} = \begin{pmatrix}(1 - \gamma)(\Phi_q + \dfrac{q}{K}\Psi_q) & (1 - \gamma)\dfrac{q}{K}\Psi_K\\ \Psi_q & \Psi_K\end{pmatrix}\begin{pmatrix}q - \bar{q}\\K - \bar{K}\end{pmatrix}$$

$$+ \begin{pmatrix}(1 - \gamma)(\Phi_{G_C} + \dfrac{q}{K}\Psi_{G_C}) & (1 - \gamma)\Psi_{G_I} & (1 - \gamma)\Phi_D\\ \Psi_{G_C} & \Psi_{G_I} & 0\end{pmatrix}\begin{pmatrix}G_C\\G_I\\D\end{pmatrix}$$

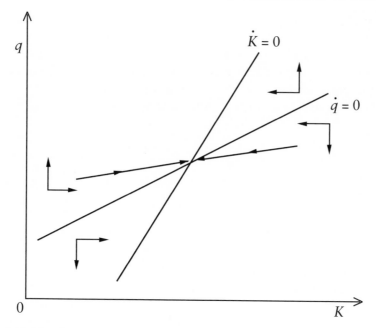

Figure 16.3 The dynamics of the two-sector economy

where the derivatives are evaluated at $(\bar{q}, \bar{K}; 0, 0, 0)$. It is shown in the appendix that if the production function of the consumption good is locally Cobb-Douglas, $\Phi_q > 0$, $\Phi_K = 0$, $\Psi_q > 0$, and $\Psi_K < 0$. It is also shown that $\Phi_{G_C} > 0$, $\Phi_{G_I} > 0$, $\Phi_D > 0$, $\Psi_{G_C} > 0$, $\Psi_{G_I} = -1$, and $\Psi_D = 0$.

In the steady state $\dot{q}$ and $\dot{K}$ are zero so Φ and Ψ are zero. Conveniently, the $\Phi = 0$ equation determines the steady-state value of q independently of the $\Psi = 0$ equation for negligible values of D, G_C, and G_I, so the steady state is unique.

It is shown in the appendix that in the K–q space both stationary loci are upward-sloping, as illustrated in Figure 16.3. Consider first the $\dot{K} = 0$ locus. Given q, and thus v, a rise in K will lead to an equiproportionate rise in L_C and thus the supply of the consumption good; the rise in K also leads to an equiproportionate rise in wealth and thus to an equiproportionate rise in the demand for the consumption good and fall in labor supply. Since L_C rises and L falls, L_I falls, the supply of the capital good declines, and since the demand for the depreciation allowance δK increases, $\dot{K}$ becomes negative. At this higher level of K, a rise in q is necessary to free some labor from the consumption-good sector as well as to increase the total supply of labor, so as to increase the supply of the capital good and make $\dot{K}$ equal to zero.

Consider next the $\dot{q} = 0$ locus. Given q, K affects $\dot{q}$ only by way of the last term in the numerator, which involves $\dot{K}$. According to the argument, presented above for the $\dot{K} = 0$ locus, given q, a rise in K will result in a declining capital stock and thus declining q. Again, according to the argument presented above, a rise in q is necessary for $\dot{q}$ to become zero.

It is easily shown that the $\dot{K} = 0$ locus is steeper:

$$(16.32) \qquad \left.\frac{dq}{dK}\right|_{\dot{K}=0} = \frac{-\Psi_K}{\Psi_q} > \frac{-\dfrac{q}{K}\Psi_K}{\dfrac{q}{K}\Psi_q + \Phi_q} = \left.\frac{dq}{dK}\right|_{\dot{q}=0}$$

It follows that the system has a unique, stable saddlepath, as shown on the phase diagram in Figure 16.3. The saddlepath is upward-sloping and flatter than both stationary loci. For any given capital stock, the saddlepath gives the unique equilibrium price of capital, which is increasing in the capital stock. This is intuitive since it implies that a sudden reduction of the capital stock would lead to a rise in the price of the consumption good, which is capital-intensive, and thus to a rise in the rate of return of capital. L_C immediately drops and since K is also lower consumption drops. L increases and thus L_I increases to replenish the capital stock. In the long run, the economy returns to the initial steady state.

We now turn to the analysis of the effects of three fiscal policy experiments in this two-sector model, which is the main focus of this chapter. We study the effects of a permanent increase of government debt as well as the effects of a tax-financed permanent increase of government purchases in the two sectors. As has been the practice up to now, most of the algebra is presented in the appendix.

PERMANENT INCREASE OF THE GOVERNMENT DEBT

Consider a one-time, unanticipated increase in the government debt D which is transferred equally to all agents. In all subsequent periods the government raises enough taxes to cover the interest payments on the debt. The principle is never paid back. It is shown in the appendix that the $\dot{q} = 0$ locus shifts down while the $\dot{K} = 0$ remains unaffected, as illustrated in Figure 16.4.

Consumers now have a higher after-tax income equal to the amount μD, which they receive from the insurance companies. Higher income induces higher consumption demand and lower labor supply, as both con-

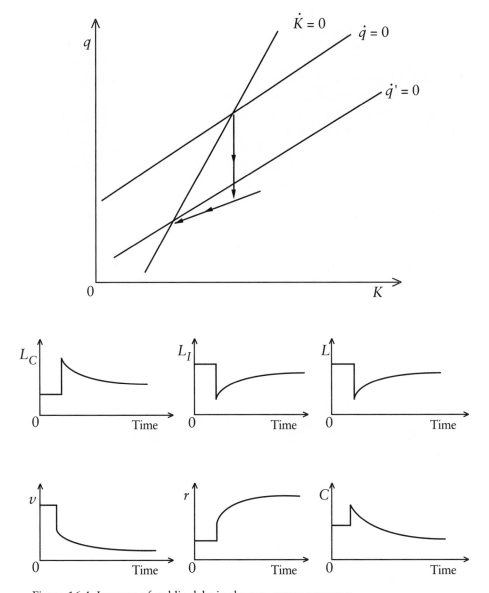

Figure 16.4 Increase of public debt in the two-sector economy

sumption and leisure are normal goods. The excess demand for the consumption good causes its price to increase, that is, it causes q to drop. Recalling that wage equalization between the two sectors amounts to $v = \omega q$, the drop in q causes a drop in the real wage and an increase in the rental. This is in the spirit of the Stopler-Samuelson theorem: a drop in the price q of the labor-intensive good results in the drop of real wages and an increase of the rental. The drop in real wages reinforces the desire of agents to supply less labor. The interest rate, which is equal to $(R(q) + \dot{q})/q$, may rise or fall depending on whether the increase in the rental, expressed as a ratio to the price of capital, is larger or smaller than the anticipated capital losses (Figure 16.4 shows the case where the interest rate increases). As shown in Figure 16.4, consumption immediately rises, total employment falls, the real wage falls, and the rental increases. A lower real wage implies a lower capital-labor ratio in the consumption-good sector, and since capital is fixed in the short run, employment in the consumption-good sector expands and the higher demand for the consumption good is satisfied. Since L drops and L_C increases, employment in the capital-good sector declines.

The convergence of all the main variables to the new steady state is shown in Figure 16.4. L_C initially overshoots its long-run value to support the temporary consumption boom that results from higher debt holdings, and L_I and L undershoot their long-run value. Compared with the initial steady state, in the new steady state consumption and the capital stock are lower, total employment is lower, employment in the consumption-good sector is higher, employment in the capital-good sector is lower, the price of the capital good is lower, real wages are lower, and the interest rate is higher.

Compared with the one-sector model, the effects of an increase in government debt differ in several aspects. In the short run, consumption increases and total employment falls in both models. In the one-sector model, lower employment is accompanied by an increase in the real wage as the demand price of labor (the marginal product of labor) increases. In the two-sector model, employment is higher in the consumption-good sector, so the demand price of labor and thus the real wage declines. In the long run the two models lead to the same conclusions.

PERMANENT INCREASE IN G_C

Consider now an unanticipated permanent increase in government purchases of the consumption good, which is financed by an increase in taxes so that the budget is balanced. It is shown in the appendix that both stationary loci shift down but the $\dot{K} = 0$ locus shifts down by more, as illustrated in Figure 16.5.

As soon as the new policy is implemented, demand for the consumption good by the government increases from zero to G_C. Higher taxes reduce the consumers' income, so their demand for the consumption falls and labor supply increases, as both consumption and leisure are normal goods. The rise in government expenditure crowds out some consumption but the crowding-out is not complete so $C + G_C$ increases. The excess demand for the consumption good brings about an increase in its price so q drops. The drop in q implies a drop in the real wage v and a rise in the rental and the rate of interest r, which is again the Stopler-Samuelson effect. Lower v implies a lower demand price for labor in the consumption-good sector, so employment in the consumption-good sector L_C increases and the higher demand for the consumption good is satisfied.

With regard to total employment there are two opposing effects: on the one hand lower income stimulates the supply of labor, and on the other hand the lower real wage depresses the supply of labor, the net effect being an increase in labor supply. To confirm that the income effect dominates, recall that L_C rises and note that L_I also rises, since K is increasing immediately after the new policy is implemented. Actually, employment overshoots its new, higher, long-run value and then declines toward that value.

Higher government purchases of the consumption good, which is capital-intensive, leads to higher investment. So in the case of higher government purchases of the capital-intensive good, the two-sector neoclassical model yields the same conclusion as the one-sector neoclassical model, namely that higher government purchases crowd investment in rather than out, and this takes place despite a rise in the rate of interest.

The paths of all the variables to the new steady state are shown in Figure 16.5. Compared with the initial steady state, in the new steady state consumption is lower, the capital stock is higher, employment in both sectors is higher, the price of the capital good is lower, the real wage is lower, and the rate of interest is higher. The one-sector and the two-sector model give the same qualitative predictions, both in the short and in the long run, in response to a permanent increase in government expenditures in this case.

PERMANENT INCREASE IN G_I

Consider an unanticipated, permanent increase in government purchases of the capital good, which is financed by higher taxes in order to balance

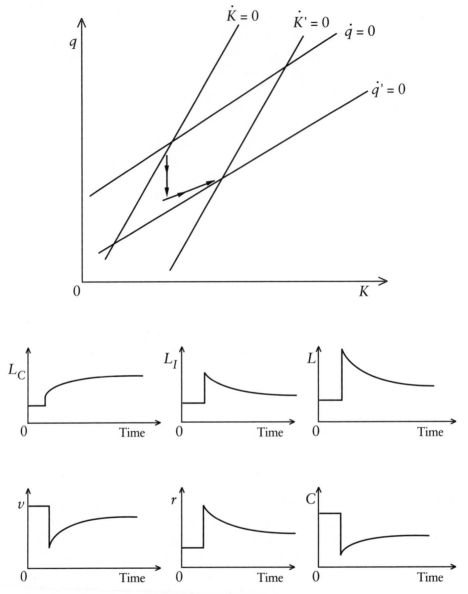

Figure 16.5 Increase of government purchases from the consumer-good sector in the two-sector economy

the budget. It is shown in the appendix that the $\dot{K} = 0$ locus shifts down while the $\dot{C} = 0$ locus remains unaffected, as illustrated in Figure 16.6.

When the new policy is implemented, demand for the capital good increases by G_I. The imposition of higher taxes implies lower consumption demand and higher labor supply, as both consumption and leisure are normal goods. So an excess demand for the capital good and an excess supply of the consumption good develops. To clear the market, the price of the capital good q increases, which implies that the reward to the factor used intensively in the capital-good sector increases, so the real wage increases and the rental as well as the rate of interest fall. On the one hand, higher v implies lower employment in the consumption-good sector. On the other hand, higher v reinforces the increased labor supply so total employment increases. Since L increases and L_C falls, employment in the capital-good sector increases. The increased demand for the capital good by the government is met with higher output but also with some crowding-out of investment as $\dot{K}$ becomes negative. The decline of the rate of interest in response to higher government purchases of the capital good is contrary to standard theory and may seem puzzling. However, once it is viewed as a response to the rise in the price of the capital good, it is simply a consequence of the Stopler-Samuelson theorem. This feature of the model is consistent with the Penati-Barro observation that the real rate of interest declines during wartime periods when the government increases its purchases of capital goods.

The convergence of the variables to the new steady state is shown in Figure 16.6. Compared with the initial steady state, in the new steady state consumption and the capital stock is lower, employment in the consumption-good sector is lower, employment in the capital-good sector is higher, and total employment is higher. In the new steady state the price of the capital good, the real wage, and the rate of interest return to their original levels. This is because in a steady state where D and G_C remain at their original level of zero, the $\dot{C} = 0$ equation is a function of K/L_C alone:

$$(16.33) \quad \left[r\left(\frac{L_C}{K} \right) - \rho \right] F\left(1, \frac{L_C}{K} \right) = \mu(\mu + \rho) q\left(\frac{L_C}{K} \right)$$

so the capital-labor ratio in the consumption-good sector and thus the real wage, the rate of interest, and the price of the capital good remain unaffected.

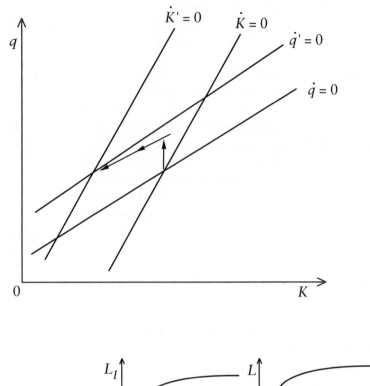

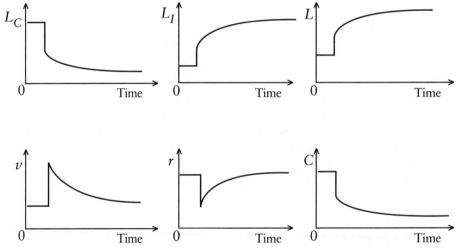

Figure 16.6 Increase of government purchases from the capital-good sector in the two-sector economy

TECHNICAL PROGRESS

In this section we extend the model to include equiproportionate labor-augmenting technical progress in the two sectors and study the behavior of the economy under two experiments. First, we study the effects of a one-time increase in productivity in both sectors. Second, we study the effects of an increase in the rate of productivity growth.

Let $A_t = A_0 e^{\lambda t}$ be a measure of labor productivity; lower-case l, l_C, and l_I actual total employment, employment in the consumption-good sector, and employment in the capital-good sector, respectively; and upper-case $L = Al$, $L_C = Al_C$, and $L_I = Al_I$ the corresponding variables for effective employment. Furthermore let $k = K/A$, $c = C/A$, and $F(K, L_C) = AF(k, l_C)$. Straightforward application of this notation leads to the following two dynamic equations in q and k:

(16.34)
$$\dot{q} = \frac{\left[\rho + \mu(\mu + \rho)\dfrac{qk}{F}\right]q - (F_k - q\delta) + \dfrac{fq}{kc}(\omega l_I - \delta k)}{1 - \dfrac{F_l^2}{F_{ll}F}}$$

$$\dot{k} = \omega l_I(q, k) - (\lambda + \delta)k$$

where $F = F(k, l_C)$ and the fiscal-policy variables have been set to zero for simplicity. Using the new notation and defining $\Phi(q, k)$ and $\Psi(q, k)$ analogously to equation (16.29) above, the system is expressed as

(16.35)
$$\dot{q} = \frac{\Phi(q, k) + \dfrac{Fq}{kc}\Psi(q, k)}{1 - \dfrac{F_l^2}{F_{ll}F}}$$

$$\dot{K} = \Psi(q, k) - \lambda k$$

By a similar argument as in Section 16.3, it is straightforward to show that both stationary loci are upward-sloping, that the $\dot{k} = 0$ locus is steeper than the $\dot{q} = 0$ locus, and that the economy has a unique, stable saddlepath as shown in Figure 16.7. In the steady state, actual employment in both sectors is constant whereas effective employment and the wage are growing at the rate λ and so is the capital stock and consumption.

We now turn to the study of the behavior of the economy under changes in the level of productivity A and the rate of growth λ.

First, consider an economy with $\lambda = 0$ which is in the steady state

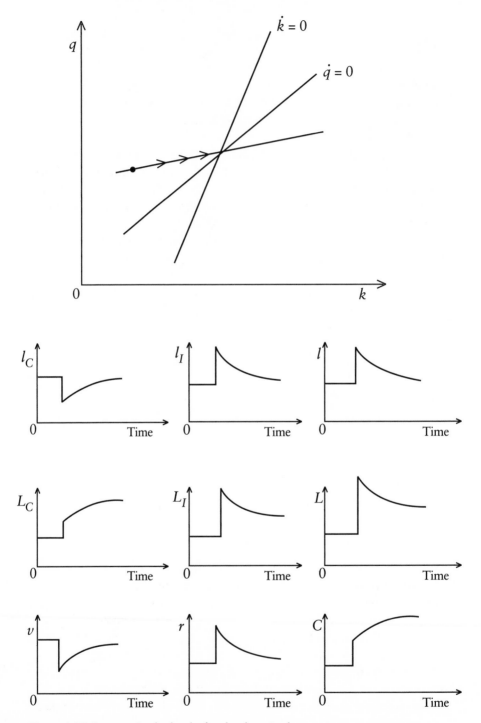

Figure 16.7 Increase in the level of technology in the two-sector economy

and experiences an unanticipated permanent increase in A. It follows from (16.35) that neither stationary locus shifts, so the economy finds itself on the saddlepath at a lower k and a lower q, as shown in Figure 16.7. The economy has now relatively little capital, so the price of capital has to drop in order for the return to capital to increase, given that the capital-producing sector is labor intensive. Equation (16.61) in the appendix implies that l_C is increasing after the shock, and since it will eventually converge to its original steady-state value, l_C drops after the shock. However, effective employment in the consumption-good sector L_C rises after the shock since the drop in q implies a drop in K/L_C. Equation (16.49) implies that total employment l rises and so l_I also rises; trivially, total effective employment and effective employment in the capital-good sector also rise after the shock. Since L_C rises, consumption also rises after the shock. Finally, the rate of interest rises both because the rate of return to capital rises and because there are anticipated capital gains.

The convergence of the main variables to the steady state is shown in Figure 16.7. In the new steady state, actual employment and the rate of interest are unaffected while effective employment, the capital stock, and consumption have increased in proportion to the increase in productivity. In conclusion, a one-time increase in labor productivity has a transitory expansionary effect on the economy.

Consider now an economy in steady state with a constant rate of productivity increase at the rate λ which experiences an unanticipated permanent increase in λ. It follows from (16.35) that the $\dot{q} = 0$ locus remains unaffected and the $\dot{k} = 0$ locus shifts up, as shown in Figure 16.8.

With k predetermined in the short run, the drop in q leads to an immediate rise in l_C and a drop in l_I and total employment l. In the long run q and k converge to lower values. The long-run effect on l_C is ambiguous, as there are two opposing factors: on the one hand the declining q exerts an upward pressure on l_C, and on the other hand the declining k exerts a downward pressure on l_C as labor becomes relatively less productive. This ambiguity carries over to the long-run effect on l_I and l as well. In conclusion, an increase in the rate of productivity growth has a contractionary effect, at least in the short run.

16.3 Commentary

This chapter has analyzed the dynamic and steady-state effects of fiscal policy in a two-sector general-equilibrium model with finitely-lived agents. The finite horizon implies that the level of national debt directly affects consumption and allows for the steady-state interest rate and real wage

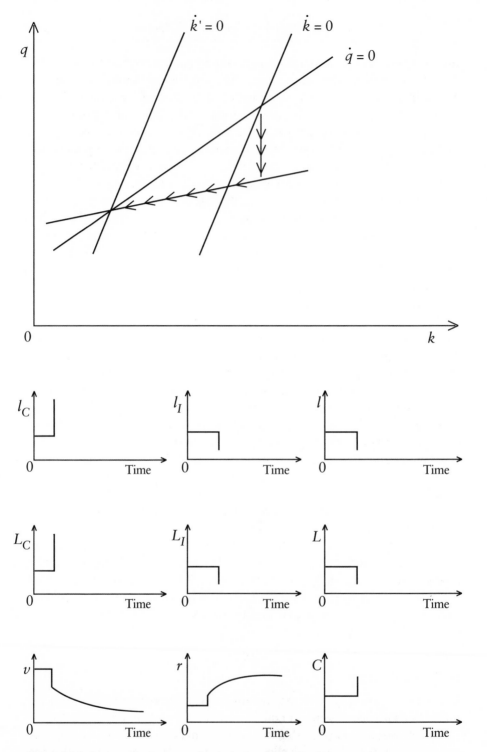

Figure 16.8 Increase in the rate of technical progress in the two-sector economy

to depend on policy. The two-sector structure of production made possible the distinction between government purchases directed to consumption goods as opposed to capital goods. The composition of government purchases was shown to be of crucial importance with regard to its impact on the economy.

It was shown that an increase of the national debt serviced in all subsequent periods by higher taxes creates a temporary consumption boom, contracts employment, leads to a higher rate of interest, and crowds out the capital stock.

A tax-financed permanent increase in government purchases of the consumption good, which is capital-intensive, leads to higher employment in both sectors. The increased demand for the capital-intensive good leads to an increase of its price and thus the return to capital. In the short as well as in the long run, higher government purchases of the capital-intensive good crowd in investment despite the rise in the rate of interest. In this case higher employment is accompanied by a lower real wage, as is the case in the one-sector neoclassical model.

A tax-financed permanent increase in government purchases of the capital good, which is labor-intensive, also leads to higher employment, despite the fact that employment in the other sector declines. In this case investment is crowded out by higher government purchases. The increased demand for the labor-intensive good temporarily increases its price and thus the real wage increases and the rate of interest declines, approaching their initial values asymptotically. This feature of the model is consistent with the observed low real rates of interest during wartime periods of high government purchases of capital goods. In this case higher employment is accompanied by a higher real wage.

It is important to emphasize that the two-sector structure of production does not lead to the empirically implausible conclusion of the one-sector neoclassical model, which implies that higher employment must be accompanied by a lower real wage. The two-sector neoclassical model implies that a higher level of employment is consistent with either a lower or a higher real wage, depending on the composition of demand. The composition of government demand is crucial because while labor supply expands in either case, owing to a negative income effect, labor demand also expands when the purchases are directed to the labor-intensive sector and thus the real wage is driven up.

The short-run effects of labor-augmenting technical progress on the two-sector neoclassical model differ sharply depending on whether the productivity increase is in the level or the rate of growth. A permanent increase in the level of labor productivity has an expansionary effect on employment, whereas a permanent increase in the rate of productivity growth has a contractionary effect.

We conclude with some comments and suggestions. First, our assumption that the capital-good-producing sector does not use any labor takes the Uzawa capital-intensity assumption to its extreme and is clearly unrealistic. Our conjecture is, however, that since demands and supplies are continuous, the main results of this paper would continue to hold if the capital-good-producing sector used both inputs, as long as it continued to be (sufficiently) labor-intensive. Nevertheless, the model should be investigated under the opposite capital-intensity assumption.

Second, most of the results obtained with finitely-lived agents apply also in the infinite-horizon case, with the exception of the effects of the public debt, which is inconsequential under Ricardian equivalence. The effects of a permanent increase in government purchases of either good are the same in the two cases, except that in the long run the wage and the rate of interest return to their initial value determined by the modified Golden Rule in the infinite-horizon case.

Third, the model can shed some light on the question of whether the contemporaneous expansion of employment is larger when the increase in government purchases is temporary as opposed to permanent. Barro and Hall argued that it is, but that argument was later refuted by Aiyagari, Christiano, and Eichenbaum in the context of a one-sector neoclassical model; our one-sector model is in agreement on this point with the result of the three authors. In our *two*-sector model the contemporaneous impact on employment is also smaller when there is a temporary as opposed to permanent increase of government purchases of the *capital* good, but the reverse is true when the government purchases are directed to the *consumption* good. (This can be verified from examination of Figures 16.5 and 16.6.)

Finally, the model should be extended in at least two directions. First, distortionary as opposed to lump-sum taxation should be introduced. Second, public goods, such as law and order, roads, and ports, should be allowed to affect the level of productivity. These questions are left to further research.

Appendix: Mathematical Analysis

THE ONE-SECTOR CASE

We will analyze first the dynamical properties of the system and then turn to the comparative-statics exercises discussed in the text.

Dynamics.   The dynamics of the model can be reduced to two differential equations in consumption and the capital stock. For simplicity, it is assumed that the production function is locally Cobb-Douglas and given by $F(K, L) = L^\gamma K^{1-\gamma}$. From the first-order condition (16.8), employment can be expressed as a function of consumption and the capital stock, $L = L(C, K)$, with the partial derivatives evaluated at the steady state given by

(16.36)
$$L_1 = \frac{\partial L}{\partial C} = \frac{-L}{F - (1 - \gamma)\delta K} < 0$$

$$L_2 = \frac{\partial L}{\partial K} = \frac{(1 - \gamma)(F - \delta K)\dfrac{L}{K}}{F - (1 - \gamma)\delta K} > 0$$

The system becomes

(16.37)
$$\dot{C} = \left[r\left(\frac{K}{L(C, K)}\right) - \rho \right] C - \mu(\mu + \rho)[K + D] \equiv \Phi(C, K; D)$$

$$\dot{K} = L(C, K)^\gamma K^{1-\gamma} - \delta K - C - G \equiv \Psi(C, K; G)$$

The first-order Taylor approximation around the steady state with D and G equal to zero is

(16.38)
$$\begin{pmatrix} \dot{C} \\ \dot{K} \end{pmatrix} = \begin{pmatrix} \Phi_C & \Phi_K \\ \Psi_C & \Psi_K \end{pmatrix} \begin{pmatrix} C - \overline{C} \\ K - \overline{K} \end{pmatrix} + \begin{pmatrix} 0 & \Phi_D \\ \Psi_G & 0 \end{pmatrix} \begin{pmatrix} G \\ D \end{pmatrix}$$

where the derivatives are evaluated at the steady state. Denoting the derivative of the interest rate with respect to the capital-labor ratio by r', the expressions in (16.38) are given by

(16.39)
$$\Phi_C = r - \rho - r' \frac{KCL_1}{L^2}$$

$$\Phi_K = \frac{Cr'}{L} \left(1 - \frac{KL_2}{L} \right) - \mu(\mu + \rho) < 0$$

$$\Psi_C = F_L L_1 - 1 < 0$$

$$\Psi_K = r + F_L L_2 > 0$$

$$\Phi_D = -\mu(\mu + \rho) < 0$$

$$\Psi_G = -1 < 0$$

Φ_K is negative because KL_1/L is less than 1. All the other expressions can be unambiguously signed except Φ_C.

Φ_C is negative for low values of the mortality rate μ. The proof is as follows. Φ_C is a continuous and increasing function of the steady-state marginal product of capital denoted by $\bar{F}_K$ for the purposes of this proof:

(16.40)

$$\Phi_C = \bar{F}_K \left(1 - \frac{\gamma}{1 + \dfrac{\gamma\delta}{\dfrac{\bar{F}_K}{1-\gamma} - \delta}} \right) - \rho - \delta$$

with

$$\frac{d\Phi_C}{d\bar{F}_K} = \frac{1}{1 + \dfrac{\gamma\delta}{\dfrac{\bar{F}_K}{1-\gamma} - \delta}} \left(1 - \gamma + \frac{\gamma\delta}{\dfrac{\bar{F}_K}{1-\gamma} - \delta} - \frac{\gamma^2\delta\bar{F}_K}{(1-\gamma)\left(\dfrac{\bar{F}_K}{1-\gamma} - \delta\right)\left(\dfrac{\bar{F}_K}{1-\gamma} - \delta + \gamma\delta\right)} \right)$$

$$> \frac{1}{1 + \dfrac{\gamma\delta}{\dfrac{\bar{F}_K}{1-\gamma} - \delta}} \left(1 - \gamma + \frac{\gamma\delta(\bar{F}_K - \delta)}{\left(\dfrac{\bar{F}_K}{1-\gamma} - \delta\right)^2} \right) > 0$$

Upon substitution of $C = F - \delta K$ into the $\dot{C} = 0$ equation, it follows that the steady-state interest rate and marginal product of capital $\bar{F}_K$ is a continuous and increasing function of the mortality rate μ. In particular, when the horizon is infinite so μ is zero, we have that $\bar{F}_K = \delta + \rho$ and for μ positive we have that $\bar{F}_K > \delta + \rho$ and increasing with μ. Since Φ_C is continuous and increasing in $\bar{F}_K$ and $\bar{F}_K$ is continuous and increasing in μ, it follows that Φ_C is continuous and increasing in μ. When μ is zero Φ_C is negative, since $\bar{F}_K = \delta + \rho$. Since Φ_C is continuous and increasing in μ, it is also negative for low values of μ and in this case the system has a unique, stable saddlepath as inspection of the signs in (16.38) confirms. The possibility that Φ_C becomes positive as μ gets closer to 1 cannot be excluded. Should that happen, the $\dot{C} = 0$ locus becomes upward-sloping and flatter than the $\dot{K} = 0$, at least before μ gets too close to 1. In this case the system is unstable. We concentrate on the case where the system is stable, that is, in the case where Φ_C is negative.

Increase in government debt. The steady-state effects of a permanent increase in D can be computed directly from (16.38):

$$(16.41) \quad \frac{d\overline{C}}{dD} = \frac{-\Phi_D \Psi_K}{\Delta} < 0$$

$$\frac{d\overline{K}}{dD} = \frac{\Phi_D \Psi_C}{\Delta} < 0$$

$$\frac{d\overline{L}}{dD} = L_1 \frac{d\overline{C}}{dD} + L_2 \frac{d\overline{K}}{dD}$$

$$= \frac{-\gamma \Phi_D L[\gamma \delta F + (1 - \gamma)(F_K - \delta)\delta K + (F_K - (1 - \gamma)\delta)\delta K]}{\Delta[F - (1 - \gamma)\delta K]^2} < 0$$

In the new steady-state consumption, the capital stock and employment are lower. Since both C and L fall, the lefthand side of the first-order condition $C/(\overline{H} - L) = v$ falls, so the real wage falls and the rate of interest increases in the new steady state. It is straightforward to show using (16.38) that the $\dot{C} = 0$ locus shifts down while the $\dot{K} = 0$ locus remains unaffected and so the dynamics are shown in Figure 16.1.

Increase in government purchases. The steady-state effects of a permanent increase in G are also computed from (16.38):

$$(16.42) \quad \frac{d\overline{C}}{dG} = \frac{\Psi_G \Phi_K}{\Delta} < 0$$

$$\frac{d\overline{K}}{dG} = \frac{-\Phi_C \Psi_G}{\Delta} > 0$$

$$\frac{d\overline{L}}{dG} = L_1 \frac{d\overline{C}}{dG} + L_2 \frac{d\overline{K}}{dG} > 0$$

In the new steady state consumption is lower, the capital stock is higher, and employment is higher. Since consumption falls and the capital stock increases, the rate of interest increases in light of the $\dot{C} = 0$ equation. So the real wage falls.

Along the adjustment path both C and K are rising. Since K is rising, for a given wage rate the supply of labor is falling, owing to a positive wealth effect, and the demand for labor is rising, because the productivity of labor is increasing. We provide a sufficient condition for L to decline along the adjustment path in terms of γ, which is the share of labor in total output. This condition is that γ is greater than or equal to 0.5. The proof is as follows. Differentiating L with respect to time and using (16.36), the rate of change of L can be expressed as

$$(16.43) \quad \frac{\dot{L}}{L} = \frac{C}{F - (1 - \gamma)\delta K}\left[(1 - \gamma)\frac{\dot{K}}{K} - \frac{\dot{C}}{C}\right]$$

$$= \frac{C}{F - (1 - \gamma)\delta K}\left[\rho + \gamma\delta - (1 - \gamma)\frac{C + G}{K} + \mu(\mu + \rho)\frac{K}{C}\right]$$

Along the adjustment path G/K is above its steady-state value, since K is rising. It follows that a sufficient condition for $\dot{L}$ to be negative along the adjustment path is that C/K is also above its steady-state value and is falling along the path to the new steady state. So $\dot{L}$ will be negative if the slope of the saddlepath is smaller than 1. We derive a sufficient condition for this to be true.

The negative eigenvalue of the Jacobian of the system is

$$(16.44) \quad \lambda = \frac{\Phi_C + \Psi_K - \sqrt{(\Phi_C + \Psi_K)^2 - 4(\Phi_C\Psi_K - \Phi_K\Psi_C)}}{2}$$

and the slope of the saddlepath is $\Phi_K/(\lambda - \Phi_C)$. After some straightforward algebra we arrive at the following condition:

$$(16.45) \quad \frac{\Phi_K}{\lambda - \Phi_C} < 1 \Leftrightarrow F > \frac{1 - \gamma}{\gamma}C$$

A sufficient condition for this inequality to be satisfied is that γ is greater than or equal to 0.5, since output is greater than or equal to consumption.

THE TWO-SECTOR MODEL

Again we begin with the dynamic properties that are basic to the behavior of the economy modeled.

Dynamics. The dynamics of the model can be reduced to two differential equations in q and K, which are repeated here for convenience:

(16.46)
$$\dot{q} = \frac{\Phi(q, K; G_C, D) + \dfrac{Fq}{KC} \Psi(q, K; G_C, G_I)}{1 - \dfrac{F_L^2}{F_{LL}(F - G_C)}}$$

$$\dot{K} = \Psi(q, K; G_C, G_I)$$

We want to approximate the system linearly around the steady state that obtains when D, G_C, G_I, and T are zero, that is, around $(q, K; G_C, G_I, D) = (\bar{q}, \bar{K}; 0, 0, 0)$. For simplicity we assume that the production function of the consumption good is locally Cobb-Douglas and is given by $F(K, L_C) = L_C^\gamma K^{1-\gamma}$ and denote the marginal products by F_L and F_K. We first compute some useful partial derivatives:

(16.47)
$$\omega q = F_L(K, L_C) \Rightarrow L_C = L_C(q, K) \qquad \frac{\partial L_C}{\partial q} = \frac{\omega}{F_{LL}}, \frac{\partial L_C}{\partial K} = -\frac{F_{LK}}{F_{LL}}$$

(16.48) $\dfrac{H - L}{C} = \dfrac{1}{v} \Rightarrow L = L(q, K, G_C)$

$$\frac{\partial L}{\partial q} = -\frac{\omega}{F_{LL}} + \frac{C}{\omega q^2}, \frac{\partial L}{\partial K} = -\frac{C}{\omega q K}, \frac{\partial L}{\partial G_C} = \frac{1}{\omega q}$$

(16.49) $\dfrac{H - L}{C} = \dfrac{1}{v} \Rightarrow L = L(L_C, K, G_C)$

$$\frac{\partial L}{\partial L_C} = -\frac{1}{\gamma}, \frac{\partial L}{\partial K} = 0, \frac{\partial L}{\partial G_C} = \frac{1}{\omega q}$$

where all these derivatives are evaluated at the steady state $(\bar{q}, \bar{K}; 0, 0, 0)$. The first-order Taylor approximation of the system around the steady state is given by

(16.50)
$$\begin{pmatrix} \dot{q} \\ \dot{K} \end{pmatrix} = \begin{pmatrix} (1 - \gamma)(\Phi_q + \dfrac{q}{K}\Psi_q) & (1 - \gamma)\left(\dfrac{q}{K}\Psi_I\right) \\ \Psi_q & \Psi_K \end{pmatrix} \begin{pmatrix} q - \bar{q} \\ K - \bar{K} \end{pmatrix}$$

$$+ \begin{pmatrix} (1 - \gamma)(\Phi_{G_C} + \dfrac{q}{K}\Psi_{G_C}) & (1 - \gamma)\Psi_{G_I} & (1 - \gamma)\Phi_D \\ \Psi_{G_C} & \Psi_{G_I} & 0 \end{pmatrix} \begin{pmatrix} G_C \\ G_I \\ D \end{pmatrix}$$

Letting $R'(q)$ be the derivative of the rental with respect to q, the expressions in (16.50) are given by

(16.51)

$$\Phi_q = \rho + \mu(\mu + \rho)\left(\frac{2 - \gamma}{1 - \gamma}\right)\frac{qK}{C} - R'(q) > 0$$

$$\Phi_K = 0$$

$$\Psi_q = -\frac{2\omega^2}{F_{LL}} + \frac{C}{q^2} > 0$$

$$\Psi_K = -\frac{C}{qK} + \frac{\omega F_{LK}}{F_{LL}} - \delta < 0$$

$$\Phi_{G_C} = \mu(\mu + \rho)\frac{q^2 K}{C^2} > 0$$

$$\Phi_{G_I} = 0$$

$$\Phi_D = \mu(\mu + \rho)\frac{q}{C} > 0$$

$$\Psi_{G_C} = \frac{1}{q} > 0$$

$$\Psi_{G_I} = -1 < 0$$

$$\Psi_D = 0$$

Noting that $R' < 0$, all the expressions in (16.51) can be unambiguously signed. The signs in (16.51) prove that both stationary loci are upward-sloping and the $\dot{K} = 0$ locus is steeper, as argued in Section 16.3.

The steady-state effects on q and K of a change in fiscal policy is computed from the solution to the system of the two equations $\dot{q} = 0$ and $\dot{K} = 0$:

(16.52)

$$\begin{pmatrix} \Phi_q & 0 \\ \Psi_q & \Psi_K \end{pmatrix}\begin{pmatrix} d\bar{q} \\ d\bar{K} \end{pmatrix} = -\begin{pmatrix} \Phi_{G_C} & 0 & \Phi_D \\ \Psi_{G_C} & -1 & 0 \end{pmatrix}\begin{pmatrix} G_C \\ G_I \\ D \end{pmatrix}$$

It is useful for the analysis below to define the determinant of the matrix on the left of (16.52) by

(16.53) $\Delta = \Phi_q \Psi_K < 0$

Increase in government debt.   The steady-state effects of an increase in the government debt can be directly computed from (16.52):

(16.54) $\dfrac{d\bar{q}}{dD} = -\dfrac{\Phi_D \Psi_K}{\Delta} < 0$

$\dfrac{d\bar{K}}{dD} = \dfrac{\Phi_D \Psi_q}{\Delta} < 0$

$\dfrac{d\bar{L}_C}{dD} = \dfrac{\partial \bar{L}_C}{\partial \bar{q}} \dfrac{d\bar{q}}{dD} + \dfrac{\partial \bar{L}_C}{\partial \bar{K}} \dfrac{d\bar{K}}{dD} = \dfrac{\omega \delta \Phi_D}{F_{LL}\Delta} > 0$

Since K is lower in the new steady state, L_I is lower, and (16.49) shows that L is lower since L_C is higher. Since q is lower, v is lower and r is higher. Finally,

(16.55) $\dfrac{d\bar{C}_C}{dD} = R\dfrac{d\bar{K}}{dD} + F_L\dfrac{d\bar{L}}{dD} < 0$

since both K and L are lower in the new steady state.

The increase in D shifts the $\dot{q} = 0$ locus down, and leaves the $\dot{K} = 0$ locus unaffected, as can be directly verified from (16.50). Thus in the short run, when the capital stock is fixed, q falls, L_C increases, (16.49) implies that L drops and so L_I drops. The capital-labor ratio in the consumption-good sector drops, so v and q drop and R increases. The interest rate, which is equal to $(R(q) + \dot{q})/q$, may rise or fall depending on whether the increase in the rental, expressed as a ratio to the price of capital, is larger or smaller than the anticipated capital losses.

We now turn to the adjustment to the new steady state. From Figure 16.4 we know that q is falling, so v is falling and R is increasing. To see whether L_C is falling or rising during the adjustment, we compute the change in the time derivative of L_C in response to the increase in the national debt. First note that (16.18) implies that

$$(16.56) \quad \frac{\dot{C}}{C} = (1 - \gamma) \frac{\dot{K}}{K} + \gamma \frac{\dot{L}_C}{L_C}$$

and (16.20) implies that

$$(16.57) \quad \frac{\dot{v}}{v} = (1 - \gamma) \left(\frac{\dot{K}}{K} + \frac{\dot{L}_C}{L_C} \right)$$

Substituting (16.56) into (16.57) and replacing $\dot{v}/v$ by $\dot{q}/q$, we obtain

$$(16.58) \quad -\frac{\dot{L}_C}{L_C} = \frac{\dot{q}}{q} - \frac{\dot{C}}{C}$$

Substituting (16.58) into the $\dot{C}$ equation (16.12), we arrive at the following expression for the rate of change of L_C:

$$(16.59) \quad -\frac{\dot{L}_C}{L_C} = \rho + \mu(\mu + \rho) \frac{qK + D}{C} - \frac{R(q)}{q}$$

We compare the value of (16.59) right after the increase of D to the value it will eventually attain in the new steady state, namely zero. Noting that D will be at the same level in the two instances and that the expression is increasing in q for small D, we conclude that $-\dot{L}_C > 0$, since q will be lower in the steady state. Therefore L_C overshoots its long-run value when D is increased and then declines toward that value.

Since both K and L_C are falling, so is C. From (16.49) it follows that L is rising and so L_I is also rising.

Increase in G_C.   The steady-state effects of an increase in government expenditure in the consumption good can be directly computed from (16.52):

(16.60) $\quad \dfrac{d\bar{q}}{dG_C} = \dfrac{-\Phi_{G_C}\Psi_K}{\Delta} < 0$

The effect on the capital stock is

$$\dfrac{d\bar{K}}{dG_C} = \dfrac{-\Phi_q\Psi_{G_C} + \Phi_{G_C}\Psi_q}{\Delta}$$

$$= \dfrac{1}{q\Delta}\left[-\rho - \mu(\mu + \rho)\dfrac{2 - \gamma}{1 - \gamma}\dfrac{Kq}{C} + R'(q) \right.$$

$$\left. + \left(-\dfrac{2\omega^2}{F_{LL}} + \dfrac{C}{q^2} \right)\mu(\mu + \rho)\dfrac{Kq^3}{C^2} \right]$$

$$= \dfrac{1}{q\Delta}\left[-\rho - \mu(\mu + \rho)\dfrac{1 - 2\gamma}{1 - \gamma}\dfrac{Kq}{C} + R'(q) \right]$$

After substitution of the expression $R'(q) = -(\gamma r + \delta)/(1 - \gamma)$, and using the $\dot{C} = 0$ equation to replace $\mu(\mu + \rho)K$ by $(r - \rho)C/q$, we obtain

(16.61) $\quad \dfrac{d\bar{K}}{dG_C} = -\dfrac{1}{q\Delta}\left(r + \dfrac{\gamma\rho + \delta}{1 - \gamma} \right) > 0$

Since q drops in the new steady state, v drops and r rises. Therefore the capital-labor ratio in the consumption-good sector drops, and since K increases, L_C must increase as well. Also, L_I increases because K increases. Since both L_C and L_I increase, L increases. Finally, the rise in both v and L implies, through the first-order condition (16.8), that C falls.

Both loci shift down but the $\dot{K} = 0$ locus shifts down by more so that q falls and the capital stock increases in the new steady state in accordance with (16.60) and (16.61). In the short run, when the capital stock is fixed, increased government purchases of the consumption good lead to an immediate drop in q and thus v and to a rise in the rental and the rate of interest ($\dot{q}$ is positive). Since v drops and K is fixed, L_C increases. L_I also increases because the capital stock is increasing after the new policy is implemented, so L increases. Since v drops and L increases, the first-order condition (16.8) implies that C falls. Government purchases crowd out some consumption, but the crowding-out is not complete since total output of the consumption good increases.

Equation (16.59) implies that L_C is increasing toward its new steady-state value, by an argument analogous to the one presented in the case of an increase in the national debt. Then equation (16.49) implies that L is falling along the adjustment path, so L_I must be falling as well. Finally, consumption is increasing, since both K and L_C are increasing.

Increase in G_I. The steady-state effects of an increase in government expenditure in the capital good can be computed from (16.52):

$$(16.62) \quad \frac{d\bar{q}}{dG_I} = 0$$

$$\frac{d\bar{K}}{dG_I} = -\frac{\Phi_q \Psi_{G_I}}{\Delta} < 0$$

Since q is unchanged, v, R, and r are unchanged, and L_C falls by the same proportion as K. Equation (16.49) implies that L increases, since L_C falls, and thus L_I increases. Finally, C falls since both K and L_C fall.

Both stationary loci shift to the left by the same amount, so q remains unchanged in the new steady state. In the short run q and thus v increase, R and r drop, and L_C drops given that K is fixed. Equation (16.49) implies that since L_C drops, L increases and so L_I increases as well. Equation (16.59) implies that since q is falling, L_C is also falling and L and L_I are rising along the adjustment path.

Increase in λ. The steady-state effects of an increase in λ on q and k are computed as follows:

$$(16.63) \quad \frac{d\bar{q}}{d\lambda} = \frac{q\Psi_k}{\Delta} < 0$$

$$\frac{d\bar{k}}{d\lambda} = -\frac{k\Phi_q + q\Psi_q}{\Delta} < 0$$

V

EMPIRICAL EVIDENCE

17

Econometric Tests of the Theory:
A Postwar Cross-Country Time-Series Study

IN the preceding chapters a new approach to unemployment determination has been developed. The approach seeks the *nonmonetary mechanisms* by which *nonmonetary* shocks operate to disturb the path of unemployment. The aim is to capture the *indefinite shifts* and *long swings* in economic activity. What broad changes in the structure of demands and supplies and the substructure of fiscal parameters (tax rates and subsidy rates) have driven unemployment rates over the decades of the postwar era? What institutional provisions have served to moderate unemployment, and what institutional developments (entitlement programs, say) have made it worse?

The theoretical challenge posed by those questions has been to model suitable intertemporal and international channels with which to complete a modern general-equilibrium theory of unemployment determination. The framework that has emerged after a considerable struggle sees the open economies of the world economy connected both by the world real interest rate set in the global capital market and by real exchange rates coming from the global tradable-goods markets.

The challenge at this juncture is to put the new framework to empirical test. There are at least two methods of testing the framework, of course. One method is to investigate whether or to what extent the new theory can account broadly for the major movements of the unemployment rate over a long historical period. The next chapter attempts a nonmonetary history of the postwar period from the perspective of the modern equilibrium, or structuralist, approach.

The other method, adopted in the present chapter, investigates whether the new framework provides an econometric model that is supported by available data. The main purpose is to see the extent to which the underlying causal factors identified by the structuralist theory influence the unemployment rates of the countries studied in the direction predicted by the theory and with a statistically significant magnitude.[1] When one considers the difficulties that some long-standard elements of macroeconomics have had with time-series data in recent decades, the thought of submitting the fledgling theory to such statistical tests may seem quixotic; however, a new theory is unlikely to receive a wide-scale hearing until it has survived some econometric testing.

A reduced-form econometric model is estimated for the purpose of testing the main conclusions of the structuralist theory. Of central interest, though not sole interest, are the three theses of the theory relating to rates of interest and asset prices. These propositions are:

- *First,* a proposition on unemployment in the individual small open economy: overseas demand and supply changes that drive up the rest-of-the-world real interest rate (say, an increased world public debt or a decreased world capital stock) thereby have a downward effect on the demand wage in the small open economy, thus a contractionary effect on its employment, and cause either an increased balance of trade or, in the customer-market setting (in which the law of one price does not apply to consumer goods), a real depreciation in consumer goods or both.

- *Second,* also regarding the small open economy: the same shocks occurring within the home economy in a customer-market setting, through their upward impact on domestic interest rates, generate an expansion of domestic employment and a real appreciation.

- *Third,* a proposition on the "representative" open economy: if such an economy experiences the same shocks on the same scale as occur overseas, there is no real appreciation, hence no expansion of labor demand on that account, and there is no depreciation either, hence no contraction of labor demand on that account; but there is nonetheless a contraction resulting from the increase of the world real interest rate. These same shocks, if equal across countries, are contractionary for the world as a whole (since they are contractionary for a representative country). In fact, unless the economies are quite varied, these shocks are contractionary for every country linked to the global capital and goods markets.

Other propositions of the structuralist theory, including its implications regarding tax rates, can also be tested with the available data set.

The econometric study here is a cross-country time-series model of the national unemployment rates in the advanced economies over most of the postwar era. The data set describes seventeen countries of the Organization for Economic Cooperation and Development (OECD) from 1955 to 1989. The variables analyzed include the national unemployment rates, the national real exchange rates, the national markups, the world real interest rate, and the world real oil price. Playing the role of causal variables are the beginning-of-year national and world public debt, national and world public expenditure, the beginning-of-year national and world stocks of capital, the national and world average tax rate, and a set of national characteristics.

It might be wondered whether the postwar data on national unemployment rates have not already been fairly well mined. Certainly the unemployment experience of the past twenty years—the great waves of unemployment, first in the 1970s, then in the 1980s, and now in the 1990s—are interpreted by many commentators as a manifestation of fundamental shifts in the equilibrium path of unemployment. Nevertheless, econometric investigations of shifts in parameters and conditions hypothesized to underlie movements in the equilibrium path of unemployment have been few; and these precious few, as their authors might agree, have each adopted a rather narrow focus and have not had a general-equilibrium model guiding their econometric framework.[2] In treating the national economies as open to the world capital market and to world tradable-goods markets, and in encompassing both the demand-supply structure and some aspects of the institutional structure, the present study is the most comprehensive econometric model of unemployment to date.

17.1 The Econometric Model and a Summary of the Main Results

The cross-section time-series model is an attempt within the limits of data availability to represent the structuralist theory.[3] Pooling the time-series data of many countries greatly increases the degrees of freedom with which to estimate the effects of national and global variables. Such pooling need not exclude cross-country differences both in the constant term and in the "deflator" by which one country's coefficients may differ across the board from another's.[4]

THE REDUCED-FORM ECONOMETRIC MODEL

The model's equations and identities are the following:

(17.1) $u_{it} = u(DOM_{it}, GLO_{it}; C_i) + d(infl_{it})$

(17.2) $DOM_{it} = (rdebt_{it}, rk_{it}, rmil_{it}, rgnm_{it}, rt_{it}, youth_{it})$

(17.3) $GLO_t = (rtbraw_t, rpoilw_t)$

(17.4) $rtbraw_t = f(rdebtw_t, rkw_t, rmilw_t, rgnmw_t, tpoilw_t, d(inflw_t))$

$$i = 1, 2, \ldots 17; t = 1957, \ldots 1989$$

A full glossary of the code names of the variables can be found in appendix 2.

Although the theoretical models determine only the equilibrium unemployment path, the data on the actual unemployment path in any country unquestionably reflect both the influence of monetary shocks and the operation of nonmonetary shocks through monetary mechanisms. Equations (17.1) and (17.4) seek to control for the consequent disturbances around the equilibrium path by introducing as an added explanatory variable the change in the inflation rate, $d(inflw_t)$, where d is the first-difference operator. The hypothesis is that unemployment is below its equilibrium path (u^*) when inflation is increasing, above when decreasing; the boost to world consumption from an episode of below-equilibrium world unemployment may be guessed to reduce, transiently at any rate, the world real interest rate.

The equilibrium path is determined by a set of exogenous variables contained in the structuralist models. These variables fall into three categories: global variables (GLO), domestic time-variant variables (DOM), and domestic time-invariant variables, or characteristics (C).

The world real interest rate is determined, as described in the closed-economy models, by the equality of world supply and demand of consumer goods. The exogenous world variables driving this equilibrium real rate are the world level of public debt, the world capital stock, world military spending, world government spending on nonmilitary goods, and the transitory component of oil prices. Government spending is divided into the two components on the hypothesis that military expenditures fall to a greater extent on capital goods and on the possibility that nonmilitary spending is less exogenous. In addition, the world price of oil is a determinant of the world real interest rate while it also affects labor demand and thus unemployment directly.

Domestic variables are, on the one hand, variables that could affect the domestic real interest rate or exchange rates and hence domestic labor demand, given the world real interest rate: these are the domestic level of public debt, the domestic capital stock, domestic military spending, and domestic spending for nonmilitary purposes. On the other hand, we have variables impacting on labor incentives and hence the wage locus: tax revenue collected through direct taxation as a proportion of household income and the proportion of the labor force between 20 and 24 years of age.

The global variables directly affecting the national variables, including the national unemployment rates, are the world real interest rate and the real price of oil.

Finally, we have a vector, C_i, of country characteristics that are not time-dependent.[5] These are variables that can affect either labor demand or incentives. Some of them reflect labor-market institutions, such as unions and legislation, while others reflect general government policy.

The structuralist tenets centering on the real interest rate are tested in three steps. These are followed by two related exercises.

Step 1 is to test whether the relevant demand and supply variables in our data set have the estimated effects on the world real interest rate that are implied by the theory—by one or more of the models constituting this body of theory at any rate. To this end we estimate the linearized version of equation (17.4) linking the world rate of interest to its hypothesized determinants. Of course, this step is just a toe in the water.

Step 2 is to estimate the effect on the national unemployment rates of the various countries of shocks to the domestic counterparts of the above explanatory variables along with the effects of the world real interest rate and the world real oil price. Hence the system of 17 national-unemployment-rate equations—essentially augmented Phillips curves—is estimated jointly, a procedure which, in view of the cross-equation restrictions imposed, is equivalent to pooling time-series and cross-section data. To repeat: Although the national data here are pooled, each country is permitted to have its own constant term *and* a "sensitivity coefficient" measuring the responsiveness of its labor market.

It would be difficult to argue that the world real interest rate is endogenous to an important degree for any of these countries—with the possible exception of the two, perhaps three, largest countries. In any case, it is an interesting experiment to substitute for the actual world real interest rate and real oil price the *fitted* values obtained by regressing these variables on the world-variable set. This experiment is conducted as a variant of step 1.

Step 3 closes the test of the three central propositions relating to interest rates by examining the *world* effect of national shocks, which is the sum of the *national* effect when the global situation is taken as given and the *global* effect (falling predominantly on the rest of the world) through the world real interest rate. In particular we ask whether, as predicted by the closed-economy version of the theory, the shocks estimated to drive up the world real interest rate are also estimated to have a *net* contractionary effect on national employment in every country in the simple case in which the shock to the world variable—say, the world public debt—is composed of identical national shocks (per unit of labor force) in all the countries in the study. This last step is necessary since certain shocks, say, expenditure shocks, could have a local expansionary effect exceeding their global contractionary effect. This step is a *calculation* from steps 1 and 2, not a separate regression.

An additional set of exercises looks into the validity of the theoretical argument that national expenditures having an expansionary effect do so through channels that increase real exchange rates and decrease home-country markups. Real exchange rates were regressed on the national explanatory variables, and these fitted rates were then used to explain comparative markups—more precisely, to check whether real appreciation tended to lower national markups compared with overseas markups.

The final exercise serves to bring in the variety of institutional differences across countries. Linear equations are estimated linking the country-specific statistics—each country's constant term and sensitivity coefficient—to the time-invariant, country-specific variables, C_i.[6]

THE MAIN RESULTS PREVIEWED

The thrust of the econometric results may be conveyed in advance of a more detailed inspection of the estimates.

In the equation for the world real interest rate, strikingly, all the explanatory variables have estimated effects consistent with the modern equilibrium theory: World wealth—capital plus public debt aggregated over the 17 countries and figured at historic real cost—drives up the world real interest rate, while the world capital stock drives it down. The *net* interest-rate effect of an increase of the world capital stock, the world public debt held constant, is negative, as predicted by the only one of the foregoing models built around physical capital.[7] The excess of the real world oil price over its past five-year moving average also performed well in filling what would otherwise have been a worrisome lacuna in the regression equation. The sole surprise is that military public expenditures are not estimated to have driven down the real interest rate, which the two-sector model suggested they would do *if* such expenditures typically fall on comparatively labor-intensive activities—the armed forces, small-scale weapons assemblies, and the like. Nevertheless, this finding is in no way troubling. In the closed-economy models introduced above, namely the investment-in-customers model and the investment-in-employees model, public expenditures on the output of firms do drive up interest rates, so no theoretical anomaly is raised by these findings.

In the national-unemployment-rate equations, the world real rate of interest is a key variable for the structuralist theory. The coefficient of that variable is estimated to have the predicted sign and to be statistically significant. Further, the size of the contractionary effect that the world real rate is estimated to have on national employment rates is rather appreciable. A numerical example, recorded in detail largely to facilitate understanding, not to measure reality, will illustrate. Consider a 5 percentage-point rise in the interest rate—an increase of .05 in the rate as decimal, or a 500 basis point increase in financial-market terms. A real rate increase of this magnitude generates over the first subsequent year a one-half percentage-point increase in the national unemployment rate of the country—namely, Australia—whose sensitivity coefficient is the standard. However, the ongoing response in hiring rates, working through the lagged dependent variable, raises the ultimate effect on the unemployment rate to 1.1 percentage points. In France, to take a contrasting example, the initial impact is only .35 percentage points, as its sensitivity is only three-quarters that of Australia's. But persistence is greater in France, and the ultimate effect is 1.4.

It may be mentioned here that when the fitted world real interest rate was substituted for the actual real rate, the coefficient estimates in the national-unemployment-rate equations changed hardly at all. The importance of interest might have been stronger had a measure of the expected real *long* rate been available. Experiments too late to include here confirm that property, but the larger coefficient is roughly counterbalanced by the lesser responsiveness of the long rate. The significance of the explanatory variables in generally improved though.

The other global factor, the real price of oil, was also statistically significant. The *t* ratio of the coefficient was about the same as that of the coefficient of the real interest rate. Of course, the oil price has fluctuated even more spectacularly than the interest rate over the past two decades.

As predicted by the customer-market model, an increase in national consumers' wealth, given the world variables and the other national variables, is expansionary—though only mildly so.[8] Symmetrically, an increase of the domestic capital stock, given national wealth, is contractionary for domestic employment. It is also contractionary on balance when the national public debt is held constant: evidently the wealth effect on domestic demand of additional capital owned by nationals does not cancel altogether the substitution effect on labor demand of additional domestic capital, as firms meet customer demands with less labor.

A parallel finding is that increased national government purchases of output are also expansionary for employment. The customer-market model also serves to interpret that finding.

The national-tax-rate variable used, a rather broad and inadequate measure, was found to be importantly contractionary—a result all the more remarkable when one considers that this variable may pick up the non-resource-absorbing part of government spending, which is expansionary except under Ricardian equivalence. That finding is consistent with the structuralist theory here if nonwage incomes—entitlement payments received under welfare programs, the nonpecuniary services of owner-used property, capital gains, and income from overseas assets—are taxed at lower rates than wage income or if they elude the tax authority's net. Two strands of confirmation on the importance of tax rates for wage payments are some subsequent calculations with national time series (available for all but two of our countries) indicating that payroll taxes were strongly contractionary while indirect taxes mattered little if at all—both as predicted by the theory.

The last step was to calculate whether, according to the estimates, the *total* effect of certain worldwide shocks on national unemployment rates—the indirect effect through the world real interest rate and the direct effect of the national part of the world shock—is in the direction predicted by the theory. Consider, for example, a $1,000 increase of public debt per worker in all countries, hence also in the world-public-debt variable (which is in thousands of 1980 dollars per unit of world labor force). The effect on the world real interest rates is to increase it by .0215 as a decimal—that is, by 2.15 percentage points, or 215 basis points. This increase is to be multiplied by 9.4402, as shown in Table 17.2, to obtain its next-period impact through this world route on national unemployment rates. In Australia, the effect is .203 percentage points—that is, 20.3 basis points.

The national-unemployment-rate effect of the increase in public debt holdings of Australians alone is −0.043, or −4.3 basis points; so the *net* short-run impact there is .160 percentage points, or 16 basis points. In France, where the sensitivity coefficient is .74 times that in Australia, the same net impact produces a sensitivity-adjusted increase of .118 points in the unemployment rate, or 11.8 basis points. The net *long-run* effect in Australia is .372. In France, where persistence is stronger, the ultimate effect is .472, or 47.2 basis points.

In fact, between the end of the 1970s and the mid-1980s, the world public debt increased by approximately $4,000 per worker. If nothing else in the world had happened and had France not increased at all the debt holdings of its own nationals, the short-run impact would have been .601 percentage points, and the long-run effect would have been 2.403 percentage points—quite a large effect.

Several other findings are of considerable theoretical interest and of historical or policy-making importance. These findings, however, will emerge in the inspection of the regression estimates.

17.2 The Econometric Estimates

We begin with the estimates of the world real interest rate equation, then proceed to the explanation of the national unemployment rates.

TEST OF THE DETERMINANTS OF WORLD REAL INTEREST RATES

The estimated equation in Table 17.1 shows the world real rate of interest to be determined by the stock of world public debt, the stock of capital,

Table 17.1   The world real interest rate equation

$$rtbraw_t = -0.1602 + 0.0215(rdebtw_t + rkw_t) - 0.0266\,rkw$$
$$(0.0424)\quad(0.0005)\qquad\qquad\qquad(0.0009)$$

$$+\ 0.1818\,rmilw_t + 0.0795\,rgnmw_t + 0.1330\,tpoilw_t$$
$$(0.0039)\qquad\quad(0.0039)\qquad\quad(0.0254)$$

$$-\ 0.0009\,d(inflw_t)$$
$$(0.0014)$$

Note: Standard errors in parentheses; OLS estimation method; $n = 32$, $R^2 = 0.85$, s.e. = 0.0091, $F = 25.44$, DW = 1.89, White-$F = 0.383$, mean of dependent variable = 0.0154.

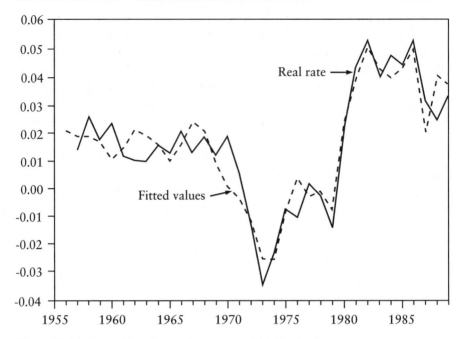

Figure 17.1 The world real rate of interest and its fitted values

government expenditures, and transitory changes in the price of oil. Also included is an inflation-shock term that is intended to capture some of the higher-frequency movements, especially those of a monetary character but not only those.

Residuals are both free of autocorrelation and heteroskedasticity. The equation explains more than 80 percent of the variation in the interest rate.

If the public-debt and the capital-stock variables are separated, the former comes out with a positive and the latter with a negative coefficient, less significant than above.

The first difference of public debt—the world central government deficit—turned out to be insignificant when added to the equation. Thus the interest rate is not correlated with the change in the public debt, only the level, as current non-Ricardian models predict.

From Figures 17.1 and 17.2 and the estimated equation, one can see that the increase in world interest rates in the period 1979–1989 is explained by the movement of the price of oil, by the level of public debt, and also to some extent by government expenditures. Oil prices dominate until around 1982, but the public debt takes over in the period thereafter. Simultaneously there is a sharp increase in the level of government expenditure starting in 1979 also. In other periods no more than one of these three variables has a high value: government expenditure in the late 1960s and oil prices in the mid-1970s.

THE NATIONAL UNEMPLOYMENT EQUATIONS

This part contains the joint estimation of equation (17.1) for the 17 countries. After substituting definitions (17.2)–(17.3) into the equation and imposing cross-equation restrictions, we obtain

$$(17.5) \quad u_{it} = c_i[a_i + b(rdebt_{it} + rk_{it}) + c \cdot rk_{it} + d \cdot rmil_{it} + f \cdot rgnm_{it}$$
$$+ g \cdot rt_{it} + h \cdot youth_{it} + i \cdot rtbraw_t + j \cdot rpoilw_t + k \cdot d(infl_{it})]$$

The coefficient restrictions imply that the *ratio* of any two coefficients is the same across countries. Thus the countries differ only in the degree

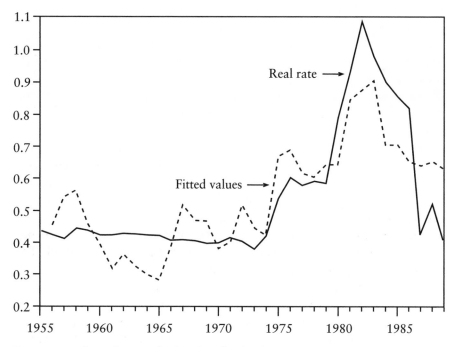

Figure 17.2 The real price of oil and its fitted values

of sensitivity of their labor markets, as reflected in the slope of the labor demand and the wage locus, and the intercept term, a_i. The coefficient c_i is a measure of this labor-market sensitivity.

Because of adjustment costs, firms respond partly with a lag to changes in the righthand side variables. It is assumed that a simple geometric lag representation is sufficient to capture this effect. This requires the estimation of only one additional coefficient, which is the parameter of the lag distribution. The equation is now as follows:

$$(17.5') \quad u_{it} = k_i \cdot u_{it-1} + c_i[a_i + b(rdebt_{it} + rk_{it}) + c \cdot rk_{it} + d \cdot rmil_{it}$$
$$+ f \cdot rgnm_{it} + g \cdot rt_{it} + h \cdot youth_{it}$$
$$+ i \cdot rtbraw_t + j \cdot rpoilw_t + k \cdot d(infl_{it})]$$

On the basis of a prior estimation the coefficient of lagged unemployment, k_i, was constrained to take the same value for countries belonging to the same group of countries. One group is Europe excluding Scandinavia, the second group is Scandinavia, and the third is North America. Japan and Australia were treated separately.

The equations were estimated jointly using iterative, nonlinear, weighted least squares. This method corrects for cross-equation heteroskedasticity by weighting each equation by an estimate of the inverse of the standard error of the equation.[9]

An iterative Cochrane-Orcutt procedure was used to correct for any possible autocorrelation of residuals over time. Given the presence of the lagged dependent variable, autocorrelation would lead to inconsistent coefficient estimates if not corrected for.[10] The estimation results follow in Tables 17.2 to 17.4. (A related estimation in Table 17.5 will also be taken up.)

Table 17.2 reports the coefficients of the explanatory variables. A number of features are worth commenting upon.

The equality of the coefficients of the two types of government expenditures was tested and could not be rejected at the 95 percent level. This restriction was then imposed in the final estimation.

All coefficients have the expected sign, or at least one that can be readily rationalized. An increase in wealth tends to decrease unemployment. So does an increase in government expenditures. Direct taxes as a proportion of total household income, the proportion of youngsters in the population, and the capital stock turn out to increase unemployment. Most important,

Table 17.2 Estimates of the coefficients of the time-series variables in the
national-unemployment equations

Variable name	Coefficient estimate	Standard error
$rdebt_{it} + rk_{it}$	−0.0430	0.0262
rk_{it}	0.1194	0.0473
$rmil_{it} + rgnm_{it}$	−0.1981	0.2086
rt_{it}	8.8014	3.2425
$youth_{it}$	11.2476	5.7815
$d(infl_{it})$	−0.0408	0.0141
$rtbraw_t$	9.4402	3.0743
$rpoilw_t$	1.7249	0.5336

Note: The dependent variable is u_{it}; $n = 32$; and the estimation method was iterative, nonlinear weighted least squares.

both the world real rate of interest and the real price of oil have negative effects on employment. All coefficients are significant at the 95 percent level, with the exception of public debt and public expenditures. The former has a coefficient with a *t*-statistic of around 1.64 and the latter a coefficient with a *t*-statistic of around 0.95. The low significance of public expenditures comes as a surprise. Yet the sign and size of the coefficient is a robust feature of the data, not sensitive to the inclusion or exclusion of any variable.

Indirect taxes, calculated as the ratio of tax revenue and private consumption, were also tried in the estimation. The coefficient turned out to be insignificant and was omitted.

Data on payroll taxes, calculated as the ratio of the sum of social-security and pension-funds contributions to total private-sector wage payments, were available for 15 of the 17 countries. This variable had a very significant, positive coefficient ($t = 2.28$) but was not included in Table 17.2 because of its limited coverage.

A net foreign assets series for most of the countries was added to total wealth in a separate estimation. Even though net foreign assets tended to be considerable compared with some countries' stock of public debt, this did not affect the results above.[11] Owing to gaps in the series for many of the countries, this variable was omitted.

Table 17.3 shows the country-specific coefficients. The size of the sensitivity coefficient, c_i, across countries conforms to common past impressions. The Scandinavian countries have low values while others, such as Spain, the United Kingdom, and the Netherlands, have a high value. The

Table 17.3   Estimates of the constant term, sensitivity, persistence, and autocorrelation of residuals in the national-unemployment equations

Country	c_i	a_i	k_i	AR(1)
Australia	1.0	−3.88	0.57	0.10
Austria	0.30	−3.15	0.75	−0.02
Belgium	0.99	−3.47	0.75	0.29
Canada	1.56	−1.90	0.22	0.61
Denmark	1.43	−4.38	0.53	0.54
Finland	0.79	−3.40	0.53	0.63
France	0.74	−2.95	0.75	−0.14
Germany	0.82	−4.50	0.75	0.13
Ireland	1.00	−2.69	0.75	0.30
Italy	0.45	−1.71	0.75	0.26
Japan	0.15	−0.54	0.69	0.15
Netherlands	1.48	−4.65	0.75	0.38
Norway	0.31	−2.40	0.53	0.59
Spain	1.88	−2.57	0.75	0.30
Sweden	0.35	−2.68	0.53	0.50
United Kingdom	1.39	−3.15	0.75	0.07
United States	1.35	−1.56	0.22	0.50

relatively high value for the United States and Canada is deceptive. The estimates of the coefficient of lagged unemployment is low for these two countries, indicating that the effect of shocks is more immediate than elsewhere. Hence the cumulative effect of shocks is smaller there than in the high-unemployment European and Asian countries. Japan, not surprisingly, has a low value of the sensitivity coefficient. However, the coefficient of lagged unemployment is rather high for that country.

Table 17.4 contains the unadjusted coefficient of determination of multiple regression and the standard error for each of the countries. Also included is the mean value of unemployment for the period 1957–1989. These vary from 1.73 percent for Sweden to 7.05 percent for Spain.

Of greater interest, perhaps, is the correlation of the national unemployment rates with the unemployment rate in the rest of the world (*urw*). The latter is calculated for the years 1955–1989 using the national labor forces as weights. The unemployment rates are highly correlated over time. The main exceptions seem to be the Scandinavian countries and Austria. The U.S. unemployment rate also has a correlation coefficient lower than

Table 17.4 Selected statistics of the national unemployment rates

Country	R^2	Standard error	$\bar{u}$	$cor(u_i, urw)$
Australia	0.92	0.91	4.38	0.96
Austria	0.92	0.51	2.28	0.72
Belgium	0.98	0.68	5.82	0.97
Canada	0.88	0.97	6.82	0.93
Denmark	0.94	0.96	4.81	0.94
Finland	0.84	0.86	3.40	0.76
France	0.99	0.39	4.65	0.92
Germany	0.95	0.71	2.97	0.92
Ireland	0.97	0.96	8.56	0.90
Italy	0.95	0.44	5.13	0.60
Japan	0.93	0.19	1.85	0.79
Netherlands	0.98	0.70	4.76	0.98
Norway	0.53	0.65	2.23	0.44
Spain	0.99	0.65	7.05	0.90
Sweden	0.69	0.34	1.73	0.67
United Kingdom	0.97	0.77	5.50	0.95
United States	0.72	1.02	5.96	0.65

the average. Italy too has a very low value of the coefficient, though this is tied to the very high unemployment in the period 1955–1963; if these years are excluded, the coefficient has the value 0.85. Thus unemployment rates have to a large extent moved together in the industrialized countries. But individualized shocks and unequal responses to common shocks seem capable of differentiating a country's unemployment experience from the crowd. This is a result of our two global factors, of course, but the apparent correlation across countries of several of the national variables must also play a part.

The interest-rate and oil-price variables are endogenous for the world as a whole, of course. The rationalization for their inclusion in the reduced-form equation is that for each country the degree of endogeneity is much smaller than for the group of countries as a whole. Nevertheless, to the extent that one country can affect the world real rate or oil prices, this results in biased estimates.

To check how serious the bias is, the fitted values for the interest rate and oil prices were used in the estimation. The fitted values for the interest-rate variable, *frtbraw*, are taken from the estimates in Table 17.1. Those

Table 17.5   Estimates using the fitted real interest rate and oil price in the national-unemployment-rate equations

Variable	Coefficient estimate	Variable	Coefficient estimate
$rdebt_{it} + rk_{it}$	−0.050	$youth_{it}$	12.568
rk_{it}	0.110	$frtbraw_t$	9.799
$rmil_{it} + rgnm_{it}$	−0.150	$fpoilw_t$	2.867
rt_{it}	4.487		
$d(infl_{it})$	−0.022		

for the oil-price variable, *fpoil*, are taken from a regression of the oil price on world public debt, the world capital stock, military expenditures, and other government expenditures.[12]

The new estimation of equation (17.5′) yielded similar, though not exactly identical, point estimates. Hence there is a slight bias in our estimates above, but no qualitative difference seems to arise because of it. The most important coefficients had the values shown in Table 17.5. Using the fitted values of the world interest rate and oil price yields consistent estimates of the coefficients but not of their standard errors, so our calculations of the latter are not reported.

The first difference of GDP inflation, or the second difference of the GDP deflator, is included as a proxy for demand shocks. A potential problem is that supply shocks cause co-movements of prices and unemployment. In order to check the significance of this element, we included the first difference in the rate of change of nominal oil prices in the equation. The coefficient of this variable turned out to be negative, as was the coefficient of the inflation-shock variable. Thus the negative effect of high oil prices on employment seemed to go through the level and not the rate of change of prices.

An alternative way of taking out the influence of monetary shocks is to use period averages. Thus, one can take averages of the included variables over business cycles and estimate the unemployment equations with the second difference of the price level omitted. This was done, and the simple least-squares coefficient estimates turned out to be almost identical.[13] This would suggest that treating monetary shocks with the inflation term above is a reasonable way to proceed.

Explaining the sensitivity coefficients.   The country constants, a_i, and the sensitivity coefficients, c_i, were included in the unemployment equations in order to prevent omitted, country-specific variables from influenc-

Table 17.6 Regression of the sensitivity coefficients on national characteristics

Variable	Coefficient estimate	Standard error
constant$_i$	−0.409	0.464
bendur$_i$	0.018	0.048
labexp$_i$	−0.032	0.014
replace$_i$	0.017	0.005
corp$_i$	0.082	0.032

Note: The dependent variable is c_i; estimation by OLS method; $n = 17$, $R^2 = 0.61$, adj. $R^2 = 0.49$, s.e. $= 0.37$, $F = 4.77$.

ing the results. Therefore one is forced to omit all time-invariant variables. Having shielded the main coefficients of interest from possible bias, we now turn our attention to the vector C_i. Estimates of a simple linear equation linking the sensitivity coefficients, c_i, to the elements of the vector are shown in Table 17.6. In interpreting such estimates one should bear in mind that the existence of any relevant, omitted variable that is correlated with one or more of the elements of vector C_i will make the estimates biased.

Undoubtedly, many of these explanatory variables are endogenous and respond to changes in the unemployment rate. This applies especially to the duration of unemployment benefits and labor-market expenditures.

Tarantelli's index of the centralization of wage-bargaining, or corporatism, designated by *corp*, turns out to be significant. Thus countries which have very centralized wage-bargaining show the least sensitivity to shocks. This is a result of some importance since this variable is presumably fairly exogenous. The corporatism index is also important in that, without it, few of the other explanatory variables are significant.

The variable *labexp*, which shows public expenditures on labor-market programs per unemployed worker as a proportion of output per worker in 1987, also turns out to be significant. Thus shocks seem to have least effect on unemployment in those countries spending the most on such programs. In addition, the replacement ratio turns out to be significant: the higher is the ratio of unemployment benefits and wages, the more sensitive the labor market. However, the duration of unemployment benefits is, disappointingly, insignificant at the 95 percent level.

UNEMPLOYMENT, EXCHANGE RATES, AND MARKUPS

An important part of the theory tested here is the behavior of real exchange rates and markups. These two variables were of course excluded from the

Table 17.7   Regressions for the relative markup and relative unemployment

$$\frac{mu_{it}}{(\Sigma w_{jt} \cdot mu_{jt})} = a_i + \frac{mu_{it-1}}{(\Sigma w_{it-1} \cdot mu_{it-1})} - \underset{(0.0003)}{0.0021} \,(re_{it}^c - re_{it-1}^c)$$

$$\frac{u_{it}}{(\Sigma l_{jt} \cdot u_{jt})} = b_i + \frac{u_{it-1}}{(\Sigma l_{jt-1} \cdot u_{jt-1})} + \underset{(0.2408)}{0.6229} \left[\frac{mu_{it}}{(\Sigma w_{jt} \cdot mu_{jt})} - \frac{mu_{it-1}}{(\Sigma w_{jt-1} \cdot mu_{jt-1})} \right]$$

Note: Statistics under the coefficient estimates are standard errors.

reduced-form equations above. The reduced form could in practice represent many structural forms. Though estimation of the full structural form is beyond the scope of this chapter, a look at the behavior of exchange rates and markups is ventured below.

First, markups will be related to the behavior of real exchange rates. The theory predicts that an appreciation in the real exchange rate, in making the price of competing foreign goods lower, reduces markups. The ratio of the real exchange rates based on the price of consumer goods, re^c, and unit labor costs, re^u, will be used as a measure of relative markups across countries. For each country the ratio is equal to a ratio of the country's markups to a weighted average of other countries' markups.[14] Table 17.7 displays a regression that makes *relative* markups a function of real exchange rates, re^c. It was estimated over the period 1963–1987 for the countries in the sample, with Austria and Ireland omitted for lack of data. The method of instrumental variables was applied, using the domestic variables that affect only the demand side of the labor market as instruments ($rdebt_i$, $rmil_i$, $rgnm_i$). The variable w_i denotes the weights.

The theory predicts that unemployment and markups are positively correlated. In order to test this hypothesis we estimated an equation linking the ratio of a country's unemployment and unemployment in the rest of the world to the country's relative markup, as defined above. This regression is also displayed in Table 17.7. This companion equation was estimated for the same 15 countries using the same instruments ($rmil_i$, $rgnm_i$, $rdebt_i$) for the period 1963–1989. The national labor forces were used as weights in calculating the unemployment in the rest of the world for each country.

Both equations had to be estimated in first differences because when they were estimated in levels the coefficient of the lagged dependent variable was not significantly different from unity.

The results suggest that markups react to movements in the real exchange rate in accordance with the theory. The t-statistic of the coefficient of the first difference of the real exchange rate is equal to -7. They also indicate a positive relationship between markups and unemployment. The t-statistic of the coefficient of markups is 2.6.[15]

17.3 The Findings Assessed

Clearly it would be impossible to look back on the foregoing results without some degree of satisfaction. What is most remarkable about these findings is that there were no fundamental failures of the theory, only a handful of mild surprises that could readily be understood in terms of the theory and hence did not require a revamping of the theory.

On the other hand, the economy is so complex an organism, so to speak, that it would be naive in the extreme to imagine that, at long last, the true macroeconomic model of equilibrium employment determination had been discovered. A question that permanently looms over any such research as this is whether the results interpreted as favorable to the theory are in reality the expression of some mix of other theories, some likely to be old and some *not yet known*.

An occasional objection to the structuralist interpretation of this evidence is that the contractionary effect of fiscal stimulus in one part of the world on employment in the rest of the world, though derivable from structuralist models, can be explained as well by monetary models containing sluggish nominal wage behavior and a Bretton Woods system of fixed nominal exchange rates—if the monetary authorities in the country where the stimulus occurs are unable or unwilling to delay its impact on real interest rates. That objection suffers from three weaknesses. First, Bretton Woods provided an adjustable peg for exchange rates, not fixity, and money wage rates were left free to speed up or slow down, both adjustments driving exployment toward the natural rate—nothing like an ultra-Keynesian single-currency fixed-wage model. Second, that part of the transmission of contraction occurring through the monetary channel is captured in the regression equation here by the first difference of the inflation rate, leaving only the structural effect on the natural rate itself to be picked up by the explanatory variables of the structuralist type. Finally, the objection offers no hint of how to interpret along monetary lines the other counter-Keynesian finding—that a worldwide fiscal stimulus through public debt or expenditure causes a global contraction. It remains true, as acknowledged, that the results are not certainties.

One of the large question marks is the heavy weight that the customer-market model is asked to bear in explaining many of the results. Are the flows of customers across borders so slow as to make this explanation valid? And even if many customers are slow to move, the estimation procedure at present does not contain the constraint that asymptotically all customers move as they would do in a frictionless world market. Unfortunately we lack data on the national stocks of (domestic and foreign) customers. The shortage of data on stocks of net foreign assets also frustrates efforts to obtain a logically complete description of the international links. The omission of consumer durables, both from the theory and the econometric model, is also a worry. And so forth.

But, though there remains some uncertainty whether the family of structuralist models tested here is largely or importantly right, how much greater must be our doubts, in view of these findings, about the other *existing* theories of the world's slumps and booms! The findings, it must be insisted, flatly contradict at central points the only existing alternative theory of unemployment—the *monetary* approach, begun by Keynes—in both its closed-economy and open-economy versions. Specifically:

- A *worldwide* increase of public expenditure (aggregate or nonmilitary) was *not* found to be expansionary, except possibly over the time (if such exists) when the inflation is rising in response, contrary to the Hicks-Hansen model. The same is true of a worldwide increase of public debt.

- A *national* increase of public expenditure and of public debt was *not* found to be expansionary abroad, subject to the same qualification, contrary to the Mundell-Fleming model with flexible exchange rates.

Prudence requires putting aside the Keynesian approach for the time being in favor of taking up the structuralist approach. If structuralism should at some point prove unsatisfactory, we would be free to move on.

Appendix 1: Procedures and Results of Other Studies Compared

The objective of this appendix is to point out a few related studies. These are, on the one hand, studies of capital-market equilibrium and the determination of real interest rates and, on the other hand, labor-market studies.

The simple world-interest-rate equation shows that the world real rate is positively correlated with the level of central government debt, the transitory component of oil prices, and the level of government expenditures. Such a simple regression does not prove causality but is indicative of possible links between the variables. These links have been studied by Robert Barro and Xavier Sala-i-Martin, Michael Beenstock, and Dirk Morris.[16] All three studies use annual cross-country postwar data.

Barro and Sala-i-Martin use a framework similar to the one used in the unemployment equations above and look at the determinants of world investment demand and desired saving in an integrated world capital market. They estimate a set of reduced-form capital-market equilibrium conditions for 9 countries with all coefficients constrained to take the same value except for the constant term. The presumption is that each country's real interest rate differs from a world real rate by a fixed constant term. Their results suggest that high stock prices, which drive up investment demand, and a high ratio of expenditures on oil consumption to GDP, which tends to lower desired saving, make the world real rate of interest increase; also, and most important for our purposes, that a high level of world public debt reduces world desired saving and hence drives up the real interest rate. They did not, however, find a significant relationship between world government spending and the world real interest rate.

Beenstock estimates a structural model of the world economy, treating the industrialized countries and the developing countries as two separate blocks. His simulations suggest that the level of public debt affects the real interest rate by affecting aggregate demand as in our model.

Morris estimates, using OECD aggregates, a simple linear equation linking the world real interest rate to various monetary and nonmonetary variables. He concludes that both public debt and public expenditures affect the world real rate of interest positively.

A recent paper by Alan Manning looks at the forces affecting equilibrium unemployment. The motivation is similar to ours in that he tries to explain the long-run rise in unemployment in most OECD countries in the past decade or so.[17] Using a different theoretical framework, he tests for the effect of real interest rates on unemployment by estimating augmented Phillips curves for 19 OECD countries for the period 1956–1985. He does not, however, impose any cross-equation restrictions, nor does he test for the determinants of cross-country differences. His is thus a pure time-series study. Manning finds evidence for a negative relationship between employment and real interest rates for nine out of ten countries for which the coefficient was significant.

Finally, the impressive volume by Richard Layard, Stephen Nickell, and Richard Jackman contains an abundance of labor-market studies.[18] These vary from pure cross-section to pure time-series models. A few of the variables that are crucial to their results can be found in the following section. Some turn out to be significant in explaining cross-country differences. Since their theoretical framework differs in fundamental ways from that of the present paper, it seems that the importance of these variables is compatible with a wide range of economic theories.

Appendix 2: The Data and Their Sources

Definition of variable	Symbol	Source of data
Working-age population	*wap*	OECD, *Labor Force Statistics*
Labor force	*ℓ*	OECD, *Labor Force Statistics*
Population	*pop*	IMF, *International Financial Statistics*
Number of people between the ages of 20 and 24	*age2024*	ILO, World Bank Data Base
Unemployment	*u*	OECD, *Economic Outlook*[a]
Central government debt	*rdebt*	IMF, *International Financial Statistics,* and national sources
Government consumption expenditures	*rgc*	IMF, *International Financial Statistics*
Military expenditures	*rmil*	Stockholm International Peace Research Institute
Direct taxes as a proportion of household income	*rt*	OECD[b]
Indirect taxes as a proportion of private consumption	*it*	OECD[b]
Social security taxes as a proportion of private-sector wage bill	*ss*	OECD[b]
Pension fund contributions as a proportion of private-sector wage bill	*pf*	OECD[b]
Net foreign assets	*nfa*	OECD[b]

Definition of variable	Symbol	Source of data
Capital stock proxy table[c]	*rk*	Summers and Heston, *World Data Set*
Unemployment benefits duration (1985)	*bendur*	U.S. Department of Health and Social Services[a]
Replacement ratio (1985)	*replace*	U.S. Department of Health and Social Services[a]
Labor market program expenditures (1987)	*labexp*	OECD, *Economic Outlook*[a]
Corporatism index	*corp*	E. Tarantelli, *Industrial Relations*, 1986
Relative consumer prices in dollars	*re^c*	OECD, *Economic Outlook*
Relative unit labor costs in dollars	*re^u*	OECD, *Economic Outlook*
Nominal interest rates (three-month treasury bill rates)[d]	*tbra*	IMF, *International Financial Statistics;* OECD, Main Economic Indicators; and national sources[e]
Consumer price index	*pc*	IMF, *International Financial Statistics*[e]
GNP/GDP deflator	*pgnp*	OECD, *Economic Outlook;* Center for Economic Performance, OECD Dataset[a]
The real price of oil[f]	*rpoil*	Citibase[e]
The nominal price of oil	*npoil*	Citibase[e]

Derived variables:

Measure of age distribution of population	*youth*	Equal to *age2024/pop*
Real interest rate	*rtbra*	Equal to *tbra* − consumer price inflation
A rolling average of oil prices (five-year-backward)	*ppoil*	Calculated by author
Transitory component of oil prices	*tpoil*	Equal to *rpoil* − *ppoil*
Public expenditures on nonmilitary goods and services	*rgnm*	Equal to *rgc* − *rmil*[g]
Payroll taxes	*pr*	Equal to *ss* + *pf*

Note: All values are written on a per-augmented-labor-unit basis. The labor force measure used is a 5-year rolling average of the OECD annual labor force data. The rate of labor-augmenting technical progress is determined such that the output-augmented labor unit ratios in the United States have no trend—assuming that the U.S. was close to steady state during the period. In calculating the growth rate the sample was split in 1973. This gave a higher rate in the period 1955–1973 (1.82 percent) than in 1974–1989 (0.9 percent).

World variables are calculated as the weighted average of the country variables, the weights being the share of the country's labor force in the world labor force. The only exceptions are the world rate of interest, which uses GDP-shares as weights, and the oil-price variable, which takes the U.S. value unchanged. World variables have names ending with w.

a. Taken from R. Layard, S. Nickell, and R. Jackman, *Unemployment: Macroeconomic Performance and the Labour Market* (Oxford: Oxford University Press, 1991).

b. Data provided by John Martin and Jorgen Elmeskov, OECD.

c. The World Table gives the capital stock (total capital, including residential construction) and output for 1979–1987. The capital-output ratio in 1979 and the output level in 1955 are used to find the capital stock in 1955. A 5 percent depreciation rate and investment data from the World Table are then used to calculate the capital stock in future years. The 5 percent rate makes the capital-output ratio for the U.S. trendless for the whole period 1955–1989. On the assumption that the U.S. was not far from steady state in this period, this rate is then applied to the other countries.

d. Money market rates for France and Japan.

e. Data provided by Robert Barro, Harvard University.

f. Ratio of U.S. PPI (Producers' Price Index) for crude petroleum to overall U.S. PPI.

g. Countries: Australia, Austria, Belgium, Canada, Denmark, Finland, France, Germany, Ireland, Italy, Japan, Netherlands, Norway, Spain, Sweden, United Kingdom, United States of America.

18

A Concise Nonmonetary History
of Postwar Economic Activity

THE world unemployment rate has exhibited broad movements of re-markable magnitude since the last world war.[1] Starting from a figure around 5 percent toward the end of the 1940s, when the capital stock had been put back together following the wartime damage and dislocation,[2] the world unemployment rate reached record-breaking lows in the mid-1950s and again in the 1960s—about 2.5 percent at the bottom; where-upon it turned around, finding a plateau of 5 percent in the second half of the 1970s, a zone around 8 percent in the mid-1980s, then a partial recovery, and most recently a return to high rates in the early 1990s.

How are we to account for these wide swings? It must be a dread of every economist to be asked by a layman, "since you are an economist, perhaps you can explain to me why the economy has been in a slump (boom) for so long."[3] On high-frequency fluctuations we can speak with presentational confidence, parroting "effective demand" whenever weekly retail sales or freightcar loadings go up or down, since we believe "effective supply" rarely moves sharply and inconspicuously. Understanding the forces beneath low-frequency movements involves real demands and sup-plies, and puts more importance on identifying the underlying shock or shocks rather than merely categorizing them as in some sense demand-side or supply-side.

To account for the long swings in unemployment one needs the casual relationships provided by a theory, of course. The structuralist framework here provides such a theory, generating the implications that if the world public debt increases the employment rate is ultimately reduced, if the world capital stock goes up the employment rate is ultimately increased, and so forth; and there is now the econometric evidence supporting these conditional predictions in Chapter 17. But if we are to avoid unwieldiness our theories have to remain narrow in scope, with few causal mechanisms and a small typology of exogenous forces. So a theory, though econometrically sound, may happen to shed little light on actual events (like the proverbial streetlight not placed over the lost object). Hence the need is for a theory fortunate enough that its implications explain a large portion of the actual data—such as the recorded unemployment rates in recent decades.

It is further desirable that a theory manage not just to have a good batting average, as measured perhaps by its R-squared, but also to hit well in the clutch. We would like a theory to do well at explaining the data at the big opportunities—to illuminate the major movements.

Can the highlights of the postwar fluctuations in employment be explained to a large or important degree by those causal factors and mechanisms portrayed by the theory? The structuralist approach will not "graduate" to the status of an empirically functioning theory until it passes this last trial: to tell a plausible story of employment in recent decades.

The purpose of the present chapter, then, is to give an accounting of the long swings of the world unemployment rate since the last world war. Years ago, Milton Friedman offered a monetary history of fluctuations in the United States, and occasional supplements have since been issued by the heir apparent to this monetary tradition, Martin Feldstein.[4] It is fair to say that those histories interpret fluctuations as deviations around a constant natural rate.[5] A structuralist history such as that offered here instead interprets the low-frequency movements of unemployment as vicissitudes in the natural rate itself. But if monetarists will refrain from adding low-frequency fluctuations to their *explananda,* and the structuralists will cede the high-frequency fluctuations to the monetary models, the two approaches to history can be considered complementary rather than rival.

The history here will be similarly informal, in places somewhat speculative. A contrasting precision is presented by some charts plotting the steady-state unemployment rate predicted by the econometric model of the previous chapter and decomposing the predicted level into the influences of the main causal factors incorporated into the econometric model.

As our canvas is the international economy or those parts of it tied to the global capital market, rather than a closed (and completely integrated) national economy, we will also want to take note at places of the heterogeneity of the experience of the countries composing the world aggregate.

18.1 The Several Epochs since World War II

The years immediately after the close of World War II were a period of restarting institutions and mending the capital structure in the economies that had suffered extensive war damage and dislocation. This period of so-called reconstruction went on in some countries longer than in others, of course. For the collection of advanced economies as a whole, though, we may safely view that process as having been largely completed in three or four years. The response of the world economy to various shocks, that is, begins to resemble the response over the whole postwar era by the late 1940s, and so our history begins there.[6]

It is convenient to divide the span of time being examined into distinct subperiods, or epochs. Yet the number of these periods to define and their demarcations remain somewhat arbitrary.

NORMALIZATION: THE END OF THE 1940s TO THE LATE 1950s

Although world data for this period on capital stock, public debt, and so forth are not very reliable, where available at all, the scattered national data and the impressions of observers of the world's economies in these years suggest that this first epoch was driven by the low levels of the capital stock relative to the augmented labor force, and the high level of the world public debt relative to the augmented labor force, with which the period started. Over this period, the world public debt subsided to lower and lower levels, and the world capital stock recovered to its normal range, with the result that the shadow prices of the assets in which firms invest tended to rise over the period and there was a corresponding tendency for the equilibrium path of the world unemployment rate to be falling.

Questions arise, it is true, about that interpretation. If the public debt and capital stock were critical, why, since the world public debt was at an all-time high and the world capital stock presumably at an all-time low, was the world unemployment rate not extraordinarily high at the beginning of this period? The answer may be that some other factors nearly counterbalanced the magnitude of the public debt and the scarcity of capital. The level of public expenditure was low, compared with the heights reached decades later; if it operates typically to drive interest rates up and thus to contract equilibrium employment, that could have saved this period from being one of extraordinarily high interest rates and helped to moderate the high unemployment rate that would otherwise have been experienced. Another counterbalancing factor was the low level of tax rates in that period, which also operated to moderate the unemployment rate, according to the modern equilibrium theory.

Another question about the above interpretation centers on real interest rates. It is not abundantly clear from the data that the world real interest rate started moderately high and proceeded to fall, a movement that would corroborate the asset-price story of the decline of the world unemployment rate. Part of the explanation may be that the moderate inflation rates of this period were not fully discounted in expected nominal rates of returns on assets and hence in nominal interest rates. The public had to learn that governments would come to believe that they could keep unemployment low by systematically producing moderate inflation, and it could be that the learning process was not nearly complete until the middle or late 1950s. In some countries, interest-rate ceilings may also have helped to keep bill rates low.

From the perspective of the theory being fitted to the data here, the Korean War is an interesting episode in this period. An adequate treatment of this subject cannot be offered on the present occasion. It may be commented, though, that the very low unemployment rates found during this period in the United States despite so little pickup in price inflation and so little rise in the rate of (nominal) wage inflation as well are consistent with the implication of the theory that the expenditures of the U.S. government in prosecuting the Korean War served to contract the equilibrium unemployment rate itself. There may have been little or no rise of the actual employment path *over* the equilibrium path in this period.

A GOLDEN AGE: THE END OF THE 1950s TO THE EARLY 1970s

The record shows the world unemployment rate reached new lows in the mid-1960s before returning to the moderate level with which it began the period. Some of the *initial rise* in the world unemployment rate is explained by the disinflationary monetary policies put in place in several countries at the start of this period, so the equilibrium world unemployment must have fallen less sharply in the early 1960s than the actual rate, if it fell at all. A good theory will have the feature that it does not predict a large change for the equilibrium path in one direction or the other in this period.

Judging from the fitted path of the world unemployment rate in Figure 18.1, our equilibrium theory "predicts" almost no change in the world rate throughout this period. More accurately, the fitted path shows a small decrease to midperiod—a much smaller decrease than the actual path,

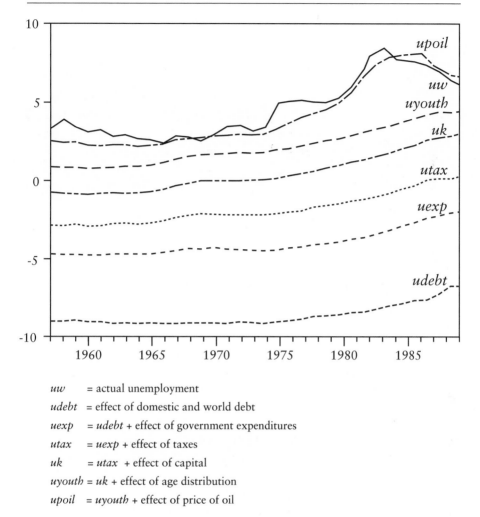

uw   = actual unemployment

udebt   = effect of domestic and world debt

uexp   = *udebt* + effect of government expenditures

utax   = *uexp* + effect of taxes

uk   = *utax* + effect of capital

uyouth = *uk* + effect of age distribution

upoil   = *uyouth* + effect of price of oil

Figure 18.1 The world unemployment rate, its fitted values, and their decomposition

which must have been elevated by the disinflationary policies of some countries in the first years of the period, as just suggested; this is followed by a somewhat larger increase of the fitted path to the end of this period, leaving the fitted unemployment rate a little higher than it began.

The decompositions in Figures 18.1 and 18.2, the details of which are left to an endnote, indicate that the continuing decline of the world public debt (relative to the augmented world labor force) continued to operate toward lowering the unemployment rate.[7] The continuing but weaker

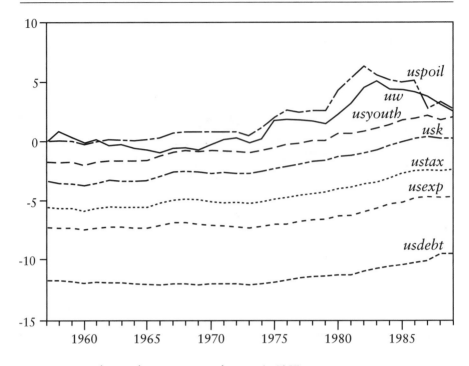

uw = actual unemployment – unemployment in 1957

usx = predicted steady state with actual values of explanatory variables – predicted
      steady state with 1957 values of explanatory variables (see Figure 18.1 for
      definition of variables)

Figure 18.2 Decomposition of the fitted steady-state unemployment rate

growth of the world capital stock relative to the augmented labor force
operated in the same direction, but weakly. In this period the declining
real price of oil is another force tending to reduce world unemployment.
But the steeper rises of government purchases and of tax rates now operate
more strongly in the opposing direction, in contrast to the first period. If
the decomposition is accurate, they manage to impart a net upward effect
on the fitted unemployment rate, relative to its starting value, by the end
of the period.

The world aggregate unemployment rate covers a considerable diver-
sity of national experiences over this second period. While the world rate
touched bottom in 1966 and was nearly as low again in 1968, the unemployment rate in France reached its low in 1963 and rose strongly over
the rest of this second period. The unemployment rate in the United States

hit its low still earlier, in the 1950s, and was generally much higher in the 1960s; without the influence of rising inflation of largely monetary origins toward the end of the decade, it doubtless would have been markedly higher than it was. If we paint with a pretty broad brush, we may say that in Europe and Japan unemployment continued to fall well into the second period while in the United States there are signs of a steady rise of the equilibrium unemployment rate throughout the period.

It is not possible to consider at length whether the sort of equilibrium theory developed here can serve adequately to explain these two contrasting profiles of unemployment. An attempt to do so might begin with the premise that the growth of the American labor force proceeded at a lower rate in this second period than earlier, as Depression-born entrants were relatively few, with the implication of weaker investment demand; in Europe, economic growth and investment demand held up better.[8] One effect in the United States is that the capital-goods sector faces lower real prices. Another effect is real exchange-rate depreciation, which invites higher markups. A third effect is a tendency toward faster or at any rate largely maintained wealth accumulation (by a work force having few young dissavers) with which to finance continued American export surpluses and increased budgetary deficits, the effect of which is to drive up the equilibrium wage locus. All these effects in turn have the consequence of driving up the American unemployment rate, while in Europe the same tendencies are weaker or absent or we find the reverse tendencies.

Much later, in the 1980s, it is in Europe that the labor force is growing at a slower rate than the other countries. As a consequence, it is Europe that suffers the reduced demand for nontradable capital goods, the real depreciation, and the unfavorable wage-setting locus—all developments tending to drive up unemployment in Europe. (There was also a lesser fiscal stimulus to investment in Europe than in America and a lesser decrease in the supply of national saving in Europe, which also tended to generate a real depreciation and to increase unemployment, as in the Fitoussi-Phelps thesis.)

Yet, it should be noted, slower labor-force growth operates through the hiring/training cost channel to decrease the unemployment rate somewhat. So the upshot of this factor is ambiguous. Perhaps the net balance is tipped toward employment contraction when account is taken of the side effects of the comparative slowdown of the labor force in the United States: a comparative slackening in the decline of the public debt per unit of labor force and a comparative speedup in the capital-labor ratio. Some young workers who would otherwise have arrived to man the new machines and to buy the public debt did not show up. (Recall from Chapter 17 that an open economy's debt-worker ratio is domestically expansionary and its capital–labor force ratio likely to be contractionary, as suggested in Chapters 12 and 13.)

THE OIL SHOCK: MID-1970S TO THE EARLY 1980S

Perhaps it will cause no surprise that, according to the decomposition calculations depicted in Figure 18.1, the oil-price increase of 1973 was the most important shock for the equilibrium path of the world unemployment rate over this period.[9] Owing to the role of the lagged dependent variable in the calculation of the equilibrium path, the calculated equilibrium path displays a gradual increase in response to this shock.

Historians of this period have all overlooked the strong effect, operating through the world real interest rate, of the marked reversal in the path of the world public debt on the equilibrium path of the world unemployment rate. This factor appears to be at least half as important as the first oil shock.

Another neglected factor in this period is the slowdown in the pace of world capital accumulation in relation to the augmented world labor force. Undoubtedly some of this decline can be attributed to the oil-price increase and to the increase in the public debt. Of course, some of the latter may itself be attributable to the oil-price increase. In any case, it is interesting to see how an oil shock can set in motion a train of accompanying effects that, operating through various channels, reinforce the contractionary impact that is the direct effect of the oil-price increase.

Public expenditure and tax rates do not seem to be forces driving the world unemployment rate in this period. However, in some countries, there is a marked increase in taxation, which may have imparted an upward trend to their unemployment rates.

DISTURBANCES TO REAL INTEREST RATES AND OIL PRICES: 1981 TO 1989

The growth of world public debt, which had gotten underway in the mid 1970s, quickened sharply in the early 1980s. There was also a significant increase in the world level of public expenditure. The world real interest rate, which had recovered to a normal range by 1980, soon soared to levels rarely seen for a prolonged spell in the mid-1980s. These shocks gave impetus to a major increase of the equilibrium unemployment rate. It could be said that this demonstration, based though it necessarily is on fragile econometric estimates, is a confirmation of a central theme, perhaps the most important theme, of the modern equilibrium theory developed here.

This increase came on top of the significant increase already in store owing to the occurrence of the second oil shock in 1979. The decomposition calculations underlying Figures 18.1 and 18.2 imply that this oil-price increase was a more important shock for the equilibrium path of the unemployment rate than the real-interest increase. But by 1986 or 1987 the real price of oil was back to its level of the early 1970s. So it was largely the high real interest rates lasting over most of the decade that account for the high equilibrium unemployment rates in the late 1980s.

A mildly surprising finding, in view of the tax revolts of the 1980s in the United States and Britain, is that some of the rise of the world unemployment rate in this period comes not from oil or public debt or public expenditure but from the rise of direct-income tax rates.

In this third period too there is a contrast to be noted in the experience of the United States and the rest of the OECD countries. The possible consequence for unemployment in Europe relative to that in the United States of the relatively slower labor-force growth in Europe has already been noted. In Figures 18.3 and 18.4 we find corroboration of the importance for the unemployment rate in a sample European country, namely France, of the rise of the world real interest rate in the 1980s, as first argued by the Fitoussi-Phelps thesis.[10] The evidence suggests that the real-interest factor was of the same order of magnitude as the second oil-price shock. The exact calculations using the econometric estimates suggest it was about two-thirds as important.

Two problems have been raised about this interpretation of the striking contrast between the United States and the rest of the OECD countries in this period. One is that share prices on the stock markets of the world rose sharply, beginning at various times in the first half of the decade, a fact hard to reconcile with calculations that real interest rates were high in the period. In this view, required real interest rates came back down after the brief run-up in the early 1980s. It is more plausible to look to other sources of stock-market reevaluation than to a supposed recovery of real interest rates to lower levels. It could be that with the prospect of the conquest of inflation, or at any rate a large part of it, stocks came to be seen as assets that could be held without a capital-gains tax on that part of the nominal-price increase corresponding to an unchanged real price. It could also be that the "equity premium" that the prospective rate of return on equities had to offer formerly was simply adjusted downward through a widely

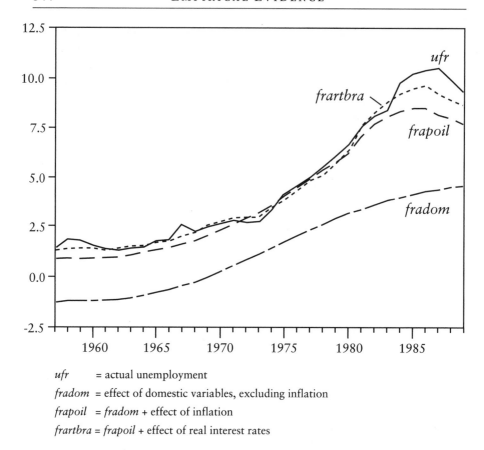

ufr   = actual unemployment

fradom = effect of domestic variables, excluding inflation

frapoil = fradom + effect of inflation

frartbra = frapoil + effect of real interest rates

Figure 18.3 Decomposition of French unemployment, assuming a steady state in 1957

agreed shift in conventional thinking among professional portfolio managers at large financial firms.[11]

The more serious problem is the possibility that the rise in share prices represents a fall in the cost of capital through equity finance that in an appropriate sense approximately offsets the rise in the cost of capital through debt finance that the increase of expected real interest rates on bond and loans represents. It has been argued by Barro that there was, on balance, no net, or aggregate, increase in the cost of capital in the 1980s.[12] This view flies in the face of the traditional view that firms face great difficulties in financing investments importantly through equity issues, with the consequence that they are importantly dependent on loans, commercial paper, and bonds.[13] There is also the point that if share prices are seen as high enough to make a share issue attractive, firms may use the funds to buy bonds or retire debt rather than to invest in new capital.[14] In any case, this revisionist position, it should be noted, makes its argument by counting internal financing as equity financing. Why should a company be assumed to regard the cost of capital financed internally as equal simply to the return on shares when the shareowners would allocate any dividends received to bonds as well as shares? If internal financing is undertaken in large part in order to qualify for additional debt financing and if the amount of additional debt financing that firms are willing to do is a func-

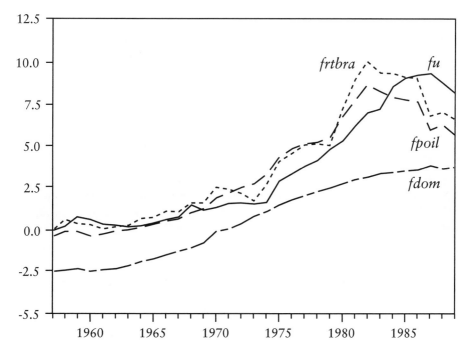

fu = actual unemployment – unemployment in 1957

fdom = predicted steady state with actual values of domestic variables – predicted steady state with 1956 values of domestic variables

fpoil = *fdom* + effect of inflation

frtbra = *fpoil* + effect of real interest rates

Figure 18.4 Decomposition of French unemployment, steady state assumed for all years

tion of the expected real rate of interest on debt, then the cost of capital via equity financing is important only to the extent that firms issue shares, which has not been important as a method of financing until the past couple of years.

THE EARLY 1990S

The decade of the 1990s has begun with extraordinary events. The iron curtain was lifted. The Wall separating East Germany and West Germany was torn down, which led finally to the unification of the two countries and which came to symbolize the reintegration of the countries of Central Europe into the international economy of the West. The Soviet Union dissolved into separate countries, some of which have embarked on a transition to a private market economy. Latin American countries began radical reforms, while East Asia and the southern part of China continue their extraordinarily fast growth.

Although a quantitative analysis of this last period in the nonmonetary history must await the collection of additional data, a few surmises are now in order. The striking behavior of real interest rates is, once again, a central feature of this period. A rather widely held impression, shared by the author, is that the major rise of investment demand and decline in the supply of saving in (united) Germany, especially if combined with the opening of the world capital market to Latin America and China, among other new bidders for the world's supply of saving, goes far to explain why real interest rates have not subsided much, if at all, in the 1990s in relation to their levels toward the end of the 1980s. A contrary view points to the small size of the investment levels in these areas of the world in relation to the volume of world saving. Of course such measurements are germane. It can be argued, nevertheless, that the world real interest rate can be driven up sharply if the marginal claimants to the world's supply of saving suddenly see investment to be much more profitable than was the case before.[15]

In addition, the public debt has continued to climb, causing a further increase of world real interest rates and the equilibrium unemployment rate. Moreover, the capital stock outside the "new areas" just discussed has undoubtedly continued to slow relative to the augmented labor force, so that a factor formerly helping to oppose the rise of real interest rates and the world unemployment rate is now weaker.

In the OECD countries, the fiscal stance is another contractionary influence. There has been some slight tendency for higher tax rates in the West in this period, especially in the United States.

Against this background it is not surprising that the world unemployment rate, which had been tending downward in the late 1980s as world real interest rates subsided, has resumed its climb, reaching levels that are well above those in the 1970s though not at the record highs reached in the 1980s. A further rise of unemployment rates within the European Community, almost to previous peaks, a cyclical rise layered on top of stubbornly high natural rates of unemployment, occurred in 1992 and 1993. The well-accepted explanation of this rise, however, is the aggravating response of monetary and exchange-rate policies to the increase of the natural rate of interest in Germany caused by unification. This cyclical elevation will subside, barring new shocks.

It is not possible to forecast the future without having a way to predict the course of the underlying causal factors. It may be ventured, though, that it is unlikely the 1990s will see a concatenation of shocks—the oil shock as well as the disturbances to the world real interest rate—such as was experienced in the 1980s. There is a good chance, therefore, that this recent slump, which is in some respects an extension of the previous one, will remain milder than the extraordinary depression of the 1980s.

VI

CONCLUDING NOTES

19

Notes on Classicism, Etc.

ECONOMICS is not governed by the pendulum of opinion that historians see or think they see in national politics. There is no likelihood that a theory discredited by new evidence or overtaken by new ideas will be restored for a time to its former popularity by subsequent events.

Nevertheless, an economic theory sometimes comes back, rather transformed yet similar enough to support much of the policy doctrine that it had previously sustained. Newly arriving ideas may happen to fill a void or repair a defect in a discarded theory, making possible at least a partial reconstruction of the theory and its doctrine.

In twentieth-century economics, the most famous case in point is the revival of the mercantilist perspective of preclassical times brought about by Keynes's theory of employment. In the chapter "Notes on Mercantilism" in his *General Theory,* Keynes argued that his theory lent new weight to the mercantilists as against the classicals who had triumphed over them. The Reverend Malthus is the sympathetic anti-hero, a warmly drawn figure next to Hume, Smith, and the darkly portrayed Ricardo.[1]

What motivated Keynes to make this connection is uncertain. In acknowledging that in his differences with the traditional theory there had been some anticipations, notably the reigning doctrine little more than two hundred years earlier, he may have thought to increase receptivity to the radical break he was advocating. Another reason may have been that the discussion enabled him to establish where his precursors had fallen short, thus to identify for readers his own value added. These are perhaps two of the reasons why any author cites the literature.

The theory of unemployment developed in the present work also has a parallel to an earlier theory—the classical conception of employment determination found in Smith to some extent and more fully in Ricardo.

Classical theory, meaning the literature from the classical period to Marshall and his successors that is based on the postulate of perfect information, is one of the whipping boys of the present volume, it is true, as it was in the *General Theory*. (Keynesian theory, being based on money and problematic features of the market economy of a nominal character, is another—and more proximate—target of the present work.) Yet it will be seen that the classical conception as it finally evolved in Ricardo, eventually to be displaced by the neoclassical paradigm, is rather analogous in a formal way to the approach to unemployment set forth here. One can think of the structuralist theory here as reconstructing the classical model, which had been left poorly founded and problematic, to make it work.

In looking back to forerunners, Keynes's review stopped first at his most recent precursor, the gifted monetary crank Silvio Gesell, a Buenos Aires banker by trade. In *The Natural Economic Order* Gesell had hit upon the point that if the marginal efficiency of capital went negative, the employment effect could be neutralized by an equal algebraic decrease in the nominal and real rate of return to holding money via a tax on money holdings. Then the worsened outlook for capital goods would not precipitate an attempted flight from capital to money, depressing capital-goods prices and disrupting their production.[2]

The nearest precursors to the employment theory here were, in an important respect at any rate, the supply-siders of recent decades. The more sophisticated the author examined, and the closer the examination, the more we find a perspective and a developed body of analysis significantly distinct from the structuralist theory presented here. The less the message has been sophisticated by linkups to neoclassical notions, the more the doctrine strikes a structuralist chord.

Among these looser writers the one most serving the purpose here is the amateur fiscal theorist Jude Wanniski, a New York journalist by profession. Wanniski is our Silvio Gesell, if anyone can be. In his interesting book, *The Way the World Works,* the premise is that any decrease in the demand price of labor, net of taxes on labor paid by households or firms, destroys jobs and reduces the after-tax wage rate).[3] In particular, an increase in the rate of tax on labor, either the labor income of households or the labor outlays of firms, will operate to reduce employment. His thesis is that the surge of tax rates in the Western countries over the postwar era accounts to an important degree for the trend toward slowing employment. The Great Depression in the United States is largely attributed by Wanniski to the sharp rise of tariff rates in the Smoot-Hawley Act.[4]

The general public could only have interpreted the analysis as referring to the unemployment rate. It must also have been understood to refer to durable effects, not to effects depending on misexpectations. So the message received was that increased tax rates on labor, in reducing the after-tax wage rate that firms can pay, push up the equilibrium unemployment path. Indeed, this seems to have been Wanniski's intuition.

In fact, the theoretical mechanisms articulated by the professional theorists in the supply-side movement were entirely neoclassical and referred not to unemployment but instead to labor-force participation (to which employment was equal along an equilibrium path). The supply curve of labor was presumed to be not vertical in the neighborhood of equilibrium, as might have been assumed to be a satisfactory approximation, but rather upward-sloping, so that a downward demand shift would have the contractionary effect on employment that was assumed by the doctrine. With regard to a tax increase on labor, the argument for a contractionary effect could be rested on stronger grounds: if the budget was to remain with an unchanged deficit or surplus and public expenditure was increased as a result, the change in expenditure might (by offering free some goods formerly purchased) have a sort of income effect offsetting the income effect of the tax bill. Further, under Ricardian equivalence, of course, even if public expenditure was to remain on an unchanged course, some or all of the income effect of the tax increase would be offset by the expected income effects in the opposite direction from prospective tax reductions later on. Either way, the remaining substitution effect would be decisive, causing a contraction in the amount of labor supplied and hence in employment. Yet, empirically, the massive expansion of the public sector and corresponding rise of tax rates has not been accompanied by a secular decline in labor-force participation. There *has* been an erratic yet pronounced increase of the unemployment rate in most countries over the postwar period, but there was no mechanism in the supply-side broadsides by which the expansion of government pushed up unemployment.

The missing element in Wanniski, therefore, is a theoretical foundation for moving from the demand price of labor to the rate of unemployment. There is no notion of real-wage resistance with which to bridge the gap. Further, without a suitably general treatment of real-wage resistance, the doctrine was vulnerable to attack. If reductions in the demand price of labor caused by tax-rate increases aimed to finance larger government are contractionary, why has not the secular rise in the demand price of labor caused by continual technical progress and investment served to offset and overwhelm the contractionary effect on employment, just as it has apparently managed to keep after-tax wage rates rising?[5] Neither was there a suitably general view of markup behavior. Hence it was not clear why the imposition of a tariff, the impact of which (at given markups) must be to reduce the real income from wealth in the same proportion that it reduces the real wage rate (corresponding to a given product wage) and hence not to raise the product wage required for labor-market equilibrium, would have a contractionary effect. Still, a glimmer of structuralist theory is there.

There were other elements that, if not logically missing, were notable for their absence in Wanniski's perspective and that of the supply-side school in general. The obsessive preoccupation with the role of taxes in determining employment, a single-cause model reminiscent of the crudest kind of monetarism, left no space for consideration of all the other structural forces that have driven real interest rates, real exchange rates, and undoubtedly employment rates in the past two decades.

To retrieve the beginnings of structuralism we have to rewind past the long neoclassical period, from Debreu and Samuelson through Marshall, Edgeworth, and Mill, to the two giants at the beginning of the classical period, Smith and Ricardo. Their models of the labor market bore a resemblance in differing ways to the conception of real-wage resistance on which the present structuralist theory is based. From their approach they derive a doctrine on the effects of government expenditure, taxation, and public debt that is recognizably structuralist at important points.[6]

In this classical model, the after-tax wage is supposed, following any disturbance, always to return asymptotically toward some invariant level called the "subsistence wage." Hence a tax on wage income or wage payments leads to an increase in the product wage to the employer. As the product wage is the relevant cost of labor, the consequence even in the short run is a decrease in the quantity of labor demanded. In the short run there is also a reduction of the profit rate. In an open economy, the squeeze on profits causes an outflow of capital until the after-tax profit rate is again equal to that overseas. In a closed economy, there is a similar reduction of capital accumulation tending to restore the profit rate. Since the capital stock is reduced, the long-run effect is a further reduction of employment. In both cases, the burden of the tax on labor is ultimately borne by rich consumers and/or landowners.[7]

The main thesis that Smith and Ricardo based on this model is that "too high" a balanced-budget level of public expenditure would drive up the required product wage, as the taxation fell wholly or partially on labor, with the result that employment would fall, followed by capital disinvestment. "The declension [that is, decline] of industry, the decrease of employment for the poor, the diminution of the annual product of the land and labour of the country, have generally been the effects of such taxes," Smith wrote.[8]

A casual reading might lead to the interpretation of the subsistence wage as a rigid equilibrium level of the real wage, departures from which are rather quickly erased with the adjustment of expectations. In that model of wage determination there is no role for the supply of labor except to determine unemployment. If the labor force is taken to be a constant, meaning that the supply of labor in the Marshall-Walras sense is perfectly inelastic with respect to all variables, the implication is that any reduction of employment caused by decrease labor demand is equivalent to an increase of unemployment. This sort of model would follow from a conception of the subsistence wage as a biologically determined wage that the workers require to get to work and to produce efficiently—a level below which it would not be cost-effective for employers to pay.[9] With a contraction of the demand for labor as a result of some adverse shock, workers would be idled, hence unemployed. They would not be capable of working, not at any rate in a cost-effective manner, at the level to which the market-clearing would fall. It is this conception, or specification, of the subsistence-wage mechanism that seems a precursor of the treatment of wage behavior in the theory developed here.

To be faithful to what Smith and Ricardo wrote, however, it is necessary to distinguish between them. Smith did not have real-wage resistance, whether overlooking it or rejecting it. Instead he conceived the subsistence wage entirely as the wage necessary for viability of the population. Smith saw infant mortality as providing a mechanism by which population growth or shrinkage would drive the after-tax wage back to its so-called subsistence level. Ricardo referred to the marriage rate as a mechanism governing the asymptotic behavior of the wage. (But Ricardo later differentiated his view from that of Smith, as discussed below.)[10]

Smith's interpretation of the subsistence wage, and his corresponding specification of the model, was unsatisfactory on many counts. For one, it failed to show how one could account for secular growth of the after-tax wage. By the nineteenth century the wage had long since escaped the orbit of the biological minimum consistent with zero-growth reproduction. For another, the model led to the position that government expenditures that were not "wasteful" from the point of view of the workers would serve as a sort of supplementary wage payment, thus lowering the wage rate that the workers required from work—a view substantially (if not in every case) opposite to the position that would follow from the theory set forth here, in which public expenditures substituting for private insurance and self-help would tend to drive up the optimal incentive wage. Most strikingly, because it assumed that there was no immediate real-wage resistance, only an asymptotic tendency, the model had no place for an immediate employment effect of fiscal shocks.

An irony in this dissatisfaction over Smith's model is that it could have been revised to escape the first limitation, which was as much the cause of its demise as any. He could have foreshadowed a rather important trick in the theory here by supposing that there is a reproduction-rate function that, other things constant, is increasing in the wage, but decreasing in wealth, and homogeneous of degree zero in the two. Then it could have been argued that in the event a shock boosts the demand price of labor, and hence the wage jumps up (by the whole distance needed to maintain employment, as they saw it), reproduction jumps likewise but so does the rate of wealth accumulation. As wealth grows, the wage rate necessary to restore reproduction to the zero-growth level likewise grows, owing to the properties of the reproduction function. A new zero-growth state is approached in which wealth, the wage, and the subsistence wage are all up in the same proportion. This modification of the model would not have remedied the other two defects, though.

Had Smith been pressed to reflect more on how wages are determined in the near term, he might well have come to argue that the wage has to gravitate to the level that the employers find necessary for least-cost production in view of its health, morale, and inducement effects on their employees. He would have seen that such a model could deliver the short-term real-wage resistance necessary for a theory of near-term employment effects of shocks to the demand for labor, which they would have welcomed.

Ricardo, arriving later, had the opportunity to think about the limitations of Smith's formulation. The notion of an incentive wage could have become a part of his thinking, and with it the idea that this required real wage is rather resistant to increases in unemployment, even if it was not a theory with which he would have felt familiar and comfortable, and hence inclined to make explicit. In any case, something did happen in Ricardo's thinking.

It is clear, despite some controversy, that Ricardo ultimately breaks away from Smith's formulation in which the real wage, though demographically stabilized, is always flexible and hence prevents unemployment. Ricardo in the third and final edition of his great work throws real-wage resistance into the model he uses to discuss the short-term effects of certain shocks on unemployment. It is given no explicit foundation but it is clearly there in the famously problematic chapter, "On Machinery."

THE RICARDO CONNECTION

In this chapter Ricardo goes well beyond the political economy of taxation to consider the effects of technical change and capital accumulation. How such shocks affect the demand for labor and hence unemployment according to Ricardo may be compared with the implications of the structuralist theory. In the two-sector structuralist model of the closed economy, it will be recalled, an increase in the capital stock is seen as reducing the real rate of interest and thereby driving up the demand wage and thus, very possibly, employment too, notwithstanding a reverse effect operating through the stock of wealth (as distinct from the income from wealth). In that case, a one-time permanent technical advance triggers a transitory contraction of the employment rate. The theory appears to tilt toward the conclusion that a permanent increase of the rate of technical progress (of Harrod-neutral type) also causes an immediate contraction of employment, followed by an ambiguous after-effect as the subsequent shrinkage of the capital stock as a ratio to augmented labor, a contractionary effect, pulls against the shrinkage of wealth as a ratio to the wage, which is expansionary. What parts does Ricardo anticipate and where does he differ?

Today Ricardo's view of the effects of these shocks on labor demand is remembered largely for its anxious view of technological advances. Ricardo worried that these advances would often be so extremely labor-saving as to generate an absolute decrease in the demand wage, not simply a decline relative to the demand rental on capital. In this way Ricardo evidently expressed his apprehension that technical advances often damaged labor on impact. The modeling of technical progress as always Harrod-neutral in the present development of the structuralist theory has led to the rosier view that one-time advances, if contractionary, are only transiently so. However, Ricardo's glum impression is duplicated by the structuralist theory with regard to a continuous stream of technical progress. There the anticipation of progress in the future at once drives up the real rate of interest required by consumers at a given level of present consumption, with the result that capital values are reduced and hence investment and employment are contracted. The mechanism of so-called job destruction could also be brought in to reinforce the conclusion that steady progress costs something in the form of higher unemployment.

These are different mechanisms from Ricardo's reliance on the factor-saving slant of technical change.

Empirical knowledge about the factor-saving bias of technical change is so scant that little can safely be said on this difference of view. There is little evidence, certainly, that technical advances are usually or frequently very labor-saving. Further, the stylized facts of economic growth continue, as they have done for decades, to support approximate Harrod-neutrality. If there is any weighty evidence to the contrary it is a recent finding that, in Europe at least, technical progress has been capital-saving on the Hicksian definition, hence capital-saving on the Harrod definition in an aggregative framework if the elasticity of substitution is less than one—a deviation in the other direction from neutrality than Ricardo's.[11]

There seems also to be an internal problem in the Ricardian apparatus. If technical progress *is* predominantly very labor-saving, Ricardo must explain how in his model the wage tends to rise over time so as to conform to the stylized facts of secular growth—to the stylization before real wages nearly stopped growing in some countries two decades ago. It is fairly clear he regards the accumulation of a given type of machinery as expansionary for employment, so it can be argued that the same process is sufficiently strong to pull up wages on balance, overcoming the downward push imparted directly by technological progress. Yet Ricardo had not apparently thought about how to avoid the corollary implication of an ever-rising employment rate accompanying the ever-rising wage. The role of wealth or the income from wealth in pushing up the required wage as technical progress and capital accumulation are pulling up the demand wage is not in Ricardo. The machinery chapter fails to imbed its treatment of the short run in a setting of secular growth.

Let us sum up. Ricardo's modeling of real wages and how various shocks drive employment and investment presented puzzles and limitations aplenty. Yet it was unmistakably a structuralist sort of theory—his own idiosyncratic one. Further, the doctrine he moved toward, on the effects of tax rates, the public debt, and the technology, foreshadowed many of the conclusions derived here through models of other structural mechanisms. Ricardo, then, is the outstanding precursor of the structuralist theory of employment.

20

Economic Policies to Which the Structuralist Theory Might Lead

THE body of structuralist models of employment developed in this book raises the important question of what policies governments would do well to adopt toward employment changes that are believed to be caused by long-lived structural shifts in the domestic or global economy. What should countries do when some of them or all of them find themselves in a structural slump or boom?

The American public showed its consternation recently when it perceived that President George Bush, confronted by the evidently structural stagnation of the 1990s, had no more promising and adequate a remedy for it than Herbert Hoover had for the Depression of the 1930s. Readers of this examination of structuralist theory would be likewise consternated if this volume remained silent on the policy question. The issue has to be joined. Yet numerous pitfalls await any attempt at formulating appropriate policy toward structural fluctuations in today's global economy.

What follows is an informal reconnaissance of the terrain, not the construction of a formal model, which can come only at a later stage. A more systematic discussion of the policy issues than the one given here would specify the normative premises of the analysis. The analysis here is tacit about the social-welfare function both to get on with the discussion and because the suggestions and conclusions reached seem unlikely to depend on any special properties of the welfare function.

The purpose of this final chapter, then, is to begin the necessary discussion.

THE PASSIVIST FALLACY

There is a tendency, it must first be noted, a tendency already quite pronounced in Europe, to stymie any efforts to use structuralist employment theory for policy purposes with a misunderstanding.

The position is often taken, both by foes and misguided friends of the structuralist perspective, that if the cause of high unemployment, or for that matter low unemployment, is structural, there is nothing that social and economic policy can do to reduce it.[1] Recommendations by economists regarding the present slump have come to be put into two categories according to that very characteristic. "One [view] is to let stagnation run its course; . . . and that process cannot be artificially rushed. The other argues for an artificial stimulant."[2]

The fallacy in this view is that although the structuralist perspective assumes that the equilibrium path of unemployment is determined by the economy's current structure, however good an approximation that assumption may be, it does not follow that interventions by the government do not alter that structure. The government is part of the structure—it determines the size and composition of public expenditure, the pattern of tax rates, the prospective path of the budgetary deficit, the current stock of public debt, and more.

This error in interpretation brings to mind earlier episodes of misunderstanding over terms. When Wicksell dubbed as the "natural rate of interest" his concept of the rate of interest that enterprises could afford to pay in financing their investment, there was no possibility he could have meant to convey that this interest rate was a pristine element of nature not susceptible to intervention by man. He meant only that it was incapable of being raised or lowered by the central bank. When Friedman coined the term "natural rate of unemployment" he meant only, as the author also meant in his discussions of the same concept, that this equilibrium rate, though evolving and fluctuating with real forces, was invariant to the price level and the inflation rate generated by monetary policy.

A more reasonable position, and perhaps the thought behind the position that the government cannot be expected to combat increases in equilibrium unemployment, is that, although there are things the government can do to make unemployment worse, there are no avenues open to the government by which it can lower unemployment that do not cost too much ground in the pursuit of other objectives. The premise is that the government is initially at a constrained optimum. On that premise, it could then be argued that when a shock occurs, the direction in which the government adjusts its controls in response is of second-order importance; its controls are already in the neighborhood of the optimum. (This is the so-called envelope theorem.)

It would be a new fallacy, however, to conclude that when the structure of the economy shifts unfavorably by a discrete amount, pushing up non-negligibly the equilibrium unemployment, no response by the government is perfectly optimal. Large shocks require correspondingly large policy responses, and the optimal policy-response functions are not flat. Structuralism does not offer grounds for passivity in policymaking.

There is some truth to a broader proposition, that the optimal response to shocks is conservative in a well-defined sense. Suppose that the social payoff to employment is concave, the function giving the cost of the policy instrument setting convex. Then, even without any consideration of risk, the optimal response does not go as far as to restore the employment rate from its post-impact level, resulting before any policy response, all the way back to its pre-shock level. The optimal response is calculated to return the employment partway to its original level.[3] If there is a feeling among some that optimal structuralist policy would show very little responsiveness to shocks, the assumption underlying it may be that the marginal cost of stepping up the policy instrument is sharply increasing.

The real problems on the structuralist agenda are the identification of the appropriate governmental instruments to use in responding to shocks. We may as well go straight to the case of open economies joined together by the global capital- and tradable-goods markets.

If a shock, internal or external, causes some countries to suffer a higher equilibrium unemployment path, there are a number of countermeasures that any of these countries, acting alone, could take to reduce its unemployment. Some of these measures are reminiscent of Keynesian doctrine. A cut of direct tax rates (which are predominantly on labor income), government spending held constant, we found to be expansionary, both theoretically and empirically. Empirically it seems to be the case that an increase in public expenditure across the board, with direct taxes as a ratio to income unchanged, serves to generate at least a transient expansion. Some consideration should be given also to global balanced-budget cutbacks, which structuralist models incline us to view as globally expansionary, contrary to the Keynesian view. A non-Keynesian sort of measure, employment subsidies, also warrants a close look.

20.1 The Trouble with Unilateral Keynesian Therapies

To the Keynesian remedies there is a structuralist objection, a traditional anti-Keynesian objection, and an internationalist objection.

THE IMPORTANCE OF THE STRUCTURE OF THE RESPONSE

Public spending and tax cuts used as a tool against structural slumps are not without structural hazards. Governments make individual decisions on individual expenditures, not across-the-board spending decisions. In the Keynesian view, every dollar of resource-using public expenditure, no matter to what goods or services it is directed, is equally expansionary as any other dollar of public expenditure, and, somewhat similarly, each transfer payment is expansionary in proportion to its impact on consumption demand. But in the structuralist perspective, some expenditures would have far less impact on the derived demand for labor than others—purchases of tradable goods from the consumer industries, for example, and purchases that would generate little anti-protective real appreciation. A similar problem afflicts tax-rate reductions. Possibly all of these have a transient expansionary effect through their impact on domestic spending and thus the real exchange rate and ultimately markups; but not all have the same effect on the real demand price of labor and the real supply price of labor through their impact on relative prices and the mix of after-tax earned and unearned income.

THE PROBLEM OF TIME INCONSISTENCY

These two kinds of policy responses, both Keynesian-looking, are also subject to a familiar anti-Keynesian objection: the enlargement of the deficit stores up trouble for the future. At one level this objection ought to carry little weight. If there are endogenous mechanisms tending to restore employment at least partway to its former level, and these self-stabilizing mechanisms are not necessarily short-circuited by the government's response to the shock, it seems plausible to think that some sacrifice in future welfare is justified to ease the burdensomeness of the present. At a deeper level, however, there are grounds for worry. In its approval of deficit spending, the Keynesian school unleashed the perplexing time-inconsistency problem. The problem is that the policy of temporary fiscal stimulus may do more harm than good if it is not vanishing (or, in a growing economy, if it is not declining fast enough) as the slump comes to an end through its own endogenous dynamics; but the benefit of each year's stimulus is front-loaded, the costs in the form of debt burdens deferred, so the current benefit of prolonging the stimulus may make it politically infeasible to reduce the stimulus as much as is required for the policy to yield an overall gain. This difficulty becomes acute if the endogenous dynamics turn out to make the slump wholly or largely permanent, for then the pain of withdrawing from the fiscal stimulus has to occur in a setting of a continued slump, not recovered (or returning) prosperity.

Absolute judgments may be dangerous here. Not all countries have been unable to resist temptation all the time, so it is not obvious that there would be a gain from a self-denying ordinance against deficit spending, even assuming that such a clause could be strictly or satisfactorily enforced. And there might be some damage from cynically passing legislation known to be difficult to enforce. Still, if there is a way of supplying the desired expansionary impact without building in problems for the future, that would be all to the good.

ADVERSE EXTERNALITIES FOR THE REST OF THE WORLD

From the structuralist perspective, the most serious objection to borrowing the Keynesian responses—a general spending increase and a general tax cut, not to mention a balanced-budget general increase in spending—is that such unilateral actions by a large country or a large collection of small countries may have adverse repercussions on the rest of the world. Expenditure increases (in the present case government expenditures) that, in a one-sector model, fall upon the output of firms or, in a two-sector model, fall on the output of the consumer-good sector or directly on the services of labor have a positive impact on the real interest rate. Tax-rate cuts may also have a net positive effect on the rate of interest. The consequent upward push to world real interest rates has the beggar-thy-neighbor effect of causing a contraction of employment abroad. When many countries engage in the stimulus, the effect is also to cancel some of the expansionary effect or, in many cases, to more than offset the effect that each national stimulus would have had if it had been unaccompanied by similar stimuli overseas.

By way of clarification it should be admitted that a decrease of employment in the rest of the world does not in every conceivable case represent a loss of welfare. If, as a result of a boom overseas, employment there could be considered too high, a policy response to the contractionary effect in the home country or countries under discussion that drives up real interest rates around the world some more—sending the ball back to the other court, as it were—could actually be regarded as beneficial, by cooling off the boom overseas. But, as an empirical matter, there seem to be few booms that, even in the country of origin, cause more harm than good. In any case, a clear social cost of the "redoubling" of real interest rates by countries responding with Keynesian fiscal countermeasures is that it puts a further burden on third countries that are not able or willing to adopt the same policy response. In concrete terms, had Europe in the 1980s imitated some of the fiscal stimuli to investment and to consumption enacted by the United States—not all of the tax changes merely fueled demand, of course—the result would have been a worse rise of the real interest rates confronting Latin America, Eastern Europe, and indeed the whole rest of the world.

It is immediately necessary to recognize that countries in the rest of the world will have less to complain about if the country adopting the Keynesian remedy can be seen as merely offsetting a contractionary impulse in private consumption demand at home, for then there is no clear net positive effect from the demand shock and the policy response taken together. The same is evidently true of a domestic shock in the form of a reduced foreign demand for some country-specific export. A net positive beggar-thy-neighbor effect arises when the contraction of employment in the home country is the result of an external quasi-cost shock operating through the global capital market to raise the real rate of interest—the shock taken up by Fitoussi and Phelps. This sort of shock is pretty plainly among the major disturbances, perhaps the largest disturbance, to have struck Europe, Canada, and Latin America in the 1980s, and this same kind of shock may have turned about on the United States in the 1990s, so it is an important enough case to be considered.

On this analysis, the near-universal tendency to look toward Japan for unilateral fiscal stimulus whenever the rest of the world finds its employment rate sagging is utterly misguided. The sole exception that it is possible to see at this stage in the development of the theory is that an increase of public expenditure on *capital goods* tends to lower the real rate of interest, not to raise it. That result of the closed-economy two-sector model strongly suggests that when an open economy engages in increased public expenditure on a nontradable capital good, it does not thereby raise the world real rate of interest, it reduces the interest rate. But the introduction of customer markets into the model may be capable of overturning that result. Empirically we found (without reporting) that public expenditures in a country, both military and nonmilitary, generate a real exchange appreciation, and global public expenditures of both types raise the world real rate of interest.

Notwithstanding these remarks, one can only be puzzled that, in the 1990s, several countries have responded to contractionary forces with accelerated measures to *cut* their budgetary deficits. It would be prudent to postpone these measures in the hope that the external climate improves.

20.2 Helpful Unilateral Measures

There are two measures to combat a structural slump that do not have (not as apparently, at any rate) the consequences for national wealth in the future and for real interest rates in the rest of the world that the Keynesian responses exhibit.

The anti-Keynesian balanced-budget variant. Keynesian habits of thinking direct us to conceive of a balanced-budget expansion of the public sector as a plausible way to end or moderate a durable structural slump. But this might be a counterproductive response even when one country acts alone. Although the net effect may not be theoretically determinate, the empirical experience seems to be that balanced-budget increases of public spending are contractionary—an anti-Haavemo-Wallich effect— not expansionary, as Keynesian economics was shown to imply by Haavelmo and Wallich. The contractionary effect of the tax-rate increase seems to be sufficient to outweigh the expansionary effect of the increased government spending, at least from the medium-term and long-term perspective of equilibrium theory.

Thus structuralist theory points to *balanced-budget reductions* of tax rates and spending as a candidate for deployment against long-term slumps. Such a policy response to a domestic slump would have the virtue, as advertised above, that it would not be at the expense of the national wealth owned by future generations. Also, while tending to restore employment at home (provided the impact on domestic supply outweighs the impact on domestic demand), it would operate to reduce, not raise, the real rate of interest overseas. Hence it would not have the drawback of Keynesian fiscal stimulus to demand that, if the domestic contraction is the result of an upward impulse to real interest rates overseas, like-situated countries not adopting the same policy would suffer an even worse contraction or, if they all were following that policy, their joint stimulus would be largely self-cancelling. However, the balanced-budget policy of reverse stimulus does not escape another of the difficulties considered above, and there is a new difficulty to which Keynesian policies of stimulus were not subject.

The distinctive difficulty with that policy is that its *near-term* employment effect through the Keynesian monetary mechanism will work in the undesired direction to contract employment rather than to expand it. The answer to that conundrum would seem to lie in monetary policy. If the balanced-budget fiscal shift is accompanied by militantly easier money, the Keynesian countereffect can be held in check.

The other difficulty, encountered by across-the-board stimulus as well, is that the magnitudes of the effects of such a policy response may be seriously misgauged, and even the direction of effect could depart from the average. Even over the medium term, therefore, there would have to be adjustments in the policy dosage, especially the first time the policy is tried. In the near term, just how much monetary stimulus would be required (measured in units of the money supply or even the nominal rate of interest) to offset the counterproductive Keynesian demand effect of the fiscal contraction would also be unknown; it too might be contingent upon the exact structure of the cutbacks in public expenditure and reduction in tax rates. Such monetary-fiscal maneuvers would greatly increase uncertainty, thus dampening business plans for expansion and thus depressing present output (through the three asset channels). For a country to adopt such a strategy alone would require considerable courage, and only political leaders already in favor of such a shrinkage of the government are apt to be attracted to it.

A role for employment subsidies. A more reliable policy response serving to restore employment following an external cost shock while not having a clear tendency to further drive up real interest rates overseas is the application of employment subsidies. These may be financed by across-the-board increases in tax rates.[4] There is already a moral-philosophic case for employment subsidies targeted at the low end of the wage scale to bring the rewards for work not having a high scarcity value more nearly in line with the requirements of economic justice.[5] The suggestion here is that, with a system of employment subsidies in place, it would be natural to add a cyclical supplement that varies with disturbances to macroequilibrium in an employment-stabilizing direction.

There has been recent discussion of the idea to permit jobless workers to transfer their unemployment compensation entitlement to enterprises willing to employ them. A proposal by Dennis Snower would allow transfers to a firm equal to its net increase in employment.[6]

20.3 Thinking about International Coordination

The safer course may well be an international policy approach rather than a unilateral approach. Two international approaches may be distinguished, however, one involving coordinated national behavior enforced through multilateral agreement or understanding, the other involving bilateral agreements resembling trade agreements between pairs of countries.

The Bilateral Approach

Until an appropriate and effective multilateral approach can be organized, hopes for a better coordination of national policies must depend upon spontaneous deals struck by one country with another. Much of what passes for multilateral cooperation may be the product instead of such bilateral (or in rare cases trilateral or quadrilateral) interactions.

A large country finding one of its policies damaging to another country can generally modify the policy that causes harm in return for a modification of another policy by the latter country in such a way that there is a mutual gain. Both give something to get something more valuable. Through the perception of such opportunities we can expect that a large country will try to persuade each of several large countries that it can afford to make a larger concession with each additional country willing to contribute a concession of its own.

The following may serve to illustrate the possibilities of reaching a mutual gain—an Edgeworth improvement—by trading policy concessions. Consider a two-country world in which one large country, as a result of some exogenous cut in tax rates or increase in government spending, is driving up the world real rate of interest and thus contracting employment in the other large country. Then there may be room for a mutual gain through a concession by the second country, such as the enactment of increased employment subsidies or a reduction of investment tax credits (or other competitive pro-growth measures operating at the expense of foreign countries). This would have the effect of lowering the real interest rate and increasing growth in the first country, in return for the first country's agreement to scale back its tax cuts or its public spending, which would serve to moderate the fall of employment in the second country.

Alternatively, in the same two-country situation, the countries might find a mutual gain through a scaling back by the first country of its tax cut or its public spending in return for steps in the same direction—tax increases or public spending cuts—by the other country. The essential idea is to ensure that a sort of trade in policy-instrument settings takes place to the point where the marginal conditions are such that no country has an interest in offering a further concession to obtain one in return.[7]

It would not be easy for a global planner or the architect of an international system of coordination to come close to the bilateral, or Edge-worthian, efficiency that bilateral bargains in such a setting might well achieve. The countries themselves will usually know best where their own benefits and costs lie, though political considerations may seriously distort the use that the countries make of their free choice.

Yet not much in the way of a satisfactory world order can be grounded on such spontaneous bilateral exchanges of political concessions. In the global economy of the present age, after the three largest economies, the output and wealth of the next country trail off rapidly; about half the output of the advanced economies is produced by these much smaller countries. The typical country among these is too small to take individual actions that would affect perceptibly the real interest rates and real currency values of the largest countries, so there is nothing a small country could do to win a perceptible concession from the large country rocking the global-economy boat. Further, any of the larger countries would find its incentives in feigning a lack of interest in a policy bargain that would cost it a concession in order to be a free rider.

THE MULTILATERAL APPROACH

The desirability of a system in which nations could bind themselves to act multilaterally is easy enough to illustrate. Suppose the block of countries suffering from reduced employment owing to some real shock comprise *all* or at least the preponderant part of the world economy. It makes sense in that event for them to respond by *reducing* the (possibly enlarged) levels of public expenditures (those falling on the consumer-goods industries at any rate), not raising them, in order to cause a reduction of the world real interest rate and thus a net increase in employment rates. The competitive compensatory government spending in the 1980s may have been a mal-functioning of the world economy as bad as the competitive devaluations of the 1930s, the ill effects of which seem less certain now to many than they once did. It is clear, at any rate, that international arrangements that build in a *stimulus* to consumption or investment spending in response to a fallen level of employment are not going to be part of a satisfactory global policy system to treat slumps.

The operational question is what incentive-compatible arrangements can be drawn up that would do some good. There could well be some skepticism that the governments of the world can be expected to be capable of inducing themselves to behave multilaterally, taking into account their effects on the rest of the world, rather than unilaterally. The Bretton

Woods system lasted little more than two decades, and other schemes have not gotten off the drawing board.

In the prescription for multilateral control of employment levels and nominal exchange rates emerging from the Bretton Woods agreement, each country of the cooperative system is obligated to fix its exchange rate with the dollar and, having both a fiscal and a monetary instrument available, is at the same time free to control the level of economic activity. The obligatory part of the system could have been sustained in various ways: by guarantees of international lending or cost-sharing to encourage a member's support of exchange-rate fixity in the face of currency weakness or else by sanctions a member would anticipate if it failed to maintain exchange-rate fixity—except under the circumstances delineated by so-called fundamental disequilibrium. In practice, little or no cost-sharing or sanctions seem to have been provided, and in fact most currencies saw their exchange rates against the dollar adjusted numerous times (until the weakness of the dollar itself caused the system to fall).

The system embodied in the famous Swan diagram is, in a way, rather isomorphic. Here each member of the group is to use two tools, one the exchange rate and the other the level of public expenditure, to achieve balance on current account, called external balance, and "full employment," called internal balance.[8] External balance is here the obligatory target, since it is not generally in the self-interest of a particular country, while internal balance means the employment level that is best for the country. (Here as in the Bretton Woods system only $N - 1$ of the N countries can have an external target, the Nth country needing to accept passively the outcome of their actions.) Apparently we are to conceive of the countries in the group as having an instrument they are willing to divert from its normal use to that of a disciplinary device for rewarding obedience or punishing disobedience to this obligation.[9] This system, apparently, has never been instituted on a world scale, though some readers may find its balanced-trade feature reminiscent of the old European Payments Union.

These models of international cooperation will strike any reader abreast of modern macroeconomics as quaint in their innocence of the natural-rate hypothesis and even of the Phillips curve. (As already noted, their assumption of international rewards and sanctions to encourage obedience to international obligations is problematic. Yet these survive as illustrations of the continuing intuitive attraction of the idea of more cooperative international relations among countries in the same global boat.)

Is there a loosely analogous system that can be used for coordination of the *equilibrium* (or *natural*) levels of employment and other *real* indicators in the global economy? There do seem to be a number of such systems, and perhaps the class of schemes pointed to below are worth talking about. In bringing up these schemes I do not mean to be making a proposal. (How much more comfortable to examine others' proposals!) The sketches below are ideas for discussion and, if not rejected, for modification or, if rejected, for use as stepping stones to better ideas. A technical remark is that in these schemes the decentralized allocation of each tool to one target or desideratum is more an expository device than an essential feature.

To begin, consider the following system: Monetary or (nominal) exchange-rate policy would be allocated to the achievement of a monetary objective such as nominal price or wage stability or exchange-rate stability; this is the Keynes-Friedman dimension and is of little relevance to the choice of the nonmonetary policy instruments if they are chosen solely or mainly for the medium-term future. Total tax revenue would be planned to balance the government budget; this formulation may be thought of as a proxy for a fuller analysis of the Ramsey problem of optimum national saving. The aggregate level of public expenditure would be guided by the Samuelsonian calculus of current public goods as seen by the legislators; capital expenditures by the public sector on education, research, equipment, and so forth would be determined by the usual cost-benefit tests; and the configuration of transfer payments would answer to the political dictates of the welfare state. Two instruments or classes of instruments are left to attend to two remaining goals. An *investment subsidy or tax,* such as the investment tax credit, would be geared to the *external imbalance* as measured by the deficit or surplus in the international current account; if foreign countries ran current-account deficits, they would be expected to increase their investment taxes or reduce their investment subsidies to moderate their external deficits, and those with the current-account surpluses would be expected to moderate their external surpluses by the opposite measures. *Subsidies for the employment of labor,* especially low-wage labor, would then be used to modify—rather than to restore to some predetermined norm—the current *equilibrium rate of unemployment.*

The direct part of the impact of, say, decreased fiscal stimulus to invest in a country is to decrease its international current-account deficit both by diminishing the inflow of imported capital equipment and, in lowering the prospective real rate of return on capital, by engendering a real depreciation, thus generally discouraging imports and encouraging exports; the consequent reduction of tax rates to keep the budget balanced would have an indirect impact undoing some of its distortionary supply-side effects and thus working in the opposite direction but not by enough, it is assumed, to offset the direct impact. This is the obligatory part of the package. Each country is asked to moderate the burden it places on the others through the world capital market when shocks cause it to draw upon the balance of saving over investment occurring in the rest of the world. Bulges in the current-account deficit are to be viewed with the same opprobrium that used to attach to swollen surpluses in the Keynesian era. The "locomotive" of investment and dissaving is seen as pulling in the wrong direction.

The impact of increased subsidies to employment is to increase the rate of employment, provided that the financing through higher tax rates is not specially tilted toward labor income so strongly as to have a nearly offsetting effect. It might be noted that there is no beggar-my-neighbor effect of such a subsidy. The employment-expanding balanced-budget increase in the employment subsidy rates by one country, in causing a real depreciation there, operates to reduce markups and thus to expand employment in the rest of the world; the increase in supply is greater than the increase in absorption, which (antithetically to Keynesianism) induces a competitive increase in supply abroad.

How would such a system have worked in the past? To respond to the current-account deficit resulting from the cut of tax rates and the increased military expenditure in the 1980s, the United States would have had to reduce its fiscal stimuli to investment, not increase them, in order to lower the upward pressure on real interest rates in the rest of the world; the effect of that in turn on the investment subsidies abroad would drive the current-account deficit only partway back toward where it was. There would be a reciprocal concession worth something to the United States in the form of an increase of employment subsidies by the other countries, which in spurring supply more than demand overseas would serve to lower real interest rates. Somewhat similarly, events in Germany leading to increased public expenditure and private investment demand in the 1990s would prompt it to enact an investment tax or reduce investment tax credits in order to cushion the impact on real interest rates and employment in the rest of the world.

The above system is illustrative of a set of systems having some similarities. Another version would allocate to the aggregate *balanced-budget public expenditure level,* rather than the investment tax credit, the task of moderating the current-account balance, thus responding to a domestic demand surge with austerity in public goods rather than in investment; the investment stimulus would be freed to pursue a domestic goal. Yet another version would aim to moderate the current account by adjusting the *mix of public expenditure* between consumption expenditure and capital expenditure; again, employment subsidies are left to serve the domestic objective.

The basic property of all these approaches is that some national policy instrument is drafted in the interest of the community of nations, requiring a departure by that instrument from the setting, or level, that would best serve the country's self-interest, given the actions (as distinct from the threats of reward and punishments) of the other countries. The intention is always to dampen shocks to the global capital market, thus slowing its reallocations of capital—but not checking them.

These sketches of a policy system among countries made interdependent by global capital and goods markets, if it has any attraction, will have to be followed up by more extensive analysis. A question needing investigating is whether, for any of these systems, the particular one-to-one allocation of instruments to targets indicated would exhibit desirable stability properties. Another complication is that, if any of the dynamic models employed in this volume is adopted as the setting for such an analysis, an intertemporal approach to optimal cooperative policy will be required.

Once the thrust of the above schemes is understood, the imagination races ahead to others, some of which may be superior. A tax on current-account deficits, the proceeds to go for paying a bounty on current-account surpluses, would appear to be as good or better a way to discourage drawing upon the saving of the rest of the world and to encourage supplying net saving to the rest of the world. Another scheme, in imitation of the TIP plan to hold down wage increases, would require signatories to the international agreement to purchase enough one-dollar rights to run a deficit of the desired size from those willing to run surpluses; but it is not obvious how to make such a scheme effective since, if it is actual surpluses that must be paid for with rights, there will always be just enough rights supplied by deficit countries to meet the demand for rights at a zero price. In contrast, the former scheme imposes, through an agreed international administration, a positive tax price to be paid for deficits even if there is no excess demand for them.

20.4 Commentary

It is time to summarize. Whatever the multilateral system to be considered, employment subsidies or some instrument performing like them seem the most cost-effective means to counteract low levels of employment. If employment subsidies are not convenient, there are a few other instruments that could substitute for increased employment subsidies: A balanced-budget cut in transfer payments is perhaps the best candidate, especially those welfare-type transfer payments that make working and holding a job less desired; an across-the-board cut in public expenditures is also a plausible prospect; and the mix of public expenditure between labor-intensive and capital-intensive goods is another, though somewhat risky vehicle. There is some appeal to requiring the public to give up transfers and public goods in the interest of expanding employment when the unemployment rate is enlarged—certainly if the slump is seen to be temporary and perhaps even if not.[10]

What is paramount in any case is that across-the-board *increases* in government spending, and especially balanced-budget increases, are *not* to be used since they have the beggar-thy-neighbor effect of lowering employment abroad while raising it at home—the latter, generally speaking, by a lesser amount than the former—so that if all countries engage in that policy response to low employment, the consequence is a further general reduction of employment rates.

There are grounds for hope, however, that the choice of a policy response to low employment rates will prove of less critical importance than it has in recent years. In future decades the problem of high unemployment may abate. Once real interest rates fall back to the neighborhood of 3 percent, around which they seemed to center for many decades, workers will not have such plump cushions, their own and their relatives', provided by the various incomes from wealth as exist today. In a book that keeps looking over its shoulder at Keynes, it is impossible not to recall his prophecy that years of full-employment policy would bring about a steady fall of real interest incomes (and thus the "euthanasia" of the rentier class). That has not happened, at first because the Second World War and the postwar population explosion intervened and most recently because of the entry onto the global economy of the transformed economies of Asia and now the emergent economies in Latin America and perhaps soon those of Eastern Europe. But as these last stages in the close of the global frontier are completed, real interest rates and, with them, real incomes from wealth will very likely subside to the old norm and quite possibly fall to much lower levels.

At the same time we may at last be in sight of the day when public policy will shift from the social-insurance programs that have been the historical mission of the welfare state to programs for economic justice. Unemployment insurance and all the other social-insurance programs that tax away wage income and that undermine work as a way of providing self-esteem will be dismantled and the savings will be put into raising the wage rates paid for the contributions to society of the less advantaged members of the labor force.

If and when the decline of real interest rates and of the welfare state come to pass, economic life will center more nearly on earning wages and remaining employed. Workers will be attracted by decent rates of pay, and the reduced flow of unearned income and transfer income in lieu of wage income will offer less of a temptation not to work. When that happens, employment will have a far more significant place in the minds of the population, and the biases toward high turnover, shirking, and the rest, and hence toward swollen rates of unemployment, will be far weaker than in the present day.

The above scenario seems likely if the ideas here are right and they are perceived as right. The reception given to new ideas is not certain, however. In his peroration to that other (and more exciting) book, which keeps hanging over this one, Keynes called upon readers persuaded by his theory to take heart from the thought that the world is "ruled by ideas and little else." A splendid thought, and a necessary refutation to marxists and reductionist physicists who had no room for the mind in their philosophies. Yet it overlooked two sorts of error in the competition of economic doctrines.

Some theories owe their influence to the convenience of the doctrine they support and they may go on being quite influential no matter how little truth there is in them. Keynesian economics was very nearly the official theory in many governments for decades in part because of its rhetoric justifying their targeted spending programs as a support of effective demand. Supply-side macroeconomics was embraced by some governments in part at any rate as a rationale for reductions in tax rates they sought largely for other reasons—to raise the disposable incomes of voters and to deprive legislatures of revenue for spending.

The other error is the unwillingness to discover the truth in a theory. The calculus of self-interest does not draw uncommitted researchers to the testing of new theories for a simple reason. Even a small innovation along the lines of an already prevailing theory will be repaid in a huge shift of citations from the outmoded treatments to the new technique, while there are hardly any current references that an entrant into research on an untested theory can hope to divert to himself. (This is perhaps why the most central questions often go unstudied for years.) The best chance for an untested theory arises when no existing theory enjoys hegemony over the others, when the beliefs of the profession are splintered over several existing theories.

So Keynes's magnificent observation is a half-truth, though an important one. The world is ruled by the competition of ideas, but in that competition the race does not always belong to the swiftest.

Changing circumstances offer the theory here a good chance at a hearing, however. With the profession now so large and econometric skills so widespread, the supply of resources to test the theory has never been so great. In addition, the demand for a new theory in macroeconomics is stronger than at any time since the 1930s. The Keynesian theory has lost its hegemony and no other theory has managed yet to take its place. Macroeconomic research is therefore much more open to a new approach than it has been for decades. Hence there is reason to hope that if the structuralist theory of employment developed here has a great deal of truth to it, much of that truth will be ferreted out and with time be recognized.

Notes

Introduction

1. John Maynard Keynes, *The General Theory of Employment, Interest and Money* (London: Macmillan, 1936).
2. Jean-Paul Fitoussi and Edmund S. Phelps, *The Slump in Europe* (Oxford: Basil Blackwell, 1988).

1. Modern Equilibrium Theory

1. Except when the context is expressly that of the classical period, from Hume and Smith to Mill, the term *classical* should be understood to include the neoclassical period as well. Writing *(neo)classical* serves to emphasize that neither the neoclassical period alone nor the early classical period alone is being referred to but, rather, the union of the two. (Yet, as Chapter 19 argues, some early classicals, at least Ricardo, were not consistently nonmodern, especially regarding the employment relationship.)
2. Kenneth J. Arrow, "Uncertainty and the Welfare Economics of Medical Care," *American Economic Review,* 53, December 1963, 941–973.
3. William S. Vickrey, "Counterspeculation, Auctions and Competitive Sealed Tenders," *Journal of Finance,* 16, March 1961, 8–37.
4. Edmund S. Phelps, "Money-Wage Dynamics and Labor-Market Equilibrium," *Journal of Political Economy,* 76, August 1968, Part 2, 678–711. A revised version, which was less focused, appeared in Phelps et al., *Microeconomic Foundations of Employment and Inflation Theory* (New York: Norton, 1970), 124–166.
5. It could also be recognized that the employee faces the symmetrical hazard: The company that the employee has incurred various investment costs to join and adjust to may abolish his job and thus force him to incur new adjustment costs at another firm. The worker hopes the firm will not dismiss employees except for cause (the employee is costing more or producing less than the industry standards) but knows it is usually difficult to enforce such an understanding. What can be done to reduce the hazard? Certainly offering to work at a concessionary wage is not the solution. The solution discussed in the implicit contract literature, it appears, is a policy of

the firm to guarantee steady employment until predetermined retirement at a wage for active duty fixed beforehand along with another payment to apply during any temporary layoff.

6. Note that in the presence of frictions in hiring and recruiting, the process now called *matching*, the excess supply referred to in the text can coexist with excess demand—unemployment accompanied by vacancies. Hence the equilibrium need not exhibit *net* excess supply, as overemphasized in the paper.

7. Phelps, "Money-Wage Dynamics," p. 686. The argument here why the equilibrium unemployment rate is positive was not put as clearly or emphatically, perhaps, as it ought to have been. A clear treatment of the same idea, in a somewhat remote context, is found in Joseph E. Stiglitz, "Wage Determination and Unemployment in LDCs," *Quarterly Journal of Economics*, 88, May 1974, 194–227. A later paper expressing what I wanted to say is Steven C. Salop, "A Model of the Natural Rate of Unemployment," *American Economic Review*, 69, March 1979, 117–25.

8. Guillermo A. Calvo, "Quasi-Walrasian Models of Unemployment," *American Economic Review*, 69, May 1979, 102–108, and Samuel Bowles, "A Marxian Theory of Unemployment," lecture at Columbia University, April 1979.

9. For a much broader discussion of wage policy in relation to personnel staffing, see Andrew Weiss, *Efficiency Wages* (Princeton, N.J.: Princeton University Press, 1991). As Weiss uses the term *efficiency wages*, it includes wage policy to address the adverse-selection problem as well as incentive wages to deal with quitting, shirking, alcoholism, and absenteeism.

10. With respect to shirking, one answer may be that there is always the penalty of demotion available to penalize the higher-ups while the lowlier employees can only be penalized with dismissal from positions that pay above the market-clearing level, the possibility of short-term fines aside, so a smaller elevation of the wage results at the upper end of the salary scale. Another answer may be that the productivity of an executive is relatively observable, even though notoriously difficult to measure with precision. With regard to quitting, it could be that the elevation of the wage rates that occurs to deter quitting of the higher-ups prompts a smaller cutback of their employment than it would for a homogeneous work force, owing to the importance of being unimportant or because the psychic costs of fitting in at a new firm are greater for them than for persons doing work that is relatively homogeneous across firms.

2. Contrary Postulates of the Neoclassical Schools

1. This chapter can be skipped by the reader without loss of continuity.

2. See for example George J. Stigler, *The Theory of Price*, 3d ed. (New York: Macmillan, 1962).

3. A modern critic of this defense would point to the difficulty every owner would have in convincing workers that value was being received in return for such a wage reduction, and the further difficulty of workers in keeping abreast of the identity and fire experience of every factory facility and factory owner.

4. There seems to be no widely cited paper expressing such a position. See, however, Lorne Carmichael, "Can Unemployment Be Involuntary: Comments," *American Economic Review* 75, December 1985, 1213–1214, and a somewhat similar criti-

cism in Olivier Blanchard and Stanley Fischer, *Macroeconomics* (Cambridge, Mass.: MIT Press, 1988).

5. A sometimes cited discussion of various aspects of the theory of prosocial behavior by several economists and philosophers is Edmund S. Phelps, ed., *Altruism, Morality and Economic Theory* (New York: Russell Sage Foundation, 1975). Recent advances can be found in two essays: Robert H. Frank, *Passion within Reason* (New York: Norton, 1989), and Heinz Hollaender, "A Social Exchange Approach to Voluntary Cooperation," *American Economic Review*, 80, December 1990, 1157–1167.

3. The Labor-Market Equilibrium Locus in Modern Models

1. See for example John Hicks, *The Crisis of Keynesian Economics* (Oxford: Basil Blackwell, 1974).

2. Jeffrey D. Sachs, "Wages, Profits and Macroeconomic Adjustment: A Comparative Study," *Brookings Papers on Economic Activity*, 1979:2, 269–319. The paper argues that the degree of real wage resistance, a static concept, or possibly the degree of real wage stickiness, a dynamic concept, can explain the extent of the decline of employment from shocks assumed to have a nonmonetary component.

3. Steven C. Salop, "A Model of the Natural Rate of Unemployment," *American Economic Review*, 69, March 1979, 117–125.

4. Carl Shapiro and Joseph Stiglitz, "Equilibrium Unemployment as a Discipline Device," *American Economic Review*, 74, June 1984, 433–444.

5. The employment rate here and throughout this volume means one minus the unemployment rate.

6. An example that arises immediately is that in the formulation of Salop, a permanent positive productivity shock, as it pulls up the labor demand curve, simultaneously pushes up the equilibrium wage-setting curve because it raises the opportunity cost of diverting employees to training activities, and thus raises the cost to the firm imposed by an employee's quitting; in fact the two curves shift up equally, driving up the wage in equal proportion to labor productivity and leaving firms' hiring rate and the economy's employment rate invariant to the productivity improvement. The Salop and Stiglitz models of labor-market equilibrium conditions do not establish, contrary impressions notwithstanding, that the natural rate is *generally* driven down by shocks pulling up the derived demand for labor and thus lifting the real wage, since the wage-setting curve is not generally invariant to shocks that shift the labor demand curve.

7. A better approximation is derived in Richard Layard, Stephen Nickell, and Richard Jackman, *Unemployment: Macroeconomic Performance and the Labour Market* (Oxford: Oxford University Press, 1991).

8. The reason for not displaying a quit-rate equation is to escape the need for additional notation, namely a symbol for the quit rate.

9. Placing the parameter Λ in a qualitative, unspecified way in the T function has the advantage that we have the option to shut it off if we like. For example, a productivity advance that increases only Λ must increase the opportunity cost of allocating a given number of employees to training recruits. A productivity advance that in-

creases Λ and simultaneously increases the productivity of trainers in the same proportion would not shift up the T function.

10. As the previous chapter argued, the employee will shy away from the ideal neoclassical solution of paying a deposit, returnable with interest at the end of lifetime employment in the event the employee did not quit. In such a solution the incidence of the training tax is divided between labor and firms, with no unemployment arising as a by-product.

11. This maximand may be expressed as

$$vE^i - [v^iN^i + T(\zeta(\cdot)E^i, E^i)] + q[h^i - \zeta(v^i, (1 - u)v^e, y^w)]$$

a Hamiltonian function in which q denotes the shadow price applied to the rate of growth of trained employees.

12. The minimand here differs from the maximand specified earlier in the paragraph only by a constant, ΛE^i. Hence the first-order conditions for an extremum are identical in the two problems.

13. There will be some interest in relating these conditions from the quitting model to the so-called elasticity condition in the shirking model. If $E(y, x)$ denotes the elasticity of y with respect to x, the first-order condition can be written

$$1 = -E(\zeta, v^i)E(T, \tau)(T/v^iE^i)$$

Notionally, the wage is increased by successive equal one-percent amounts, each one increasing the wage bill by one percent, until the percent savings in turnover costs weighted by the ratio of turnover costs to wage costs has fallen to one.

14. A small point is that the logic of the model does not require the economy's employment rate, $1 - u$, equal E/L, since employment does not have quite the same meaning in the two contexts. If a nonnegligible fraction of employed workers were in training, hence not yet functional, because training was optimally spread out over an appreciable interval of time, a discrepancy would arise between $1 - u$, or N/L, on the one hand and E/L. This possibility is foreclosed in the present formulation, which means the training is instantaneous, though requiring massive training input.

15. A glossary of symbols used can be found at the rear of the book. Note that L, the number of workers, includes the unemployed as well as the employed workers.

16. The linear specification just examined leaves room for the quitting behavior to depend upon income from nonwage income as well. Allowing back into the picture for a moment the income from wealth, y^w, would fortify the implication of a positive slope: In the numerator, as long as y^w is increasing in $1 - u$, we have $\zeta_{13}y^w_{1-u} < 0$ if $\zeta_{13} < 0$ just as $\zeta_{12} < 0$—that is, if increased income from wealth potentiates the marginal effectiveness of an increased wage just as an increase of expected wages elsewhere do. Hence the numerator, taken with the minus sign, is positive on this account as well. In the denominator, with $\zeta_{13} < 0$, we have another positive element there too, since y^w is unambiguously decreasing in v. Hence, in this much-studied linear case, even after introducing income from wealth, the slope of the equilibrium wage locus is positive.

17. It is easy to check that, drawing on the above assumptions, the elasticity of equilibrium v with respect to $1 - u$ is equal to zero at zero employment rate and goes to infinity as the unemployment rate approaches zero.

18. Indeed it has come to be argued that this is the truth about the equilibrium wage curve—that it is quasi-vertical, for if it were not the secular productivity growth that generates nonvanishing growth of real wages would imply an ever-rightward move up the wage curve, hence a secular tendency toward lower unemployment that recessions can only temporarily interrupt. See Lawrence H. Summers, *Understanding Unemployment* (Cambridge, Mass.: MIT Press, 1990). The answer to this criticism provided by the theory is implicit in the wealth-based formulation emphasized in the remainder of this chapter. A utility-theoretic model to support that formulation is contained in Chapter 15.

19. The minimization with respect to v^i, upon putting aside terms in the Hamiltonian not involving v^i, is

$$\varsigma^i(1 - u; v^e, \Lambda) = \min[v^i + q\zeta(1, (1 - u)v^e/v^i, y^w/v^i)]\Lambda^{-1}$$

where ς^i denotes minimized unit cost at the given output.

20. The logic of this first-order condition is that an equiproportionate scaling back, say, of all the arguments such that $v^i = 1$ would magnify in equal proportion the absolute value of ζ_1, so if no such balanced scaleback has occurred the value of ζ_1 evaluated at $v^i = 1$ must be deflated by v^i to yield the correct and unchanged derivative with respect to v^i.

21. Although the impact effects on wages are general, so the first round (so to speak) of pay raises are matched and the effect on quitting through relative wages is cancelled, the marginal effectiveness of increased pay is nevertheless damped through two remaining effects: the marginal effectiveness is reduced because the wage is increased relative to employees' nonwage income (just as increased nonwage income heightens that effectiveness) and because a further small increment in pay of the same absolute size (another dollar, say) then has less economic significance than it did before insofar as the ratios do not change. So "up" is indeed the equilibrium direction here for the wage to move.

22. Recall that the term *worker* in this volume means a member of the labor force, whether employed or unemployed. Hence, in principle, the average independent income of workers could differ from that of employed workers. Incidentally, the intention has been to reserve the term *employee* for contexts in which firms have invested in their work force, such as the present context. But the rule is not always convenient to apply.

23. Equation (3.9) can be written $1 = E(\varepsilon, \theta^i)$, where the righthand side denotes the elasticity of effort with respect to the ratio. This both resembles, and is equivalent to, the Solow elasticity condition, since a one percent increase, *ceteris paribus*, of v^i implies a one percent increase of θ^i. $E(\varepsilon, v^i) = E(\varepsilon, \theta^i)$.

24. Since $\theta^e = \theta$, and hence $d\theta^e = d\theta$, the positive impact $d\theta$ is going to produce a second-round effect through the equal increase, $d\theta^e$. It is clear from inspection of (3.10) that the impact of the increment $d\theta^e$ is also positive; it is positive at any positive $1 - u$ if and only if the impact of increased employment is positive, which

is the case. But there are now two cases, that in which the coefficient of $d\theta^e$ is less than one and that in which it is not less than one.

There is obviously a range of unemployment rates low enough to ensure that the coefficient of $d\theta^e$ is less than one. (One can make the coefficient arbitrarily close to zero, in fact, by setting the employment rate sufficiently near to zero.) Over this range, our small increment to the employment rate, $d(1 - u)$, in having a positive impact $d\theta^e$, produces a second-round effect $d\theta$ on θ that is positive though smaller than the first-round impact effect already discussed. This second-round effect has a second-round effect $d\theta^e$, which in turn has a third-round effect $d\theta$ that is likewise positive and likewise smaller than the previous effect. And so forth. The sum of the infinite series of effects is obviously positive and convergent to a finite number. If we denote the coefficient of $d\theta^e$ by a and note that the other coefficient is then $a\theta/(1 - u)$, the multiplier formula for the cumulative increase in θ can be seen to be

$$d\theta = [\theta/(1 - u)][a/(1 - a)]d(1 - u)$$

So the slope of the equilibrium wage curve in the region of low employment rates at any rate is positive. The elasticity of θ with respect to $1 - u$ is $a/1 - a$. Since there is a clear tendency for the coefficient a to be monotone-increasing as $1 - u$ is increased, both the slope and the elasticity tend to be increasing in this region.

There is a possibility, however, that as the employment rate is increased a critical level less than one is approached at which the coefficient a is equal to one. As the employment rate approaches that critical level the slope of the wage curve goes to infinity. Clearly at all employment rates at which the coefficient a is one or greater there does not exist an equilibrium wage; equilibrium demands an infinite wage. If, to seize on a situation of satisfying simplicity, the coefficient a equals or exceeds one at all employment rates above the critical level just discussed, which would occur if a is monotone-increasing in $1 - u$, then there are just two intervals: In the interval of below-critical employment the equilibrium wage exists and the wage curve is rising, as discussed. In the interval of above-critical employment rates there does not exist an equilibrium wage and so the wage curve is not defined in that interval.

Is there such a critical employment rate less than one? If ε_{12} is close in value to $-\varepsilon_{11}$—they are equal in the linear case adopted in most macroeconomic models—then at $1 - u = 1$ even a small value of $-\varepsilon_2$ may be enough to tip the coefficient over the brink of one.

4. The Product-Market Equilibrium Locus and Partial-Equilibrium Unemployment Determination

1. Two other conditions related to the labor market are implicitly satisfied in the equilibrium analysis found here. One requirement is that households have the correct expectation of the wage expressed in terms of the asset, since households' labor-force participation decisions generally depend on it, as does their propensities to quit and shirk. But this condition will be regarded as a condition for equilibrium in the asset market rather than the labor market. The other requirement, which *is*

a condition on the labor market, is correct expectations about the unemployment rate, hence about the average remaining time to get out of the unemployment pool, an expectation on which firms' wage-setting depends and households' consumption demand depends. (There is an asymmetry here, for although the firms' current-period wage-setting depends mainly or wholly, according to the circumstances specified, on their expectations of the current-period unemployment rate, the future rate making little or no difference, the households' consumption demand depends nearly entirely on their expectations of the course of the unemployment rate over the course of their lifetimes, the current unemployment rate making little or negligible difference.)

2. Again, in close analogy, there are two other conditions related to the product market that are implicit in the analysis of general equilibrium developed here. There is the requirement that consumers be unsurprised by the industry price expressed in terms of the asset, as consumption plans are based on that expectation. But, again analogously, this is treated as a condition of capital-market equilibrium. The other requirement is that, if there are inventory shortages or delivery lags, consumers have correct expectations about the probability of nonavailability or the length of waiting times.

3. To put this remark another way, if current production depends only on actual current prices, unconstrained or uninfluenced by its expectations in the previous period, the firms are always in product-market equilibrium. That case happens to describe the continuous-time, no-lag models of the economy with trained employees as the asset or with physical capital as the asset.

4. It has been argued that an increased demand for products of some kinds drives up the path of the real interest rate, and the consequently increased discounting of future rentals on existing capital provides an impetus to owners of existing capital assets to increase the flow-supply of their productive services—running equipment at faster speeds and utilizing plant with less frequent maintenance. Analogous increases in the flow-supply of other factors of production, such as oil and land, could likewise be induced. The consequences could well be an induced upward shift in the marginal productivity of labor schedule, as well as in the average productivity of labor schedule, and hence an increase in the demand for labor. Juxtaposed against the equilibrium wage curve, such a derived labor-demand shift would cause an increase of the employment rate and an increase of the wage. See Paul J. Taubman and Maurice Wilkinson, "User Cost, Output and Unexpected Price Changes," in Edmund S. Phelps et al., *Microeconomic Foundations of Employment and Inflation Theory* (New York: Norton, 1970), and in a thoroughly neoclassical context, Jeremy Greenwood, Zvi Hercovitz, and Gregory Huffman, "Investment, Capital Utilization and the Real Business Cycle," *American Economic Review,* 78, June 1988, 402–417.

5. The contrasts (and similarities) between the modern structuralist approach here and the "real business cycle" models of the neoclassical aggregate approach can be drawn up by comparing the modern Chapter 9 with the neoclassical Chapter 16. Note, however, that the latter chapter goes beyond the aggregative setup commonly preferred in the neoclassical theory to consider a two-sector model.

6. An increase of the wage has a negative effect through its impact on the first argument that is stronger than its oppositely signed effect through its lesser impact on

the second argument, as will be recalled from the discussion of the turnover model in the previous chapter. (In algebraic terms, $\zeta_1 + (1 - u)\zeta_2 = -(y^w/v)\zeta_3 < 0$.) It also has a supportingly negative effect through its negative impact on the third argument.

7. The ineluctable implication is that increased q causes the demand price of labor to drop at a given employment rate. But this is *not* what happens along the dynamic path, and the steady-state wage is increased as well, as can be shown from an analysis like that in Chapter 7.

8. A formalism that follows immediately is that the maximizing policy makes the current growth rate, g_t, of the stock of employees satisfy

$$r_t q_t - dq_t/dt = \max_{g_t} [\Lambda - v - T(\zeta(\cdot) + g_t, 1) + q_t g_t]$$

The equation says that the maximized value of the Hamiltonian just equals the own interest the firm must charge itself on an asset worth the given shadow price. An immediate implication of this equation is that an increase of the required, or shadow, interest, which is the lefthand side, entails a drop of the wage. However, we want here to capture the effect of an increase of the interest *rate*.

9. This assumes that the external effect of the wage increase through the second argument of the quit-rate function, which reflects the reduced competitiveness felt when the other firms raise their wage rates, is not dominated nor exactly offset by the external effect of the wage increase through the third argument, which reflects the reduction in independent income caused by the increased general wage.

10. One may divide the lefthand side of (4.4) by q and, by virtue of (4.2), multiply it by marginal training cost in order to obtain a condition in which q appears only indirectly as a determinant of the own rate of interest:

$$(r_t - q^{-1}dq_t/dt - g_t)T'(\zeta(\cdot) + g_t, 1; \Lambda) = \Lambda - v - T(\zeta(\cdot) + g_t, 1; \Lambda)$$

The geometry of this solution for the optimal growth rate is analogous to the Ramsey-Keynes solution of the optimum saving problem. With that construction the reader can easily confirm that the equation makes g_t a decreasing function of the wage; a decreasing function of the employment rate; and a decreasing function of the own interest rate, $r_t - q^{-1}dq/dt$. The solution is shown by the tangency construction in the accompanying figure.

11. See in particular the first appendix to the revised version, which was not in every respect an improved version, just a different version, of my earlier 1968 paper of the same title: Phelps, "Money Wage Dynamics and Labor Market Equilibrium," in Edmund S. Phelps et al., *Microeconomic Foundations of Employment and Inflation Theory* (New York: Norton, 1970).

12. Edmund S. Phelps and Sidney G. Winter, Jr., "Optimal Price Policy under Atomistic Competition," in Phelps et al., *Microeconomic Foundations*, pp. 309–337. A substantial advance showing how the main features of the model survive the introduction of free entry, subject to a setup cost, is Alvaro Rodriguez, "Entry and Price Dynamics in a Perfect Foresight Model," *Journal of Economic Dynamics and Con-*

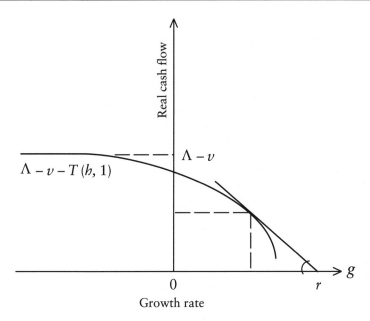

Firm's growth rate under optimal investment in employee stock (see Chapter 4, note 10)

trol, 9, June 1985, 251–271. Nevertheless the former formulation, being less unfamiliar, is followed here.

13. The loci classici are Hirofumi Uzawa, "On a Two-Sector Model of Economic Growth," *Review of Economic Studies*, 29, July 1962, 40–47, and 30, January 1963, 105–18; Duncan K. Foley and Miguel Sidrauski, *Monetary and Fiscal Policy in a Growing Economy* (New York: Macmillan, 1971), esp. 9–99.

5. Capital-Market Equilibrium, Neoclassical and Modern, and General-Equilibrium Employment

1. Some elucidation may be useful. According to the customer-market model, if the market as a whole is expanding or if the firm's relative price is such that the firm is expanding, the firm's having an additional hundred customers, say, implies that the absolute growth in the number of customers between the current moment and some future date will be greater than it otherwise would have been (proportionately greater) since the more customers a firm has the more widely the word spreads elsewhere of its existence; thus, customers at a firm have a positive own-marginal-product in producing themselves. Similarly, according to the turnover-training model, a firm having an additional hundred trained employees will optimally be training proportionately more new employees, since a given absolute amount of training over some small time interval is cheaper the larger the stock of already

trained employees, who are the potential instructors. In the two-sector model, on the other hand, having an additional hundred units of capital only serves to earn a correspondingly larger volume of rental income by causing consumer-good supply to be greater than it otherwise would have been. That is why there is a growth-rate term in the equations like (5.1) here that are found in sections 4.1 and 4.2 but not in 4.3.

2. Olivier J. Blanchard, "Debt, Deficits and Finite Horizons," *Journal of Political Economy,* 93, April 1985, 223–247.

3. The term *assets* has been reserved to refer to the physical entities whose real market values are components of wealth. A more descriptive term would be *real assets.* These assets are the elements of what is called "outside wealth," other than holdings of public debt. No simpler alternative having so far presented itself, it can only be hoped that this terminology is not too labyrinthine.

4. For extensions of the system by Blanchard, see the following two papers: Willem J. Buiter, "Death, Birth, Productivity Growth and Debt Neutrality," *Economic Journal,* 98, June 1988, 279–293; Philippe Weil, "Overlapping Families of Infinitely-Lived Agents," *Journal of Public Economics,* 38, June 1989, 183–198.

5. The astute reader might wonder why in the Blanchard-Yaari world the real price q attaching to a class of assets would matter. As long as the wealth owners receive an undisturbed flow of interest and actuarially determined dividend income, why should they care to what depths q may have plunged as a result of some increase of r? The answer must be that the term in the differential equation that introduces $qA + B$ captures the influence of the actuarial part of the income flow—the dividend—and that is μqA.

This is perhaps a useful opportunity to comment that the nonwage income variable in the quitting and effort functions, generically denoted y^w, is properly written $(r + \mu)(qa + b)$. In the lump-sum tax case, the terms involving r are offset by taxes under a balanced-budget policy, leaving the terms involving μ. That is not true in the case of income taxation or expenditure taxation, as will later be discussed.

6. Arnold Collery, mimeographed manuscript, ca. 1973.

7. Michael Kalecki, "The Principle of Increasing Risk," *Economica,* 4, November 1937, 440–446.

8. Philippe Aghion and Patrick Bolton, "A Trickle-Down Theory of Growth and Development with Debt Overhang," mimeographed manuscript, DELTA, Paris, June 1991.

9. Joseph Stiglitz and Andrew Weiss, "Credit Rationing in Markets with Imperfect Information," *American Economic Review,* 71, June 1981, 393–410.

10. Bruce C. Greenwald and Joseph E. Stiglitz, "Imperfect Information, Credit Markets and Unemployment," *European Economic Review,* 31, May 1987, 444–456.

6. Key Factors in the Structuralist Theory of Unemployment Fluctuation

1. I have in mind my own "Commodity-Supply Shock and Full-Employment Monetary Policy," *Journal of Money Credit and Banking,* 10, May 1978, 206–221. Some parallel analyses are cited there.

2. See Robert J. Barro, *Macroeconomics* (New York: John Wiley, 1984), and Edward C. Prescott, "Theory Ahead of Business Cycle Measurement," *Carnegie-Rochester Conference Series on Public Policy*, 25, Autumn 1986, 11–44, reprinted in the *Quarterly Review* of the Federal Reserve Bank of Minneapolis, 10, 1989.

3. Michael Bruno and Jeffrey D. Sachs, *The Economics of Worldwide Stagflation* (Cambridge, Mass.: Harvard University Press, 1985).

4. The reference here is to productivity shocks that, although possibly labor saving, are not "very labor saving" in the sense of actually lowering the marginal productivity of labor while nevertheless raising average productivity.

5. Robert G. King, Charles I. Plosser, and Sergio T. Rebelo, "Production, Growth and Business Cycles: I. The Basic Neoclassical Model," *Journal of Monetary Economics*, 21, June 1988, 195–232, and idem, "Production, Growth and Business Cycles: Technical Appendix," manuscript, University of Rochester, July 1987.

6. King, Plosser, and Rebelo, "The Basic Neoclassical Model."

7. Deepak Lal and Sweder van Wijnbergen, "Government Deficits, the Real Interest Rate and LDC Debt," *European Economic Review*, 29, November–December 1985, 157–191; Jean-Paul Fitoussi and Edmund Phelps, "Causes of the 1980s Slump in Europe," *Brookings Papers on Economic Activity*, 16 (2), Autumn 1986, 487–520, and chapter 4 of Fitoussi and Phelps, *The Slump in Europe* (Oxford: Basil Blackwell, 1988), 53–96; Andrew Newell and James Symonds, "Wages and Employment between the Wars," Discussion Paper 87-02, Department of Economics, University College London, London, 1987, reprinted in Phelps, ed., *Recent Developments in Macroeconomics* (Hants, England: Edward Elgar, 1991), vol. 3, 432–467.

8. The *locus classicus* is Robert A. Mundell, "The Appropriate Use of Monetary and Fiscal Policy for Internal and External Stability," International Monetary Fund *Staff Papers*, 9, March 1962, 70–79. Though the role of the external real interest rate was not the focus of the Mundell-Fleming model, its effect on the open economy was immediately clear.

9. See Robert E. Hall, "Labor Supply and Aggregate Fluctuations," in Karl Brunner and Alan Meltzer, eds., *On the State of Macroeconomics*, Carnegie-Rochester Conference on Public Policy, 12 (Amsterdam: North-Holland, 1980).

10. See Richard R. Nelson, "Full Employment Policy and Economic Growth," *American Economic Review*, 56, December 1966, 1178–92.

11. In drawing the implications of growth for employment in the neoclassical theory, one might start from King, Plosser, and Rebelo, "The Basic Neoclassical Model." However, Chapter 16 of this volume offers a two-sector neoclassical model for purposes of comparison with the two-sector modern model analyzed, in a necessarily less utility-theoretic way, in Chapter 9.

12. A more future-oriented modeling of the propensity to quit or to shirk would lead immediately to the future consequence of a positive impact on incentive wages, hence a contractionary effect through this channel, taken alone.

13. Stefano Micossi and Giuseppe Tullio, "Fiscal Imbalances, Economic Distortions, and the Long-Run Performance of the Italian Economy," Quaderni di Ricerca no. 9, University Luiss, Rome, October 1991.

14. The quitting model is less convenient here because T' is the marginal opportunity cost of training rather than the marginal payroll cost, but T' could be so reinterpreted without significant consequences.

15. A useful discussion of some of the theory and evidence is Anthonie Knoester, "Supply-Side Economics and the Inverted Haavelmo Effect," Research Memorandum 8701, Institute of Economics, University of Nijmegen, 1987.

16. Owing to the zero-degree homogeneity of the shirking function, the multiplication of all the arguments of the function by one minus the flat tax rate, which introduction of a flat income tax implies, does not affect the wage (before income tax) necessary to induce a given rate of (non)shirking at any specified unemployment rate, and it will not affect the marginal effectiveness of a "dollar" increase of the wage in reducing shirking, since if it would have meant a k percent increase of the wage-nonwage income ratio before it will mean the same k percent increase of the net-of-income-tax wage-nonwage income ratio. Hence the cost-minimizing wage (before employees' income tax) will not be affected.

17. Dirk Morris, *Government Debt in International Financial Markets* (London: Pinter Publishing Co., and New York: Columbia University Press, 1988); Michael Beenstock, "Saving, Investment and Growth: An Econometric Investigation," paper presented at the Villa Mondragone International Economic Seminar on World Saving, Prosperity and Growth, July 1990; Robert J. Barro, "World Real Interest Rates and Investment," *Scandinavian Journal of Economics*, 94, April 1992.

There is also a much-cited global study finding no such effects, after accounting for the influence of some other hypothesized causes, by Robert J. Barro and Xavier J. Sala-i-Martin, "World Real Interest Rates," *Macroeconomics Annual 1990* (Cambridge, Mass.: MIT Press, 1990). But this finding is superseded by the later Barro paper just cited.

18. The working models here have been formulated to exclude any other possible points of impact; achieving a resolution of the theoretical questions raised will be a main objective of the foundational part of this study, in Part IV.

19. John Maynard Keynes, "Can Lloyd George Do It?" (1929), reprinted in *Collected Writings of John Maynard Keynes*, vol. 9: *Activities 1922–29* (London: Macmillan/Cambridge University Press, 1981), 86–125.

20. Robert J. Barro, "Output Effects of Government Purchases," *Journal of Political Economy*, 89, December 1981, 1086–1121. See also Hall, "Labor Supply and Aggregate Fluctuations." The revised version emerges in R. S. Aiyagari, Lawrence J. Christiano, and Martin Eichenbaum, "The Output, Employment and Interest Rate Effects of Government Consumption," Federal Reserve Bank of Minneapolis, Working Paper 25, 1990, and in Chapter 16 of this volume.

21. References to the empirical literature on real rates of interest can be found in Chapter 9.

7. A Turnover-Training Model

1. This chapter is based on Hian Teck Hoon and Edmund Phelps, "Macroeconomic Shocks in a Dynamized Model of the Natural Rate of Unemployment," *American Economic Review*, 82, September 1992, 889–900.

2. See Steven C. Salop, "A Model of the Natural Rate of Unemployment," *American Economic Review*, 69, March 1979, 117–125.

8. A Customer-Market Model

1. There would have been an advantage in starting with Chapter 8 instead of Chapter 7 since, in the closed-economy case, which is of relevance for analyzing the world economy as a whole, the dynamics are made simple by the exogeneity of the aggregate stock of customers, which is convenient to treat as fixed: the firms as a whole cannot invest or disinvest in their customers, nor can the representative firm. Thus it spares us the need to analyze an adjustment path (though not in any open-economy version). A disadvantage of starting with this model is that it takes a comparatively idiosyncratic view of the economy, one having a still fairly small number of adherents. Further, starting there would require adoption of the shirking apparatus in the first of these three chapters, then its abandonment in the next, and finally its readoption in the third. The net effect of these disadvantages is clear.

2. Edmund S. Phelps and Sidney G. Winter, "Optimal Price Policy under Atomistic Competition," pp. 309–337, and Dale T. Mortensen, "A Theory of Wage and Employment Dynamics," pp. 167–211, in Phelps et al., *Microeconomic Foundations of Employment and Inflation Theory* (New York: Norton, 1970).

3. The treatment of the closed economy here is based on my "Consumer Demand and Equilibrium Unemployment in a Working Model of the Customer-Market Incentive-Wage Economy," *Quarterly Journal of Economics*, 108, August 1991, 1003–1032.

4. An earlier general-equilibrium extension of the Phelps-Winter customer market using Ricardian equivalence and giving a neoclassical treatment of the labor market (hence market-clearing wages), not the modern treatment here, is Guillermo A. Calvo and Edmund S. Phelps, "A Model of NonWalrasian General Equilibrium," in James Tobin, ed., *Macroeconomics, Prices and Quantities: Essays in Memory of Arthur M. Okun* (Washington, D.C.: Brookings Institution, 1983), 135–157. Pareto-inefficiency nevertheless emerged, which was the paper's focus.

5. Fixity in the number of firms in the face of a contractionary shock, I believe, can be defended along the following lines: When real interest rates are driven *up* by a shock, as in the cases motivating the analysis in this chapter, existing firms are induced to raise markups even though they first think it will cost them some customers (though it does not actually since they all do it); in the new equilibrium every existing firm is again at the margin with regard to gaining another customer, and any potential firm that was on the margin of entering, if there was such, will at no time see a gain from entering. The higher real interest rate makes the investment (the initial losses) entailed by entry less attractive than before.

But when interest rates are instead driven *down* a little by a shock, existing firms will want to invest a little in acquiring a few more customers if (and as long as) they do not foresee the general decline of markups awaiting them, and any potential firm that was in the previous equilibrium at the margin of entering under correct expectations, if there was such, would be drawn in by similarly incorrect expectations. However, in an earlier version of this material (cited in n. 3), I argued that "the potential firm closest to entering during equilibrium is never at the margin under correct expectations if potential firms are identical and must pay a higher investment to gain customers from a zero base than established firms must pay to gain the same number from a positive base" (p. 1007). This now clearly appears incorrect. The existing firms must pay a front-loaded cost, namely the price concession necessarily going to existing customers as well as to any new ones, when they attempt to expand market shares, while new entrants would have to pay the (different sorts of) investment costs made necessary by starting from a zero customer base. Hence it is possible to have an equilibrium time path along which those potential firms closest to entering are just indifferent to doing so while the existing firms are also indifferent at the margin about expanding. My previous thinking suffered from having forgotten the superb paper, which clarifies all these matters, by a former student of mine, Alvaro Rodriguez, "Entry and Price Dynamics in a Perfect Foresight Model," *Journal of Economic Dynamics and Control,* 9, June 1985, 251–271.

6. A revision of the model has been suggested on the ground that while customers need time to find a single seller that is cheaper than all the others, customers at a firm that becomes suddenly more expensive than the others would turn to another supplier at once. See Joseph E. Stiglitz, "Price Rigidities and Market Structure," *American Economic Review,* 64, May 1984, 350–355. But perhaps such an amendment rests on an overly literal interpretation. If there are many industries, all in customer markets, and suppliers somewhat sparse in each, it may take time for some or all customers wanting to leave their supplier in some industry to locate an alternative, especially a convenient one. (It is true, though, that the speeds of reaction ought to be modeled as asymmetric.)

7. Obviously, the number of customers per firm is a constant in the closed economy, though not in the open economy, as some nationals may have become customers of foreign firms or some foreigners may have become customers of domestic firms.

8. The lump-sum tax here is paid in installments, or the continuous-time version thereof. That tax is a subtraction from nonwage income on the assumption that the taxpayer can and must pay it out of nonwage income, whether or not he is or will be employed.

9. The envelope theorem shows that the rise in the firm's own wage on the shirking rate it experiences has no cost-raising effect. It serves only to minimize the rise of unit cost.

10. There is no additional decision problem of choosing output, as the firm will "clear the market" for its product. The Phelps-Winter paper shows that, on its various assumptions, a firm setting a price would not optimally produce either more or less than the corresponding amount demanded by its customers.

11. The demand relation here gives average expenditure by a representative cross-section of customers by wealth and (un)employment status. The assumption is that each firm, though atomistic, is large enough that it can assume it is representative in this respect by virtue of a sort of law of large numbers.

  Note also that this is not a genuine demand function, as demand by customers is generally a function of the wage rate, income from wealth, the interest rate, and perhaps wealth itself. The relationship simply says that the expenditure of the individual firm's customers is structurally related to its relative price and what these customers would spend at the other firms if they were customers there (or if the firm charged the same as the other firms charge). The implicit approximation here, I believe, is that no account is taken of the point that if the firm were to go on charging a different price, its customers would become more and more nonrepresentative, and so the static demand relationship set forth in the text would be less and less accurate for the firm to use in its optimal pricing.

12. More generally, government orders are distributed in proportion to the base-period sizes of firms. However, it is assumed here for simplicity that firms are identically structured and situated, so their sizes are equal and remain so.

13. It is implicit in this expression for the cash flows that the firm at each moment solves the static problem of choosing its wage rate to minimize unit cost, and that minimized unit cost is an increasing function of total output per family in the rest of the economy, $y + \gamma^f$.

14. Phelps and Winter, "Optimal Price Policy under Atomistic Competition," p. 317.

15. In the open-economy case, of course, the country may experience growth or decline in its stock of customers.

16. Recall equation (5.7).

17. Of course, the expectation of lifetime wages, or human wealth, by a family takes account of the probability of employment at each future point in time. A more rigorous treatment of this complication is a topic taken up in Chapter 15.

18. There was a state variable struggling to appear. This was the ratio of the average wealth held by employed persons to the average wealth of unemployed persons. But, on the grounds that this ratio cannot vary much and it is not a potent force in any case, this interesting little dynamic was suppressed. The assets of the employed per employee was set equal to the number of assets per worker, which is essentially the parameter x.

19. So, to elaborate a bit more, if there are two such "good" stationary-state solutions, there must be a "bad" one lying between them around which there is a continuum of equilibrium paths.

20. An equivalent way to express the results on the sign of the slope of the two curves in the small-government case is to say that the supply relation makes q elastic with respect to z (and thus also to y) while the demand relation shows q to be inelastic with respect to z; more accurately, the elasticity is at first less than one, then zero, and finally negative. The article growing out of the same material as the present chapter conducts the analysis in these elasticity terms. See Phelps, "Consumer Demand and Equilibrium Unemployment."

21. Paul A. Samuelson, *Foundations of Economic Analysis* (Cambridge, Mass.: Harvard University Press, 1947), 258–283.

22. In the broad Keynesian phylum of models a supply shock, such as a reduction in the supply of rainfall or oil flow-through, operates unambiguously to shrink output, but whether it contracts employment or actually expands it turns on whether the reduction caused in the marginal productivity of labor outweighs the reduction in the average productivity of labor and whether the rate of return to new investment improves or deteriorates. A succinct analysis is presented in Phelps, "Commodity-Supply Shock and Full-Employment Monetary Policy," *Journal of Money, Credit and Banking,* 10, May 1978.

23. The structure of taxation matters quite a lot, however.

24. A simulation model of physical investment and customer investment in an open-economy context by Gylfi Zoega suggests that no crucial differences appear to arise if a variable level of (physical) investment is introduced.

25. The reader might think to add, "or if the elasticity of the effort function with respect to nonwage income is small in absolute value." However, the first-order condition for the optimal incentive wage implies that the wage rate–nonwage income ratio is a function solely of the employment rate. So if nonwage income should rise by one percent, the cost-minimizing wage rate is implied to rise by the same percentage amount, no matter how small in absolute value the aforementioned elasticity.

9. A Two-Sector Fixed-Investment Model

1. The closed-economy model here descends from Edmund S. Phelps, "Pro-Keynesian and Counter-Keynesian Implications of the 'Structuralist' Theory of Unemployment and Interest under the Classic Two-Sector View of Capital and Production," Department of Economics, Columbia University, Discussion Paper 494, August 1990, presented at the 6th World Congress of the Econometric Society, Barcelona, August 1990. Its real-wage "rigidity" formulation omitted nonwage income from the shirking function. An antecedent paper based instead on real wage stickiness is Edmund S. Phelps, "A Working Model of Slump and Recovery from Disturbances to Capital-Goods Demand in a Closed Non-Monetary Economy," Research Department, International Monetary Fund, Working Paper 88/82, August 1988; published in Edward J. Nell and Willi Semmler, eds., *Nicholas Kaldor and Mainstream Economics* (London: Macmillan and Co., 1991), 360–378.

2. Hirofumi Uzawa, "On a Two-Sector Model of Economic Growth," *Review of Economic Studies*, 29, July 1962, 40–47, and 30, January 1963, 105–118; Duncan K. Foley and Miguel Sidrauski, *Monetary and Fiscal Policy in a Growing Economy* (New York: Macmillan, 1971).

3. The unwelcome complication of the quitting story in the present context is that it generates its own state variable, the stock of operational employees, which, in a model that already has a state variable in the form of the capital stock, would seriously increase the dimensionality of the model.

4. Here, we let $\hat{\varepsilon}(z/v^i, y^w/v^i) = \varepsilon(1, z/v^i, y^w/v^i)$.

5. Whether a more general specification of the way effort enters the production could be entertained without upsetting the most important of the implications of the model here has not been explored.

6. It may be helpful to think of the determination of v here in the following way. If we plot in the (v, v^i) plane the firm's reaction function showing how v^i increases with v, we are plotting the locus of points at which the Solow elasticity with respect to v^i is equal to one. Any locus along which this elasticity is a constant *less* than one lies necessarily *below* the former locus, by virtue of the second-order condition satisfied at the maximum. So as we move up the 45-degree line, starting from the origin, we at first slice through just such loci, where the elasticity is less than one, until we reach the point of intersection with the reaction curve, where (to repeat) the elasticity equals one. It is now obvious how the equilibrium v is determined, and that it is unique, given the parameters governing the position of the reaction curve.

7. This is a natural and, it seems, an unexceptionable way to represent Blanchard's device. There will be some paper gains or losses to the insurance sector if q should jump, and a rising gain (or loss) if q is rising (or falling), but the companies are never ahead or in deficit on a cash basis, and the paper gain or loss vanishes in the limit through the dividend, which is adjusted to the level of q.

8. We could work instead with the condition $v^d/q = \hat{\varepsilon}[f_1(\tilde{k}_1) - \tilde{k}_1 f_1'(\tilde{k}_1)]$.

9. As students of the two-sector model often remark, the demand price is not "diminishing" in aggregate N; it is independent of the employment-capital ratio. But shirking has made it decreasing in the employment rate.

10. Alternatively, we could work with the following equilibrium condition: $v^s/q = -[f_1(\tilde{k}_1) - \tilde{k}_1 f_1'(\tilde{k}_1)][(1 - u)\hat{\varepsilon}_1 + (y^w/v)\hat{\varepsilon}_2]$.

11. Another case in which the capital stock does not matter is when G_C and D are fixed as ratios to K. Parameterizing these fiscal influences in that way, though it is analytically convenient, would have little substantive appeal.

12. With regard to private consumer expenditures, we do not directly observe shocks disturbing the rate of pure time preference—in Keynesian terms, the propensity to consume—but rather the sum total of exogenous and endogenous movements. In contrast, variations in public expenditures are interpretable as shocks, at least to a high degree, so there is particular interest in studying the implications of the model for the effects of these shocks. The theory is more nearly operational, so to speak, with regard to public-expenditure shocks. With regard to shocks disturbing the valuation of assets in the form of capital goods, an equilibrium analysis regards them as entirely endogenous, induced by correct forecasts of shocks to productivity, preferences, and public policy.

13. We are positing here that the government debt created, and any preexisting public debt, is in the form of postal savings deposits and the like, so that its price is not free to drop. There cannot be any important loss of generality in specifying the model in this way so that there is only one asset price, not two, to take into account in the analysis of the effects of shocks.

14. A representative reference is Friedrich A. von Hayek, *Prices and Production* (London: George Routledge, 1931; 2nd edition, 1935).

15. While of presumably no empirical interest, this increase of the wage to the firms implies, taken alone, a fall of employment and hence a reduction of the rental on capital. It would not be surprising, therefore, if it were found that the rate of interest drops initially before finally rising to its new steady-state equilibrium level.

16. From the stationary-state relation $r = \rho + m(qK/C)$ one can see that the stationary consumption level equals $mqK/(r - \rho)$.

17. It should be mentioned that an increase in K_P has a direct contractionary effect on Z_C since $Z_C = [(K - K_P)/\tilde{k}_C]f_C(\tilde{k}_C)$. Hence, there is a possibility that if the increase in K_P contracts Z_C sufficiently, q may fall instead.

18. Portions of the section, particularly the second part, are based on Gylfi Zoega, "The Effect of Technological Progress and Population Growth in a Structuralist Model of Unemployment and Interest," manuscript, Columbia University, December 1990.

19. Recent unpublished work by Michael J. Boskin and Lawrence Lau develops estimation procedures leading to the conclusion that technical progress in postwar Europe has been predominantly Solow-neutral, not Harrod-neutral. It could be, of course,

that this finding will not prove robust to the introduction of additional considerations left out in their first exploration.

20. The other possibility is that progress is Hicks-neutral in the consumer-good-producing sector. But that possibility requires restrictions on the production function, and will not be pursued here.

21. Robert G. King, Charles I. Plosser, and Sergio Rebelo, "Production, Growth and Business Cycles: The Basic Neoclassical Model, II. New Directions," *Journal of Monetary Economics*, 21, September 1988, 309–341, and "Technical Appendix," Department of Economics, University of Rochester, July 1987.

22. If we work with variables which are normalized by Λ, the term δK on the righthand side of (9.42′) is replaced by $(\delta + \lambda)(K/\Lambda)$. In (9.43′), the term δK on the righthand side is replaced by $(\delta + \lambda)(K/\Lambda)$ and $[(R(q)/q) - \rho - \delta](Z_C - G_C)$ is replaced by $[(R(q)/q) - \rho - \delta - \lambda][(Z_C/\Lambda) - (G_C/\Lambda)]$. Importantly, the net effect of the change in λ in the latter equation is nil in the "classic" case. The reason is that, in such a case, the K elasticity of Z_C at fixed q is equal to one, in the light of Rybczynski's analysis of factor shifts in a two-sector world, so that the negative effect on the righthand side caused by the increase in λ via the former term, $(\delta + \lambda)(K/\Lambda)$, is exactly offset by the positive effect of the increase in λ via the latter term. (It is clear that in the more general case, in which capital is used to produce capital but with less capital intensity than is found in the consumer-good sector, the latter locus moves, shifting left as well and thus seeming to introduce an ambiguity about q, but the shift up cannot be as large as the leftward shift of the other locus, so no ambiguity arises even in the general case.)

23. The faster-wage-growth factor was introduced in a paper by Alan Manning, "Productivity Growth, Wage Setting and the Equilibrium Rate of Unemployment," Conference on Unemployment and Wage Determination, National Bureau of Economic Research and the Center for Economic Policy Research, Cambridge, Mass., October 17–18, 1991.

24. As remarked in note 19, there was an important amount of capital augmentation in the postwar period in Europe, according to unpublished research by Michael Boskin and Lawrence Lau at Stanford University in 1991.

25. N. Gregory Mankiw, "Consumer Durables and the Real Interest Rate," *Journal of Political Economy*, 93, May 1985, 353–362.

26. John Maynard Keynes, "Can Lloyd George Do It?" (1929), reprinted in *Means to Prosperity* (London: Macmillan and Co., 1933).

27. Hayek, *Prices and Production*.

10. Synthesis of the Single-Economy Theory

1. To repeat some introductory material, with regard to labor-market mechanisms there are models in which the real wage exhibits stickiness and models in which the real wage exhibits what might be called generalized rigidity (so the unemployment bears some of the disturbance, or incidence, of a shock). In addition, more than one product-market mechanism has been modeled, of course.

2. This section borrows from Phelps, "A Review of *Unemployment*," *Journal of Economic Literature*, 30, September 1992, 1476–1490. This review article examined the volume by Richard Layard, Stephen Nickell, and Richard Jackman, *Unemploy-*

ment: Macroeconomic Performance and the Labour Market (Oxford: Oxford University Press, 1991), within a wider review of the shift going on in contemporary macroeconomics.

3. The big picture, bigger than the one sketched in this volume, would also include implicit contractual understandings between the firm and its work force, particularly those workers who can be said to be employees in the sense that, as in Chapter 7, there is a bond between them and the firm.

4. Of course, in the closed economy under study, the stock of customers is naturally interpreted as the number of families participating in the economy and is therefore a constant rather than a state variable.

5. It might be added, in anticipation of a trivial implication of the models in Part III, that in the small open economy, the stock of foreign-based assets of domestic firms (namely, foreign customers) and the income from wealth held by households abroad should also increase in the same proportion.

6. Obviously, in an open economy one must also reckon on the initial invariance of the net stock of foreign customers and the initial stock of assets that households hold abroad.

7. Lest it be thought that such a mechanism seems to depend more on the supply side than is consistent with the data—when capital somehow becomes excessive we do not see the wage being driven up in accompaniment of the decrease of employment—it should be noted that the adverse effect of the reduced effort of employees also contracts the demand wage, or labor demand, so that no net decrease of the wage is strictly implied.

8. An interesting reference point is the case in which an increase of q is locally neutral for y^w. Then the increase of q has no impact on the supply wage but it still has a positive impact on the effort-adjusted demand wage, given by $V^*(q)$. That function could exhibit an elasticity well in excess of one, its value in the "classic case" under examination in the text. At the same time the elasticity of the demand wage with respect to K is small potatoes, clearly greater than minus one. It would therefore seem that the net effect of an increase of K would be expansionary in this reference case. But what is the elasticity of q with respect to K? It could be quite small. It is clear that as K goes to zero, q falls to some lower bound greater than zero. (An earthquake wiping out the capital stock would not present producers of capital with a zero price for the output they produce.)

9. It is a reasonable conjecture that the odds in favor of a net expansionary effect improve if we modify the model of firm-specific training along the following lines. In the existing model, labor augmentation leads to a proportional increase in the worth of each employee to firms, which is counterbalanced by a proportional increase in the opportunity cost of diverting employees to train newly hired ones. The result is that the wage and the income from wealth jump up likewise in proportion to the labor augmentation, and there is no impetus to increase hiring. It is more realistic to assume, however, that the opportunity cost of the employees diverted to training is not immediately increased by the final equilibrium amount, as the propagation of the new way of doing things has to be taught and mastered by the employees at the firms. That consideration points to a surge of new hiring to take advantage of the lag, or gestation period, while the new technology is being made operational.

10. The economywide labor augmentation under discussion is an equiproportionate increase of labor augmentation in the two sectors. When only the capital-goods sector experiences the technical advance, it is easy to check that the steady-state effect is to drive the wage up and to drive the rental and thus q down, which in turn reduces the wealth-consumption ratio and thereby lowers the steady-state interest rate. When the labor augmentation is solely in the consumer-good sector, the steady-state rental is driven up, pulling up the steady-state q and driving up the steady-state interest rate. It seems that both of these shocks have expansionary elements. The former, which appears to be Harrod-capital-saving, has incentive effects raising the demand wage and lowering the supply wage, the expansionary effect of which is clear. The latter, which appears to be Harrod-labor-saving, has the effect of raising the demand price of labor by pulling up q, while the incentive effects work in the contractionary direction.

11. With regard to economies that are *open* and *small,* hence facing a fixed external real rate of interest, r^*, the analysis runs more smoothly. In the extreme case in which the real exchange rate in terms of consumer goods remains invariant, as the only tradable is a consumer good and it is supplied to a perfect world market, arbitrage equates the domestic real interest rate to r^* at all times. In that case, it is impossible for q to jump, for a jump up accompanied by the prospect of decline back to the original level would imply a decrease of the domestic interest rate, putting it below the world rate, and a jump down accompanied by the prospect of a recovery to the original level would imply an increase of the domestic interest rate, putting it above the world rate; neither of these scenarios is possible. Hence, an increase of K would be *unambiguously contractionary* in the small open economy: the increase in income from wealth, assuming that K is domestically owned, would weaken employees' effort, thus lowering the demand wage and pushing up the supply wage, which would require a decrease of $1 - u$ to re-equate the two wages. Accordingly, a one-time economywide labor augmentation would be *unambiguously expansionary*: the decrease in income from wealth relative to labor augmentation boosts effort, causing v^d/Λ to increase, while that same decrease in unearned income as a ratio to labor augmentation, y^w/Λ, causes the corresponding ratio v^s/Λ to drop. (In the zone, which has been carefully excluded from attention, in which initial conditions are such that the capital-goods-producing sector has shut down, increasing K is apt to pull employment *up* since the labor demand schedule is increasing in K and independent of q except through the wealth effect.) In less extreme cases, where the real exchange rate may vary so the domestic interest rate may deviate from r^*, q will not possess this invariance to domestic shocks, but the constancy of the overseas real interest rate in the face of those shocks will serve to dampen the response of q.

    Interested readers can reflect on the implications of the initial invariance of the stock of overseas customers belonging to the open economy's firms and the stock of overseas assets held by the open economy's households. There is a loose parallel, clearly, between a closed economy's physical capital and an open economy's "capital" in the form of overseas customers. But it could well be that the stock of overseas customers is expansionary, not contractionary as domestic capital was argued to be. If these external stocks are small in relation to the size of the open economy, their initial invariance can safely be neglected.

12. It may be noted that, again in anticipation of the open-economy two-sector model, an open economy will experience no change of q in any case if, despite its altered prospects, it is too small to affect the world real rate of interest. Then there is no drop of q operating to contract employment initially in response to faster foreseen technical progress, only the slow expansion brought by the ensuing decrease of K/Λ—hence a gradual expansionary effect from the higher rate of growth of labor augmentation.

13. The references to money here have only the function of expediting the analysis. Nothing in the argument requires that the economy use money as a medium of exchange. Shares could be used as well, precisely as was sometimes done in the foregoing chapters. Incidentally, a rather careful discussion of taxes is contained in my "Review of *Unemployment*," much of which was prompted by the book discussed in that review (see note 2).

14. If there is public debt but it is not indexed to the consumer price index, the "inflation" reduces the real debt and consumption in the same proportion, leaving interest rates unchanged and thus having no impact on the investment by firms in new workers. If instead some or all debt is indexed to the consumer price level, the impact of the rise in the nominal price level is a rise in the debt-consumption ratio in real terms, hence an increase in the rate of interest, which operates to discourage firms from maintaining their stock of trained employees at its current level.

15. The journal article on which the first section of Chapter 12 is largely based does contain a parameter measuring the replacement ratio provided by unemployment-compensation legislation. See Edmund S. Phelps, "Effects of Productivity, Total Domestic Product Demand, and 'Incentive Wages' on Unemployment in a Non-Monetary Customer-Market Model of the Small Open Economy," *Scandinavian Journal of Economics,* 92, April 1990, 353–367.

16. This argument would be less persuasive if dismissal for cause did not increase the firm's insurance rate while layoffs for economic reasons did.

17. In other words, the models labeled New Keynesian have an equilibrium path, but at least a transient part of that path is a reflection of stickiness, or predetermination, in the behavior of nominal wages or prices, so that the current and future stocks of money, even though conforming to present expectations, make some difference to the equilibrium path of employment.

18. Government spending under entitlement legislation can be classified as a type of expenditure, since it represents subsidies conditional on certain actions, namely specified purchases by households, not a pure transfer payment; however, such spending has already been taken up under the fiscal heading above.

19. The term *public good* is used here in the sense of Samuelson. The term *collective good* is perhaps more descriptive but is not standard.

20. In the *open* economy, the employment-rate effects of some of the expenditure shocks may contrast with those found in the closed economy. For example, increased public expenditure in the consumer-good-producing sector will not have the contractionary effect operating through the asset-price mechanism in the two models (Chapters 7 and 9) where arbitrage keeps the real exchange rate equal to one and the domestic real interest rate equal to the overseas rate. The channels connecting wealth or taxation to the supply wage will still operate there, and if taxation falls principally on labor income the effect of the public expenditure will

be contractionary on this account. But in the customer-market model, in which the real exchange rate is effectively determined by the firms' markup decision, the initial effect could be expansionary: The increased public expenditure will generate some crowding out of private expenditure, which means a real appreciation—a rise of the price of domestic firms relative to the price generally paid overseas, or a rise of the "real price" (in units of goods of overseas suppliers). This real appreciation is not so large as to block an expansion of employment, however. If initially firms simply auctioned off the reduced supply left over after the government purchase, domestic firms would then be willing to step up output in order to cushion the fall of supplies, and thus the rise of the real price, to overseas customers lest they be lost too quickly, the overseas interest rate not having increased. The consequent rise in the derived demand for labor raises the "real demand wage" (likewise defined in terms of overseas supplies), which pulls up the employment rate insofar as workers are customers overseas, while the real supply wage is pushed down to the extent that income from wealth consists of income from assets overseas. Subsequently, the customer base erodes in response to the real appreciation and this operates, as argued in note 8, to cool off the economy and restore the real exchange rate to its normal level of competitiveness. Thus a worldwide public expenditure in the consumer-good sector may be contractionary on balance or only mildly expansionary for the world economy while the same expenditure by one country alone may be transiently expansionary or less contractionary.

By analogy, a public expenditure in the capital-good-producing sector of the open economy will not have an expansionary effect carried by the asset-price mechanism. In the two-sector model, which has an invariant real exchange rate and imported real interest rate, the effect of the public expenditure will therefore turn on wealth and taxation effects.

21. In an open economy with a real exchange rate capable of deviating from its normal level, there could be some crowding out of exports, not just physical investment, and thus a real appreciation inducing some increase of employment.

22. Two suggestive papers are N. Gregory Mankiw, "Consumer Durables and the Real Interest Rate," *Journal of Political Economy*, 93, May 1985, 353–362, and Robert Murphy, Topol, and Shleifer, "Consumer Durables," mimeographed manuscript, University of Chicago.

23. Unfortunately, many present-day writers have mixed it in with the rental cost that a firm not owning a unit of capital would have to pay to lease it. Of course, such an outside lessor would properly regard the rental as the sum of the estimated user cost and a residual pure quasi-rent.

24. John Maynard Keynes, *The General Theory of Employment, Interest, and Money* (London: Macmillan, 1936). p. 68.

25. Keynes, *General Theory*, p. 73.

26. Paul Taubman and Maurice Wilkinson, "User Cost, Output; and Unexpected Price Changes," in Phelps et al., *Microeconomic Foundations of Employment and Inflation Theory* (New York: Norton, 1970), 411–420.

27. Of course it also follows that the kind of technical advance of the Harrod-neutral type studied here, which does not require new investment for its expression, in generating a transient elevation of the real rate of interest would have a similarly expansionary effect through the user-cost channel. However, the presumption we

arrived at, it will be recalled, was that such a shock is expansionary, so the user-cost effect merely reinforces that conclusion.

28. Jeremy Greenwood, Zvi Hercowitz, and Gregory W. Huffman, "Investment, Capacity Utilization, and the Real Business Cycle," *American Economic Review,* 78, June 1988, 402–417; quote from p. 416.

29. Julio Rotemberg and Michael Woodford, "Oligopolistic Pricing and Effects of Aggregate Demand on Economic Activity," *Journal of Political Economy,* 100, December 1992, 1153–1207.

30. *A propos,* at his wartime meeting with Churchill to tell him about the bomb, Niels Bohr saw that Churchill was growing impatient with the exposition. Bohr stopped to say he could offer accuracy or clarity but not both. Which did Churchill want? Churchill selected clarity.

11. International Linkages through Investment in Employees

1. The global economy, or international economy, means here the set of economies in which all or substantially all enterprises and households are free to operate in the international capital market (both credit and equities) and the international goods market. On this definition several countries, including some large ones such as the former Soviet Union, were not participants in the global or international economy until the 1990s.

2. This section is based on the last section of the paper on which Chapter 7 was based, Hian Teck Hoon and Edmund S. Phelps, "Macroeconomic Shocks in a Dynamized Model of the Natural Rate of Unemployment," *American Economic Review,* 82, September 1992, pp. 898–899.

3. The first relationship uses the fact that $\Phi' = 1/T''$ and around the steady state, $\Phi = \hat{\zeta}$.

4. The modeling here bears some similarities to a first pass at the problem in Hian Teck Hoon and Edmund S. Phelps, "The Impact of Fiscal and Productivity Shocks on the Natural Rate of Unemployment in a Two-Country World," in *Open-Economy Macroeconomics,* edited by Helmut Frisch and Andreas Wöergoetter for the International Economic Association (London: Macmillan, 1993), 95–118. A further simplification of the model is made here in order to tackle asymmetric shocks.

5. Jean-Paul Fitoussi and Edmund S. Phelps, *The Slump in Europe* (Oxford: Basil Blackwell, 1988).

6. Like the model of the single economy in Chapter 7, the present model omits the annuity income of wealth owners.

7. It is convenient to imagine that F consists of public debt indexed to the price level. Accordingly it will be supposed that the two countries have, at least initially, a small, equal-sized quantity of public debt outstanding.

8. Since the initial value of $D + F$ is zero, a change of the interest rate has no impact on y^w and hence it does not appear in the reduced-form equations for the wage and the employment rate.

9. The rate of change of a country's q, for example, is increasing in the level of its own q, as clearly required for saddlepath stability.

10. The aforementioned two-country Hoon-Phelps paper, "The Impact of Fiscal and Productivity Shocks on the Natural Rate of Unemployment in a Two-Country World," examines such a shock.

12. International Linkages through Investment in Customers

1. The analysis that follows seems to be as systematic a consideration of the dynamics of international competition as any so far appearing in the literature. But it should be commented that the emphasis is on the main ideas rather than a rigorous statement and thorough analysis of the model, and I hope it will be read in that spirit. For research purposes one would have to study it alongside Chapter 8 and Edmund S. Phelps and Sidney G. Winter, Jr., "Optimal Price Policy under Atomistic Competition," in Phelps et al., *Microeconomic Foundations of Employment and Inflation Theory* (New York: Norton, 1970); as previously mentioned, see also Jean-Paul Fitoussi and Edmund S. Phelps, *The Slump In Europe* (Oxford: Basil Blackwell, 1988).

2. This section is based on my paper, "Effects of Productivity, Total Domestic Product Demand, and 'Incentive Wages' on Unemployment in a Non-Monetary Customer-Market Model of the Small Open Economy," *Scandinavian Journal of Economics*, 92, April 1990, 353–367. A paper with extensive parallels despite a contrasting approach to product-market pricing is Pentti J. K. Kouri, "Real Wage, World Demand, and Unemployment in a Customer-Market Model of a Small Open Economy," in Claes-Henric Siven, ed., *Unemployment in Europe: Analysis and Policy Issues* (Stockholm: Timbro, 1988).

3. When we come to discussing a world of two large countries, as in the two-country customer-market model of Chapter 10, it is impossible any longer to shield the model from the complication of that second state variable.

4. In an analysis that takes into account the dynamics of a as well as of x, the former state variable would share some of the work of bringing the real price back to one or else it would operate to make the task of the latter more difficult, thus requiring a deeper adjustment of the customer stock than would otherwise be necessary.

5. Taking the derivative of the ordinate of that curve at the initial x yields

$$(d\tilde{p}/dy^*)_{\dot{p}=0} = (r^*F_{py^*} + G_p F_{xy^*})/[-(r^*F_{pp} + F_x G_{pp})]$$
$$= \{r^*F_p[(F_{py^*}/F_p) - (F_{xy^*}/F_x)]\}/\{-r^*(F_{pp} - qG_{pp})\}$$

upon using $r^*F_p = -G_p F_x$ at the rest point. So the direction in which the curve shifts with an increase of y^* is determined by the effect on the ratio

$$F_p/F_x = [p + (D(p)/D'(p)) - c]xD'(p)/(p - c)D(p)$$

at $p = 1$, which can be seen to be x times the ratio of MR − MC to p − MC, where MR is marginal revenue and MC is marginal cost, multiplied by the price elasticity of demand. (Since MR − MC and the elasticity are negative, the expression is positive.) It is frequently assumed the price elasticity is unaffected by the increase of y^*; the flattening of the demand curve just offsets its outward shift so as to leave marginal revenue unchanged at an unchanged real price. On this assumption, increased y^* increases the critical ratio in (7.38), and thus increases the price level, if and only if it increases the firm's unit and marginal cost, ς. (That is because, as is surely not obvious, the derivative of the ratio with respect to ς is unambiguously positive if the elasticity can be taken to be constant.)

As (12.3) implies, unit cost rises if and only if, given v, there is an increase in the amount of output demanded, $D(p; y^*)x$. We just saw that the price level rises if and only if unit cost rises. It follows that there cannot have been a net decrease (or even a zero change) in the amount demanded as a result of the increase of y^*, with $D_{y^*}(p; y^*) > 0$, for that would imply a fall of cost, which would imply a fall of price, and a fall of price would add to the increase in the amount demanded directly caused by the increase of y^*; that would leave the amount demanded up, a contradiction. The reader can see immediately that the same argument rules out a zero net change in the amount demanded, for that would imply no rise of price, which would again lead to a contradiction. So there must be an increase in the amount demanded, hence in the amount of output produced (since the firms clear their respective mini–product markets). The resulting increase of cost induces a rise of the price, but that rise cannot be large enough to prevent a net increase in the amount of output demanded. (It should be unnecessary to note the terminological distinction, preserved in the more careful introductory texts, between an "increase of demand," which refers to a *shift* of the demand curve as represented by an increase of the shift parameter y^*, and an increase of the "amount demanded," which includes movements *along* the curve together with shifts of the curve.)

6. As there is an increase of employment too, thus a rightward movement along the labor-market equilibrium locus, and nonwage income in real terms is unchanged if portfolios are as cosmopolitan as consumers, the real wage is unambiguously increased. Since nonwage income in terms of domestic product is decreased by the real appreciation, however, it is not at all clear that the product wage is increased. (Recall that only a negligible proportion of our cosmopolitan consumers find themselves customers in their home country, so the product wage may fall while their real wage rises.)

7. Phelps, "Effects of Productivity," p. 365.

8. Some calculations from the above model confirming this possibility were carried out in Michael Hoel, "Comment on Phelps, 'Unemployment in a Non-Monetary Customer-Market Model,'" *Scandinavian Journal of Economics,* 92, April 1990, 363–373. The journal issue is reprinted in Bertil Holmlund and Karl-Gustaf Löfgren, eds., *Unemployment and Wage Determination in Europe* (Oxford: Blackwell, 1990).

9. It is a pleasure in closing this section to acknowledge that some of the results here have also been obtained in the customer-market model by Kouri, "Real Wage." Yet it is worth commenting that Kouri's model strays from the Phelps-Winter price-differential view in invoking the notion of "pricing to market," so it is not to be expected that the model here and Kouri's have identical implications. The attractions of the pricing-to-market view are considerable, of course; it seems realistic, and it generates some results beyond the powers of models that resist it. The question is whether that view is not quite misleading for analyzing problems having more than a short-term aspect. The Phelps-Winter model is a formalization of the

notion that firms take a long view in their pricing policy, so disturbances believed to be short-term are downplayed in the firm's current price decisions. The pricing-to-market view takes this to an extreme that I find hard to accept.

10. This section is based on Edmund S. Phelps, "Fiscal Stimulus and Employment at Home and Abroad in a Real Two-Country Customer-Market Model," *Rivista di Politica Economica*, 79, December 1989, 157–181.

11. On this definition, the nominal exchange rate is the cost of foreign currencies in terms of the home currency, and the real exchange rate is the cost of the representative production basket of foreign goods, sometimes including capital goods and sometimes not, in terms of the representative basket of home goods in production.

12. I thought to call some similar relationships "IS" equations in a paper of mine marking the fiftieth anniversary of Hicks's IS-LM reduction of Keynes's theory, "An Extended Working Model of Slump and Recovery from Disturbances to Capital-Goods Prices in an Overlapping-Generations Closed Economy: 'IS-LM' without Money," conference, IS-LM after Fifty Years, held at Aalborg, Denmark, in September 1988.

13. The proposition that the required rate of return is increasing in output, and hence output is in a sense increasing in the rate of interest, may seem contradicted on its face, since a glance at equation $(2')$ in Table 12.3 suggests that a rise of r reduces the righthand side of the equation and thus reduces the lefthand side, which is output. But this overlooks the point that the required real shadow price of shares on the righthand side is an increasing function of output with elasticity greater than one. As a result, for a small enough public debt, the curve of the righthand side when plotted in a cross diagram as a function of output slices through the 45-degree line from below. So a rise of r, in shifting down that curve, actually shifts out its intersection with the 45-degree line.

14. Robert A. Mundell, *International Economics* (New York: Macmillan, 1968).

15. Theoretically, a real appreciation has two distinct effects. One of these effects actually operates to reduce the output supplied. When foreign suppliers were supplying the same number of units of the good for a dollar, say, as domestic suppliers in A—say, 6 days in the resort hotel or 6 scoops on the ice cream cone—a decision by domestic firms to go to 5 days or 5 scoops for the same money would have represented a bigger-percentage, or relative, worsening of competitiveness than if, as a result of the increased competitiveness of overseas suppliers, the foreign suppliers now supply 7 days or 7 scoops. This effect, taken alone, says that increased supply by foreign competitors induces decreased supply by domestic firms.

The other effect operates in the reverse direction. If depreciation abroad has improved the alternatives for customers of a domestic firm, the firm will respond on this account by sweetening its offer (though not by so much as to nullify the decline of their competitiveness). Diminishing returns to sweetening a firm's terms set in more slowly the greener are pastures elsewhere. This effect, taken alone, says that increased supply by foreign competitors induces domestic firms to emulate the former by increasing their own supply. The text assumes that, empirically, the latter effect outweighs the former effect.

16. This result was arrived at, though based on a different source of a demand shock, in the analysis of the small open economy at the start of the present chapter.

17. The five-equation system behind Figure 12.3, the Equilibrium Steady State, may be written as follows:

(1) $r = \{[1 - \varsigma_B(Z_B)]/[\varsigma_B(Z_B) - MR_B]\}(-j'_B(1))$

(2) $r = \rho_B + m_B\{[Q_B(\cdot)(1 - x_{AB}) + Q_A(\cdot)s_{AB} + \beta_B]/[(Z_B - G_B)/(1 - x_{AB})]\}$

(3) $r = \{[1 - \varsigma_A(Z_A)]/[\varsigma_A(Z_A) - MR_A](-j'_A(1))$

(4) $r = \rho_A + m_A\{[Q_A(\cdot)(1 + x_{AB} - s_{AB}) + \beta_A]/[(Z_A - G_A)/(1 + x_{AB})]\}$

(5) $[(Z_B - G_B)/(1 - x_{AB})]x_{AB} = [1 - \varsigma_A(Z_A)][(Z_A - G_A)/(1 + x_{AB})]s_{AB}$

For both countries the share price function satisfies

$$Q(Z, y) = (-1/j')(-dy/dP)[\varsigma(Z) - MR]$$

by virtue of a first-order condition like (8.7), which is to be evaluated at a price level, P, equal to one and a marginal revenue, MR, taken to be independent of Z. Here $-j'(\cdot)dP/dy$ is equal to $g'(1)$ in (8.7), $j'(1) > 0$.

13. International Linkages through Investment in Fixed Capital

1. This section has certain roots in my paper, "A Working Model of Slump and Recovery from Disturbances to Capital-Goods Demand in an Open Nonmonetary Economy," *American Economic Review: Papers and Proceedings*, 78, May 1988, 346–350. There are some important differences, however.
2. Clearly this specification would be upset if the two public expenditures figuring in the relationship determining steady-state capital were so large as to imply the opposite sign for the net effect of an increase of K.
3. Students of open-economy macroeconomics will note that asset holdings located abroad has the role that is played by the real exchange rate in the Mundell-Fleming model—that of reconciling the domestic interest rate to the external interest rate.
4. Aspects of the present model are sketched and the consequences of certain shocks discussed in Jean-Paul Fitoussi and Edmund S. Phelps, "Global Effects of Eastern Europe Rebuilding and the Adequacy of Western Saving: An Issue for the 1990s," in *Economics for the New Europe*, edited by Anthony B. Atkinson and Renato Brunetta for the International Economic Association (London: Macmillan Ltd., 1991), 27–44. See also *Rivista di Politica Economica*, 81, December 1991.
5. The reason that a disturbance to the overseas real interest rate, r^* in the present notation, has no impact on y^w is that the initial value of F is taken to be zero.
6. The effects on the asymptotic unemployment rate of the changed wealth position can safely be neglected here.
7. Of course, the magnitude of the drop in the interest rate is moderated by the absence of any impact—any direct effect—of the expenditure program in A on the economy of B. The effect on the world interest rate is clearly proportional, at least

in the loose sense of the term, to the size of country *A*, which is here taken to be substantial—on the order of the size of country *B*.

14. Synthesis of the Global-Economy Theory

1. In a nutshell, using the IS-LM apparatus supplied by Hicks, the stimulus to the IS curve pulls up the nominal rate of interest, and this increase in the opportunity cost of holding idle balances fuels a rise in the velocity of money, driving up output and employment until the nominal wage and price level have neutralized this effect.

2. In this theory, fiscal stimulus tends to expand employment by driving up the real interest rate, of which labor supply is an increasing function. If the stimulus takes the form of a tax cut, there results in addition an increase of the after-tax wage rate, which may also increase labor supply; if instead the stimulus takes the form of a balanced-budget increase of government spending, this second effect clearly operates in the opposite direction.

3. We may interpet this result as predicting a contractionary effect (relative to the initial reference path) over some medium term, which would be visible to econometric analysis after the initially favorable monetary effects have been largely worked off by inflation or countervailing monetary policy.

4. For simplicity only the example here omits from this income the actuarial dividend, with the result that the public debt has no impact on the propensity to shirk (since the interest income on the debt is offset by lump-sum taxes in the present balanced-budget setting).

5. In that theory, the effect of the increased real interest rate is only to reduce domestic investment-goods purchases; capital-goods output may actually be increased to supply increased exports and substitute for imports or, if not, the reduced output will be more than offset by increased exports and decreased imports of other goods.

6. The implicit assumption here is that the government's use of labor services does not entail the investment outlays in the form of training costs that private-sector employment does or, if not, that the government nevertheless "jumps" its employment level.

7. The ambiguity-laden term *domestic demand* as used here consists of external, or foreign, demand and, if any, internally generated demand for the output of domestic firms or for the services of domestic labor.

8. The domestic firm in this context is one that uses domestic labor to service its customers, a foreign firm foreign labor.

9. It might be noted that the magnitude of the rise of the world real interest rate is an increasing function of the relative size of the country experiencing the positive expenditure shock.

15. Interest and Wealth in the Microeconomics of the Incentive Wage and Equilibrium Unemployment

1. With the term *monetary approach* I have in mind the contemporary schools emphasizing monetary shocks and adopting the postulate of a natural rate of unemployment: the New Keynesians, the New Classicals, the monetarists, and those basing Keynes's model on nonrational expectations.

2. An equilibrium path, once more, means here a path over the future along which today's expectations are going to be fulfilled. Equilibrium models, in the sense of the term here, assume that the actual path will take this course, barring unforeseen structural shifts and accidents to the state variables.

3. Another branch, much less developed, invokes real-wage stickiness. Following Lerner, we say that a variable is sticky if it is not a jump variable, which means that only its rate of change responds to a shock.

4. The interest rates and asset prices generated by the capital market are taken as given in this partial-equilibrium view.

5. The current real wage necessary for labor-market equilibrium is that economywide wage the expectation of which by wage setters will be self-fulfilling.

6. I am following Stiglitz here in saying that the real wage is rigid at least to a degree if it does not adjust enough to accommodate fully a shock, so that unemployment bears some of the adjustment. But since the wage responds instantly to disturbances, the term is plainly unsatisfactory.

7. Steven C. Salop, "A Model of the Natural Rate of Unemployment," *American Economic Review*, 69, March 1979, 117–125, and Carl Shapiro and Joseph Stiglitz, "Equilibrium Unemployment as a Discipline Device," *American Economic Review*, 74, June 1984, 433–444. A close reading of Salop discloses that the labor-market equilibrium locus implied there, though upward-sloping, is indexed by the costliness of employee training, which is an opportunity cost. In consequence, it shifts up with a permanent shock to the labor-productivity parameter in proportional fashion, as does the labor demand curve, so that the natural unemployment rate is unaffected—a point noted below. However, many *other* shocks to labor demand, if admitted to the model, would disturb the natural rate even in Salop's restrictive formulation; so he pioneered the slope after all.

8. A wage-bargaining paper closely addressed to the wage locus concept is Ian McDonald and Robert M. Solow, "Wage Bargaining and Employment," *American Economic Review*, 71, September 1981. Among insider-outsider model one finds a wage-setting locus in Assar Lindbeck and Dennis J. Snower, *Insider-Outsider Theory* (Cambridge, Mass.: MIT Press, 1988).

9. See, for example, Pentti J. K. Kouri, "Profitability and Growth in Small Open Economies," in A. Lindbeck, ed., *Inflation and Employment in Open Economies* (Amsterdam: North-Holland, 1979). Later, a number of observers speculated about an exogenous real-wage push in Europe in the 1980s.

10. The structuralist framework appears to be implicit in the oil-shock analysis by Michael Bruno and Jeffrey D. Sachs, *The Economics of Worldwide Stagflation* (Cambridge, Mass.: Harvard University Press, 1985).

11. See Jean-Paul Fitoussi and Edmund S. Phelps, *The Slump in Europe* (Oxford: Basil Blackwell, 1988), and the subsequent nonmonetary working models of the open economy by the present author.

12. See Chapters 7 and 8 above.

13. See Chapter 9 above.

14. By this point the reasons for dubbing the approach *structuralist* will be evident: It sees informational and organizational imperfections and features at the bottom of unemployment; it focuses on long-lasting or permanent movements in the unemployment rate rather than those coordination failures of short duration; it treats

unemployment as the outcome of *real* demands and supplies, not the supply of money in relation to sticky nominal wage or price levels (which are not commonly thought to be part of the structure of the economy); and, for good measure, it gives a role to the "structure" of goods demands in relation to goods supplies, unlike theories expressible in terms of aggregate demand and aggregate supply. In contrast, as is well known, the monetary approach aggregates demands, showing that a stimulus to aggregate demand is always expansionary; real business cycle theory, too, has been steadfastly aggregative virtually to the present. Hence, whatever we finally come to call this theory, it is *not* a reestablishment on new theoretical grounds of Keynesian dogma. Nor is it a variation on the neoclassical aggregative models of "real business cycle theory."

15. Salop does not make the calculation, but the property is clear. Chapter 7 shows that a *temporary* positive productivity shock has the expected effect, but not a permanent one.

16. In fact, no one proceeded to use the model to argue that the natural unemployment rate had shifted with some observed real shock, nominal shocks having been still the preoccupation of most theorists.

17. An appeal of this model has been the simplicity of its labor-market equilibrium, in which no one ever shirks! But that property does not generalize to quitting models where a no-quit equilibrium would be an absurdity. Also, that feature does not appear to generalize to a world of heterogeneous agents by age and hence wealth.

18. A worker with an indefinite run of joblessness would see his wealth and hence his consumption go to zero. To avert that implication we could introduce unemployment compensation that exhibited in real terms a fixed replacement ratio to the wage. Since that extension would not alter the results here, it has not seemed worthwhile to clutter the model with it.

19. Why not simply model the economy as having identical, infinitely lived families, as described by Ramsey, with positive discounting and a Shapiro-Stiglitz no-shirking equilibrium condition? Such is the model used by Jean-Pierre Danthine and John B. Donaldson in their working paper, "Non-Walrasian Economies" (Columbia Graduate School of Business, Research Working Paper 93, December, 1992). That model *is* worth having, but it would seem that it must suffer from Ricardian equivalence, and hence not deliver the interesting implications with regard to the employment effects of public debt and government expenditures which are important to structuralist theory. The Weil case avoids Ricardian equivalence, and the analytically harder Blanchard case does so with more realism.

20. If individual wealth were observable, and firms were permitted by law to use the data on the wealth of applying or employed workers, workers having accumulated the most wealth, by virtue of their distant entry into the labor force or a recent run of employment, would need the highest "incentive wage" to dampen their propensity to shirk, and hence would rate low in the employment preferences of the firm; some workers would be so rich that they would have to retire. If only age were observable, the oldest workers would be unemployable, forced to live off their interest and annuities. For present purposes, however, I take the shortcut of positing that social legislation enforces "equal pay for equal work" so that no firm can pay some employees less than it pays other employees, and it forbids mandatory retirement (though that would be hard to enforce).

21. That there should exist *deterministic* equations in the level and rate of change of consumption in the stochastic context here may raise a doubt in the reader. In the interpretation I suggest, however, it is the *planned* rate of change (and level) of consumption of persons in each current job status that is described by the two Euler-like equations. These plans are not stochastic. However, it could also be argued that the planned growth rates will be realized—the bump up to or down to the other path in the event of a change in job status having nothing to do with the consumption experience of a person in a *given* job status over a small interval of time.

22. Frank P. Ramsey, "A Mathematical Theory of Saving," *Economic Journal*, 38, December 1928, 543–559.

23. See William H. Press, Brian P. Flannery, Saul A. Teukolsky, and William T. Vetterling, *Numerical Recipes: The Art of Scientific Computing* (New York: Cambridge University Press, 1986), pp. 277–283.

24. This method can be found in Press et al., *Numerical Recipes*, p. 283.

16. Structural Shifts and Economic Activity in Neoclassical Theory

1. See Robert J. Barro, "Output Effects of Government Purchases," *Journal of Political Economy*, 89, October 1981, 1086–1121, or his *Macroeconomics* (New York: Wiley, 1984); Robert E. Hall, "Labor Supply and Aggregate Fluctuations," *Carnegie Rochester Conference on Public Policy*, vol. 12 (Amsterdam: North-Holland, 1980); and R. S. Aiyagari, Lawrence J. Christiano, and Martin Eichenbaum, "The Output, Employment and Interest Rate Effects of Government Consumption," Federal Reserve Board of Minneapolis Working Paper, 1990.

2. See for example Andrew B. Abel and Olivier J. Blanchard, "An Intertemporal Model of Saving and Investment," *Econometrica*, 51, May 1983, 675–692; Blanchard, "Debt, Deficits, and Finite Horizons," *Journal of Political Economy*, 93, April 1985, 223–247; Kenneth L. Judd, "Short-Run Analysis of Fiscal Policy in a Simple Perfect Foresight Model," *Journal of Political Economy*, 93, June 1985, 298–319.

3. For the origins see Hirofumi Uzawa, "On a Two-Sector Model of Economic Growth," *Review of Economic Studies*, 29, July 1962, 40–47, and "On A Two-Sector Model of Economic Growth II," *Review of Economic Studies*, 30, January 1963, 105–118; and Duncan Foley and Miguel Sidrauski, *Monetary and Fiscal Policy in a Growing Economy* (New York: Macmillan, 1971).

4. Blanchard, "Debt, Deficits, and Finite Horizons."

5. This chapter was co-authored with George Kanaginis.

6. Barro, *Macroeconomics*; and Allesandro Penati, *Money, Business Cycles, and the Real Rate of Interest in the United States*, doctoral dissertation, University of Chicago, Chicago, 1984.

7. N. Gregory Mankiw, "Government Purchases and Real Interest Rates," *Journal of Political Economy*, 95, June 1987, 407–419.

8. The finding first turned up in Phelps, "Pro-Keynesian and Counter-Keynesian Implications of the Structuralist Theory of Unemployment and Interest Under the Classic Two-Sector View of Capital and Production," Discussion Paper 494, 1990, Columbia University. A heavily reworked version appears here as Chapter 9.

9. Nonhuman wealth is increasing as long as the person is alive—there is no "hump-shaped" path for assets. This is because life expectancy is assumed to be independent of age.

10. Across steady states, higher public debt was also shown in the aforementioned paper by Blanchard to lead to lower capital stock when labor is supplied inelastically. Phelps and Shell show that if saving is a constant fraction of income, then for a given positive level of public debt there may exist two steady states, one with a low level and one with a high level of capital; they obtain the result in the text here if the economy starts from a high-capital steady state and the reverse in the other case. See Phelps and Karl Shell, "Public Debt, Taxation, and Capital Intensiveness," *Journal of Economic Theory,* 1, October 1969, 330–346.

11. A sufficient condition for employment to overshoot its long-run value and then decline toward that value is that the share of labor in total output is more than one half. In the U.S. this number is about 0.65.

17. Econometric Tests of the Theory: A Postwar Cross-Country Time-Series Study

1. Of course, the various econometric estimates represent not only a battery of tests of the modern equilibrium theory. They are of considerable substantive interest in their own right. That is because we are curious about the size of each of the coefficients as well as whether the sign accords with the theory being tested (or some other theory). And with regard to some variables, the theory does not present a tight prediction, so the "knowledge" provided by the coefficient estimate is purely empirical, but interesting, maybe even useful, notwithstanding. Such cases may constitute evidence against one or more *other* theories.

2. Among the recent econometric studies, one highlighting institutional factors is Richard Layard, Stephen Nickell, and Richard Jackman, *Unemployment: Macroeconomic Performance and the Labour Market* (Oxford: Oxford University Press, 1991). A study somewhat similar to the present one as regards the rate of interest is David Manning, "Productivity Growth, Wage Setting, and the Equilibrium Rate of Unemployment," Conference on Unemployment and Wage Determination, National Bureau of Economic Research, October 17–18, 1991. See also Warwick J. McKibbin and Jeffrey D. Sachs, *Global Linkages: Macroeconomic Interdependence and Cooperation in the World Economy* (Washington, D.C.: Brookings Institution, 1991). Among econometric forerunners one must mention, besides Sachs, the econometric work in Andrew Newell and James Symonds, "Wages and Employment between the Wars," Discussion Paper 87-02, University College, London, 1–36, reprinted in *Recent Developments in Macroeconomics,* vol. 3, ed. Edmund S. Phelps (Hants, England: Edware Elgar, 1991), 432–467.

3. The statistical analysis here was developed and carried out in collaboration with Gylfi Zoega. The design of the study and the results were first published as the Deuxième Rapport du Groupe Internationale de Politique Economique de l'Observatoire Français des Conjonctures Economiques (OFCE), *Taux d'interet et Chômage* (Paris: Le Seuil, 1993); also published as the Second Annual Report of the International Policy Evaluation Group of the OFCE, *Interest and Unemployment* (Oxford: Oxford University Press, 1993).

4. Pooling of cross-section and time-series data offers the possibility of controlling for unobservable country-specific effects that may be correlated with some of the included variables. One way of doing so is to include a country-specific constant term in each equation, which is done here. But if that were the only provision for country-specific effects, the resulting coefficient estimates would have two defects: First, all time-invariant, country-specific variables would be eliminated by the transformation. Second, some efficiency would be lost since variation across countries in the sample would be ignored. In order to deal with the former, we add a step to the estimation that links the estimated country coefficients to the observed, time-invariant, country-specific variables.

5. Characteristics can be time-invariant either because the object they measure does not change over time or because the measures of it exist for only one point in time.

6. This may of course result in biased estimates. The estimated equation for the constant terms is not reported here because it did not yield significant coefficients.

7. Possibly a stronger negative effect would have been estimated had the capital series been restricted to the business-capital stock. Our series included the stock of residential housing at real historical cost.

8. At considerable effort a time series of national wealth, including net foreign assets, was obtained for most of the countries over most of the period. It was expected that such a series, in being less responsive to debt shocks, since foreign assets would act as a partial buffer, would exhibit a coefficient that is larger in absolute value. The result obtained is the reverse, but the effect is quite small, perhaps because of errors in measurement infecting the more inclusive wealth series.

9. Since some unobserved shocks are likely to affect all countries simultaneously, the equations were also estimated using Zellner's method (SURE) to take into account any cross-country correlation of residuals. The results turned out to be qualitatively the same as below.

10. In order to prevent the Cochrane-Orcutt procedure from converging to a local minimum which is not a global minimum, a grid search was applied. Thus the procedure was started from values of the autocorrelation coefficient ranging between -1 and 1. All estimations gave the same coefficient estimates.

11. The wealth coefficient was -0.0394 (0.0200). The other coefficients did not change significantly.

12. The estimated-oil-price equation (with standard errors in parentheses) was as follows:

$$rpoil_t = -0.318 - 0.0069\,rmilw_t - 0.098\,rgnmw_t + 0.009\,rkw_t$$
$$(0.975)\quad(0.087)\qquad\quad(0.075)\qquad\qquad(0.005)$$

$$- 0.011\,rdebtw_t - 0.016\,d(inflw_t)$$
$$(0.008)\qquad\quad(0.011)$$

Estimation method by OLS; $n = 33$, $R^2 = 0.81$, s.e. $= 0.097$, DW $= 2.02$, $F = 18.84$.

13. For each country the timing of business cycle troughs was located. Averages of all variables were then taken over each business cycle, trough to trough. Equation $(17.5')$ was then estimated using these average values, the inflation shock term ex-

cluded. By doing this we hoped to average out movements along Phillips curves, as well as their shifts due to changes in expectations, leaving only changes in unemployment caused by changes in the determinants of the natural rate of unemployment.

14. The real exchange rates are calculated by the OECD. For information about the indices, including the weighting matrices used, see Martine Durand, *Method of Calculating Effective Exchange Rates and Indicators of Competitiveness* (Paris: OECD, Working Papers, February 1986).

15. It is preferable to apply an IV estimator to the latter regression after having substituted real exchange rates or markups for some of the domestic variables (namely, $rmil_i$, $rgnm_i$, and $rdebt_i$). This estimation did not turn out to be feasible.

16. Robert J. Barro and Sala-i-Martin, "World Real Interest Rates," in *NBER Macroeconomics Annual 1990*, ed. O. J. Blanchard and S. Fischer (Cambridge, Mass.: MIT Press, 1990); Michael Beenstock, "An Aggregate Model of Output, Inflation and Interest Rates for Industrialised Countries," *Weltwirtschaftliches Archiv*, 1988; Dirk Morris, *Government Debt in International Financial Markets* (London: Pinter Publishing Company, 1988; New York: Columbia University Press, 1988).

17. Alan Manning, "Productivity Growth, Wage Setting and the Equilibrium Rate of Unemployment," NBER Conference on Unemployment and Wage Determination, Cambridge, Massachusetts, 1991.

18. Layard, Nickell, and Jackman, *Unemployment*.

18. A Concise Nonmonetary History of Postwar Economic Activity

1. To be more accurate we should speak of the average unemployment rate of the OECD labor force, which is a weighted average of the national unemployment rates.

2. During the earliest postwar years of reassembly and reconstruction, the unemployment rate was even higher than toward the end of the 1940s. For noneconomists, perhaps, this observation goes without saying, since for them it is common sense that the destruction of some plant and equipment destroys jobs without creating new jobs in their place. DeSica's *Bicycle Thief*, for example, portrays a man unemployed for want of a bicycle. Neoclassical theory would say that workers without bicycles might suffer a lower wage payment, reduced by the amount of the rent imputable to having a bicycle, but not a lower employment rate. In contrast, the modern equilibrium theory is supportive of the film's economic premise.

3. In Pinter's *The Homecoming*, the philosopher begs off a philosophical question with the excuse that it is not his specialty, but a macroeconomist could hardly say that the above question is outside his field.

4. Milton Friedman, *A Monetary History of the United States* (Princeton, N.J.: Princeton University Press, 1963). See also Martin J. Feldstein, "U.S. Budget Deficits and the European Economies: Resolving the Political Economy Puzzle," *American Economic Review*, 76, May 1986, 342–346, and Martin J. Feldstein and D. W. Elmendorf, "Budget Deficits, Tax Exemptions, and Inflation," in *Tax Policy and the Economy*, vol. 3, ed. Lawrence H. Summers (Cambridge, Mass.: NBER, 1989), 1–23.

5. Constancy of the natural rate here does not mean that demographic or institutional developments do not cause the rate to move. It means only that the macroeconomic shocks under discussion generate only deviations from the natural rate, not a response of the natural (or equilibrium) rate itself.

6. The discussion here is an extension of a lecture of mine, "A Short Non-Monetary History of Fluctuations of the World Economy in Recent Decades," Central Bank of South Korea, Discussion Paper 90-7, June 1990.

7. In Figure 18.1, the fitted, or estimated, unemployment rate for 1956 and subsequent years is calculated starting from the (counterfactual) assumption that in 1956 the lagged fitted dependent variable, which in concept is the fitted unemployment rate of 1955, was equal to that in 1956—there being no way to calculate the fitted rate for 1955 since in this calculation the data began that year. Thereafter the lagged fitted dependent variable is obtainable from the calculation of the previous year's fitted unemployment rate. Probably the decomposition of the fitted rate here needs no commentary.

   Figure 18.2, by contrast, calculates each year's fitted rate on the (again counterfactual) assumption that last year's fitted rate was equal to the current year's. The decomposition here looks at the contribution of each causal factor in isolation, with no significance attaching to the intercept, only to the direction of movement. Hence this exercise is a calculation of the natural rate in the sense of the stationary value, which is the definition used in this volume.

8. The growth of the domestic labor force and of the world labor force were not incorporated into the econometric analysis in part through oversight. A subsequent extension of that analysis finds that natural population growth raises the natural rate, as my 1968 paper predicted. An attempt to estimate econometrically the role of the expected rate of long-term economic growth in unemployment determination is found in David Manning, "Productivity, Wage Setting and the Equilibrium Rate of Unemployment," Conference on Unemployment and Wages, NBER and CEPR, October 1991.

9. The importance of the world real oil price for the *equilibrium* world unemployment rate seems first to have been stressed in Michael Bruno and Jeffrey D. Sachs, *The Economics of Worldwide Stagflation* (Cambridge, Mass.: Harvard University Press, 1985). In the 1970s Keynesian models of a temporarily disequilibrating effect of the oil shock on unemployment in which the equilibrium path itself was invariant, such as those worked out by Robert Gordon and the present authors, were the recognized and formalized view. In those years the view that a permanent oil shock would have an *equilibrium* effect, such as contended later by Bruno and Sachs, would have been contrary to the dominant view of inflation as a wage-wage spiral, which had the microfoundation sketched by Phelps in 1968 and implied by Keynes in 1936, rather than a wage-price spiral, which had no microfoundations at all. An attempt to formalize a real-wage-setting locus toward the close of the decade was made in work on incentive-compatible contracts by Guillermo Calvo and the present author.

10. Jean-Paul Fitoussi and Edmund S. Phelps, "Causes of the 1980s Slump in Europe," *Brookings Papers on Economic Activity,* 16 (2), Autumn 1986, 487–520, and *The Slump in Europe* (Oxford: Basil Blackwell, 1988).

11. See Olivier J. Blanchard, "The Vanishing Equity Premium," in Second Annual Report of the International Policy Evaluation Panel of the OFCE, *Real Interest and Unemployment* (Oxford: Oxford University Press, 1993).

12. Robert J. Barro, "Pray that Real Interest Rates are High in the '90s," *Wall Street Journal,* October 1, 1991. See also Barro, "The Stock Market and Investment," *Review of Financial Studies,* 3, January 1990, 115–131.

13. In the 1980s there was very little new issue of shares, of course, as leveraged buyouts gave rise to debt issues that financed the retirement of shares outstanding.

14. The issue of shares to retire debt has become important in the past two years, but it played no role whatsoever in the 1980s.

15. I owe this point to the late Arnold Collery, to whose memory this book is dedicated.

19. Notes on Classicism, Etc.

1. John Maynard Keynes, *The General Theory of Employment, Interest and Money* (London: Macmillan, 1936).

2. Silvio Gesell, *The Natural Economic Order: A Plan to Secure an Uninterrupted Exchange of Products of Labor,* translated from the German by Philip Pye (Berlin: Neo-Verlag, 1929; German ed., Berlin, 1916).

3. Jude Wanniski, *The Way the World Works* (New York: Basic Books, 1978).

4. There is also the suggestion in the supply-side movement that a capital-gains tax, in raising the cost of capital, shifts down the demand for labor and thus contracts employment. At least this is one interpretation, the other one being that the diminished prospect of capital gains after tax will have a dispiriting effect on the supply of labor.

5. The answer that could be given on the basis of the general theory presented here is that shifts in the demand for labor born of Harrod-neutral technical advances are possibly neutral for the equilibrium unemployment rate, at least asymptotically, while increases in the tax rate on labor income, which seem to have carried a disproportionate share of the costs of the welfare state, are not neutral.

6. The description below of the classical doctrine draws heavily on Giuseppe Tullio, "Smith and Ricardo on the Long-Run Effects of the Growth of Government Expenditure and Debt," *History of Political Economy,* 21, December 1989, 723–736.

7. Ricardo differed from Smith, arguing that if land already received a zero rent the burden cannot fall on the rentier class. That is a case in which there appear to be too many rigidities for the tax to collect any revenue at all. We need not dwell on these matters, however, since the structuralist theory here does not face any such conundrums.

8. Adam Smith, *The Wealth of Nations,* ed. H. Campbell, A. S. Skinner, and W. B. Todd (Oxford: Clarendon Press, 1975), vol. 2, p. 865.

9. See, for example, John C. H. Fei, "Per Capita Consumption and Growth," *Quarterly Journal of Economics,* 79 (1), 1965, 52–72.

10. On this see Samuel Hollander, *The Economics of David Ricardo* (Toronto: University of Toronto Press, 1979), p. 383, n. 209.

11. See notes 19 and 24 in Chapter 9, above, referring to unpublished research by Michael Boskin and Lawrence Lau at Stanford University in 1991.

20. Economic Policies to Which the Structuralist Theory Might Lead

1. This position is sometimes used for an attack on structuralist theory. The argument is that slumps are remediable maladies, structuralist theory implies they are not, therefore structuralist theory must be wrong and misleading.

2. Louis Uchitelle, "Economists Offer Dismal U.S. Outlook," *New York Times*, August 31, 1992 (*International Herald Tribune*, p. 9). The part deleted reads: "[O]nce consumers and corporations work off their debts, they will borrow and spend again." Private debts are a structural factor, of course, though not one integrated into the models here.

3. In Keynesian theory, or its purer versions at any rate, an increase in liquidity preference or a decrease in the marginal efficiency of capital is usually regarded as optimally requiring restoration of employment exactly to its pre-shock level, either through monetary policy or, equivalently in the open economy, through the necessary currency depreciation. The nonconservatism here springs from the presumed costlessness of printing more money or lowering the exchange value of the currency.

4. In a closed economy, the effect of such a subsidy to firms would be to raise the wage paid to workers and to lower the real rate of interest. The effect in an open economy would be to lower real rates of interest generally in the world.

5. See my paper, "Economic Justice to the Working Poor through a Wage Subsidy," in *Aspects of the Distribution of Wealth and Income*, ed. Dimitri Papadimitriou (London: Macmillan, 1993).

6. Dennis J. Snower, "Getting the Benefit out of a Job," *Financial Times*, February 23, 1993.

7. Gilles Oudiz and Jeffrey Sachs, "Macroeconomic Policy Coordination among the Industrial Economies," *Brookings Papers on Economic Activity*, Spring 1984, 1–64.

8. Trevor W. Swan, "Economic Controls in a Dependent Economy," *Economic Record*, 36, March 1960, 51–66.

9. Since the countries would prefer not to use the instrument if the threat or promise proved insufficient, were it not for the lesson it would have for the future, the strategy is not what is called "sub-game perfect."

10. It has to be argued that the marginal beneficiaries of an increase of employment gain more the worse the jobless rate.

Glossary of Frequently Used Symbols

VARIABLES AND PARAMETERS

A	stock of the real asset owned by nationals (cf. W)
a	the national asset stock per worker (cf. w)
a	rate at which unemployed are hired
b, β	public debt in real terms per capita or per worker
C	aggregate national private consumption
c	national private consumption per capita or per worker
ς	unit cost
D	public debt in real terms
δ	exponential rate of capital depreciation
E	domestic stock of (instantaneously) firm-trained employees
e	real exchange rate, American definition ($= P^*/P$); decreases with a real appreciation
ε, e	average employee attention to work (*see* ϕ)
F	national stock of foreign assets in real terms net of the foreign stock of domestic assets
f	national stock of foreign asset holdings per capita or per worker
F^*	foreign-held stock of domestic assets in real terms net of the national holdings of foreign assets ($= -F$)
G	output purchased by the national government, in real terms
Γ_I	government purchases of the capital good, in natural units
Γ_P	government employment, in natural units
γ^f	government purchases of firms' output per firm
γ^h	government purchases of the firm's output per customer or household

h	hiring rate, or new hires per employee, gross of attrition
I	capital-good purchases
K	domestic stock of fixed capital
k	domestic stock of capital per worker ($= K/L$)
$k/(1-u)$	capital per employed worker, or capital-labor ratio ($= K/N$)
L	labor force, or labor supply
ℓ	labor force per firm
Λ	cumulative labor augmentation
λ	rate of labor augmentation
μ	death rate, or force of mortality
N	number of employed workers
n	average employment, or workforce, per firm
Ω	present value of future wage stream
o	output-capital ratio
P	domestic price level in units of the foreign good
P^*	foreign price level ($= 1$ by choice of unit)
p	relative, or real, price of a domestic firm ($= 1$ along equilibrium paths)
ϕ	in Chapter 14, shirking rate; in Chapter 15, intensity of monitoring
Q	real value of the firms' stock of assets
q	real price of the (real, or capital) asset
R	real rental per unit of the asset, or income per share
r	real interest rate
r^*	world real rate of interest
ρ	rate of pure time preference, or utility discount rate
T	tax revenue
τ	lump-sum tax per family
θ	ratio of wage rate to workers' average nonwage income
u	unemployment rate, U/L
$1-u$	employment rate, N/L or E/L
V	real wage bill
v	wage in real terms; i.e., in consumption units
W	real value of total wealth
w	real value of wealth per worker
x	stock of customers per firm; sometimes market share of domestic firms

y	supply of consumer goods per customer
y^w	average income from wealth (nonwage income) of employees
Z	total output, often Gross Domestic Product
z	total output per firm
z^h	output per family, or household
ζ	turnover rate through attrition, or quit rate

Functions

D	average cosmopolitan consumer's demand function in the open economy
ε	effort function
$\hat{\varepsilon}$	effort function having ratios as arguments
η	average consumer demand function in the closed economy
F	production function
f	demand-price function; output-labor function
Φ	gross hiring function
Ψ	per-worker nonwage income function
Q	asset-price function
T	training-cost function
V	demand-wage or supply-wage function
ζ	quit-rate function
$\hat{\zeta}$	quit-rate function having ratios as arguments

Index